HITTIN' THE JUMPER

HITTIN'
THE
JUMPER

A 60-YEAR AFFAIR WITH BASKETBALL

PATRICK DOWDALL

GOOSETOWN PRESS

WELLESLEY, MA

Published in the United States by Goosetown Press.

Library of Congress Number 2016909506

ISBN 978-0-9976902-0-0

Printed in the United States of America

First Edition

For further information, contact:

hittinthejumper@gmail.com or

Goosetown Press
129 Washington St.
Wellesley, MA 02481
781-235-0690

Cover Design by Pat King and Joyce Alpert

FOR

SUSANNE

Contents

Chapter One

A Lifelong Sport

My story begins with an end. It's 1966 in Anaconda, Montana, population 12,000. Anaconda was a smaller version of Pittsburgh back then, isolated in the Rockies, nestled high along the Continental Divide. My hometown was a company town built, along with its nearby sister city Butte, around the mining and smelting of copper. Marcus Daly founded the company and the town, helping to nurture its traditions. Daly imported workers from his homeland of Ireland, and their descendants comprised the majority of the city's residents. In many ways, it functioned more like a large village than a small city.

Is This the Last Game?

Basketball rivalries and tournaments along with Smeltermen's Day festivities were huge, well-attended pieces of our shared traditions. The town boasted itself the home of former NBA player Ed Kalafat of the 1950's Minneapolis Lakers, and more recently my hero Wayne Estes, an All-American from Utah State.

I grew up looking forward to the city championship between my parochial school, Anaconda Central, and the larger public Anaconda High when 4,000 people crammed into Memorial Gym to fervently and feverishly root for their team—"Hoosier Hysteria" Montana style. It was the Anaconda High "Copperheads" against our scrappy "Fighting Saints" of Central High. Each December, loyalties and the game's outcome would divide and unite families, neighbors and what felt like the entire city. While the Saints had enjoyed some parity with the larger school during the 1950's, in recent years we hadn't had much success in the annual city tilt, registering our last victory in 1959.

My dream growing up was to play and star on that city championship floor. I had caught on to the game at an early age and through my grade school years was considered a player with some talent. I'd spent countless hours in gyms and at alley hoops preparing myself for the big day when I would be on the floor as one of the Saints. Unfortunately, my appearances in the championship game resulted in nothing but defeats, including my senior year when I'd hoped we could overcome our usual destiny. The previous spring we had eked out a win against the Copperheads in a divisional tournament in Butte, a rare game against our rivals outside of the city championship. We certainly were extremely pleased by the victory, but it just did not have the same feel as a city championship win.

The disappointments of my final city championship loss were less than three months old when another opportunity for realization of high school basketball dreams loomed—competing in the state tournament. Besides winning the city championship, every Anaconda aspiring basketball player wanted to travel to the state tournament to play before those huge crowds against the best in the state. The Saints had come close to grabbing one of the two spots in the previous year's qualifying tournament when we finished with only one loss, but we were denied a play-off game against the other "one-loss" team since we had fallen to them in the first round.[1]

I now faced my last chance to make it to State. As we walked four blocks to Memorial Gym that Friday in late February of 1966 to play our second game of the divisional tournament, our minds were on that goal. Our odds weren't high since we had gone down to defeat the previous night, but they weren't impossible. Four victories over three days of play would position us to join the winner of the tournament as one of the two entries for the division to travel to Butte Civic Center. The first victory looked to be a breeze as we headed to the gym in our cocky stride.

Our opponents were the Wardens of Powell County High in Deer Lodge. Everyone from Montana knew Deer Lodge as the home of the State Penitentiary, and it clearly was the source of some pride for the residents since they associated their team name with the town's principal industry. Deer Lodge also is the birthplace of Phil Jackson although he never played for the Wardens. He subsequently moved to North Dakota, where he played high school and college ball before embarking on his storied playing and coaching career with the Knicks, Bulls and Lakers. The Saints had twice easily defeated the Wardens during the season, and I'd been particularly proud to rack up my high school best of 32 points in one of those games. The Wardens also were sitting on a losing streak of about 30 games stretched over two seasons. We had reason to believe they would not be viewing our game with optimism.

Despite the loss the previous night, we had played solidly over the latter part of the season, winning five of the last seven. The two losses were at the hands of Libby, the eventual state champion, and Bozeman, considered the

---

[1] Technically, the rules of the tournament were as follows. The winner of the championship game had an automatic berth. The loser of that game also had a berth unless it had not played the third place team, the winner of the consolation game. In that event, those two teams would play on Monday to decide who went to State.

power house in the state. We also had an emerging star, 6'7" junior Jim Meredith, who ultimately would attain Pac Eight All-Conference honors at Washington State. The only wrinkle in that optimistic forecast was minor dissension among some players on the issue of "ball distribution." Nevertheless, a victory over Deer Lodge was assumed, and much of the discussion on that walk concerned our potential opponents for the next morning's game.

The game began badly. The Wardens came out in a four corner offense stall. Basketball historians among you will recognize this as a favorite strategy of Coach Dean Smith of North Carolina in the 1970's, who perfected it under the leadership of point guard Phil Ford. A tactic of the pre-shot clock and pre-three-point shot era, coaches resorted to the stall when facing a more dominant opponent. With four of their players occupying the outer edges of the corners of their half of the court and the remaining guy floating in the middle, the Wardens proceeded to move from one corner to another with a player dribbling and then passing to another. The objective was to keep the ball out of our hands as the minutes ticked off. Besides killing the clock, the stall strategy aimed to catch the defense over-committed in guarding the perimeter, resulting in an easy shot around the basket. The Wardens executed the slow-down flawlessly. I remember looking up at the scoreboard early in the second quarter, flashing four to two. Shortly before the half, they lifted the slow-down. In pent-up frustration, we responded with a complete breakdown of our game. The offensive discipline carefully crafted by our coach Tracy Walsh evaporated as the remainder of the game was dominated by our impatient shooting from all corners. Any semblance of team unity evaporated. Our play was disastrous. When the buzzer sounded, the Wardens were up 67-55. Their 30-game losing streak was over, and we were out of the tournament—no possibility of State.

As I sat despondently in the locker room waiting for a trainer to cut the tape off my ankles, my only thoughts were on the proverbial 10,000 hours I had spent over the past decade—ending in such futility for my last high school game. It was an unfathomable, humiliating and wholly unanticipated debacle. At that moment, in the midst of my gloom, I could not have imagined that my basketball life essentially had just begun. I could not have pictured myself on that same date 49 years later lacing up my sneakers to play with my pick-up group, Over the Hill Basketball, with an eye to competing in the 65-69 division at the National Senior Games in Minneapolis. Playing basketball as a grandfather was not part of our lexicon in 1966.

This book chronicles my 60 years of playing the game, including those years leading up to the Deer Lodge loss and, perhaps more significantly, the following 49 years. It has been an extraordinary journey for an ordinary player, who was neither a collegiate nor professional player. Through it I have been privileged to share the courts with thousands of people, many of whom have become good friends on and off the court. It has taken me to South Bend, Cambridge, Washington, D.C., Tacoma, New York, Chicago, Boston, Norfolk and Houston, along with many other places. I have found myself playing in the neighborhood of the birth of our country and at the site of the birth of the game of basketball itself. The courts have ranged from makeshift baskets in alleys to those at elite New York venues like the Downtown Athletic Club, the home of the Heisman Trophy. Several with whom I have shared the court— teammates and opponents—became famous in politics, business and academia, and a few were former NBA players. Mostly though I have played with those not in the headlines, but whose lives inspire their fellow hoopsters. They have defined and enhanced my experience on the court, and the story that follows is as much theirs as mine.

I have played through many stages of my life, and the circumstances of each necessarily had some impact on my playing. I've progressed from being the youngest to the oldest on the court. From being referred to as "kid" to "young man" to "sir" and now qualifying as "gramps." In a near round trip, I have travelled from struggling to reach the basket with the ball because of the insufficient strength of my six-year-old body to recent years where I have come up short with my shot because my legs aren't so young anymore. If I continue to play, I expect to fully complete that round trip.

Basketball has been my constant companion through life. That life has taken me to worlds far removed from tiny Virginia City where I first was exposed to the game as the son of a coach. My formative years with the game were in Anaconda, followed by education at Notre Dame and Harvard, and legal positions in New York, Chicago and Boston. The last 31 years I've spent in Wellesley, a Boston suburb, with my wife, Susanne, raising our three sons. I have faced in each of these chapters in my life new challenges and experiences considerably different from the previous ones, but basketball has always been there. It has been my passport to enter these worlds, and it has been an invaluable ally in helping me to navigate the unfamiliar waters.

I also have witnessed the far-reaching changes in the game during these years. When my father started coaching in the early 1950's, his favorite player was Bob Cousy, whose magician-like dribbling and passing when now viewed on YouTube impresses us as entertaining and masterful, but also obsolescent. My father himself began his competitive play when there was a jump ball at center court after each basket. His older brother played in an era when the game was known primarily as a passing game since the rules limited dribbling the somewhat misshapen ball. My first basketball hero was Elgin Baylor, the precursor to the breathtakingly athletic and acrobatic game we witness today. With the increased athleticism of the game, though, there is a countervailing trend—basketball played for recreation by weekend warriors, increasingly older men and women who left behind their best athletic days dozens of years ago. The NBA finals on television and the contest of octogenarians at the National Senior Games—radically different spectacles but same ball, same hoop and same game.

Similarly, basketball has skyrocketed into a privileged spot within the American cultural firmament. Today, we have our first basketball president, whose 2008 campaign featured his affinity towards playing the game as a critical part of its electoral strategy in traditionally red states, Indiana and North Carolina, where hoops mania dominates. Famously, Michelle Obama commissioned her former college player brother to set up a game with her boyfriend Barack to get an assessment of his character. Barack passed. During the Obama administration, the weekend pick-up game on the grounds has become as regular a feature as the press briefings.

In contrast, back in the 1950's, baseball ruled. The collective attention of the nation was focused annually on the fall classic as we followed every pitch of the World Series, broadcast on black and white televisions and transistor radios. Among amateurs, battles for bragging rights, whether fought in Congressional offices in Washington or on Wall Street or among the members of the local chamber of commerce, were waged on softball diamonds. Today, annually the attention of the nation is captured by the March Madness bracketology, and now bragging rights more often are determined on the courts rather than the diamonds.

I think the reason for basketball's rise within our sports culture is that the game is fun to play and watch because it's fundamentally a team sport. Sure the game vividly showcases the athletic skills of its players, with the best frequently described as akin to ballet dancers, but victory comes only to those teams that find a way to inspire every player on the floor to contribute. It's enormously fulfilling to be part of an equation that is more than the sum of its parts and exciting to sense and watch that chemistry evolve on the court.

We've all seen NBA teams studded with a superstar (or two) yet incapable of being the last team standing after the final play-off game in June. Michael Jordan and the Bulls come to mind. For six years, Jordan was a perennial all-star prolific scorer and generally considered the best player in the league, but the Bulls came away empty each year in the play-offs. Enter Phil Jackson. As he describes it in his memoir, *Sacred Hoops,* he endeavored to instill that team with the "selfless ideal of teamwork," and its core tenet was that everyone on the team had a vital role recognized and valued by all, from Jordan on down. We all know the story—the Bulls pulled off a "three-peat," which was to be followed by another "three-peat."

The Bull's performance, based on mutual valuing among all players and for all roles, set the stage for the kind of shared trust and creative play that translated into exuberant dominance on the courts. Frankly, it's true of all the best teams I've ever played on, competing in a tough league or merely a transitory pick-up on the playground,—and true as well of all the teams and working groups of any kind I've ever been part of.

As I sat in that locker room in 1966, I could not have foreseen all that the game would give me or even the possibility of playing the game for so many more decades. None of us expected to play beyond our late 20's. The general attitude towards the limited horizon of playing basketball was reflected in a 1974 legislative study regarding inter-school activities in Montana. The report critically noted that too much emphasis was placed on sports such as football and basketball while shortchanging certain minor sports such as tennis and golf that were described as "lifetime sports." It recommended that inter-school basketball and other sports at large schools be eliminated in favor of intramural competition. In continued defiance of such expectations, today men and women in their 80's, as I observe at senior tournaments, put on uniforms and sneakers to compete with the same spirit, and occasionally the same skills, they demonstrated in their teens. It is my fervent desire that I shall be doing likewise when I reach their age.

In the words of my former grade school coach, Bill Lowney, basketball has become "a lifelong sport."

A Series of Private Reunions

This book also tells the story of another journey—the renewal of old friendships. I work out at a branch of the Boston Sports Club near my home in Wellesley. My work-out is primarily cross-training for my basketball playing, a twice a week occurrence when I'm free from illness or injury. The facility includes a basketball court with two cross courts, measuring nearly regulation size. A number of years ago I began to incorporate 20 minutes of shooting around on the court into my biweekly regimen to supplement my weights, flexibility and aerobic work-outs. At 6:30 or 7:00 in the morning, I usually had the court to myself. About six years ago, a guy with longish gray hair and a prominent drooping moustache began to show up each morning. For about 30 minutes he would walk and dribble from one basket to the other. When he got about eight feet from the basket, he would shoot the ball, almost always converting the goal. After the shot, he headed back to the other basket and repeated the pattern. His work-out included about 50 such round trips.

The two courts were separated by a removable net barrier so our paths did not directly cross. For a few weeks we each stealthily studied our early morning companion on the court. One day I was retrieving my ball by the net when he was a few feet away dribbling so he turned towards me and we started a conversation. We began with mutual acknowledgments of what the other had been doing during the previous weeks—me complimenting him on his accuracy, he responding with "My legs are gone. You're still in the game, able to shoot those three-pointers" (a little exaggeration since I have never been a three-point shooter).

As the weeks and months progressed, we managed always to carve out a little time to chat. Charlie, a year or two older than me, grew up in neighboring Brookline and played for a team that competed for the state championship in the old Boston Garden. He is a colorful raconteur and entertained me with many basketball stories and a few unrelated to the game. I always relished his penetrating, pithy remarks. One day I shared my "modest" goal of my work-outs—to get my game to where it was 10 years earlier. He profoundly assured me: "It ain't gonna happen!"

Inspired by his tales, I began to reflect one morning about some of my own basketball stories, stretching out over nearly 60 years. "This could be an interesting book," I mused and began to outline it in my head as I finished my work-out. Thinking more about my project over the next few weeks, I knew I had to contact dozens of guys with whom I had played at various stages in my life. What I did not realize was the fabulous journey I was about to embark on for the next four years as I located and spoke with so many I used to see on a nearly daily basis. In some instances, we had not spoken in 50 years. Yet, as we began talking, the intervening years melted away and it seemed only last week since we had played together

Our conversations, whether by phone or in person, were filled with nostalgic re-creations of the past. Our familiarity and intimacy with events, both significant and trivial, that occurred long ago was astounding. We shared the details of games won and lost, fellow players, tough opponents, formidable coaches, affectionate ones, referees (good and bad), gyms and outdoor courts. What the game meant to us at that stage of our life was a recurring theme. We lingered briefly on the circumstances of their leaving the game—most had, and in nearly all instances it was an involuntary departure brought about by some physical ailment accompanied by doctors' orders. I left each of these conversations feeling energized, a feeling I believe was mutual. Frequently, before saying good-bye, I was thanked for the memories.

I think that Bob Matosich, whom I played basketball with for a dozen years as a youth, best expressed what this journey was all about. As we sat in his house overlooking scenic Georgetown Lake, about 15 miles west of Anaconda, Bob observed: "I know what you are doing; you are going around and having a bunch of your own private reunions." Reunions, of course, are defined as re-connecting with those whom we have experienced life with in the past. Recon-necting with so many has been one of the unmitigated joys of putting together this story.

As I have described my basketball experiences to friends over the years, several have referred to the guys I played with as a brotherhood. I agree, but it is perhaps more accurately expressed as a web of brotherhoods. The game is played as a team, and the success in competing depends critically upon the ex-tent to which that team displays unity and cohesion. But the brotherhood ex-tends far beyond teammates and includes everyone on the court—opponents, coaches, referees and even fans. By my estimates, I have played with about 5,000 through the years—some only once or twice and others repeatedly over decades. My reunions have provided me the opportunity to revisit important members of that brotherhood, and this book has given me the enormous pleasure to record their lives from the perspective of that brotherhood.

Reunions are about people, but they also are about places. In writing this book, I've indulged in another love of mine, the history of the places where I played. When I've met with players with whom I have shared a past, we mentally return to a specific place—the town or city which was so important to us at that stage of our life. My basketball life has been shaped by the history, traditions and ethos of the communities where I played, whether they be the local basketball lore or even more generally the prevailing culture of the place. The influence of place has also been revealed in the gyms, playgrounds and garages where I played. Each possesses a separate character. Some were inspirational because of their historic connections. Others provided much comfort because of their familiarity and intimacy. A few overwhelmed with their charm. Playing hoops on a playground asphalt court as a teenager in Anaconda evokes memories distinct from intramural play at a college in South Bend or Cambridge or a lawyers' league in New York. The memories of the brotherhoods are inextricably linked to the singularity of those courts.

Reunions also provide an occasion for us to review the course of our life. At first blush, it might strike one as odd that playing a game might be a standard for such reflection. After all, in the words of Bill Littlefield, who hosts the PBS radio series on Saturday mornings, "it's only a game." Other aspects of one's life, like family, profession or contributions to society, would seem a more appropriate barometer. Yet, this game has always been there with me as I have passed through many worlds. It has been and still is my abiding passion. More than just a game, it is a fine-ground lens through which my life can be viewed and reviewed.

Certainly the circumstances of my "real" or everyday life intruded onto my experience on the court. At times there was a direct connection between the two as when I played for my firm's team or hosted clients to a pick-up group I organized. Other times, I played to escape the pressures of the real world buffeting me. In sum, my basketball experience was inseparable from what was going on with the rest of my life.

Finally, reunions inevitably bring to mind lost worlds. As much as we would like to, we cannot return to 1960 to begin anew. The memories are there, but as fond as they may be, they are only memories. Many of those who populated that long ago world are now departed, adding to the sense of loss. The institutions that shaped our lives may no longer exist. The school where my father first coached, my grade school, high school, the major industry in my home town, the three law firms where I spent a good part of my working life— all have disappeared. Telling this story of my journey has given me a treasured opportunity to recreate those worlds and my deep-seated affection for them, even if I cannot return to them.

Chapter Two

"I'm on the Ball, Dad"

My basketball journey began in Virginia City, Montana circa 1950, sitting at the end of the bench when I was three years old. I was there with my father, the basketball coach. After graduating from the University of Montana, he had found a job teaching History and Commercial (typing, shorthand and bookkeeping) classes. It was at a high school of 20 students in Virginia City, referred to affectionately by him as VC. His salary of $2,200 was increased by $200 when he agreed to coach the VC Vigilantes in basketball, both high school and grade school, women's volleyball and track.

Once a Booming Town

When our family reached its dusty streets in late August 1950, VC's best days were embedded in ancient history, at least by Montana standards—having occurred nearly a century earlier. Fortunately, its worst days also were behind it. Sparked by the discovery of gold in the beds of Alder Creek in 1863, the town's population mushroomed to more than 10,000 within a few months, and a year later VC became the capital of the recently formed Montana Territory. Many of the town's founders were vigorous sympathizers of the Confederate cause and initially called the town "Verina " after the wife of Jefferson Davis, the president of the Confederacy. When rejected by the U.S. Postal Service, the name was modified to honor the home state of the capital of the Confederates, which apparently was deemed more acceptable. By all accounts, VC was an open and wild gold mining camp similar to so many in the American West during this era. VC superseded most of them with the appearance on its streets of a number of particularly memorable figures.

Among them were the leaders of the Vigilantes, under whose moniker my father's teams played. Lawlessness in mining camps was common, but it was particularly acute in Virginia City. It was orchestrated by the only sheriff in Montana, Henry Plummer. For a number of weeks in late 1863 virtually no gold shipments out of VC successfully reached their destination as they were held up by alleged members of Plummer's "Gang of the Innocents." On the day after

Christmas, a group of citizens headed by Paris Pfouts and Wilbur Sanders organized and in ruthless fashion hanged 27 men over several weeks, including Plummer. On the particularly efficient night of January 14, 1864, five men including "Clubfoot" George Lane were hanged in VC. They were subsequently buried on Boot Hill where the simple white markers noting their name and "hanged January 14 1864" remain to this day. Even the most ardent advocates of the Vigilantes concede that at least one innocent person suffered his demise at the hands of the Vigilantes and that their general disregard of common judicial procedures was regrettable. Nevertheless, they undeniably played a critical role in the annals of Montana and VC history.

Perhaps the single most colorful individual who ever lived in VC was General Thomas Francis Meagher, appointed acting Territorial Governor of Montana following the cessation of the Civil War in 1865. His gubernatorial offices served as our family's residence 85 years later. Up to that point, Meagher had crammed into his life enough heroics and exploits for a dozen men. Born in Ireland, he was condemned to death in 1848 as a leader of the Young Ireland rebellion against English rule. Following the sentencing, he delivered a stirring "speech at the dock" on behalf of the condemned decrying English rule, a speech which subsequently became part of the canon of Irish resistance. The death sentences ultimately were commuted by Queen Victoria, and the rebels were re-sentenced to "transportation" for life to Australia. After spending a few years in relatively unconfined quarters in Australia, Meagher escaped under somewhat controversial circumstances and arrived in New York in 1852. After earning his law license, he was actively involved in various Irish causes and became a leader of the "Union" Democrats in New York. As this group typically sided with Northern interests in the pre-Civil War political battles, Meagher frequently was at odds with many of his fellow Irish.

With the commencement of hostilities, he helped to form the Irish Brigade from New York recruits. As head of the Brigade, Meagher attained much distinction and won many honors for the gallantry of him and his men on the battlefield. By all accounts, they fought heroically in many of the key battles. However, as always with Meagher, the record was not untarnished, and there have been debates over his Civil War actions. Some have alleged that at times he imprudently risked the lives of himself and his men, and he also found himself embroiled in conflicts with superior military officials over various matters.

The Irish Catholic Union Democrat Meagher, placed among the generally Protestant populace of VC and western Montana, either pro-Confederate Democrats or nativist-oriented Republicans, was bound to create an incendiary state of affairs. Among the parties Meagher feuded with repeatedly were the Vigilantes, heavily infused with members of the Masonic order. It all ended in 1867 when Meagher died while on a steamboat in Fort Benton, Montana. His body was never found, and the explanations of his death are as varied as the assessments of his life—ranging from his falling off the boat while drunk to

10

being murdered by assorted factions of his many enemies, including the Vigilantes and Irish dissidents, with an occasional reference to suicide. Whatever the circumstances, posterity has been generous to Meagher vis-a-vis his enemies as he sits triumphantly on his horse presiding over the front lawn of the State Capitol in Helena and has one of the state's 56 counties named after him.

The easy gold pickings soon disappeared in VC, followed by the loss of territorial capital status, the latter being ceded to Helena, the site of Montana's next voguish gold rush. By the mid-1870's, VC's population numbered in the hundreds. The town did experience a resurgence around the turn of the century when the dredge boat method of mining was introduced. Resembling strip mining for coal, it involved the process of upending land along the banks of Alder Creek. The remnants of the dredging still can be seen as one approaches VC from the west on Highway 287. It is a landscape filled for miles with mounds of stones on both sides of the road. The dredging shut down in 1937, and by the early 1940's VC had approached the status of a ghost town.

It was about that time Charles and Sue Bovey undertook to buy buildings in VC and reinvigorate the town. Originally from Minneapolis where his family was a prominent owner of a milling company that ultimately became General Mills, Charles attended the prestigious Boston-area prep school, Philips Exeter Academy. Despite that education, he decided that college was not for him and moved to Montana to learn the milling business. His interests, though, soon migrated to other pursuits, including furthering his interest in historic preservation, which centered on VC. At that time VC was a collection of buildings, mostly built during the gold rush, stretching along a few streets on a hillside. Many were in a dilapidated condition with the structures frequently stripped for fire wood. Bovey undertook to restore and convert them to shops and museums, and by 1950 he had purchased most of the historic buildings in town. A tourist trade emerged, and VC became a hub of vibrant activity during the summer months. The visitors converged onto the various sites along the Wallace Street boardwalk and hopped on the stage coach to climb up Boot Hill to visit the graves of the five hanged men.

The Arrival of the Coach

This was the VC that greeted my parents and their two small children, me a few months shy of my third birthday and my sister Mary Anne, born the previous March. They were young—my mother was 22 and my father was 26. A beautiful young woman with long and stylish dark chestnut hair, my mother bore the responsibilities of two children but retained the spiritedness of her high school days as a member of the socially in-group, the "Big Five." Reasonably tall for his era and of slender build, my father with his fading freckled face and traces of red remaining in his hair could easily have been mistaken for a young man hailing from his mother's native County Down, Ireland. He was

11

outgoing, a personality forged as the youngest son striving to distinguish himself in the shadow of talented older brothers. Approaching him on the street or in the halls, one would be greeted heartily with his signature "How she go?" They had spent nearly four years in Missoula with its stimulating university life, filled with veterans and their families, many of whom had been friends from their high school years. VC offered none of that life.

When they arrived on Labor Day weekend, the last day of the tourist season, the town was "roaring." My mother was stunned to discover the next day that the dusty streets were deserted. The tourists were gone, and most of the historic buildings were closed for the long winter. Worse, VC was essentially at the end of the road. The paved part of Highway 287 then ended in VC. Beyond that was a windy dirt road extending to Ennis, which frequently was closed during the winter months. A visitor travelling by bus to VC would not miss his stop since it was the last. Social life was limited, revolving around the Elks Club and the school, where basketball was a major attraction.

Adding to the local color of our VC experience were the circumstances of our living quarters that first year. We and three other parties shared the Elling House—once a grand house built by Henry Elling in 1876 that sat towards the end of Idaho Street. Arriving in VC in 1864, Elling became a prominent business man with interests in retail, banking and gold and silver investments. While not as palatial as some of the houses built in Butte and Helena, the stone-constructed Elling House with its three Gothic windows on the second floor stood out as the finest in VC. Around 1900 Elling's widow expanded the house to include a ballroom in the front. Following her death in 1924, harder times befell the home as it became a "boarding house" for multiple occupants. My mother recollects that Mr. Perry, the principal at the school, lived in the front part of the house while we occupied the old servant's quarters and the ballroom. A young man by the name of John and a chef at one of the restaurants resided in the remaining parts of the house. Each section was separated by curtains, and there was a shared refrigerator and bathroom. It goes without saying that the tenants were afforded little privacy.

My father's school looked like something out of a TV Western such as Bonanza or Little House on the Prairie. A classic square shaped two story brick building built in the same year as the Elling House, it was the successor to a two room log building. The lower level was the grade school while the upper level housed the high school students. At the time that he taught, there were four principal rooms for the high school, including a spacious central room serving many functions. Admittedly modest, the space was more than accommodating for 20 students and a handful of teachers.

The young John Dowdall was a busy man at the school. In addition to his teaching and varsity basketball coaching responsibilities, he also was the volleyball coach for the girls, the basketball coach for the grade school team and the adviser for the Annual, the school newspaper, the Junior Class Play and the speech team, among others. His picture is ubiquitous in the yearbooks.

The principal reason he was hired, though, was his ability to coach boys' basketball. His first foray into the job market a year earlier had taught him that "history majors were a dime a dozen." He returned for an additional year of schooling to pick up the "business" classes to make himself more marketable. He went into the interview with the VC board quite nervous about his ability to answer questions on the business subjects but discovered they had little interest in those credentials. "Hell yes, I can coach basketball" was his response when the question was posed, and he was hired.

Young Coaches in Small Towns

When he assumed the coaching job at VC, the game of basketball in Montana was just emerging from its "wild west" stage. Thirteen years earlier, just as he was entering high school, the game had been radically altered with the elimination of the "jump center" after each score. The rule change was to revolutionize the game with a flood of strategies based on speed and quickness. The plodding ritual of returning to the center with the focus of winning the jump after each successful basket was replaced with the immediate possession of the ball and the possibilities of a quick basket at the other end. Montana high school games, typically with scores in the teens prior to 1938, now featured scores that routinely were double the previous tallies. However, the arrival of World War II with its scattering of former high school players (and future coaches) around the globe for the various theaters of war postponed the full fruition of the revolution in Montana until the late 1940's.

The war also impacted the pool of coaches as the average age of the coaches climbed during the war. Coaches frequently had been recruited among local businessmen and others not affiliated with the schools, a trend that continued throughout the war. The long-time coach at VC had been Dale Kisling, who ran a local grocery store. Following the war and with the benefits of the GI bill, many young former high school athletes enrolled in the state's colleges and universities. They were to be the coaches on the bench guiding the Montana high school basketball teams in the 1950's and 1960's, who became so much a part of my life. The ascendancy of these young war veterans into the coaching ranks received a major boost when the Montana High School Association issued an edict that all coaches must be teachers at the schools they coach. Young coaches were in demand!

The marriage of the recent graduate coaches with Montana small town residents was not always a blissful one. One of my favorite stories involved Jack, former teammate of Ben Tyvand. Jack was having a tough season in Townsend, a small town of approximately 1,000 residents located about 35 miles east of Helena. As the half-time buzzer sounded for the end of a not particularly inspired 16 minutes for the Bulldogs, the fans were fulsome in their expression of dissatisfaction with the coach. In the confines of a small gym with the fans essentially intermingled with the team's bench, their rather indelicate remarks were nothing akin to catcalls from an anonymous and dispersed crowd—they were personal and directed. Having earned his spurs growing up in the tough environs of the streets of Butte, he was not inclined to tolerate such behavior. Turning to the fans, who undoubtedly included members of the school board and other teachers, Jack retorted: "You can't make chicken salad out of chicken shit," and departed defiantly to the locker room. I don't know how the Bulldogs played the second half, but the board apparently did not appreciate candor and honesty as he was not sitting on the bench for the first game of the next season.

The coaching opening in VC, in fact, resulted from a much-talked about incident involving the previous coach—invariably referred to as the night the coach left the players on Pipestone Pass. At that time the Pass was the section of US Highway 10 that traversed the Continental Divide outside Butte. Since VC was on the east side of the Divide it was necessary to cross Pipestone en route to Butte, Anaconda, Missoula and other destinations in Western Montana. It was a windy road with a number of hairpin turns, and the drop-off to "below" was steep.

Jerry Lightfoot, one of the team members, tells the story like this. The Vigilantes had played in the District tournament and were headed home in two cars. Jerry had secured a seat in the back of the coach's car where he could sleep. At some point beyond Pipestone, he awoke to find the car considerably less crowded than when the trip began. He discovered from the only other player remaining that several had been dumped out of the car on the Pass by the coach. They apparently had been complaining about his driving, particularly the speed at which he was (barely) finessing some of the curves. As the griping became more vocal, he slammed on the brakes and told the complaining players to get out of the car. He then drove off without them. The ejected group hitchhiked to Cactus Junction at the top of the Pass and found a phone to arrange a pick-up up by one of the parents, reaching VC nearly at dawn. Hence the vacancy for the coaching position.

In contrast, the relations between my father and the VC residents were uncontentious. All conversations I've had with former players and students have resonated with comments such as we were "so lucky to have him" or "he taught me so much" or "we were so sorry to see him go." One player described him as like a "big brother," which made sense since he was only a few years older than they. One former student and player was particularly grateful for the skills he learned in the commercial classes because those skills enabled him to secure a position as clerk typist, saving him from the Korean battlefield when he was drafted into the army following graduation in 1953. In contrast to some contemporaries, he was a young coach who resonated with his players and fans even though his record was far from stellar.

Meagher Bravado and Vigilante Ruthless Efficiency

One of the smallest schools in the state, VC struggled to be competitive. It was part of District D of the Southern Conference of Class C with its fellow district members being Sheridan, Twin Bridges, Ennis, Harrison, Lima, Boulder and Whitehall. Nearly all these schools were larger, and a couple were among the best in the state for Class C contenders.

In November 1950, inspired to combine the undaunted spiritedness of Meagher and the ruthless efficiency of the Vigilantes, my father began the practices for his first coaching season to make his mark in District D. By all accounts, particularly his, the team's performance was more heavily weighted towards spiritedness and was a little light on ruthless efficiency. In fact, the ruthless efficiency too often was found to reside with the opposing teams. In his later years, he would regale us with stories about his experiences with the Vigilantes, mixing humor and fondness for those days of less than mediocre performance on the court. I tended to view some of his tales as hyperbole, the entertaining stories of an Irishman. What I have discovered these past few years is that he wasn't exaggerating!

By the numbers, it was a formidable schedule for those two seasons with victories against tinier Harrison the only likely successes in conference play. The box scores reveal too many blow-outs with scores like 75 to 30. They were a team with a limited talent base due to the size of the school, and during his years that outlier athlete who occasionally pops up in small towns didn't emerge. These were ordinary guys spending their winter months in a gym to uphold the tradition of the Vigilantes to field a team for their classmates, parents and fans. There are some hints that the losing seasons did take their toll on him. According to Jerry Lightfoot, when my father started coaching, his demeanor was gentlemanly—a la legendary UCLA coach John Wooden—but by the end of his tenure he resembled a raging Bobby Knight, throwing chairs and all. On one occasion, out of exasperation he led them out of the gym and down the snowy street to repeatedly run up and down a hill.

As the years passed and the VC years became more distant, the frustrations were forgotten and only the humor remained when he recounted his tales. One of his favorite stories involved the District tournament in Deer Lodge. According to him, even with every male in the school essentially required to play basketball, it was a struggle to maintain a respectable size roster. As the February tournament approached, he lost several players—one broke his leg, another turned 20 and became ineligible, a third "ran off and got married," and illness felled a fourth. Almost overnight, his roster was reduced from ten to six for the District. In a game that otherwise was not going well, one of the players fouled out so he was down to five. Then another fouled out, and as he headed to the sidelines there remained but four black and red jerseys on the court. When my father looked down the bench, the only other body in his sight, other than the two who had fouled out, was me. He had to go with the four on the court since I was not in uniform. After the referee who had called the last foul became aware of the consequences of his whistle, he made his way over to the bench apologizing: "Gee, if I knew the kid had four fouls and you had no one left, I would have never called it." Unfortunately, there are no rules to reverse a foul. Needless to say, the game did not fall in the win column even though the Vigilantes went foul-less for the remainder of the game. In reflecting on that game, one of his former players provided an insightful angle about the team's limited pool of players. Their tendency to be tight on personnel did not escape the notice of opposing coaches. In his view, certain teams would engage in a particularly physical style of play to generate fouls, and to avoid fouls the VC players would be inclined to not play aggressively.

It was common for me to accompany my father to the gym to attend the practices as his "assistant." With his busy schedule, it was a way for him to spend some special time with his son. I have vague but pleasant memories of walking down the alley on a later winter afternoon to the gym with him. As was the case at the District tournament, I also found myself in the prized position of sitting on the bench during the games and accompanying the team into the locker room during the half-time.

The centerpiece of any half-time break is the pep talk. For one of the mid-season games, it had been a dismal first half for the Vigilantes, and they were trailing badly. Even by the Vigilantes' standards, it was a sub-par game. As he later repeatedly told us, in the locker room he really "laid" into the team for their lack of production. He subjected them to his "Knute Rockne" speech, always his description when he referred to a rousing "give them hell" inspirational talk. No, this speech did not end with "Win one for the Gipper." Rather, it culminated with the more proverbial: "Who the heck [hell?] is on the ball out there?" After a very brief silence in the locker room, there arose the timid voice of a little boy from the corner: "I'm on the ball, dad." As everyone in the locker room turned their attention to me, I guiltily pointed to the ball I was sitting on. The tenseness of the locker room dissipated with the ensuing laughter.

He never mentioned whether the speech or the humor made any difference in the performance of the Vigilantes in the second half. I would like to think that those talks did inspire his players (and me). In later years, my sense of competition was inspired and nurtured by many, but I think it all began with absorbing those half-time "Knute Rockne" pep talks with the spirit of Meagher and the Vigilantes hovering above.

Those who knew my father as a genial Irishman might assume the Wooden demeanor would fit his on-court personality better, but I think the Knight actually is the better analogy. His was a fiery competitive personality. I witnessed this competitive spirit in full display in the summer of 1973 shortly after his 49th birthday, when my cousins and I convinced him to join us in a pick-up game. He reluctantly agreed to play but once in amazingly threw himself full-hearted into the game, including diving for a couple of loose balls on the playground black top. His performance was a revelation to me since I rarely had the opportunity to observe his competitiveness as he typically shied away from such games. Yet, I should not have been surprised since I sat in on those half-time speeches. Furthermore, it was in the genes. I recall his stories about his own mother, an otherwise proper woman with the Victorian mores of her generation, huddled at the table listening to the Saturday broadcasts of Notre Dame football games in the 1930's and cheering fiercely.

Playing in the Harrison "Gym"

As might be expected, the quality of high school gyms in small towns back then was far from first rate. Bucking the trend, VC did have a "state of the art" gym, which had been built a few years earlier with the combination of WPA funding and volunteer labor. The white wooden frame building, which still sits at the corner of Idaho and Van Buren streets, was about two blocks or so from the school. The width of the floor accommodated about five or six feet on either side of the out of bounds lines and the second level had chairs for spectators. Unlike many gyms built in the 1920's and 1930's, there was no running track on the second level creating an overhang over the playing court. The ceiling was spacious with plenty of clearance for the ball. Moreover, during his tenure an electric scoreboard was installed—financed by a junior prom fundraiser. As former player Norm Dixon described it, "it was fancy for the times."

The words "fancy" and "state of the art" were not words that would be used to describe the gym in Harrison, a town of about 150 residents nestled along U.S. Highway 287. The tiny gym was located at the back of a bar, used most of the time as a dance floor, and to no surprise was a frequent topic of his VC stories. During the game, patrons would roam in and out of the gym with drinks and cigarettes in hand. The room filled up with so much smoke and dust that by the end of the game, according to a former player, it was difficult to see the basket at the other end of the court. This was true even though the length of the gym was quite short, half the dimensions of a standard basketball court. The low ceiling provided insufficient clearance for passes. With virtually no space between the court lines and the walls, the few brave spectators were forced to stand along the wall or at the entrance. From the standpoint of the Vigilantes, though, all the gym's limitations apparently helped their game since they always left Harrison with a win.

I recently visited Harrison to try to locate the bar/gym of family lore, but I was informed at the single window post office that Harrison's only bar had burned down about 15 plus years ago. Walking to the site, I found the broken foundations of two adjacent buildings, the back set of which could not have exceeded 25 by 45 feet. (By comparison, a standard high school floor measures 84 feet by 50 feet.). I had found it!

Harrison remains to this day a small farming community by the side of the highway but now houses a few blocks up the road a modern regulation sized gym proudly displaying a sign outside proclaiming it is the "Home of the Wildcats." It is a beautiful facility, but I can't help feel that something has been lost. Gone are the days of stories of high school ball players sharing the court with bar patrons, tales affectionately being re-told 65 years later.

Treatment by an Iconic Doctor

At the end of the first year in VC, my parents decided to extract themselves from the chaotic conditions of the Elling House and to move to the second floor back apartment of a red brick building at the corner of Wallace and Main Streets. Known as Content Corner after its original owner, the building dated back to the 1860's. Notably the rooms comprising the two apartments on the second floor served as the territorial capital offices for Meagher and his aides. But the spirit of the Vigilantes was not far away from the former Meagher premises. Across the street was the so-called "hangman's building," which in its half-constructed state had served as the gallows for Clubfoot George and others in 1864. Similarly, from the edge of the porch extending the full length of the building, one could gaze at the apex of Boot Hill a few hundred yards away. Similar to the Elling House, Content Corner today is listed on the National Register of Historic Places. That means that prior to my fourth birthday I had the privilege (though my mother might dispute that characterization) of living in two places on the National Register—something I have not been able to duplicate in the last 60 years.

When we moved in, the first floor was occupied by Bob's Place, an establishment that sold a variety of goods, including hardware, groceries, snacks and featured one the town's watering spot—a long bar. The proprietor Bob Gohn, whose family had conducted various businesses at the site since 1883, was blind, having lost his sight when has was young in a mining explosion. Bob was an "institution" in VC. Everyone marveled at his ability to run the store and in particular to mix the drinks despite his lack of sight. Bob's most remarkable attribute, however, was his ability to recognize voices—even after the lapse of many years, a feat I saw him reliably perform when I'd returned years later. My father walked in and delivered his standard greeting "Bob, how she go?" and within a few seconds, Bob called out "John Dowdall!"

That summer after his first year of coaching my father sustained a foot injury that effectively ended his own basketball play. With no school commitments during the summer months, he signed up to work on the construction of the new Ennis highway. Early on, a construction tractor ran over his foot breaking several bones, putting him in a hospital in Ennis and ending the much-needed summer income. Charles Bovey, the father of Virginia City's revival and tourist industry, came to the aid of our family. He showed up at the door shortly after the accident in his usual uniform of work clothes with tools hanging on his belt. Although Bovey's familiarity with us was scant, he generously offered my mother a job in the gift shop on the boardwalk to replace the lost income from the accident.

Despite the misfortune of his injury, my father was incredibly lucky to be treated by the local country doctor who would go on to considerable fame in the area of orthopedics. Located in Ennis, Dr. Ron E. Losee was the only doctor for miles. His was a general practice begun two years earlier out of his log cabin home. A Yale Medical School graduate, Losee later attained world-wide distinction for his pioneering techniques in treating damaged anterior cruciate ligaments, known more popularly as ACLs. In particular, he was known for developing a test to determine whether the ACL was torn, which became known as the Pivot-Shift Test or the Losee Maneuver. He also devised innovative surgical techniques to repair the damaged knee.

Losee had settled in Ennis after he left Connecticut with his wife and two-year-old daughter in a 1942 Ford Army Jeep headed to a destination "somewhere west." He'd chosen Ennis, home to "600 people and 600,000 trout," after meeting with a group of the town's citizens. His practice began immediately despite the technical deficiency of lacking a license, which he didn't receive until six months later in May 1950. As he describes it, no one cared or ever asked to see his medical diploma or license. They were interested simply in being cared for. At his urging, a modest hospital with five beds was built, which opened its doors (sort of) in August 1950. Reflecting the unconcluded state of construction in those first months, Losee describes the first delivery of a baby at the hospital taking place on an unfinished door supported by two sawhorses!

My mother, who has very fond memories of Losee, was impressed with the degree of care and quality that he displayed in treating the wounded coach, something that was to characterize his long career. While Losee would have been issued his license when he treated my father, he would have had limited experience treating patients requiring setting a cast on such a severely broken foot—particularly one run over by a tractor. So, after he set the leg, he sent my father to Butte to have more experienced physicians check his work.

Losee, still alive at 96, has cut quite a figure in Ennis for the past 65 years. He describes himself as a socialist and an atheist—not common views in rural Montana—and in one interview with the *Bozeman Daily Chronicle* he set forth the rationale for his political views: "the sick and injured have to pay billions to the insurance bosses." As my father would say, Losee is a "character," exhibiting an unconventionality that he always prized. It's fitting that they came together for that brief period in the early 1950's.

Vigilantes or Wildcats?

In August 2011, I visited VC with my family to meet with the gracious, engaging and knowledgeable town historian Evalyn Batten Johnson. In her late 70's, she resides about a stone's throw from where she grew up. In the interim, she has travelled the world, living in Washington D.C. and many other places around the country. Her published work, *Images of America: Virginia City*, is an authoritative text of the town's history filled with priceless photographs. Evalyn's VC roots are revealed in her charming manner, but a short conversation with her also makes clear that she's seen, and understands, the outside world. She was a student during our VC time, and her older brother Bill played on the basketball team.

With her guidance, we toured the abandoned school, the gym, our quarters at Content Corner (now returned to their original office functions) and the museum. The museum's section on the school included a few pictures with my father, but what really struck my attention were two short articles in the local paper *The Madisonian*. In one edition, the team was referred to as the "Vigilantes" and in another as the "Wildcats." Evalyn and Norm Dixon claimed they were the "Wildcats" despite my father's continual references to them as the Vigilantes. I was surprised since I had seen the Wildcats sign in Harrison, and it is rare for Montana high school teams in such close proximity to bear the same nickname, particularly when they are in the same division. The competing references to the team puzzled me—were they the Vigilantes or the Wildcats?

Former players John Sprunger and Jerry Lightfoot solved the mystery for me. Shortly before we arrived, Virginia City was looking for new uniforms, but their tight budget dictated that they be thrifty. Either the principal or the coach came across a great deal on uniforms. A team that shared the black and red colors of the Vigilantes had ordered new uniforms, but for whatever reason failed to take delivery. These uniforms with the right colors but the wrong name (Wildcats) were sitting in inventory with an eager seller. Undeterred by the labeling and motivated by a bargain, the school purchased them. Thus, the Vigilantes became the Wildcats, at least on the uniforms. It was a detail ignored by my father—to him they were always the Vigilantes.

Who Made the Wrong Basket?

On a visit with my mother a couple of years ago, we spent some time mining her memory of the VC years. She mentioned a player who'd scored at the wrong basket, putting up two points for the opposing team at the beginning of the game, but she could not identify the embarrassed cager. She also recalled the names of some of the players: Jerry Lightfoot, Bill Barrett, the Williams' brothers and Dave Gilligan. Dave, whom she thought was one of the better players, was a guy she believed still lived in Missoula. We called his home that day and learned that he had recently passed away, but his widow Carma invited us over that very evening.

Because she had recently broken her leg, Carma instructed us to ring the bell and let ourselves in. Eager to talk about her husband, she proved to be a treasure trove of information. A delightful woman in her early 70's, Carma is herself an author, having written a number of books on genealogy and at least one scholarly article on biology, "Occurrence of Fusarium on Leach Pine Cells from the USDA Forest Service Nursery, Couer d'Alene, Idaho." When I asked how she had broken her leg, she said it occurred in a race. Intrigued, I inquired further and asked for details. Carma responded heartily: "it was a race between a car and a bicycle!"

Sitting on the couch with her casted leg on the adjacent chair, she directed me to room after room to locate assorted books and documents. One of the books she asked me to look at was a genealogy of Dave's family and a history of his life. What a life it was! Dave and his sister had been born in Butte, the children of a miner and his wife who'd died when her children were quite young. Following her death, their widowed father concluded that he was not capable of caring for them and sent them to the state orphanage in Twin Bridges in 1943.

While there, Dave developed an interest in and aptitude for basketball and starred for the orphanage team. His playing came to the attention of Dale Kisling, then the coach at VC. As Dave described it, he was "recruited to play" for the Vigilantes. I had to chuckle at that comment. I've observed at times the unscrupulous high stakes recruiting of middle school players by top-ranked private schools in Massachusetts and elsewhere. The notion of VC "recruiting" in the late 1940's certainly does conjure up a vastly different image from what we witness today.

Kisling was offering Dave the opportunity to leave the orphanage. However, there was the matter of his younger sister, and the 17-year-old Dave said he would leave only if they also found a foster home in VC for his sister Hazel. Kisling located a second home, and they both moved to VC in 1948, two years before we arrived. The book also gave me a glimpse of Dave's humor. Scribbled on his graduation class photo of Dave and five girls was his notation "I graduated in 1951 with five girls and myself, the only boy. How could I be so lucky?" There actually was another guy in the picture: my father.

After reviewing Carma's collection of photos and clippings from Dave's life, I asked her if she could remember any of his basketball stories. She said: "Oh, he always talked about the time he made a basket on the wrong end. He was so nervous because they were playing Twin Bridges. He said that the coach was so mad at him for doing that." My mother and I laughed—we'd found our guy.

I mentioned to Carma that I'd seen a reference to Dave having been a POW during the Korean War. Her response, "Oh my goodness, I was married to that man for 20 years before I found out he had been a POW." Then began her bone-chilling story of what Dave had finally confided to her. After 13 days of captivity, he and two others escaped from the Chinese imprisonment near the Korean-Chinese border. Fortunately, one of the others, a Native American from Minnesota, was very knowledgeable about grubs and shrubs, which sustained them for several weeks. During the day, they hid in the trees so they would not be detected by the Chinese, at times convoying a few yards away. They moved on at night when the possibility of detection was less. They finally came upon the house of a Chinese man who at great personal peril befriended them, fed them and gave directions so they could return to their comrades. After 35 days officially missing, they finally made it back to the American lines.

The escape from captivity was not the only heroics he displayed. He fought in the protracted battle of Heartbreak Ridge, a battle that has worked its way into the chronicles of U.S. military history because of the exceptionally high casualties on both side. For his service in Korea, Dave was awarded the Bronze Medal and the Purple Heart. The Korean experience, she told me, had profoundly affected him: "He never wanted to talk about the war and would never go to any war movies until I finally convinced him to see *Saving Private Ryan*." His reaction to the award-winning Tom Hanks movie: it showed it as it was— "all arms and legs flying."

I left grateful for an evening spent in the company of the remarkable Carma and the chance to encounter Dave Gilligan, albeit posthumously, through her stories. It was a moving tribute to a man who as a youngster had made a shot at the wrong basket playing for the Vigilantes 65 years ago, forever cementing his place in the "Dowdall Family Basketball Lore."

Farewell to the Vigilantes

As the end of our second VC year approached, my father decided it was time to move on. He was following a common pattern of teachers and coaches in Montana at that time. One would secure entry into the high school system through a job at a small school and then work to seek a position at a larger school, hoping ultimately to teach or coach in one of the schools in the larger cities. For him, the next step was to be Beaverhead County High School in Dillon, about 25 to 30 miles away southwest of VC "as the crow flies", but closer to 60 miles driving along Highways 287 and 41 in the valleys abutting the majestic Ruby Range.

My father's experience in VC was life-defining, as his stories so clearly indicate. Not only was it his first professional job, but it was one that enabled him to have a prominent role in both the school and the community. His faithful attendance at the reunions during the years, sometimes acting as the master of ceremonies, and his reliable visits to "say hello" to Bob Gohn were a testament to that. It is true that the VC years did not foster a burning desire to be a career high school basketball coach. Yet, I know he took pride in the continuing references to him in the local newspaper *The Madisonian* as "Coach Dowdall," even when it was an article about the Junior Class play.

As for my mother, the VC experience was a tough one. For a 22-year-old woman with two small children, the town was small and isolated, and she very much missed the lively Missoula scene. Yet, it was not all negative. She recalls with fondness the high school girls, who were only a few years younger than she. On Saturdays she frequently would "pile them in the car" and drive to Sheridan, about 20 miles away, to go shopping. In our second year, she developed a close relationship with Pearl Beardsley, the county clerk, who lived in the front apartment at the Content Corner building. It was a friendship that far outlasted our VC residency. She retains a remarkable memory of those years, the good and the bad, the humorous and the sad.

For me, VC remains a mosaic of recollections. One of my most enduring memories is riding my tricycle down the boardwalk from our home to the gift shop where my mother worked and then into Bob's Place on the return trip. As for basketball, I have various indistinct memories of being in the gym and on the bench but none specifically of any games. Those early VC experiences in that gym were surely the genesis of my passionate, and what has been described at times as fanatical, attachment to being on the court shooting, not sitting on, that ball.

Chapter Three

Cheering On the Beavers

The move to Dillon meant that we now were in the B Conference, reflecting Dillon's status as a mid-size town by Montana standards with a population of 3,268 in 1950. If Virginia City was a nearly depleted mining community turned tourist attraction, Dillon was a "cow town." It was the center of the extremely productive farming and ranching operations spawned by the fertile soil of the Beaverhead Valley. I remember with great affection walking a half block down East Morse Street to South Atlantic Street., the town's main thoroughfare, to watch the cattle drives. For a five-year-old, it was a remarkable sight to see for the first time hundreds of cattle being driven through town, the air filled with their symphony of mooing, as the cowboys on their horses kept them restricted to the streets so as not to traverse the sidewalks onto a front yard. Following their departure we kids marveled at the pot-marking and scent deposited on the streets. The town also was noted for its three day rodeo over the Labor Day week-end, known as the "biggest small town rodeo in the world." That was the essence of Dillon.

Founded as a railroad town in 1880, it originally bore the name Terminus, being the end station of the Utah and Northern Railroad. After the line was acquired by the Union Pacific and extended to Butte, the town was renamed after Sidney Dillon, president of the UP. It soon became known as a wool-shipping center, suggesting that sheep herding was prominent in the area, unusual in cattle country in view of the historic battles between the cattle and the sheep interests in nineteenth century Montana.

In moving to Dillon, we also lost the distinction of living in homes now listed on the National Register, but our first rental on East Orr Street certainly had the feel of "historic" in that the kitchen stove was fired by coal and wood. Our life on East Orr Street was to last only a year when we moved to the most comfortable quarters of my parent's married life to date. An attractive bungalow on East Morse Street with a full porch and plenty of room for the family became our new home. Sitting in the middle of the kitchen was a sparkling gas stove.

Lessons in Competition from the Freshman Coach

Dillon is the seat of Beaverhead County, named after a large rock formation overlooking the Beaverhead River, about 20 miles south of town. The formation strongly resembles the profile of a beaver's head. When Lewis and Clark passed through the valley and came upon the rock, their Shoshone guide Sacajawea knew she was close to home because her tribe had so named it. Following upon the theme, the athletic squads of the school were the "Beavers."

At Beaverhead County High School, known commonly as Dillon High School, my father's coaching duties were limited to "freshmen coach." He also was the teacher of Spanish, Bookkeeping and Civics-Economics and most intriguingly the sponsor of the ski team. I am not certain what his responsibilities were with respect to the ski team, but I am confident that they had nothing to do with instruction since to my knowledge he never was on a ski slope his entire life.

As far as the freshmen coach responsibilities, that too is somewhat of a mystery. The yearbook does not include any pictures of a freshman team. Neither of the other coaches, George Scott and Ben Tyvand, have any recollection of his duties, but the yearbook includes a picture of the three of them captioned as the "coaches." I also have many memories of accompanying him to the gym and the football field for practices and remember in particular playing with the basketball in the gym—dribbling, throwing and sometimes kicking it to a friend, "treated" to spending the afternoon with the freshmen coach's son. My father's responsibilities most likely consisted of running intra-squad practices for the freshman to prepare them for inter-school competition their sophomore year. It assuredly was not a role that would prompt the local newspaper to refer to him as "Coach Dowdall," but the demotion in the coaching ranks was not discernible to me. I continued to hold his position in high esteem and proudly bore the special distinction of "coach's son".

I do not recall receiving any instructions from my father on the mechanics of basketball or any other sport while he was freshman coach. I was the recipient, though, of keen lessons on competitiveness by him, whether or not they were intended as such. While the seeds were planted when I was the half-pint audience for his half-time "Knute Rockne" speeches, his lessons were predominantly "delivered" on the checkerboard. We began our checkers games when I was in kindergarten, and inevitably I was the tearful loser. "Why don't you let him win a game?" my mother would implore, and he would always reassure her it was good training for me. I eventually did win some of those games although it is unclear whether my skills improved that much or he came around to her position and let up his competition. Without a doubt those lessons of defeat made their mark. When I began to play ball a couple of years later, I approached every game with a consuming desire to win, regardless of how trivial

25

the meaning of the outcome. Predictably, what followed was not always an example of being a good loser.

The Blue and the Gold

The other major lesson from the Dillon years was loyalty to a team—I became an ardent fan of the Beavers. Since my father was not the head coach, I had lost my cherished position on the bench and the privilege of going to the locker room during half-time. I sat in the stands, but I was not to be disappointed since there were compensating advantages to sitting in the bleachers rather than on the floor. From that vantage point I was to be introduced to the pageantry of 1950's Montana high school basketball. As a Class B school, we possessed deeper resources, which meant the Beavers played in a larger gym, and importantly much more went on in that gym during the games. In contrast to the VC gym, the Beavers' facility offered eight to ten rows of rising benches on each side of the floor. The cheering section for the Beavers was on one side of the floor and the opposition was on the other. A photo from the era shows the bleachers filled with zealous fans standing with clenched fists raised toward the rafters. I was surrounded by fans who shared my commitment to the Beavers cause!

The stands enabled me to see all the action on the floor, not only the game but the rest of the spectacle surrounding the competition, the "blue and gold," the cheerleaders and twirlers, the band and the rabid fans. In contrast to the red and black of the Vigilantes, the Beavers assumed the colorful combination of blue and gold and everywhere I looked my eyes feasted on those colors. They were not limited to the uniforms of the players, but were to be found on the "Beavers" insignia, the "BCHS" inscribed on the floor, the wall banners and the protective mats hung on each end of the court.

To appreciate the true brilliance of the colors we only had to look to the cheerleaders. I was fascinated by the young women on the floor costumed in their blue and gold blouses or sweaters and matching skirts, with their blue and gold megaphones appended to their arms. With their contagious enthusiasm, they served as the emotional intermediaries between the action on the court and the cheering fans, seemingly monitoring both simultaneously. Before the tip-off and during time-outs and the half-time, the cheerleaders under the inspiration of "yell queen" Louisa Piazzola, would lead the fans in various cheers and songs. They complemented their vocal calisthenics with spirited and vigorous routines involving jumping, handsprings, legs splitting, twirling and other acrobatic maneuvers. Their blue and gold-clad bodies were in perpetual motion. Regardless of the contortions of their bodies, they never stopped smiling. Their skirts were long, corresponding with the fashions of the day with the hems falling somewhere between the knee and the ankles. However, as they spun around, the skirts lifted and occasionally displayed the blue or gold "bloomers," a sight of unending fascination for the six-year-old spectator in the stands. From his bedazzled perspective, nothing could surpass the magnetic and entrancing glory of those cheerleaders.

A critical accompaniment to the cheerleaders' efforts was the band, ensconced within the cheering section. The Beaver's band had many functions, such as playing at official events and performing a few thematic programs during the year (e.g., Christmas or spring). An abbreviated section performed as the "dance band" at proms and mixers. One of their most valued duties was to play at the football and basketball games under the guise of the "pep band." And plenty of pep was provided by that ensemble of approximately 30 brass, wind and percussion instruments, ranging from the tuba to the piccolo. Their repertoire included a number of marching tunes and other anthems that elevated the level of energy among the Beaver fans, but the rallying point for the faithful was the school song.

Nearly all schools in Montana had their own "fight song," usually based on the well-known melody of a college anthem. For the Beavers it was the "Maine Stein Song," made famous by Rudy Vallee on the radio in the late 1920's. With the band playing the melody imported from the Down East country, the Beaver fans, young and old, stood and sang:

> On to vict'ry Beaverhead,
> We fight for the blue and gold.
> Take the ball and keep it goin'
> Show them that you're blue and gold
> Rah Rah Rah
>
> We will win the game this time
> Rain or shine or cold.
> So on to vict'ry Beaverhead,
> Fight for the blue and gold.
> B E A V Beavs!

Rudy Vallee's rendition of the Stein Song (captured on YouTube) was good, but it did not compare with the rousing version of the song emanating from the Beavers' gym.

The pageantry reached its apex during the half-time when the band and cheerleaders moved to the center of the court where until a few minutes earlier the valiant Beavers had contended with the visiting opponents. Their mission was to provide us a change of pace: a medley of entertainment to relieve the tension from the first half play. The band would play a number of songs around a theme that was not necessarily related to basketball or the Beavers, affording the band leader an opportunity to display a broader and more creative range. Joining the band and the cheerleaders for the half-time "show" were the twirlers and flag swingers, a group of eight to ten young women with batons and blue and gold flags moving in synchronized fashion. Most amazing of all was the sight of the leader dressed in white hurling the baton high into the air and then catching it as it came down—without missing a beat.

As I think back on the half time show during those games, I am somewhat reminded of the role of the "comic relief" scenes provided by Shakespeare in his tragedies. He usually would insert these scenes after dramatic moments in the play to release some of the escalating emotional tension and to provide amusing entertainment before the story continued. Similar benefits were afforded the fans during the half-time performances. Certain emotions would have erupted from the first half of play—nerves on edge if it was a close game, exhilaration if it was a Beavers' blow-out and despondency if the Beavers had performed miserably. Whatever the prevailing emotion, the spectacle was a welcome fifteen minute release and distraction before the players positioned themselves around the half-court circle for the second half tip-off.

The mascots, the school songs and the school colors defined the 1950's Montana pageantry. There was a sense of proprietary ownership among the fans with respect to these symbols of their zealotry. The mascots, reflected in the schools' nicknames, were particularly esteemed for their uniqueness, and much creativity was exhibited in searching out the perfect rallying point for the allegiances to their team. Animals, particularly Montana natives, were favorites, but the names team uniforms displayed also reflected the diversity of the state's industries (Engineers, Locomotives, Sheepherders, Savage Heat, Refiners, Miners, Loggers, Beeters, Prospectors, Wardens).

The range of school songs was more limited, probably reflecting the smaller universe from which to choose. "On Wisconsin" was the runaway leader with 35 schools adopting the charging rhythm and stirring lyrics of the Big 10 favorite. In second place with about 25 adherents was the Notre Dame Victory March. In contrast, the Maine Stein song was selected by only a few. Blue and gold were the most popular school colors, a combination rivaled only by maroon and white.

The blue and gold had another significance for me; it also appeared on the uniforms of another team in the Beavers' conference, the Anaconda Central Saints. As a loyal fan of the Beavers, my six-year-old self reserved special contempt for the hated Central Saints. Not only did they expropriate "our" colors, but my mother's younger sister attended the school, and Aunt Ann took every opportunity to tease me about the rivalry, abetted by my Uncle Fr. Bill. Their provocations included teaming up to bellow out the Anaconda Central Victory March song (a re-working of Notre Dame's), and together they took great pleasure in reminding me of the last time the Saints beat the Beavers. From time to time, I also had to endure the receipt of a "gift," representing some memento of the Saints when Aunt Ann came for a visit. It was all in good humor, but I was a loyal fan and a humorless six-year-old defender of my team's honor. Unsurprisingly, their playful jesting cemented my attachment even more vigorously to the cause of the Beavers.

Lost in all this bantering was that the Saints were my parents' alma mater. More amazingly, I certainly could not have imagined that ten years later I would be wearing the blue and gold uniform of the Saints, competing against the blue and gold of the Beavers.

Two Coaches and One in the Wings

As for the Beavers' success on the court, we experienced two remarkably different seasons. During the first, the Beavers lost more games than they won, which included losing decisively to such Class B rivals as Deer Lodge and Anaconda Central. More embarrassingly, we lost by a score of 65 to 47 to Twin Bridges, a member of the lowly Class C to which VC belonged. The following year was a saga of triumph and excitement. With a dominating second half of the season leading to capturing the divisional tournament championship, the Beavers were catapulted into the state tournament. While they disappointingly were quickly eliminated at State, I was thrilled with the season, which became the catalyst for my first ambition in basketball, to someday play for the Beavers.

Like my father, both basketball coaches at Dillon were recent university graduates who had been War veterans. The Beavers' experience of head basketball coach George Scott reflects well the vagaries and uncertainties of coaching in Montana during that era. At only 5'7", George had compiled an impressive basketball resume before taking over the coaching reins. His high school team from Columbus, a relatively small town in central Montana, won the 1945 state B championship. He entered the army after high school and ended up stationed in Alaska. With military matters quiet as WWII was winding down, he was able to compete on three army teams that played a full schedule in the military leagues in the future 49th state.

After being discharged, George played guard for the Montana University Grizzlies despite his size. He initially was not hired to coach the Beavers when he received his teaching contract for Dillon in 1951. That all changed when in August he received a call from Lou Rocheleau, the Dillon basketball coach and a teammate from the Grizzlies. Lou had just been hired as the varsity basketball coach at Missoula Sentinel, one of the largest schools in the state, placing him in a position of power and influence. "I have recommended you for the job," Rocheleau told George. His recommendation was sufficient, and George assumed the position of head coach three months after graduating from college. George was to learn that success in coaching required more than being able to draw up x's and o's.

The five years that he spent in Dillon had its share of valleys and peaks, as reflected in my two years of cheering for the Beavers. As George pointed out to me, such cyclicality is bound to occur since the major determinant of a coach's success is the talent, which varies from year to year in a small town. The championship year buoyed his position, but the uplift was temporary as the record for the following year was mediocre. Shortly before the opening of the ensuing school year and 18 months after returning from the state tournament, a friend warned him of an impending "plot" involving, among others, the new school principal, some school board members and the coach at Western Montana College (a few blocks from the high school) to replace him at the end of the season. The coach to-be-in-waiting was a recent graduate who had played forward for the Western basketball team, Pat Curran.

According to the script, the designated replacement was being hired to teach English and to serve as the assistant coach in basketball and football before being promoted. Disregarding such intelligence, and too much of a novice to understand that alliance building is important, George considered it inconceivable that after his recent success such a turn of events could occur. Unfortunately for him, the season went poorly as his team of limited talent lost six games in the month of December. As the tough season came to a conclusion, he was informed that his teaching contract was being renewed but not his coaching contract. The man who had orchestrated the remarkable season that had nurtured my engagement with the game was dismissed. As had been disclosed to him before the season began, the board hired Curran. George declined the teaching contract and moved on to Red Lodge, which both offered a fresh start and put him much closer to his recently widowed mother.

When I met George a couple of years ago, he was a remarkably "young" 86 year-old sitting in his golf attire after having completed a round for the day. As he reflected on those events nearly 60 years ago later, he commented on the requisite political skills for a successful coach: "I didn't know enough to go to the school board meetings; after that I always made it a point to know the school board members." He apparently learned the lesson well because he followed up the Dillon experience with nearly 30 years of success without being fired again. His was a story I was to witness repeatedly. Coaching at the high school level involved considerably more skills than technical knowledge of the game or even being able to motivate 16- and 17-year-olds. Adroit political and personal relations skills were even more critical. It was a tough assignment for young guys who had only recently completed their college studies and were unaware of the many forces that impacted the key role of Coach in a small town.

The other basketball coach was Ben Tyvand, who guided the B squad, known affectionately as the Tyvand Bombers, but his principal contributions to the Beavers' sports program was as coach of the varsity football team. A star running back and captain for the Montana Grizzlies, Ben's first job after graduation was the head football coach position at Dillon. His teams on the gridiron in Dillon were extremely successful, so the circumstances of his departure from the school were considerably happier than George's. He was elevated up to the vaunted AA conference to assume the position of varsity football coach for the Anaconda Copperheads. In contrast to George Scott, I remember Ben well from our Dillon days because he was a good friend of my father's and his daughter Charlene was a classmate of mine in kindergarten.

Two of these three coaches, Ben Tyvand and Pat Curran, were to re-enter my life dramatically in later years. I also was to witness up close the devastating firing of each from their coaching position in those years.

Benny Reynolds: Dillon's Best Athlete

Ben Tyvand also was responsible for delivering to the Beavers Dillon's greatest athlete of that period, Benny Reynolds. I did not watch Benny on the basketball court competing for the Beavers because his athletic exploits were featured in another arena. He was a champion cowboy, and it's certainly appropriate, in view of its traditions, that Dillon's best athlete of the era was a rodeo hero.

In recruiting Benny, rodeo considerations were not on Ben's mind; rather, he recruited Benny to play football. Having grown up on a ranch near Melrose, equidistant between Butte and Dillon, Benny had the choice to attend either school, and he had opted for Butte. One day Ben was alerted that there was a "big kid" from Melrose who was attending Butte High. At the first opportunity, Ben hopped into his car and drove north 45 minutes to the Reynolds' homestead. He left an hour later with a commitment from the strapping 6'3" teenager to spend his senior year at Beaverhead High.

To Ben's disappointment, after a couple of practices, Benny decided that football was not for him. Still wanting to showcase Benny's natural athletic talent, Ben did get Benny involved a little with basketball that winter. It was in track, though, that his athletic abilities most shone. Because of his size, Ben originally targeted Benny for the "weight" events such as the shot put and the discus, but he also discovered that he had decent speed.

Early in the season at a meet in Hamilton, Benny won the 100-yard dash. Benny's blue ribbon in the event surprised Ben since Benny was not his number one sprinter. He became even more perplexed when he looked down at his watch—it revealed a winning time of 11.0 seconds, much slower than it should have been. He then examined the track and saw that there was a thick layer of newly laid cinder rock. In contrast to the other runners who became mired in the sloppy surface, Benny had been able to power his way through to win the race. Impressed with the victory, Ben approached Benny about spending the night with the group that would head up the valley to Corvallis. "Can't do it," Benny replied. "Why not, Benny?" Ben responded. "Who's gonna feed my horse?" Benny asked rhetorically. After some negotiations, Benny put in a call to his home to enlist the aid of the family to feed the horse.

As it turns out, feeding that horse was critically important for Benny. Within a few years of high school graduation, he was awarded the Rookie of the Year honors by the Rodeo Cowboy Association. This distinction was followed three years later when he captured the title of World Champion All-Around Cowboy. Spanning four decades, Benny attained success in rodeo that has been matched by few others, resulting in his induction into the Pro Rodeo Hall of Fame. Benny never did play under the Blue and Gold as Ben envisioned. Rather, the stage for his athletic exploits moved considerable beyond the gyms and fields of Beaverhead High where I sat through so many games as a Beavers fan.

It was not rodeo alone, though, that transformed Benny into a Montana folk hero. His numerous appearances in 1958 on the popular television quiz show, *Name that Tune* offered him a much wider audience. With his classic cowboy hat and chiseled features epitomizing the original Marlboro Man, his drawled "Yep" and "Nope" in conversation with the host George DeWitt made him a national celebrity to all watching him on the black and white screen.

In early 2014, Benny left behind all his honors and celebrity when he died at age of 77 while loading hay bales on his ranch. Through the years, he retained a deep affection for his old coach Ben. At a Beaverhead High reunion a few years back, Benny with that highly marketable smile approached Ben and warned him "you're not going to like this" as he planted a big kiss on his cheek.

No Longer a Coach's Son

After two years of coaching the freshmen and serving as the sponsor of the ski team, my father applied for an opening to teach history, commercial and Spanish at Anaconda High School. It was a move eagerly awaited by my parents since they were returning to their roots, family and friends. When he told me that we were moving to Anaconda, my first question was whether he was going to be a coach. To my utter disappointment, his answer was that he was not. He then added, unfathomable to me at the time, "I never really liked coaching." My privileged status as the son of a coach had ended with that decision.

I believe I had a discussion with him at some point as to why he did not like coaching, but I remember little of it. Certainly the relations between school boards and parents had nothing to do with it because he was revered in Virginia City and as freshman coach in Dillon he would've "flown under the radar." Perhaps the time commitment with modest compensation was the reason. Frustrations with losing may have contributed to his feelings, but that had ended in VC. Ultimately, I think he was not destined to be a coach, a profession that requires a real passion to endure both winning and losing seasons in a pressure-filled environment where success is dependent upon the performance of teenagers.

Whatever the reason, he never coached another team at any level, and I was to move on to playing the game under the guidance of other coaches and mentors, official and unofficial. Many of them were outstanding, and I was the beneficiary of their excellence and generous attention to me.

Chapter Four

Smelter City Legacy

As our family travelled from Virginia City and Dillon, the approach to Anaconda was from the east. Snaking along the windy old U.S. Highway 10 from Butte, the Anaconda Stack became majestically visible as we curved around a hill shortly before Crackerville, eight miles from Anaconda. My sister Mary Anne and I always played a game as to who first saw the Stack, the winner being the one who could blurt out the words a millisecond before the other. Even from a distance, smoke from the Stack could be seen day and night trailing down the valley towards us in the car. When the wind blew the wrong way, that smoke descended on the town. Part of the experience of living in Anaconda was periodically detecting the sweet taste of arsenic on our tongues.

Under the Big Stack: A Hard-Living Town

The defining characteristic of Anaconda was that Stack. The town was known as the "Smelter City," with the east side dominated by the copper smelter on the "Hill," rising perhaps two or three hundred feet from the valley floor where the town sat. Officially named the Anaconda Reduction Works, the smelter extracted copper ore from the rock mined in Butte 23 miles away. Looming atop the apex of the hill was the Stack that projected 585 feet in height and measured 86 to 60 feet in diameter. As every Anacondan knew, the Stack was the tallest in the world and could engulf the entire Washington Monument within its dimensions.

Traveling today on the arrow-straight four lane Highway U.S. 10A, one drives by Opportunity and then comes upon the road sign for "Wisdom" with an arrow pointing to the left. To reach Anaconda, you continue straight ahead another three miles. The Wisdom sign is a reference to a town located in the noted Big Hole valley with its extraordinary fishing holes and fertile ranch land. Nevertheless, my Boston family always has been amused that one must bypass Opportunity and forsake "Wisdom" to visit dad's hometown.

Shortly beyond the Wisdom turn-off you reach Anaconda's second most striking landmark—a massive black slag pile that stretches a mile and a half and reaches the approximate height of an eight story building. A by-product of the smelting process, the 40 million tons of slag began to accumulate decades ago. By the 1950's it was a formidable sight of peaks of pebbly molton rock unrelieved by vegetation. Continuing into Anaconda, the blue-grey south-western horizon is dominated by the ridges and summit of Mt. Haggin, part of the Continental Divide that rises to a height of 10,607 feet. A contrapuntal note to the grittiness and assault upon nature represented by the smelter, Haggin reminded us that we were in fact in the midst of the majestic northern Rocky Mountains. Following beyond Haggin, the Divide leads to the Pintler area, one of the most spectacular wildernesses in the country (and one that was relatively undiscovered by tourists during my Anaconda days).

The scenery was spectacular, but as kids we lived and played on the streets of Anaconda. Similar to its sister (always competitive and sometimes feuding) city of Butte, Anaconda was known as a place where people worked hard and in the afterhours engaged in even more vigorous recreation. Fellow Montanans considered it a tough city, a reputation I never fully was aware of until I was in high school and began to meet my contemporaries from other parts of the state. Accordingly, it is appropriate that one of the most prominent athletes to emanate from Anaconda was Roger Rouse, who twice contended for the light heavy weight boxing title in the 1960's and to my knowledge was the only person from Anaconda who was the subject of a profile in *Sports Illustrated*.

Founded in 1883, the town had not yet reach its 75th birthday when we arrived. Our founder Marcus Daly was an Irish immigrant arriving in New York penniless at the age of 15. In 30 years he would become one of the richest men in the world. The source of his wealth was the mining and smelting operations of the company he founded, the Anaconda Company, the most notable of the copper companies that rose to prominence during the latter part of the 19th century. The spectacular rise coincided with the development and spread of electricity with its requirements for copper to form wiring. Attracted by the nearby water and timber resources, Daly found the Anaconda site to be an ideal one for the reduction of the copper ore mined in Butte.[2] It certainly was con-siderably more convenient than Swansea, Wales, where the ore previously had been smelted. The town attracted a large number of Irish and then Croatian and Serbian immigrants to work initially at the Old Works smelters on the north side of the valley's opening. Operations switched to the Hill around the begin-ning of the 20th century. The city was a favorite of Daly's also because it of-

---

[2] There is some uncertainty about the origins of the name. Most agree that the original "Copperopolis" was rejected for Anaconda. It also is clear that there are no Anaconda snakes existing in the area. Some attribute the name to the "snake-like" valley the town sits in. The most likely explanation is that it was named after Daly's Anaconda mine in Butte, which in turn probably was named by a Union-supporter manager who remem-bered a newspaper article in which Grant was described as surrounding the Confederate army like an "Anaconda."

fered an ideal setting to build a magnificent racetrack for his favorite horses to compete against some of the best in the Northwest and beyond.

Besides the Hill, the Anaconda Company had one other major operation in Anaconda, the Butte, Anaconda & Pacific Railway, or the BA&P as everyone referred to it. As the name suggests, originally there were outsized ambitions to establish a line extending from Butte westward for about 600 miles, but the tracks never made it farther than 15 miles west of Anaconda. Included among its operations was the carpentry shop that employed my mother's father.

As was typical in western mining and smelting towns (particularly those populated by European immigrants), liquor was an important element in daily life, and the town's social scene revolved principally around the bars and the high school athletic games. And bars there were in Anaconda; no less an authority as *Sports Illustrated* credited Anaconda in its article on Roger Rouse with having "possibly more bars per capita than in any other city in the U.S." The *SI* writer reported 37 within the city limits—an astonishing number for a population of 12,000, and I thought the reporter missed a few in his count.

The liquor business had been part of the history of my father's family in Anaconda. At one point, my grandfather Michael J. Dowdall, originally from County Derry, Ireland, owned two establishments, both of which ultimately failed. According to my father, my grandfather was "too generous" to his friends—translated, that meant too many free drinks were forwarded in their direction. As I remember the protocol, for a customer the third or fourth drink would "be on the house." That practice presumably was breached by my grandfather with a more favorable fraction assigned to his customers. I don't know for certain when his businesses failed, but my first memories of him in the early 1950's were seeing him walking west on Fifth Street to the Washington Elementary School where he worked as a janitor.

Michael Dowdall's involvement in liquor sales preceded his ownership of bars. According to family lore and confirmed by at least one publication, he walked around the neighborhood with a baby carriage delivering home-made whiskey to the neighbors during Prohibition. For a few years, my infant father helped play an important role in the deliveries. As the youngest child, he rode in the buggy with the bottles hidden beneath him. Apparently, Baby John's growth and eventual graduation from service as the baby in the buggy did nothing to discourage the continuation of the business. The enduring presence of that buggy intrigued neighbors, as described in a book on the town: "People in the family would push a buggy. Well, we knew there was no baby in that family, but they were pushing a buggy. It was an Irish family [Dowdall] and they would make deliveries....You could never stop to look at the baby! I thought maybe they had a new baby in the family and would love to see it! 'Oh we can't show the baby to anybody' [laugh]"

That entrepreneurial spirit also was exhibited by my mother's forebears. Her great grandfather Ed Devine migrated to Anaconda in the early

1880's and established one of the first non-Company grocery stores on East Third Street at the current site of Carmel's Bar. As reflected in a photo around 1900, the store sold "hay, grain, bran, wheat, oats, flour, etc." It appears also that the fermented products of such grains were on the shelves, as evidenced by a number of newspaper ads in the 1890's informing the residents that Devine's was introducing to Anaconda some of the finer liquor products—"previously available only in Butte."

While Anaconda was known as a tough city, it also was an incubator of churchmen and scholars. As I was growing up, it became clear to me that the vast majority of the priests in the diocese of Helena originated from either Butte or Anaconda, including my two uncles. Anaconda also was the hometown of both bishops of the diocese during my youth, Joseph P. Gilmore, presiding from 1936 until his death in 1962 and Raymond G. (Dutch) Hunthausen thereafter.

Hunthausen was a classmate of my uncle Father Bill's from first grade through the Seminary. Their close friendship meant our whole family took pride in a connection to a man whose accomplishments and integrity made him a larger-than-life figure to many. Hunthausen had been an outstanding athlete in Anaconda and at Carroll College, where he also served as both the football and basketball coach during the 1950's. Dutch, as everyone referred to him, was very much a man of the people. Following his consecration as bishop of the Helena dioceses, Jack Lodell, the Juvenile Probation Officer, confided to a group of us that in his school days, "Dutch was the toughest guy on the block." As bishop and later archbishop in Seattle, Dutch stalwartly represented the spirit of Vatican II, of which at the time of this printing he is the sole surviving American delegate. Through some lean times, he advanced the principles of the progressive wing of the Church on matters of social justice and war and peace, objectives which again have returned to the forefront of the Church's mission under Pope Francis.

While Archbishop of Seattle, he also entered the political arena as he announced that he was withholding 50% of his income taxes to protest stockpiling of nuclear weapons. Responding to certain right wing critics provoked by his liberal Vatican II policies, including special ministries to gays, the Vatican led by Cardinal Ratzinger (later Pope Benedict XVI) voiced its displeasure and temporarily re-allocated some of his authority to a newly appointed Auxiliary Bishop. Perhaps the most disturbing aspect of the affair was the failure of Hunthausen's peers, the American bishops, to defend him from the Vatican onslaught. Led by Cardinal Bernard Law of Boston, the bishops failed to loyally back their colleague in 1986. It should come as no surprise that 15 years later the misplaced loyalty of Law and others was glaringly on display in connection with the clerical sexual abuse scandal. A devoted churchman, an outstanding human being and a terrific athlete—Dutch came from a mold that increasingly is disappearing among his peers, and we very much considered him "ours."

Anaconda also was a fertile ground for developing scholars in the '50's. One of them, Thomas Flynn, also was ordained a Catholic priest, and as an altar boy I was honored to be part of his "First Mass" in Anaconda. After a short stint teaching at Carroll College, Flynn moved his academic interests across the country to Columbia University where he earned his Ph.D. in philosophy with a specialty in French existentialism. For most of his academic career, he has been a professor at Emory University in Atlanta, a university with Methodist roots.

It was through Methodism that Lester Thurow arrived in Anaconda when his father became the minister of a Methodist congregation. Lester graduated from Anaconda High in 1956, and for a number of decades, he was one of the most highly visible economists in the country, the dean of the M.I.T. Sloan School of Management and the author of many highly regarded works that frequently challenged orthodox thinking. During his student days in Anaconda, he shared the distinction with others of being taught typing by my father. While I've always followed Lester's career with some pride in sharing a hometown, I don't remember his days in Anaconda since I was too young. I do vividly recall his younger brother Glen, also a spectacular student, and particularly embedded in my memory is his high school graduation where he garnered so many honors. These made an impression on the younger ambitious me. He followed his older brother to Williams College and then to Harvard for a Ph.D. in the Government Department. In contrast to Lester, who was a prominent liberal economist, Glen studied political theory, converted to Catholicism, and ultimately became the provost at a decidedly conservative Catholic school, the University of Dallas.

It's hard to describe just how foreign these distant Eastern institutions seemed from the Anaconda of my days, but to know there were others with the ability to bridge that gulf was fascinating to me. In fact, Glen became one of the first doctoral students of Harvey Mansfield of Harvard, with whom I had the opportunity to study a decade later.

The Old Hoop at St. Paul's Playground

In mid-summer of 1954, our family of four continued its tradition of moving to a new residence each year when we arrived at 414A Locust Street. The A indicated that it was the "back" house on that lot, a common practice in Anaconda. From my standpoint, it was a particularly advantageous location since our kitchen window looked out across the alley to St. Paul School, where I was to spend the next eight years. Strategically, the house abutted the nearly half block asphalt-covered playground for the school, so I was in the position of being able to peek out that kitchen window any time of the day to check out the activity. This was particularly useful in the morning when I could assure myself that I wasn't missing any of the pre-school play. Near the southeastern corner of the playground, about 20 yards from our door was a basketball hoop. It was a sorry looking one with the pole slightly bent and the backboard and rim loosely secured. I never saw a net adorn that rusted rim.

The forlorn structure was rarely used, but it became my first "hoop" as I began to spend much of my free time there with my newly acquired rubber ball. Initially my shot was the underhanded scoop shot, but eventually I graduated to the over-handed shot as I gained more strength and experience. I discovered it was a matter of securing the ball in the left hand and then using the entire body, particularly the legs, to push the ball up with the right arm so that it sailed above the 10 feet needed to clear the rim. My shooting percentage was dismal in those early days, but as the year progressed I approached respectability. The action around the hoop was mostly shooting around although occasionally another kid would show up so we could play a one-on-one game. By the end of the year, I was hooked on the game.

Basketball did not engage my fellow students before the school bell and during recess. Rather, the favored game was a bastardized form of soccer, played with a basketball that had been drained of nearly all its air. The game was open to anyone who wanted to play, which at times seemed to include all the boys in the school. En masse we chased the lumpy ball from one end of the schoolyard to another. Lacking a "net" or its equivalent, points were scored when the ball crossed designated goal lines. On one end the line was clearly delineated since it was the sidewalk, while at the other end a rather fuzzy border separating the playground and the alley was designated. Our large kitchen window was only a few feet from the "goal line," and situated next to the window was our kitchen table. During one memorable noon hour when my father was dining during his lunch break, he suddenly found himself presented with a deflated basketball and broken glass on his plate. The eighth-grader who had scored the goal was duly apologetic and arranged for a new window. The makeshift rules committee made modifications to the definition of the field to avoid any future disruptions of my father's meal.

The popular game in the winter was "last one up," a version of "pump, pump, pull away." A dictionary of children's sports defines this as a type of tag game. That was not how we played it. On St. Paul's playground, it was a game of tackling—smacking down guys on the snow packed ground. All players (usually comprised of all the boys in the school) would run from one goal line to another to avoid being tackled by the defenders with the game ending when no one was left standing. After the final person was tackled, the call of "last one up" would be heard, and everyone ran back to the initial goal line. The last person to cross the line was relegated to the defense to begin a new game. It was rough and the state of our clothes after recess or even in the morning would not pass muster as "Sunday best." My hoop stood in the midst of these games, but somehow avoided incurring damage to itself or the players.

Around the time I reached the fourth grade, the Benedictine nuns who had assumed responsibility for the school outlawed the game as well as the soccer. The playground then became a considerably less interesting place to play for several years until a new basketball hoop was installed, a story for a later chapter.

Basketball Heritage

When my parents moved back to Anaconda, they looked forward to renewing and deepening old friendships that went back to their grade school days. They also knew that they were moving to a town where basketball was a prominent part of its heritage. The tradition of the game was steeped in history as Anaconda High, known by many as AHS, had played in the first two Montana high school championship games in 1911 and 1912. While they ended up the runner-up in the inaugural game with a loss to Billings by the score of 27 to 20, in the second year the quintet of Guy Burnett, Ed (Jimmy) Hauser, Granton Sullivan, Charles Flood and Joe Kelly demolished Flathead County High School by a score of 49 to 13. That team featured arguably the first basketball superstar of Montana—Hauser, who scored 38 points in the title contest, a truly remarkable feat at a time when basketball was characterized by low scoring. The Copperheads were to follow up with state championships in 1934 and 1948 in the highly competitive Class A Division and second place finishes in 1936 and 1940. The 1948 team featured the celebrated future NBA player, Ed Kalafat.

The Central Saints, however, had enjoyed the most recent state championship success in 1951 with a victory of 54 to 50 over Ft. Benton (the site of the mysterious drowning 80 years earlier of Governor Meagher of Virginia City). While Central resided in the less competitive Class B, in that championship year they defeated the Class A victors, Flathead Braves, not only once but twice by margins of 12 and 5 points. The coach of the Braves was John Cheek, who when we arrived in Anaconda was the Copperheads new coach and was to remain in that position for decades.

The symbol of basketball preeminence in Anaconda was Memorial Gym, where I played my last high school game and suffered that devastating loss to Deer Lodge. Built as a memorial to the city's war dead in 1950, the gym was one of the largest basketball venues in the state at its opening with a capacity of about 4,000. It was a remarkable building for a town of that size. Its grey concrete hulking presence, resembling in some respects the Brutalist architecture style that was to become prominent during the 1950's, occupied nearly the entire east side of the 600 block of Hickory Street in an otherwise residential neighborhood. It was to become an important destination of mine for the next dozen years.

And then there was the city championship. It was a rivalry that spanned 50 years until Anaconda Central was closed in 1973, and the stories surrounding the game were passed down through generations—fathers, uncles, older brothers and even grandfathers. The role of the city championship in defining Anaconda's basketball heritage cannot be overstated and accordingly will receive a deservedly full treatment in the next chapter.

Am I a Copperheads Fan or a Saints Fan?

Soon after moving to Anaconda, I was faced with a major decision—which high school team was to gain my allegiance. With the tradition of the city championship and the impassioned loyalties generated by the schools' fans, a decision had to be made. It was a complex decision for a seven-year-old brain to process. My father was a teacher at Anaconda High, so that presumably should be the choice. On the other hand, both my parents were alumni of Anaconda Central, and my Aunt Ann was a senior that year. To further complicate matters, my father was not the only family member who was an employee of the public high school. My Grandmother Kantack, who had been widowed in her mid-40's, was a janitress at the school. Her boss was Michael O'Leary, who had been the Copperheads basketball coach for nearly two decades, but she was an ardent Saints' fan. Yet, I had spent the prior two years as a diehard Beavers fan and an antagonist to the Saints, and such loyalties died hard. When the Beavers visited the city to play Anaconda Central in football and basketball that year, I secretly rooted for the Beavers. Simply moving away from Dillon was not going to change the deeply attached loyalties nurtured during those formative years. Ultimately those loyalties did fade, though, and I had to directly confront my dilemma.

Ann certainly did her part to convert me to the Saints. She brought me to numerous football and basketball games (as well as her softball and volleyball games), and we always sat in the front row of the Saints cheering section, a prerogative enjoyed by seniors. She was not a cheerleader, but it seemed that she always was directing the cheerleaders with the authority of one who, at least by my estimation, was the best female athlete in her class. Ann was important, but it was my Grandmother Kantack who had the greatest influence on where my new loyalties were to be directed.

A fervent, no, a rabid sports fan, she looked to me, her eldest grandchild, to be her companion for all the home games, football and basketball. Grandma Kantack, lived alone with a yappy, territorial little dog named Midgy. She was a tall and big woman who loved to spend an occasional evening with her friends at the Copper Club. She also loved to laugh and was gifted with a voice that could carry in a crowded gym. But her life had witnessed many tragedies. She lost her parents when she was in her twenties and her husband while in her forties, forcing her into the workplace as an attendant at the state mental hospital in Warm Springs and then to her janitorial duties. Having enjoyed a pampered and privileged life as an only child, evidenced by a photo at two in her elegant frilly dress with dainty shoes and pet dog, she could not have envisioned the back-breaking labor she would face in her mid-fifties to support herself. Going to the gym or the field was an emotional escape from a tough daily grind, and I was to share the joys of the game with her for several years.

The evening always began with a dinner for the two of us featuring ample portions since she was always concerned that I wasn't being fed enough by my mother, her daughter, an accusation my mother viewed alternatively with derision and humor. It's likely that my grandmother was sharing with me a bit of indulgence for us both. Following dinner, she and I would walk the 10 or 15 minutes from her house on West Seventh Street to Mitchell Stadium for the football games or to Memorial Gym for the basketball. We walked in every kind of weather since she never learned to drive. At the games, she was vocal with nary a "bad" official call or questionable "behavior" on the part of the opposing team or its fans escaping her attention. Ann reminded me that when a tournament was scheduled to be held in Anaconda, the rest of the family colluded to keep her from attending over concern that she "might have a heart attack."

As we walked home, we would re-hash the highlights of the game, which might be the superb performance of one of the players, a turning point in the game or the bad calls of the referees (and there were always plenty to recount). Needless to say, I followed her lead on team loyalties: she was both a Copperheads fan AND a Saints fan except for the one time each year they met—then she was not a Copperheads loyalist. That quasi-Solomonic resolution of team loyalties for me was facilitated by my father leaving teaching after a couple of years to join the Daly Bank as an assistant cashier so he was no longer a teacher at Anaconda High and by her janitorial duties being switched to the Junior High School.

This ritual of dinners followed by games began when I was in the second grade, the year after Ann graduated, and continued until about the fifth or sixth grade when I started attending the games with friends. Looking back, I can imagine her sadness at letting me go since I'd become her protégé in fandom, although I am sure she recognized the inevitability of my deserting her for friends. I imagine that kid thought he could always return again with his grandmother to that shared love of sitting together in those bleachers, cheering and shouting. Now I can recognize the finality of our chapter together in the stands, and I'll always cherish the memories of those weekends together.

A Very Important Year

That first grade year was a memorable one for many reasons, in the classroom and on the playground. I began somewhat academically "behind" many of my classmates. Their kindergarten instruction had been a little more advanced than mine, but I was fortunate to have the instruction of Sister Joseph Marie and was able to catch up quickly. A remarkable and engaging woman from rural Minnesota, she was a dedicated teacher and imparted to me an insatiable love of reading. I could find Sister working in her classroom every day of the week. By crossing our alley to "help" my teacher, I was provided books on a daily basis. This opportunity had the same formative effects as shooting baskets at the lopsided hoop. From that first grade year, reading and basketball became lifelong passions.

Coming to live in Anaconda was especially fortuitous for me for another reason. My uncle Father Bill Morley, my mother's cousin who was raised as a brother after his parent's death, invested a considerable amount of time in me. A big man, probably about 6'3" and always somewhat overweight, he was not an athlete but was a major sports enthusiast. He also was an avid reader, particularly on politics and current events and had an abiding interest in the theatre, especially Broadway musicals. He spent countless hours when I was young educating me in those areas of his interest—showing me his books, summarizing a recent article in *Time* or *U.S News and World Report* or playing the *Sound of Music*, *Hello Dolly* or other current Broadway hits. He loved to devise what he called the Twenty One Thousand Dollar Question game, tossing out questions on the world and state capitals, rivers and mountains and presidents. Looking back, I appreciate how mightily I benefited from these childless teachers so invested in tutoring me, Sister Joseph Marie and Father Bill.

An incident that was to have long-lasting significance for me occurred late in the school year at the threshold of the building and the playground. There were two bells that rang before the opening of classes. At the first bell, we were to assemble in line at the door that led down the steps to the basement level. There were two classrooms for the first graders, and for the most part I knew only those in my classroom. On the other hand, those who had attended kindergarten at the school were apt to have a number of friends in the other class.

One day as we were in line, several boys from my class came over to me and indicated that I needed to "fight" this guy in the other class, whom they described as "really tough." His name was Bill Matosich, compact and muscular even at the age of six, who was immediately recognizable by his shock of bright red hair, undoubtedly reflecting the Scottish heritage of his mother. Why I was chosen for this endeavor is not entirely clear—whether they thought I was a patsy who would be a punching bag or whether I was believed to have the best punch to uphold the honor of the class. In any event, we took a few harmless swings at each other, and then the second bell rang. Those few punches were my introduction to Bill, to whom I was to be tethered in athletics for the next 12 years. They were to be years of alternatively competition and collaboration and at times both simultaneously.

As my first grade came to a close, my parents made the decision to own a home for their growing family with a third child due in December. They found a house at 105 Pine Street, next door to my friend Ed Palakovich, a house that we were to call home for the next 14 years. Initially I had conflicting emotions about the move. I loved living across the alley from the school. In addition to providing an opportunity to monitor the activities on the school grounds, it also was very convenient for inviting friends over. My commute would increase from 10 seconds to 10 minutes of walking. On the other hand, while only seven, I did have some vague understanding of the benefits of home ownership, and I also began to appreciate the attractions of living next door to a classmate.

Prior to the move, my parents hosted Ben Tyvand, their friend from their Missoula and Dillon days. Ben recently was divorced and needed a temporary place to stay for part of the summer while he established himself as the newly hired football coach for the Copperheads. Both around 30, Ben and my father were close friends and drinking buddies. I can remember on more than one occasion my mother being unhappy with both of them because of the late hour that they finished up their socializing. For nearly the entirety of the summer, our sofa in the living room became Ben's bedroom.

From the standpoint of my mother, Ben's stay soon extended far beyond the temporary stage. She firmly informed my father that Ben was not to join us at the new house. Ben did assist in the logistics of the move in that he recruited John Cheek, the basketball coach, to help. The "heavy lifting" of the move in late August was generously undertaken therefore by the two Copperhead coaches and my father, the history/ business teacher at the public school. The overwhelming presence of the Copperheads muscle in effecting the move had no impact, however, on the settlement with my grandmother on team allegiances.

The legacies of the two coaches in Anaconda proved to be radically different. Cheek went on to enjoy a Hall of Fame career until he retired more than 25 years after that move. Within a couple of years, Ben was to suffer a humiliating ouster at the hands of the School Board after a few so-so seasons—his first major setback in his life of athletics that had been saturated with triumphs. He had the misfortune of coaching when the Copperheads lacked enough superior talent for the super-competitive AA division. I also suspect that his innate shyness prevented him from doing the necessary self-promotion and friendship building like attending School Board meetings. He may also have been a victim of Anaconda's basketball dominance; a few excellent athletes, who could have been assets on the football field, opted to play only basketball.

Ironically, it was in basketball that he enjoyed his greatest success in Anaconda. In his final year, he coached the Fabulous Frosh basketball team that went undefeated and was to become one of the great teams in Montana basketball history. That was a team incidentally whose roster featured a number of outstanding football players, including all state center Wayne Estes. They would form the nucleus of a strong football team for a few seasons after Ben's departure. Ben was a victim of unlucky timing, and he never coached another Montana team. With his spirits weighed down by the firing, he crossed the border to Wallace, Idaho, where he was revered by parents and players alike for his 19 years of coaching the Miners. A couple of years ago, a scholarship in his name was set up by his former players.

What my mother did not realize, and could not have known at the time, was that she was kicking out of the house that summer of 1955 someone with whom she would one day share 40 years of marriage. My parents' marriage ended in 1969 after 23 years of marriage. Five years after the divorce, she received a call from Ben, who told her that it had taken a couple of years for him to screw up the courage to telephone her. They were married two years later—a marriage that terminated just short of their 40th anniversary when Ben died last December at the age of 94.

Chapter Five

City Championship: The Tradition

My personal introduction to that marvelous institution, the city championship, occurred during the winter of my first grade year. I don't remember whom I rooted for at that game although my Aunt Ann probably had me buried in the heart of the Saints' cheering section. I also certainly did not appreciate the significance of THE game to Anaconda's culture. That was to change as I became gradually immersed in the city championship tradition as part of my basketball training. Every winter for the next dozen years, I was first a spectator, and then a player, in the annual rites of the city championship.

Everyone who could showed up for the game, regardless of whatever ferocious weather the western town high on the Continental Divide would dish out. Those who couldn't show up listened to the play by play action announced on radio station KANA, self-described as the "first lady of radio." The numbers that filled the Memorial Gym to capacity were impressive, but they do not remotely capture the intensity of the experience shared inside the gym. From 15 minutes before the tip-off until the sounding of the final buzzer, the thundering noise was unabated with dueling school songs and fierce partisan reactions to every play.

As was traditional at games, there were separate seating sections for the fans of each school. This led to a dilemma for a married couple who attended different schools. Were they to sit separately or would one risk being seated in the midst of hostile territory? Regardless of the decisions made, stories were legendary about couples who did not speak for a month or so in the game's aftermath. Tensions among neighbors also were common. Margaret Herbolich, my grandmother's neighbor and good friend, had a couple of sons playing for the Copperheads. Despite their otherwise close friendship, the days surrounding the game each year revealed a thornier dimension to the women's friendship. During the game, the physical intensity and fatigue of the fans in the seats sometimes mirrored that of the players on the court. Most notably, the game claimed at least one casualty in the 1950's when a fan suffered a fatal heart attack.

The central role of the city championship in the Anaconda culture can be best understood with the help of a little history; it was that history that we were continually reminded of each year as the date for the GAME approached. It was a history we could not avoid since on a daily basis we interacted with many of the former giants of the games who continued to walk among us on the street s of Anaconda.

A Midget Playing a Passing Game with Tossers

The rivalry between the two schools began rather modestly in the early 1920's—about 11 to 12 years after high school basketball was regularized in Montana through the efforts of the Montana High School Association[3] The game was played at the Daly Gym, which was to host the classic for the next 27 years. In 1923 the *Anaconda Standard* headline reported "Silver and Blue Wins City Title" while noting in the secondary headline that "St. Peter's Squads Play Fine Game but are Outclassed by Opponents." There is no reference to the Copperheads, just the "Silver and Blue," reflecting the school colors. Similarly there is no reference to the Anaconda Central Saints, but rather it is "St. Peter's," the former name of the school since it was housed in the upper floors of the elementary school for St. Peter's parish. The headline suggests a bit of condescending affection towards St. Peter's by referring to their "fine game" but ultimately observing they were "outclassed," a pattern that was to continue for a number of years as the larger public school dominated the series.

As the headline suggests, two games had been played. The preliminary game featured the Silver and Blue girl's first team defeating the St. Peter's female team by a score of 9 to 1—an event occurring more than 45 years prior to the enactment of the vaunted Title IX. Basketball for girls arrived in Montana almost as early as it did for the boys. Most notably, in 1904 the girls' team from the Fort Shaw Indian School, which has been hailed in print and on the screen, travelled to the St. Louis World's Fair to compete and be declared the World's champions. The Montana experience reflected the national trend of popularity of the game among female students. Soon after the game was invented by Dr. James Naismith in 1891, girls at northeastern colleges were found on the court in their full length bloomers. The Anaconda schools sponsored female teams for a couple of decades before they were phased out in the late 1930's and early 1940's.

The body of the article revealed the characteristics of a game barely resembling today's. It was a "passing and shooting game" played by "tossers." The substantial deficit for the parochial school quintet was attributable to hav-

---

[3] I am deeply indebted to Anaconda's unofficial basketball historian, Tom White, who generously provided to me his compilation of newspaper stories reporting all the Copperheads-Saints games.

ing "missed many passes." However, deficient passing was not the sole reason for the low scoring. The players failed many times "to connect with the hoop," and the score was "no indication of the numerous tries they had for counters." The game described sounds more like a soccer game with players passing to position the ball for the best percentage shot. As it turns out, the first game organized by Naismith in Springfield, Massachusetts bore a strong resemblance to soccer with nine players on each team and the final score a soccer-like 1 to 0. Also, the ball originally used by Naismith for his peach basket was a soccer ball, soon abandoned for one made from panels of leather stitched together with a rubber bladder inside.

Despite the box score tallying only 15 field goals, the game did include at least one spectacular offensive display; the "prettiest basket of the evening" was "shot from center floor by McCarvel, midget forward of the parochial school." That apparently was the sole success of the "midget forward" as it was noted he was unable to "gain his footing" due to the "close guarding" of the opposition. Consistent with the existing rules, only one referee was employed to maintain order. Substitutions were sparse with the Silver and Blue playing seven and only six from St. Peter's seeing any action. This was attributable in part to the existing rule that a player could re-enter the game only once, a right established only three years earlier.

St. Peter's Blue and Gold did not experience any more success during the next few years, including 1927 when the Anaconda five "hung another scalp on its belt" as they trounced the cross-town rivals by a score of 37 to 5. Success for the upstarts was to occur in the following year, though, when the "Catholic lads" prevailed—by a score of 25 to 23. The victory was attributed to a strong defense, which forced the Silver and Blue players to shoot from far out on the floor, and the winners' "eagle eye" for the baskets. Also, credit was given to the "flashy" guard Jenkins who "had a canny faculty for dribbling down the floor into the vicinity of the counting stations."

The description of Jenkins' dribbling is surprising. In the early years of the game, it was not a highly regarded skill; Naismith's original thirteen rules made no reference to dribbling. It seems to have evolved out of the practice of players passing the ball to themselves. In 1900 the new rules addressed the matter by providing for only one dribble (to be executed with two hands), but lest the dribbler derive any advantage from his maneuver he was prohibited from shooting. Eight years later the dribbler was permitted to shoot, but the double dribble was made illegal. At the time of Jenkins' heroics, dribblers had come under attack. The National Association of Basketball Coaches came into existence in 1927 when the then central governing body for the game announced a change that would have essentially eliminated the dribble. The dribble was saved, but a complementary rule was instituted: the charging foul. The source of the controversy therefore may have been that dribblers on the court resembled more their contemporary on the gridiron, Bronko Nagurski, than the elegant Bob Cousy of a generation later.

It was nice to break into the win column, but for the East Enders that was to be their last victory for a number of years. The following year the Silver and Blue reclaimed the championship with a thumping. The game featured an unusually high level of scoring for the period with the victors prevailing 58 to 25. The game also was notable in that a total of 24 players were recorded in the score book. One of those was "Dowdall," who "played a nice game at guard." The reference was to my uncle, James P. Dowdall, who scored 6 points as a sophomore reserve.

Lefty, as everyone called him, was an excellent athlete, with particular skills as a left-handed baseball pitcher. He also was a star student. Following the Irish tradition of giving one son to the Church, he was ordained a priest 10 years later. His affability, physical prowess and keen political sensibilities extended his sphere of influence well beyond the church. He seemed to know everyone in the state and beyond. Besides physically building, with the help of volunteer labor, three churches, he also served as the first president of the priest's senate of the diocese of Helena. Throughout his career, he was unfailingly dedicated to the cause of economic development, a major issue in Anaconda and Butte, dominated by one company whose payroll levels were shrinking. He also was known for his ecumenism as two of his closest friends in Anaconda were Father John Caton, pastor of the Episcopalian church, and Reverend Howard Huff of the Methodist church. He seriously considered running for governor of Montana in the early 1960's. He had the skills and charm to be a winner in an era when the country had just elected its first Catholic president. Most gratifying, he was a regular feature at my high school games.

Things did not improve for the Saints during the next few years. The city championship games in 1932 and 1933 were blow-outs of 44 to 10 and 50 to 20 respectively as the Silver and Blue fielded some of its strongest teams in its history. One player of note for the underdogs was Dan McKittrick, future mayor and neighbor. Most importantly for me, he was to be the installer of a basketball hoop at his family's garage, where I was to spend countless hours.

The victors in these years were the fabled "Wonder Team" quintet of Mike Devich, Cat Thompson, Paul Chumrau, Bill Lazetich and Charles Miller. They lost the state championship in an over-time game to Butte High by a score of 31 to 29 in 1933, but it was a temporary setback. They captured the state championship in 1934 when they upended Missoula by 11 points, and to dispel the doubts of any skeptics they vanquished the Montana University freshmen team. Losses to the Wonder Team were no embarrassment.

The *Standard's* coverage of the game noted an offensive move by Devich, described as a "one-arm overhead circus shot," most likely an early variation of the hook shot. The report also described for the first time the nature of the half-time entertainment, the Soldiers' Memorial Band of Anaconda High.

Copperheads vs. Saints

The 1934 game was significant also because it was the first such game in which the AHS five were referred to as the Copperheads, replacing the Silver and the Blue as their nickname. A few years earlier, the press had begun to refer to St. Peter's as the "Saints" or the "Fighting Saints."

The Wonder Team had moved on, but the Copperheads continued to dominate, so that by the final buzzer for the 1936 game their record was 13-1 in the series. Certainly, if a memorable tradition was to evolve, a movement towards parity was required, and that began with the next two games. The Saints broke the Copperhead's streak with back to back victories by a total margin of three points. These games also featured the introduction of two referees and a record number of foul shots, and the two probably were related. With the prolific whistles, for example, 19 free throws were registered in the score book for the 1937 contest.

The Walsh and Domitrovich families were well represented in these games. In one, the Saints' squad had six players who saw action and this included three Walsh's and two Domitrovich's. The two families did transfer back and forth between the schools. One of the Walsh's on the squad had been a Copperhead as a freshman. The following year Thomas Domitrovich changed schools to face his brother Joseph, the captain and high scorer for the Saints. To further complicate the family loyalties, the nephew of the two brothers Stanley Duganz also played for the Copperheads.

The 1937 game also was the first played under the new rules whereby the center jump after each score was abandoned, and the teams responded with 70 points. The two losses were a rocky introduction to the city championship for the new Copperheads' coach, Mike O'Leary, who was to oversee one state championship and many contending teams during his long tenure as the coach. The Copperheads returned to their winning ways in 1939, which continued for most of the next decade. However, the Saints won a couple during that period and a number of losses were close scores to fuel the escalating fan interest in the series. The intensity of the competition was reflected also in the number of fouls called by the "cage arbiters." The rough play reached its apex with the 1943 game where the Saints were whistled 25 times while the Copperheads were called for 20 fouls. A year without a Copperheads victory was 1940, when no game was played because of the conflicting schedules of the two teams.

The first two games of the century's fourth decade are of particular interest to me since my father was the left forward for the Saints. In the 1941 contest, the Saints went down to their first defeat of the season 36 to 27. So intense was the fan cheering that on many occasions the players couldn't hear the officials' whistles. As for my father, he had 4 points and appeared to have played the entire game. This game also had historical significance in that it was the first city championship that dropped any reference to St. Peter's. The name of the school officially became Catholic Central High, which eventually morphed into Anaconda Central High, the name I identified the parochial school with.

The Copperheads repeated in the following year in an extremely close contest that was tied six times, including in the final minutes. For the Saints, much of the offensive punch was provided by the two forwards, accounting for 20 of the team's 29 points—my father (9) and Jimmy Reardon (11), who was to later enjoy a successful coaching career. The detailed account of the game in the *Standard* includes a number of descriptions of shots made by the various players, including the five free throws of my father, who is referred to as the "diminutive Saints forward." I am sure he did not appreciate the comment since while not tall by today's standards, his height was above the average of his contemporaries—just shy of 5'10". The reference may have been to his build since I know that he was quite thin. A few months later he was drinking generous amounts of carrot juice in his barely successful attempt to meet the minimum weight requirements for the Navy. The half-time ceremonies included the now established tradition of an appearance by the Soldiers Memorial Band of AHS. We can be assured the fare included a healthy dose of patriotic tunes by the aptly named band since the game was played in the shadow of the attacks at Pearl Harbor. Nearly all the players in this game soon were to find themselves exchanging basketball uniforms for those with military stripes.

The remaining games of the 40's continued the dominance of the Copperheads with their prevailing in five of the seven games although two of the victories were squeakers with only a point or two separating the squads. One of the Saints victories occurred in 1944 in a low-scoring game of 20 to 18. The photo of the winning team has many faces who were familiar to me 15 to 20 years later, including Joe McGinley, John "Sandy" Mehrens, and Dick Clifford. My mother was a classmate of Clifford, "the smartest in her class." A Maryknoll priest based in Peru, he returned periodically during my boyhood to eloquently describe to us at St. Paul's Church his mission work. These visits inspired me for a time to aspire to a life of dedication and high adventure as a Maryknoll missionary. McGinley, another classmate of my mother, initially studied for the priesthood but returned to Anaconda before ordination. His melodious tenor voice, particularly as applied to such favorites as *O Holy Night*, made Christmas Mass of my childhood a solemn and special event. Beginning in 1951, Sandy Mehrens represented Anaconda in the Montana House of Representative and the Senate, covering the years of my youth.

Heroics at the Memorial Gym

As the 1940's began to wind down, it became increasingly evident that the Daly Gym was overtaxed to host the city championship. The small dimensions of the court were not adequate for the all-out competitive play annually on display. Typical was one game described as "thrill-packed" and a "wild melee," with 40 to 50 fouls whistled. The gym also was not able to accommodate the rabid fans, who wanted to become active partisans in the burgeoning tradition. Prior to the 1948 game, school authorities advised fans to get there early since the game was drawing more people than the confining gym could hold. The 1,000 fans squeezed into the gym for the game certainly was a violation of all existing fire codes and probably made conditions right for a stampede. To the rescue came the opening of the Memorial Gym, which coincided with the Ed Kalafat years.

When the Memorial was opened, it frequently was referred to as "the House that Kalafat built," borrowing from the popular reference to Yankee Stadium as the "the House that Ruth built" or, perhaps more aptly for Anaconda with its large Catholic population, to the Notre Dame football stadium as "the House that Rockne built." My own view is that the gym was the House that the City Championship built. On February 1, 1950, a few weeks after the opening of the gym, it was the site of the title game that was played before a paid attendance of 2,092. As might be anticipated, the main story was the big guy who scored 29 points with ten field goals and went nine for nine from the "charity line." If he hadn't fouled out in the fourth quarter, the tally surely would have been much higher. I've thought that it was unfortunate that the school authorities didn't delay the opening of the new gym for a few weeks so that the inaugural game would have been the city championship

With the departure of Kalafat, the championship crown for the next two years was to belong to the Saints through victories by a cumulative margin of three points. In the low-scoring 1951 contest, the Copperheads lost an early lead and then went down to defeat in overtime through the conversion of two free throws by Leo Mehrens. According to some accounts, the gym squeezed in 5,000 fans for that game, which would have represented an astonishing 40% of the entire population of Anaconda. The number probably is a little inflated since the consensus view is that capacity (with spectators standing in the aisles) was about 4,000. Despite the loss, the Copperheads should have been pleased with their performance for that Saints' team went on to win the state Class B championship and twice beat the Class A champions. In the following year, in another low-scoring game, the Saints eked out a victory of 41 to 40.

The 1952 game was to mark the last city championship game in which the Copperheads were coached by Mike O'Leary, who for health reasons retired. During his tenure extending back to the mid-30's, he had met seven opposing coaches for the Saints. The following autumn brought John Cheek to the helm, and in a game held a few days before Christmas the Copperheads regained the crown by a score of 45 to 27. The high scorer of the game, however, was center Jim Hogan of the Saints, who tallied 17 (including 11 free throws) of his team's 27 points. Following a common pattern for Saints' standouts, Hogan went on to play at Carroll College, where his coach was Anaconda native Father Raymond "Dutch" Hunthausen. Hogan later followed in the footsteps of Dutch and was ordained a priest. For a significant part of his active ministry, he was pastor at Christ the King parish in Missoula, which originally served as the Newman Center for the University students. The Hunthausen influence extended beyond the basketball court as Hogan's ministry steadfastly advanced the progressive spirit of his mentor and coach.

The cruelest of the games for the Saints fans was the 1957 contest in which the Saints blew an eight point lead headed into the final quarter. With the clock running out, reserve guard Milt Smith threw up a shot from beyond the center line which went through the nets as time ran out to send the game into overtime. The Copperheads outscored the Saints in the extra quarter to prevail 62 to 60. There remains to this day considerable disagreement about Smith's intentions when making that winning shot. Some have alleged that he actually was making a long pass to Bob Hurley, the top scorer for the Copperheads. Others have contended that Smith had been dribbling at midcourt without realizing the time and then was forced into a desperation shot/pass. Regardless of the back story, the bottom line is that he made the shot and was the hero of the game.

The game recalled by all of us to this day was played five years later. By all objective standards, the Saints were superior. Its front-line consisted of Bill Sullivan, who was to play for the Montana Grizzlies after high school, my mentor Bill Molendyke and the formidable John Chor. At that point their conference play record was one loss against seven victories. In contrast, the Copperheads, weakened by having graduated the prior year nine seniors, including Wayne Estes, fielded a relatively inexperienced team. The Saints led for most of the game as we'd all predicted, but never by more than four points until the lead was stretched to 47 to 42 with about two minutes remaining. The Copperheads managed to narrow the lead to 48 to 46 with six seconds left in the game. Following the Saints possession in which they failed to score, "Big John" Stipich, an outstanding football player whom Cheek had recruited to play basketball that year, took the ball and drove the entire length of the floor. Resembling a fullback busting through the line and then the secondary for a 30 yard touchdown, he converted a lay-up and sent the game into overtime. The extra period was anticlimactic with the Saints scoring only two and the Copperheads four to grab (steal?) the victory. As an eighth grader intending to enroll with the Saints the following September, the loss was crushing.

In between Milt Smith and John Stipich, the two schools split the series with the Saints winning in 1958 and 1959 and the Copperheads led by Wayne Estes coming out on top in the next two years by significant margins. With the 1959 victory, the Saints had enjoyed a very successful run in the city championship—winning four of the nine, and as many would contend the Saints should have had the edge. If it hadn't been for that cursed Milt Smith shot!! It was an impressive record in view of the sparseness of victories in the early decades of the rivalry, and the parity during the 1950's contributed immensely to the scenes I have described at the Memorial Gym. The Saints fans had to wait another six years before their squad prevailed over the Copperheads (albeit in a non-city championship game)—a victory by a team on which I got to play a major role.

Chapter Six

McKittrick's Garage

Once we made our move to Pine Street, it quickly became clear to me that the overriding distinction of our new quarters was its proximity to McKittrick's garage. Across the alley and about 20 paces from our front door, the garage hosted a backboard and hoop far superior to the battered St. Paul's hoop. For the next several years, McKittrick's garage was my basketball home. I became a "McKittrick's garage rat."

The Best Court in Town

In the 1950's, the introduction of basketball to young people almost always took place at hoops installed on the side of garages, mounted on the wall or the roof. I think that this may have been a phenomenon related to the mass movement of post-war Americans into single family homes that began that decade. Basketball manufacturers such as Spalding tapped into a lucrative market whereby owning a hoop became a distinctive and symbolic component of the expanding American dream. In Anaconda and elsewhere, there remained baskets at playgrounds such as the Lincoln, Bryan and St. Peter Schools, but increasingly we gathered for play at garage driveways.

With their proliferation, a continual quest to find the best court emerged. My future coach Bill Shea recalls dribbling down the streets with his friends looking for a garage that was free or had a good game they could join: "we would have that ball bouncing in front of us and then pass off to another while scouting for an open court." A hierarchy among the garages clearly existed with the concrete or asphalt courts being considered superior to the ordinary alley dirt variety. Many vied for the distinction of the best. Shea mentioned "Skipper" Kelly's as being the best court near his home. Bill Lowney, another one of my future coaches, lived next door to the Bollingers, who had a popular one. Some have referred to the Devich's, built for the four sons of Dr. Devich, a member of the famed Anaconda "Wonder Team" of the 1930's. Many have cited Callan's garage at the corner of Third Street and Willow Street, the home of Dr. Terence Callan and his eight children. The best feature of that court was that there was a concrete surface connected to the sidewalk providing for an extended court that also had the optimum surface, smooth and flat.

These were all good courts, but to my mind there was no doubt as to the best basketball court in the city—McKittrick's garage. After my early experience with the wobbly misshapen hoop at St. Paul's, I particularly appreciated that the rim was extraordinarily firm. According to Pat McKittrick, the oldest son of Dan and Kay McKittrick, the steadiness of that rim was attributable to bolting the basket from the inside of the garage by his father. Dan McKittrick combined fatherly duties to his four children with his responsibilities of mayor of Anaconda from 1949 until his untimely death in September, 1955. Son Pat remembers the scene well in 1950. With the Notre Dame football game blaring from the car radio, his mother stood on a ladder holding the hoop in place while his father tightened from inside the garage. The sturdiness was field tested periodically by a ball rocketed up by his cousin, Jimmy Murphy, who later in the decade was to star at Anaconda Central and the Montana State Bobcats. Besides the sturdy rim, the basketball always had a net, thanks to the beneficence of the McKittrick family.

From a physical standpoint, the most remarkable aspect of the garage was the potential size of the playing court. Unlike most garages, which had the entry from an alley, McKittrick's garage doors faced Pine Street, which effectively extended the court to the middle of the street. The side lines of the court similarly could be extended with no barriers until our property line was reached on the far side of the alley. The expansiveness of the court, including the sloping street from the middle to the driveway, did come at a price—the unevenness in the level of the playing surface. As a result, a shot taken at the basket with its regulation 10 feet height might be effectively a few inches more or less than that standard height. That variability actually may have given us training in hand/eye coordination as we had to scope out the effective height of the hoop from our shooting position.

There was another feature that made McKittrick's unique. As Paul Greenough, a classmate who spent many hours at McKittrick's, commented, the "thing about McKittrick's is that they had that light." The obvious advantage to having a street light was that we could play at night, but the light played a more significant role in our games. It sat within the perimeter of the playing court regardless of how the out of bounds line was defined. This led to creative uses of the pole as it fulfilled the role of another player, both on offense and defense. Alternatively it could be used as an immoveable pick as formidable as any set by Wes Unseld or as an additional defensive player to help out in the event our guy drove around us.

Despite or because of its imperfections, I was instantly captivated by the physical lay-out of the court. What really impressed me, though, were the guys who played there. For that fall of 1955 and for many years thereafter, it was the preferred court of the high school players. The guys I watched on the floor at Memorial Gym on Friday and Saturdays would show up at McKittrick's on Saturday and Sunday afternoons in their jalopies to enjoy a few hours of pick-up basketball. All my heroes were there: Pat McKittrick, Ray Arvish, Marty Sells, Jimmy Sullivan, Jimmy Murphy, Bob Lemon—only a few of the names that graced the court at McKittrick's during those years.

Periodically peering out the window in anticipation of their arrival, I immediately would be out the front door with my basketball at the first sighting. To my utter amazement, they would let me "play" with them. That usually meant that at some point of the game they would let me take a shot, but for a second and third grader it was a crowning moment. Not only that, these guys I worshipped on the court soon knew my name. I became their basketball "pet." I really don't know why they were so tolerant of me. Perhaps they enjoyed providing a thrill to a little kid they liked. Maybe I pestered them enough to play that they relented by giving me the shot or two. Or it could have been gratitude for chasing down loose balls that went out of bounds. Regardless of their motivation, 60 years later I still cherish the memories of "playing" with the high school stars of the day.

I was not the only one who had such an experience with the high school guys at McKittrick's garage. Tom Greenough, Paul's older brother who later became the co-captain of one of the great teams of Montana basketball history, remembers currying favor with the high school players by bringing the best ball to the court. It was a golden rubber ball with a good grip, gifted to him by his uncle who had played at Creighton University. Exempt from the requirement of shooting free throws, Tom was permitted to play in the first game. While his playing might be limited to that first game, he too remembers the thrill of being able to share the court with the high school players.

Pine Street courts had a tradition of high school stars bestowing their attention on budding basketball enthusiasts. Prior to the installation at McKittrick's garage, there was a popular basket at the corner of Pine and Commercial Streets, about 100 feet from our house. Across Commercial Street on the BA&P property were two "car barns," which were used to store excess rail cars. Installed on one of the barns was a hoop, which was a destination point for high schoolers in the late 1940's, including Ed Kalafat. When he was six, Pat McKittrick would walk down to the car barns to "join" in the games. Frequently there was a price for his inclusion as he would be sent on an errand to ask his mother for a jug of water. After loyally walking down the block to fetch the water over a period of weeks, each time looking longingly at the game, he ultimately was rewarded with a special invitation. One day the players sent Pat home with a different request. Could he accompany them to the White Spot, the popular root beer drive-in at the east end of town? Permission granted, the proud young Pat jumped into the car with Kalafat and friends for the drive down Park Street for his root beer.

When we were older, we took on the mantle of generous treatment of the younger generation. According to Tim McKittrick, about six years younger than me, my friends and I similarly let him "play" in our basketball and football games when he was a little kid and he particularly remembers my advising him to stand next to the light pole in a football game to catch a touchdown pass. I look back and realize that I did, in fact, grow up with brothers, big and little; they just were not ones my mother had to cook for!

A Game to a 100

When the high school players were absent, McKittrick's was the neighborhood gathering point for eight months during the year. The gang included Bob and Bill Matosich, whose house was a block away, the Carlsons who lived across the alley from us, and Ed Palakovich, who lived next to me. Paul Greenough often made the two block walk from his house. Slightly older were Tom McKittrick and Bill Molendyke, who lived across the street from the garage. Sylvia McKinley also was included in the group and held her own, an excellent athlete in sports then available to girls. That core group was supplemented by friends. We could be found at McKittrick's day and night, after school and on weekends. If Malcolm Gladwell was right about putting in 10,000 hours before you are able to claim mastery, we chipped away at that assignment. In putting in those hours, we were following in the footsteps of the older guys we admired so much.

At the garage, we played nearly every variation of game that existed (and then some), a number of which were facilitated by the size of the "court." As for the traditional game, depending upon the number, it could vary from one on one to the full five on five with the overflow watching to get on the court next. The game of 21 was popular whereby the first shot counting for three was lofted from the middle of the street, the second from wherever it was caught for two points and then the one pointer from the agreed-upon free throw line. Naturally, the game of HORSE always was popular.

In a recent conversation, Bob Matosich recalled most vividly the game of "100." That game didn't ring a bell with me, so he explained. "We'd start a game to end at 20, but if it reached 20 and I was ahead, you would declare that the game should end at 30." Being a good sport, he would agree to extend it the additional 10 points. Well, you get it. "I remember a number of the games going to 100 before they finally ended—you never lost," he ribbed me. Obviously something had rubbed off from listening to my father's half-time "Knute Rockne" speeches at Virginia City and losing all those checker games.

Both Bob and Bill Matosich were excellent athletes in all sports with an imposing toughness, undoubtedly the result of their pattern of settling sibling disputes by retreating to their basement for a "few rounds." Because of their pugilistic skills, the rest of us were wary of challenging them on those grounds. After my introduction to Bill in that first grade line, I faced off with him a couple times over the intervening years and generally found myself on the short end of the stick.

Personality-wise, however, they were considerably different. Bob was tactful and diplomatic, as evidenced by his patience with the 100-point games. Bill was the outspoken "in your face" type, and he was very good at provocation. It was as difficult for anyone to come out on top in verbal jousting with Bill as it was in a round where fists were involved. He would not have agreed to play any game to 100. I think the two reflected the respective components of their heritage. Bob would've distinguished himself in the diplomatic corps of the Austro-Hungarian Empire, whereas Bill would have served well as a warrior under the Scottish hero Braveheart.

The comparison of their greetings when I interviewed them illustrates the difference. When I met Bob at his house in the Georgetown Lake area, he amiably commented about my arranging "private reunions." Later that evening, I met Bill in an Anaconda bar. It was fairly dark, and failing to account for the passage of time, I searched the crowd at the bar for the familiar red hair. That did not get me very far since he and I now share the same color—gray. Having the advantage of spotting me first, I heard his familiar voice from the direction of the bar: "What did you do—wear your church clothes?" He still had that facility for the put down—needling me about now being an outsider in my own hometown. Dressed in unremarkable khakis and a sports shirt, I looked, in fact, no different than the next Joe on Anaconda's streets, but Bill still had that ability to knock me back by playing aggressive offense.

Learning from Bill Molendyke

Four years my senior and living across the street in a house whose front door was probably 30 feet from the end of the court, Bill Molendyke had multiple roles in my life He was my good friend, basketball companion, surrogate older brother, coach (both figuratively and later actually) and a closely-watched model to emulate. His influence on the development of my game was immeasurable.

He and I spent countless hours together on the court. These included many games with the McKittrick's gang and sometimes it was a one-on-one, which he invariably won. Of most value was his teaching me various techniques he was learning in organized ball. Dribbling, lay ups and getting the right spin on the ball were just a few of the tips he taught me. In later years, the jump shot and driving to the basket were to be added. The successes I had in playing organized basketball in my early years owed much to Bill.

Bill also served as a model of rising through the ranks of competitive ball. His example was particularly inspiring because Bill's was a spectacular rise as a classic "late bloomer." During those McKittrick years, Bill was not one of the most highly regarded players of his class. By the time he was playing varsity basketball for the Saints, his position vis-a-vis his peers had changed radically. In those earlier years, he was tall but only relatively. Also, he concentrated mostly on basketball, and more attention was focused on those who played multiple sports. I watched with great pride as he rose in prominence and vicariously participated in his successes as he became the 6'4" center for the Saints. He was a source of motivation to practice continuously so I could follow his path to high school varsity play.

Like most Anacondans, Bill and I never let a little weather get in the way of whatever we wanted to do outside. With an elevation of over 5,200 feet and situated off the slopes of the Continental Divide, the yearly snowfall in Anaconda was staggering. The snow could commence in September, a notable example being my senior year when we received six inches on September 1, and the last flurries fell in May, or maybe early June. This gave Bill and me rich opportunities to bond with shovels in hand at the basketball court.

Shoveling that snow was part of the ritual of playing the game. On many occasions our crew numbered several; other times it might be just Bill and me. As soon as the last snow flake fell, I'd pass through our gate with the shovel in hand to find Bill emerging with another shovel and the same destination in mind. Shoveling skills were as highly regarded at McKittrick's as making a layup. Tom Greenough recalls his calling card to get onto the court with the older guys was not only his particularly impressive Creighton basketball, but also his shovel. A product of the BA&P Railroad's shop where his father worked, Tom was eagerly greeted when he showed up with that shovel after a major snow fall. Regardless of size of the crew or the depth of the snow, which at times led to a truncated court bordered by snow piles, we shared with all those kids playing the game in the northern climes the joint effort and camaraderie of uncovering that frozen surface beneath the snow.

One of the disadvantages of playing on the court after the snowfall is that it was impossible to get all the snow off the ground. Sometimes we'd be required to wear gloves, which made it difficult to get a good grip on the ball. When we'd toss off the gloves as the temperatures warmed, our hands became covered with mud. We'd clean them on the nearest surface, McKittrick's garage, which typically was smudged with hand prints for most of the winter. Occasionally we would buff snow over the prints, an imperfect solution and no adequate substitute for a bucket brigade of soap and water..

McKittrick's garage also provided me with an opportunity to bond with my father over the game that he'd introduced me to in Virginia City. When he returned from work at the Daly Bank about 5:30, he had to cross the court to reach our house. If he found me at the court without a game, he'd put out his hands for a pass. Standing in his suit on the street, he'd launch the ball with a high arc from 20 feet, and more often than not it would go through the net. His shot was the one hand set shot, invented by Hank Luisetti of Stanford in

1936 when my father was in sixth grade. It would soon overtake the traditional two-handed push shot to become the standard for two decades until superseded by the jump shot. My father was part of the vanguard that had mastered the shot, which was evident twenty years later in his coat and tie.

On occasion, he would come out in game attire to give me some competition. They were low-key games and bore no resemblance to the father/son grudge matches described in excruciating detail by Pat Conroy in his novel *The Great Santini,* so unforgettably portrayed on the screen by Robert Duvall and Michael O'Keefe. Disconcerting to me, he continued to beat me until a far later date than he should've—it may have been a son ambivalent over trumping his father or, more likely, that damn set shot of his from way beyond sunk me.

The Fifth Grade Competition

In Anaconda, competitive play for basketball and football began in the fifth grade. I eagerly awaited our first basketball practice in November 1958. Joining us at that practice were our coaches, who were no strangers to us since both were high school juniors who played for the Saints: Bill Shea and Bill Lowney. Because of the size of St. Paul School, the Recreation Department determined that our fifth grade should field two teams. I am not certain on what basis they divided the class but it clearly was not an equitable split. Our team included four of the eight players from our class who were to be varsity starters for the two schools in our senior year in high school: Bill Matosich, Paul Greenough, John Cheek and myself.

Shea and Lowney were following the tradition in Anaconda whereby high school players would coach grade school and junior high teams. All four years of my pre-high school teams were headed by a high school player, and I coached an eighth grade team from my freshman through senior years. Lowney was a star of the Saints so we felt privileged to have his presence on the bench. The majority of the coaching duties though fell to Shea since Lowney's team responsibilities sometimes conflicted. As a coach, Shea was emphatically focused on teaching and even as a high school student had a professorial manner. He clearly was not a screamer on the bench and rarely left the seat even when things were not going well. He also demonstrated remarkable restraint and insight into how to coach for someone so young and didn't attempt to control all action on the court. His pre-game and time-out talks always were characterized by a methodological and analytical tone.

Recalling his coaching debut 55 years ago, Shea remembers having to figure out how to handle his two rivalrous key players—Bill Matosich and myself. "At times, you were at each other on the court," he recalls. Shea did find a way to move us to put aside our squabbles and roll forward as a team. He also remembers Bill challenging him if Bill disagreed with him. Since Shea's sister

Susan ended up marrying Bob Matosich, the two have had ample opportunity to rehash the experiences of the coach and the player back in 1959.

With a good team and two outstanding coaches, we were ready to launch against a competitive group of teams. Starting from the east end of town was Bryan School with Bill Hill, a prolific scorer; two blocks away was St. Peter's, which was anchored by Pat McMahon and Jim Sullivan. Moving westward was Lincoln with the formidable Dave Nielson and Daly School with the very athletic Charlie Spangler. The most geographically western school at that time was Washington with Ken Boyer. Our games were played at the Daly Gym, the site of the city championship for so many years. Built in 1906 in memory of the recently deceased Marcus Daly, the gym was the center of much of the youth activity in Anaconda. The basketball floor, which was encircled above by a running track, also hosted girls' volleyball and the weekend youth center dances.

My most salient memory of that fifth grade basketball year was the points' competition between Hill, McMahon and myself. After each game we scoured the scorebook to review our individual points recorded. About half way through the season, a contest emerged with the outcome not determined until the final game. After the final whistle, Hill was the winner with 112 points while I had 105 and McMahon was third with 103. A funny, insignificant detail to recall these many years later—it may have been because it coincided with our street address at 105 Pine, but I wonder if it wasn't because I heard on the radio on December 1, 1969 that my draft lottery number for the Selective Service was a most unfavorable 105. A number which held fond memories suddenly became ominous.

While some trivia still adheres to my brain, I couldn't remember who brought home the fifth grade championship that year. Bill Hill solved the mystery a few years ago when he mentioned he'd found his Bryan School trophy. Of the various players from the competing schools during that fifth grade basketball season, I probably knew Hill as well as anyone since he and I had played the previous two years on the same baseball team, and our competitiveness developed as teammates. Our team in the C League for nine- to eleven-year-olds was the Anodes, named after the two feet by three feet copper slabs that emerged as the end product of the smelting. For those three years, the conversation between Bill and me was dominated by the issue of who was the better pitcher. Fortunate for the team, there was the presence of Ralph Villa, who was a far better pitcher than either of us. The Hill/Dowdall debate on baseball pitching was inconclusive, but as for basketball, it was conclusive—Bill took home the championship trophy and won the scoring contest for that fifth grade season.

Games were played on weekday afternoons so our stands typically weren't filled with cheering parents. Most fathers were working during those hours, and with large families most mothers had other obligations to their children. One person who was a fixture in the bleachers for our games was my grandmother. She often scheduled her break from janitorial duties at the adjacent Junior High when she knew my team was on the court. She was thrilled that her oldest grandchild was competing. Spotting her in the bleachers at the tip-off always spurred me to play my best, not only in recognition of her sacrifice to make it over, but also because I knew I could count on her subsequent game summary and analysis.

Whose Trophy is it Anyway?

Our sixth grade year probably represented the height of collaboration between Bill Matosich and myself, although it was not wholly free from competition. The successes of that year began in football. Bill and I worked well together, helping each other on our alternative runs as the two halfbacks. We were undefeated through the regular season, but we had to wait until early December to claim the championship. The title game between the two top teams in the standings was repeatedly postponed because of a series of heavy snow storms. When the game finally was played against Lincoln, we prevailed on a field at Mitchell Stadium frozen solid and ringed by snow banks. With the unfriendly turf, the game was a physical challenge, particularly when it came to tackling Dave Nielson, the biggest kid in our class, who seemed to be carrying the ball for Lincoln on every play.

Our winning ways continued into the basketball season. One advantage from the prior year is that we picked up Tom Hedge, who gave us that quickness we had lacked during the fifth grade season. The remaining starters were my long-time friend Paul Greenough, with his steady control of the ball and strategic shooting skills, and John Cheek. It was a competitive five that we were able to field for those weekday afternoon grade school games. The strength of the team was borne out by the 14-2 record during the season, the top of the standings. Similar to the football, there was a championship game with the second place team, which again was Lincoln led by Nielson. That game was the most memorable part of the season, not so much because we won but rather because it was played at the Memorial Gym. We felt like full-fledged ball players as we sprinted onto the floor to begin our warm-ups.

Shea returned to be our sole coach for this season, and we benefitted even more from his calm and methodical style as he continued to manage well the conflicting personalities on the squad. The most formidable challenge he faced, though, was what can be the most vexing one for an amateur coach at the grade school level—substitutions. As I was to learn many years later, coaches at the instructional level are faced with the twin, and at times conflicting, demands of winning and providing all players with a fair share of playing time. In the case of our squad of 14, he handled it admirably despite some squawking when we were taken out. He managed to secure the crown at the same time while being fair about providing quality playing time for everyone.

It was traditional for champions of the various grades to be feted after the conclusion of the season at a banquet. The story of our banquet and the aftermath can best be told through the transcript of the conversation between Bill Matosich and myself in May, 2012, (fully 52 years after an event for school kids) as we sat at the Locker Room bar in Anaconda:

Pat: Do you remember that after we won the sixth grade championship there was a banquet—I think at the AOH Hall.

Bill: I do remember.

Pat: Do you remember that there was a trophy?

Bill: Yes. [Pointing to the recorder] Keep going; I think I know where this is going.

Pat: Shea gave the trophy to me to bring to the school.

Bill: [Smiling] And I took it from you.

Pat: Yes you did. I was walking up Park Street and you grabbed it, saying that you were entitled to it.

Bill: But I gave it back to you.

Pat: No, you didn't.

Bill: Yes, I did!

Looking back, I think he may be correct. He certainly kept it overnight and I remember him arriving at the school yard cradling the trophy and wearing a big grin. He then may have handed it over to me, no doubt on the instructions of his no-nonsense Scottish mother, to carry into the school for display in the trophy case. Of course, the school's trophy belonged to neither of us!

Seventh Grade Blues

The seventh grade year did not begin well, and it started on the first day of school. Our class was reduced to about 50% of its size from the previous spring. Most of the blame for siphoning off classmates lay with the actions of my uncle, Father Lefty Dowdall. In the late 1950's, Bishop Gilmore had asked him to undertake the establishment of a new parish, St. Joseph's, to serve the rapidly expanding west end of town. As he had done previously in Three Forks and Stevensville, he was expected to physically build the church and school with volunteer labor. The school was ready by the fall of 1960, and about 40% of the class moved about a mile west to the new quarters.

The remaining departees had a far shorter trip--about two blocks down Fourth Street to the public junior high school. While it was an established tradition for some families to transfer their sons and daughters to the public schools after the sixth grade, it caught me completely by surprise. Most stingingly, among the transferees were old friends Paul Greenough and John Cheek. Moreover, they represented two of the first five on our champion basketball team of the prior winter. My parents tried to console me, but they also reminded me that Cheek's father was the Copperhead's coach, and Greenough's older brother Tom was playing for the team. Later I learned Cheek was quite surprised too when his parents told him he was switching to the junior high since "as a good Catholic boy" he always thought he was going to Central. Greenough always knew this was part of the plan.

The loss of these two in the seventh grade reflected patterns of school selection in Anaconda. The religious demographics of Anaconda leaned heavily Catholic, constituting about 60% to 65% of the population. In contrast, there were two (soon to be three) Catholic grade schools compared to five public schools, and the Central's enrollment was about 50% of Anaconda High. Thus, a substantial number of Catholic students were enrolled at the public schools, and the largest percentage was found among the high school population. This reflected the movement of many students from the parochial grade schools to the public junior high. Parents made this choice for various reasons. For many it was a matter of family tradition. If the parents attended A.H.S, the odds were that the children would. If the father had been a star athlete, that choice was nearly inevitable. Athletics could be the critical factor for sons who had talent since the Copperheads competed in the more prestigious Class AA while the Saints played in the less competitive B. The High School also had a more extensive curriculum and array of extracurricular activities, such as a band and debate. For others, it was a simple matter of economics since Central charged tuition.

The second major disappointment occurred at my first basketball game in November. I did not score a single point in a game. I came home dejected and expecting sympathy from my mother when I told her the news. Her answer: "I'm not surprised. I never see you practicing anymore," as she pointed in the direction of the garage. I immediately began a regiment of daily playing, and from that low point my basketball playing steadily improved as I enjoyed a positive trajectory over the next three years. It was a rise that had everything to do with coaches, mentors and role models I encountered during those formative years, and, of course, my mother's reminder that no one gets better without practice.

One night early in my seventh grade year a noisy group of high school students played late into the evening at McKittrick's. It was an evening that marked the end of an epoch. The next day as I walked by the garage I noticed the rim had come loose, loose enough to make the basket totally unusable. Recollections vary as to why. Maybe Kay McKittrick had had enough of hosting such gatherings and instructed her son Tom to do the deed or perhaps the players the night before had damaged it. Regardless of the reason, I was crushed by the loss of "my" court, that which had been my home for the previous several years.

An Homage to McKittrick's Garage

McKittrick's had been the scene of such important mentoring for me. It was our camp without walls, tuition fees, fancy uniforms or paid counselors, but it functioned better than any sports camp I've seen since. Somehow the examples of teaching and consideration by the older players were absorbed by us all, right along with learning how to compete in a game with our neighbors. In the process we became basketball players, and learned how to find our place to contribute to a team. Nothing can compare with the education I received at McKittrick's.

When all is considered, the success of the garage was attributable to the public-spiritedness of the McKittrick family—whether it involved assuring there was a net on the basket, gracefully lending their property to us or suffering patiently dirt marks on the doors. Kay McKittrick also served as a clearing house for mothers calling to locate their sons since it always was assumed they likely would be playing basketball on the 100 block of Pine Street. Without them, it would have been merely a basketball hoop, not a transformative experience.

The McKittricks are long gone from that neighborhood, but that sense of public-spirited remains. All three McKittrick boys became lawyers and have practiced in Great Falls, Montana's second largest city. Pat played basketball at Carroll College as one of the first to receive a "full ride" scholarship for playing the game. When he was in high school and I was about 10, my father always would point to Pat as an example I should follow: "Every time I see Pat," he noted, " he gives me a big smile and greets me with a 'hello, John, how are you doing.'" Those interpersonal skills my father admired served Pat well when he was selected by his peers to be the Speaker of the Montana House of Representatives from 1975 to 1977. After barely losing in the Democratic primary to a member of a long-established family in Montana politics for a seat in the U.S. Congress, Pat has concentrated on his litigation and labor law practice. One of his specialties has been the representation of unions, for which I am certain that his father, the former labor leader in Anaconda, looks down proudly from his perch in heaven. Over the years he has served on a plethora of commissions, boards and committees, including: the Montana Board of Investments and the Catholic Campaign for Human Development.

Tom, three years younger than Pat and in the same class as Bill Molendyke, attended law school at Gonzaga University, many years before Gonzaga became a perennial basketball contender on the national stage. After a stint as an assistant commonwealth attorney in Virginia, he eventually joined his older brother in Great Falls. His private practice, however, was to be of a limited duration as he was appointed in 1983 to the position of a district court judge for Cascade County and was subsequently reelected five times. While on the bench, he has served as President of the Montana Judges Association and as a member of various judicial related boards and commissions, including the Sentence Review Board of the Montana Supreme Court. Tim followed in the footsteps of his brothers by playing for Anaconda Central, getting a law degree and moving to Great Falls where he currently practices with Pat. My classmate Eileen has remained in Anaconda, where she is a tireless promoter of Anaconda and a prime mover behind the organization of our class reunions every five years.

****

We ultimately did solve the problem of what would succeed McKittrick's when a new hoop appeared at St. Paul School. Installed near the southwest corner of the school building, it featured a sturdy pole, a firm backboard, a durable rim and a chain net. The playground asphalt provided an even surface and the placement of the hoop provided an ample playing court. By our standards, it was first class, rivalling an indoor gym—a model of efficiency and the latest technology. The St. Paul's court soon became a favored site to play and attracted crowds similar to those seen at McKittrick's a few years earlier. I spent many hours at the school court and owe much to its existence, but the court could not replicate the quality of the soul of McKittrick's.

Returning to Anaconda recently, I drove over to Pine Street. As I surveyed the old court, I was struck both by the modest size of the garage and the unevenness in our playing court with those prominent dips. The hoop is now entirely gone but the street light remains. As I let my mind's eye wander, a familiar sight came into view—teenagers (with a few younger) in 50's clothes bouncing basketballs and shouting at each other on the court, all participants in a basketball camp as fine as ever there's been.

Chapter Seven

Coaches, Mentors and Role Models

My basketball story had met its first real setback. Somehow, I had fallen behind in developing my game and hadn't even noticed it until I was brought up short by that scoreless game. Responding to my mother's admonitions, I returned with more determination to practicing, but what critically shaped my game over the next couple of years were the people who came into my life. Their teaching and examples gave me skills I've relied on all my life—and not just for basketball.

George Hagerman: Rebounding Specialist

George Hagerman was a diminutive guy, 5'5" at the most, and he took his game of basketball seriously. He showed up regularly at St. Paul's court when he was 19 and I was in the seventh grade. That might seem like a big age gap, but in those days guys would find a game when they were free and stayed with it if it gave them the competition they wanted, regardless of the demographics of the players. George typically fit these games in after his work as an orderly at Galen Hospital so he often would show up to play still dressed in his loosely fitting white uniform. He sometimes brought along his younger brother Jerry, who was friendly, outgoing and mentally-challenged but always welcomed into our games because of his enthusiasm for play and his nice shot from about eight to ten feet. Since he was recently married, George's petite wife sometimes came along too and sat in the car watching our play.

George was one of the best rebounders I've ever met, unequalled at the attendant skills of blocking out and positioning the body. George always chose to guard me, three inches taller than he, because he viewed himself as a "big man" and played as one. I didn't present much challenge, however, on the rebounding front since I devoted little energy to the craft. I was at the age where the gratifications of shooting and scoring were paramount. One day George turned to me and with that laser beam expression in his eyes and in a tone of ridicule mixed with exasperation exclaimed: "You can't rebound for shit! You don't know how to use your body underneath." And it was true—despite being a few inches shorter, he unfailingly out-rebounded me.

That day began my lessons on the court at the Hagerman Clinic. Sometimes he told me how to block and position, but mostly he showed me with his play. His dressing-downs might occur after a play but more likely followed the winning shot for the game when he would take the opportunity to bluntly assess my skills. He repeated a simple rule: "Never allow your man to get between you and the basket." Unless it's a bad bounce, he continued, anyone so positioned will either snag the ball coming off the rim or backboard or will be fouled by the opposing player trying to "go over the back" to get the ball. He emphasized the key to positioning was the use of the butt. With the arms and legs spread at the right distance to establish balance, the most effective blocking out consisted of taking a crouching position and extending the rear end into the body of the opposing player. What I discovered was that this both prevented any further progress by him to the basket and allowed me to detect which direction he would move if he tried to get around me.

George's instructions were accompanied by dramatic demonstrations. Like any good teacher, he'd invite me to apply what I learned while he employed all his counter blocking to frustrate my actions. At the time these sessions seemed endless, but slowly I absorbed his instructions, and frankly I have never forgotten the lessons of those clinics 55 years ago. From time to time, I've been secretly satisfied to hear a game begin with a member of the opposing team exhorting his teammates: "Keep Pat off the boards." For those remarks, I am deeply indebted to George Hagerman, my unlikely instructor of rebounding.

It took decades of play to fully understand his gift to me, and I'm sorry that I never thanked him personally. A few years ago I decided to track him down to say thanks, something that should've happened in high school. Sadly, I learned that he'd died, but in my search I did discover that George had excelled at a profession for which his basketball skills would have provided an enduring foundation—he became a labor leader. While at Galen where he spent 16 years, he became a field representative of the American Federation of State and County Municipal Employees, known as AFSCME. This led to his selection as the executive director of the Montana council for AFSCME. In his obituary, it was observed that his "true passion was his work representing the union." If that passion approached the tenacity he displayed on the basketball court, I am certain that his leadership reflected that singular focus that I witnessed long ago. I can envision well that Hagerman determination as he filed a lawsuit, that blunt delivery when he addressed his members or lobbied legislators on pending legislation or his unrelenting effort to prevail, even when out-sized by his opposition.

Bill Lowney: The Definition of Intensity

Bill Lowney, a soft-spoken and modest man of slender build was a terror on the court and he was my junior high hero. Bill had coached me in fifth grade, but what I learned most was from his example on the court in the Saints' uniform. He played with fire and intensity, and I loved to root for him because anyone could see he played with 110% effort. My father heartily approved of my choice, and classmate John Cheek also revered him. A glance at his face during the game told the whole story—he was a player passionately committed to winning. He never failed to chase down a loose ball, grab the rebound that seemed out of reach or execute a steal. He seemingly was involved in every play. He didn't shy away from verbal engagements over calls. His was a playing style that both Cheek and I aspired to.

Bill broke his jaw in a game early into the season of his senior year. After a four week hiatus, he returned to the line-up to play for the remainder of the season with a boxer-like head protector that provided a look of extra menace on the court. During his playing absence, the Saints struggled without their star and ended up ranked third during the regular season. With Bill returning to 100%, they won their two preliminary games at the divisional tournament and then confronted Dillon for the championship. The game came down to the final ten seconds when the Saints drew up a play for a shot by Bob Lemelin. He missed, and as Bill modestly described it, "I was lucky to have the ball come to me and I put it up for the winning basket." We of course all knew that in typical Lowney fashion, he had maneuvered himself aggressively into that position to grab the offensive board. Some might say that the conference championship was gained through a combination of divine intervention for the propitiously named Saints and Lowney hustle, but I would afford much more credit to the latter.

Following his high school days, following the steps of so many from Anaconda, Bill took his basketball game to Helena to play for the Carroll College Saints. When I first saw him play for Carroll, he had switched from the forward position to guard, transferring his basketball toughness to that position. His four year career proved to be eminently successful, and he was inducted into their Hall of Fame.

Next for Bill was the seminary, where he pursued studies for the priesthood as did so many star athletes from Butte and Anaconda. While some might be skeptical that an aggressive competitor was the ideal candidate for the priesthood, Bill merely had to look around to see many who had preceded him in moving from the athletic uniform to the Roman collar—his bishop was Dutch Hunthausen and his pastor my uncle Lefty Dowdall. Athletic accomplishment in earlier life was seen as superior training for leadership in the church and the world. Competitive toughness and idealistic piety were not seen as incompatible in the Catholic culture of the 50's and early 60's where I grew up. Their example was inspirational, and I too aspired to the priesthood for many of my boyhood years as I worked on my basketball skills.

When Bill arrived at Mount St. Bernard's Seminary in Dubuque, he found many other aggressive athletes among his fellow seminarians. He was named the Recreation Director after he floated some proposals for basketball play. Tough as his days of basketball had been with the Saints, Bill described the Seminary games as the toughest he'd ever recalled, including "lots of fights." He attributed part of the play to the "repressive" atmosphere of the institution that still had pre-Vatican II remnants. As part of his basketball reforms, he instituted the three second rule and brought in referees for the hard-fought games among the future priests.

Following ordination, Bill was assigned to Anaconda Central as the Assistant Director and Athletic Director but ultimately left the priesthood and married, as did so many of that era. Bill taught and found ways to remain active in the church along with his wife, fellow Anacondan Karen Callan. Now retired and in his 70's, Bill continues to demonstrate that spirit of generosity that led him to the priesthood as he donates his time to Missoula's Soup Kitchen and Meals on Wheels.

Bill has made basketball an important part of his life throughout, playing in leagues and pick-up games (often with lifelong friend Bill Shea). A tiger never changes his stripes and both Bills told me an amusing story of Bill Lowney during his priesthood years getting thrown out of a church league for "aggressive" play on the courts. I'm certain my father would approve mightily. Today Bill is on the court three times a week playing at his old school with guys considerably younger than he.

Bill Molendyke: Master Instructor

Bill and I had already had had a long and close relationship through my grade school years. He'd fulfilled important roles for me as surrogate older brother, tutor and fellow alley rat at McKittrick's. During that seventh grade year, he was to assume several new roles: coach of my team, a guide into the intriguing world of varsity high school basketball and my instructor in the art of the jump shot.

With the graduation of Bill Shea, our St. Paul team was without a coach, and Bill swiftly filled the void. Since his brotherly-like investment in me was the principal reason for his undertaking the duties, much of his coaching focus was on me. I experienced both the benefits and burdens of that focus. Bill held me to a higher standard, being tougher if my effort at practice did not meet his expectations or if I made any "bonehead" plays in the games. He did not hesitate to take me aside and gently (or sometimes not so gently) point out where I was falling short and how I could remedy such deficiencies. The lessons from his coaching began my path to maturity as a player.

That year coincided with Bill's elevation to the position of starting center for the Saints. I never missed a home game and would occasionally hitch a ride with the Molendyke's to see him play away. As the center on the Saints team, Bill played the position that I hoped to have in high school, and I intently

70

scrutinized his every action on the court, taking particular pride in all his accomplishments as my friend and McKittrick's garage "camper." Bill starred on a team that crushed two of its opponents at the state tournament, only to lose two games by a cumulative five points, including a four point heartbreaker to Wolf Point, the state champions. I reveled in having access through Bill to the locker room wisdom of his coach Pat Curran and in feeling I was on the "inside" of the team's doings. One day that could be me out on the floor, I dreamed!

Bill was a skilled practitioner of the jump shot, and I was to be his pupil that seventh grade. In 1960, the jumper was not universally employed. The issue of who invented the jump shot is hotly contested among basketball historians with at least half a dozen veterans being credited. Some claim that a version of the jump shot was first introduced by John Miller Cooper in the early 1930's. Others point to a version of the shot regularly featured by such legends from the 1940's as Jumpin' Joe Fulks, Kenny Sailors and Whitey Skoog. The jump shot as we know it today, though, did not emerge as a central part of the game until the mid-1950's. The principal reason for that was the arrival of Bob Petitt, the first great practitioner of the classic jump shot, who began his NBA career with the St. Louis Hawks in 1954.

The set shot, one-handed or otherwise, dominated previously. The jump shot offered several advantages in comparison to its predecessor. The most obvious was that the ball could more easily be launched over the outstretched hands of the defender. With the set shot, the shooter's feet remained on the ground, and the release of the ball usually was at chest height. In contrast, the jump shooter was in the air with the ball released above the head. Since the set shooter's shot was a more available target to block or harass, the best of the lot moved farther to the perimeter to distance themselves from their defender. Showcasing its flexibility, a properly executed jump shot could be taken in the midst of traffic around the basket.

Another advantage, less obvious to the outside viewer, is that the jump shot provides more balance to the shot. Through the jump, an equilibrium of the body is created that is more stable than two feet wedded to the ground. The body also becomes synchronized with the ball being released. A jump shooter can feel the energy move up through the body from the feet to the finger tips—the shot is the product of the entire body in synchrony.

As the Anaconda Central Saints' center, Bill had become skillful at shooting the jumper and had analyzed the move so he could break it down to teach me. I remember his words as if they were pronounced yesterday: "As you jump, you raise the ball above your head, and then you release the ball just after you reach the top of your jump." The first two steps made sense to me, but the last did not. "Why wouldn't I shoot the ball as I was rising in the jump or at the top?" I asked. "Wouldn't that give me more power in the shot?" It appeared counter-intuitive to me. Bill explained the body balance realized through his method and then demonstrated over and over again how the shot was supposed to work. I finally was able to "get it," and by the middle of the seventh grade season, I had developed a credible jump shot. Thanks to Bill, this provided me with an immediate competitive edge since it was not common for seventh graders to be shooting the jump shot. His tutoring provided me with lifelong benefits on the court as the flow of the Molendyke jump shot has remained with me all these years.

Bill graduated and continued to play first for Carroll College and then Western Montana College in Dillon where he was top scorer. He then moved on to Oregon where those instructional skills that had proved so valuable to me were put to use in the 80's when he coached the girls team from Helix, a small community about the size of Virginia City, to consecutive State B Championships. Serving as School Superintendent in Tillamook from 1985 until his retirement, Bill's family also got to be the beneficiaries of his coaching—one of his sons became a top scorer for Oregon high school basketball and proceeded to play for the Air Force Academy.

Wayne Estes: Master of the Hook Shot (and Virtually Every Other Type of Shot)

Wayne Estes casts a long shadow. He was a giant of a ballplayer literally and figuratively, 6'6" and 250 lbs. He was massive, and yet he could move like a ballroom dancer out on the court. He had an open face with soft features which led some to tag him "Baby Huey." Wayne was, to my mind, the best player in the history of Montana high school basketball where he played for the Copperheads. There were other greats: Anaconda's Ed Kalafat, Missoula's Mike Lewis, who subsequently was a star at Duke and then played in the ABA for a number of years and the University of Montana's Larry Krystkowiak, who was the Big Sky Conference MVP for three years and played for about 10 years in the NBA. None of these matched the combined high school and collegiate performances of Estes, punctuated with his first team All-American selection in 1964, an honor shared with Bill Bradley, Cazzie Russell and Rick Barry.

He was born in Virginia City, and my father might never have left the Vigilantes if he'd had the chance to have Wayne on his team, but he didn't since Wayne's family moved to Anaconda long before we arrived. He early developed a love for the game and developed his shooting eye through countless hours of practice in his backyard. Wayne became known as a great shooter, but he also was respected for his toughness. Tom Greenough recalls that a friend moved to become Wayne's new neighbor. Tom's friend assured him that his new buddy Wayne "can even beat you up." Interestingly, he did not show early promise in the height department. A photo of his seventh grade champion team, on the questionably named Junior High Shrimps, reveals him as the shortest of the four players standing in the second row. Even by his freshman year, two team-

mates slightly exceeded him in height. Twelve months later he'd reached 6'6'''
and would eventually top 250 lb.

It was during his freshman year that Wayne's skills began to command
the attention of basketball followers. Playing guard, he was the anchor of the
Fabulous Frosh. As coach Tyvand commented many years later, "he could hit
from anywhere on the court." The mainstays of the team were Greenough, Ace
Brown, Jim Devich, Mike Crum, Tom White, Pat Connors and Jack Schultz, all
of whom were to journey with Wayne through their glorious rise to a Montana
powerhouse. In their senior year, they went undefeated during the regular season, cruising to a record of 22-0, becoming the first team in AA history to accomplish such a feat. That they were unexpectedly defeated in the second game
of the state tourney in no way tarnishes the Estes career that included 1432
points over the three years and countless rebounds. During his senior year, he
averaged 23.8 points per game in the pre-three-point era.

By rights, Wayne should've been deluged with college recruiting offers,
but Montana schools just didn't seem to recognize their home-grown talent
with the word coming out that the coaches at the two universities considered
him too "fat." Their passing on Wayne was a decision they were to sorely re-
gret. Utah State came through with a scholarship offer, and Wayne headed to
Logan in the fall. It was a great fit. We were treated to an initial glimpse of that
when Wayne returned to town for Christmas break weighing 25 pounds less
and covered in sheets of muscle. The "new Estes" was the talk of the town and
in particular was a subject of conversation among us aspiring eighth graders.

While we Anacondans always knew Wayne was good, the rest of the
world got a taste of his talents in the next three years (freshmen were not eligi-
ble to play varsity then). He scored 2001 points for an average of 26.7 points
per game, pulled down 893 rebounds (11.9 per game) and converted on 85.6%
of his free throws. There were seven games in which he scored 40 points or
more. That reconfigured body, unleashing all that playing ability, was converted
into a top level collegiate player, and all of us in Anaconda watched our native
son with pride.

The Wayne I remember most fondly, though, is the one I encountered
in the summer of 1962, prior to my freshman year in high school. It was on the
baseball diamond, and not the basketball court, that I met him. That summer I
was playing for a team called The Jokers where I got to re-unite with my grade
school teammates Greenough and Cheek, along with Bill Matosich. The recreation director, "Black" Pat Connors hired college guys to do the umping, and
that summer it included Wayne, who had emerged as a star on the Utah State
freshman team, and my old coach, Bill Shea. Hanging around the City Commons when not playing, we combined watching the games with ingratiating
ourselves with the umpires whose indulgence could make the difference on a
call for a "safe at first" infield ground ball—a shortstop's bobbled error or a too
hot to handle hit. For us, the stakes were high since a favorable ruling boosted

our batting average and hence our position in the competition for the highest average.

One day in mid-summer while watching, Wayne ambled over to me and commented: "I understand you are a pretty good basketball player." I grunted something that seemed appropriate for a 14-year-old being approached with such a question from someone of Wayne's stature. I don't know who had given him the information, but it probably was Shea. Wayne then asked me which school I was choosing—the Saints or the Copperheads. Grimacing at my response, he argued his reasons for choosing the public high school, ranging from a better program to the virtues of coach John Cheek. Thus began a highly flattering recruiting effort by Wayne to entice me to change my school decision, one that was to extend for the remainder of the summer—an utterly heady experience.

Thereafter that became the principal theme of our interactions at the Commons when I was not lobbying for a scorer's call on my "hit." Most memorable was a day he took his infield umpire position a few yards from my position at second base. Getting into his ump's crouch with hands on knees and pulling down his cap, he looked over at me with that broad grin and started quietly crooning the Copperhead's school song: "We're Loyal to You AHS," sung to the tune of the University of Michigan Loyalty Song. After a few bars, he broke into laughter. I struggled not to join him in the humorous moment and concentrated on staying alert for a ground ball that might head in my direction.

Another highlight that summer was his inviting me to tag along with him and Mickey Gee, one of his high school buddies, to the carnival. Anaconda's carnival was a highly-anticipated event, and it was a thrill when Wayne and Mickey showed up in our alley that night in Gee's stretch 50's sedan. We must've cut quite a figure as we rushed from one ride to another: Mickey was an impish 5'6" in height, and Wayne towered over everyone—I was the rising ninth grader with his tongue hanging out in awe.

Clearly, the most persuasive pitch Wayne offered was a promise that "once you give me the word you are going with the Copperheads, I will take you up to the gym every night and we'll work on your game." Coach Cheek had given Wayne the key to the Memorial Gym, and he generally played every evening with a group of guys, which might include Shea and Bill Lowney, as well as some of his former high school teammates. That summer the group also included Ron Harris, generally acknowledged to be the best player for the incoming Copperheads team. Wayne's offer was a tough one to reject; to be tutored by someone of his stature would have been the realization of one of those impossible dreams, but I absolutely was committed to attend the Catholic school.

Despite my recalcitrance, he did graciously invite me to play a couple of times at the gym. My memory of the first is most distinct. Besides Wayne, there was Harris and Gee. The first game I played was a one-on-one against Wayne—

a game to 11 that I would win if I scored a single point. I did not. I failed to even get a decent shot off. Following the game, I felt both humbled and privileged; I had performed miserably, but after all I was going against Wayne Estes. I then got to play on his team in a two-on-two that we won since it didn't make any difference who was paired with Wayne.

The most lasting memory of that evening was the clinic that Wayne gave me on the art of the hook shot. The hook shot, even at the height of its popularity, has always been a specialty shot. Most credit its origins to the renowned "clown prince" of the Harlem Globetrotters, Goose Tatum, who at times took the shot from great distances without looking at the basket. Most practitioners of the shot, though, were centers shooting within the vicinity of the basket, "in the paint" as it today is popularly referred to. Wayne had perfected his hook shot about a decade before Kareem's sky hook became part of the basketball lexicon. It was a complex move and a beauty to behold, executed by this huge man with delicacy and deadly accuracy.

The essence of the hook shot is a release of the ball over the head by a player whose body is positioned perpendicular to the basket, and Wayne methodically went through the steps to teach me how to get to that shooting position. He first demonstrated the shot from inside the key: he'd received the ball with his back squarely facing the basket, then he shifted his weight to his right foot, followed by a swing back to the left foot, which would be rotated 90 degrees counter clockwise. Concurrent with that shift, the arm was extended with the ball in the palm of the hand until the arm was nearly rigid. The position of the body was critical to this shot as it formed a revolving plane between the ball and the defender, forming a shield against anyone having a notion to block the shot.

Wayne also spent some time on the mechanics of the release; the ball was to move from the palm of the hand to the fingers and then off the fingers with plenty of spin as it headed to the basket. The other hook shot that he demonstrated was similar to the sky hook identified with Kareem. From the top of the key, he would take a dribble or two down the right lane of the key and then launch the hook shortly before he reached an imaginary line extending from the backboard. This probably was Wayne's favorite shot; it was deadly and it was nearly impossible to defend.

I didn't get to realize an immediate benefit from this instruction since my high school coach, as did so many of the era, frowned on the shot and wanted us to focus on the basics. However, the Estes' hook shots and certain variations on them were later to serve me well for more than forty years. His time spent teaching me the hook became an enduring gift.

The following summer after a headline-driven sophomore year, Wayne returned to umpire. Finding him at the Commons, I immediately noticed his ankles were wrapped in bands of green leather containing five pounds of pellets on each leg. Wayne told me they would help him jump higher so I decided on the spot that I, too, needed ankle weights. As soon as the package arrived a couple of weeks later, I strapped them on and wore them everywhere. Oblivious to both curiosity (my sister Mary Anne's friends) and derision (my cousin Mary Jo who took pains to distinguish her cool self from dorky old me), I continually wore those weights for the next three summers.

I'm sorry to say I didn't see Wayne as often that summer because I no longer was spending much time on the Commons since I had moved up to the next age bracket for baseball, the American Legion team. Within 18 months he was to die as a result of a freak accident. Prior to the last regular season game of his senior year, Wayne found himself 47 points shy of reaching the 2,000 points mark for his career, which would have made him the first person in Utah State history to reach that goal. He scored 48 in that game putting him over the top. After speaking with his parents to celebrate the remarkable milestone, he and a couple of friends drove off to a pizza parlor and came across a car accident. Getting out to investigate the crash, Wayne's forehead brushed against a downed utility wire, instantly killing him. The news hit Anaconda with the devastating effect of a hurricane as the front page headlines the next morning in the *Anaconda Standard* were juxtaposed with the news of the basketball record and the tragedy.

There are many ironies associated with Wayne's death in addition to the juxtaposition of the triumphs on the court and the tragic event. Some have asked whether he would have been brushed by the wire if he were a few inches shorter. A few written accounts surfaced as to whether Wayne had a "premonition" of death; cited for such theories are the life insurance purchased shortly before the end of the season and an unusual amount of nervousness exhibited before the game. The story I find most chilling is an anecdote from Bill Shea. After a summer basketball session at the gym, Wayne accidentally put his finger in the open cigarette lighter slot. Recoiling from the shock, he confessed to the others in the car: "Electricity, it really scares me."

I missed the funeral at Memorial gym on the following Saturday, attended by 4,000 people. The Saints departed on Thursday afternoon on a road trip to Libby and Kalispell for weekend games. Before the team departed, we stopped by to pay our respects at Finnegan's Funeral Home. As I looked at the inert body filling the coffin, the image that came to mind was Wayne hunched over between first and second base with that big smile tilted towards me singing "We're loyal to you AHS…."

John Cheek: Maestro at the Bench

John Cheek is the Montana coaching legend who holds the high school coaching record for most wins in Class AA. If Bill Lowney represented to me the uniquely competitive player, Cheek epitomized the quintessentially competitive coach, with an intense commitment to winning. As a kid, I had reverentially observed him at the Memorial Gym where he coached the Copperheads' games, including those during the years Estes was playing. He was never my coach, but I learned much about winning from my seat in the stands.

Coach Cheek was a fixture in his role as the Copperheads' head basketball coach for 30 years. He stood commandingly near his bench throughout games. He was notable for his communicating in broad gestures to his players and the refs, much like a great maestro before a large orchestra. He certainly shouted, but while we couldn't always hear his words above the fray, his posture and facial expressions could be read a mile away. They could be outrage at an undeserved call—which included wide-mouthed open-eyed surprise and disgust with arms raised in protest. Or he could be spied shrugging his shoulders with his hands down and palms raised as he queried a player: "What was that?" Coach never left room for misinterpretation of his opinions or intent. His players failed to comply at peril to their playing time.

Cheek's fiery and competitive nature was no doubt forged during his hardscrabble childhood near Dillon. As a war veteran he attended the University of Montana and served as the team captain for the 1947-48 season. From all accounts, his playing style was "take no prisoners," which extended to even the most mundane practices. George Scott recalled being on the punishing end of play during frosh/varsity match-ups when he was assigned to guard the senior Cheek. Another story that surfaced at the time of Cheek's death was the game in which his college coach found Cheek missing from the court action only to discover him duking it out with a heckling fan up in the stands.

Upon graduation, Cheek was offered two intriguing career opportunities that give one an idea of the range of his early promise: a scholarship to Georgetown Law School and a potential contract with the Boston Celtics. He turned them both down and became the head basketball coach and assistant football coach at Kalispell, one of the larger schools in the state. His success on the court was remarkable, but his tenure was cut short. As his son John told me in 2011: "He won two state championships and then he was fired." Incredulous, I asked: "Why was he fired?" and John didn't know. I decided to try to solve the mystery but still don't have anything for certain. One story was that Cheek didn't play the son of a School Board member—something that would've violated his determination to do your best to win. More commonly cited was that the long-time football coach Frank Little had a falling out with Cheek and delivered an "this town is only big enough for one of us" ultimatum to the Board. They decided Little was indispensable. Hired the following season by Anaconda, Cheek was to remain at the helm for nearly 30 years until his retirement in 1980.

During his long career coaching the Copperheads, Cheek required no less commitment to winning from his players than he had from himself. As Tom White, one of Estes' teammates, described him, "He was really intense. If the ball went on the floor, it belonged to us. If it was in the air, it was supposed to be ours." Son John described him in this way: "With Dad it was all black and white; as a result you either loved him or hated him." Cheek's intensity evoked both awe and fear in his players. One recalled, "we were scared to death of him." Another player, considered one of Cheek's stars, described being ordered to sit off the bench next to the cheerleaders for the opposing team as punishment. Cheek was a yeller and a perfectionist, but as former Copperhead player Tom White commented, "He taught basketball. He'd yell at you, but it was always to correct something." Other times he would take a different approach. "If he didn't like something, he'd just glare at you," recalls another. Yet, one former player remembered him chewing out a player, which was followed by a wink to another as he turned his head from the chastised player.

Practices were characterized by endless repetitions of offensive and defensive plays until it was perfected. As my contemporary John Harold observed, there was nothing complicated about what they did. "No team playing us would be surprised at what they saw on the court. We always were man to man on defense and we ran a couple of plays." The practices also included numerous drills to foster an aggressive approach to the games, and many laps were run if a player failed to measure up. At the practices there were no favorites, and the rules applied to everyone, including his son John (and John might contend, more to him). His ultimate objective of these practices was to win games and those who fell into the category of loving him understood this. John Harold summarized his team's reward: "With him you just assumed that you would win, and you were very disappointed if you did not."

He drove his players, but after years of being dealt hands of varying strength, he pretty reliably molded his teams into winning machines, particularly by tournament time. He believed that he could inculcate a spirit of winning— and he did. Coach Cheek did his job for his school and his players as he believed it should be done.

Standing by the bench, Coach Cheek engaged in a continual dialogue, verbal and non-verbal, with the referees. Frank (Frog) Hull, one of Montana's Hall of Fame referees, described a game against Butte Central in which the first three calls went against the Copperheads, and Cheek thought that Frog missed a couple of calls for the Copperheads. As Frog ran by the bench, Cheek yelled to him "When are you going to make a call?" Frog turned to him and responded: "Here's a call for you," and gave him the T signal for a technical foul. Cheek reacted by yelling that he would never hire him again to referee. Three days later Cheek relented (or perhaps he had forgotten his vow to not hire again) and called a satisfied and amused Frog to work out the reffing schedule for the upcoming weekend.

For Cheek, referees were combatants on the court, but they also were good friends and members of the basketball fraternity. His son John tells of a game he watched at age nine. Seated right behind the bench, he listened to his father vociferously cajole and criticize the two referees from Butte, Glen Welch and Jim Wedeen. John thought to himself: "Dad must really hate these guys." Within a few minutes of the Cheeks' arrival home after the game, there was a knock on the door, and to the utter astonishment of young John, in walked Welch, Wedeen and their wives. They had been invited by Coach to have a post-game dinner before returning to Butte.

You might wonder, though, why the coach of our cross town rivals is in my pantheon of personal greats. Certainly, from my earliest observations on, I learned much about winning from him. But there is more. He revealed a side of himself to me that was kind, paternal and generous, and that impacted me all the more because I knew of his ferociousness.

Most impressed in my memory are two incidents associated with the athletic field. Cheek accompanied our Jokers' baseball team to Hamilton to provide transportation and assist in the coaching. Late in a game where I'd been floundering and after I'd managed again to not reach first base, my reaction was not exactly sportsmanlike, even for a 14-year-old. At the end of the inning, Cheek approached me, put his hand on my shoulder and gently reminded me that such was not appealing behavior; "you are better than that, Pat" he counseled. I have to think that, despite all the stories about his toughness on players, I wasn't the only beneficiary of that type of coaching.

The other incident occurred a few years later on the track field, which was shared by the two rival schools. I was a long jumper (then called a broad jumper), and I typically practiced at the jumping pit without a coach because they were spread thinly among the athletes. One day I turned around to find Cheek standing on the runway quietly observing after I'd taken a practice jump. He made some thoughtful suggestions for improvement and stayed to watch me incorporate his tips into the next few jumps. He then moved on back to his own squad as unobtrusively as he had arrived. As I think back on the incident, I'm touched by the magnanimous gesture of someone who was not my coach but also was the father of a son who similarly competed in the broad jump event, frequently against me in track meets.

As seems appropriate, Cheek's coaching career ended on his own terms—he retired. In a profession where one was proverbially hired to be fired, lasting nearly 30 years in that era of Montana high school basketball is an incredible feat. Not that there didn't emerge recreational grumbling from time to time about dismissing him. Bob Matosich, teacher and part-time bartender at Club Moderne, remembers some of that. Back in the 70's this was one of the best watering holes in Anaconda for discussion about the state of local sports, and it wasn't hard to stir up a little controversy about one thing or another. On occasion, the basketball coach would come under critical scrutiny. When Cheek walked in traditionally around noon, though, some detractors of his couldn't get their coins on the bar quick enough to buy him a drink. When it got down to it, Coach commanded respect.

Chapter Eight

Joining the Ranks of the Saints

One day towards the end of my seventh grade season, an unexpected figure showed up to watch our game. A tall serious-looking guy with an intensely erect bearing, a crew-cut and a distinctive black eye patch, Pat Curran was the new basketball coach for the Saints. After the game, I asked Bill Molendyke about Curran's presence. Bill said he'd invited him to come see my jump shot (which Bill had been instructing me in), but Curran came and went without a word.

The Firing of Pat Curran, the Enigmatic Perfectionist

All of us grade schoolers had been quite familiar with Curran for several years. We had closely observed the Dillon Beavers' coach at Anaconda's Memorial Gym, walking back and forth with that precise military bearing in front of the their bench. To our surprise, at one point his appearance was altered—his handsome face was marked with the black patch. He'd lost an eye due to an accident involving a malfunctioning starter gun at a track meet, and he seemed to us to be more imposing now, exotic and enigmatic. We referred to him with a mixture of irreverence and awe as the "coach with the black patch."

Looking back, I recognize Pat as the most fascinating and elusive character I have met through my days in sports. Jack Oberweiser, with whom Curran coached both on the football field and the basketball court at Central, described him "as the most knowledgeable man in any sport he coached." All that was true, but for me the source of fascination was his complexity, wrapped in an aura of mystery. He was not a native Montanan; most believed he hailed originally from Minnesota, but there was less certainty about his formative years leading up to the Dillon job. It was thought that he had attended and played for St. Mary's in California, and George Scott recalled playing against him in the military basketball league in Alaska. His arrival in Montana seems to have been in the early 1950's. Ben Tyvand's earliest recollection of him was playing in a men's basketball league in Butte: "quite a player whom no one had ever seen before." Ben thought he had played at the Montana School of Mines in Butte, but George Scott insisted that he played a year at the University of Montana. It is firmly established that he finished his college playing days at Western Montana College in Dillon.

To the surprise of all of us, Curran's black patch became a regular presence on the home bench of the Memorial Gym when he made his move from Dillon to Anaconda. We eagerly sought out stories from the high schoolers playing under him about this guy who would be our coach in a few years. They responded with tales of his disciplined and perfectionist approach to the game and his absolute intolerance of any slackness or lack of commitment to win. We probably didn't need to be told those things about his coaching since they were all expressed in that quiet and solemn face on the bench.

A reliable subject of chatter about Curran's teams among fans and players was the underhanded free throw—he required nearly all his players to shoot this increasingly obsolete shot from the charity line. In the early days of basketball, the underhanded shot was a common sight on the court, even for field goals, but by the 1950's the shot had become a relic. For most of us, the shot reminded us of our younger days when it was the only way we could get the ball up to the rim; at times, we derisively referred to it as a "sissy's shot."

If we looked around the NBA, we didn't feel any better about the technique. Wilt Chamberlain was the only player who used the shot for his free throws, and he was a notoriously poor shooter from the line. Despite this, one player after another on a Curran team stepped up to the line and released that ball as it sat near their knees. Perhaps unknown to Curran, a powerful advocate for the unorthodox approach, Rick Barry, was working his way through high school as we watched Curran's players. Barry, credited with being one of the greatest free throw shooters of all time, claimed that the underhanded shot produced a mechanical release less subject to variability—the body always was in a "totally natural position" when the ball was released. This rationale would have appealed to Curran, the apostle of discipline. Discipline was his cardinal virtue both in coaching and teaching, something he may have come to value after a rather disorderly approach to completing his own education.

Curran's coaching would be described as methodical and all business. He had a dry wit, and he wasn't quick to deal out compliments. Jack Haffey remembers an incident well illustrating this trait in Curran when he was a back-up center/forward on the talent-laden 1961-62 team as a junior. Haffey recalls his moment of glory that year when he received the assignment to play against Dillon's best center, thanks to Coach Curran's temporary displeasure with starters Molendyke and John Chor. Jack seized his chance to make his mark and got the best of his star opponent with an outstanding game. The next Monday's film review of the game, typically accompanied by highly critical comments from the coach, captured Jack's most brilliant moments. Jack waited while Curran remained silent on his performance. When the film concluded, Curran quietly and ironically noted: "If we had known better, we wouldn't have assigned such a pushover to Haffey!" High praise even if a grudging backhanded compliment. Jack also recalls Curran's pre-season speech to the parents with the players in a line behind him. The message was clear—he was boss.

That same year an inter-squad game between the freshmen team and the B squad upset the logic of the universe by handing the younger players a win. For Curran, the English teacher, the Great Chain of Being had been sundered similar to the upending in Shakespeare's *King Lear*, and it was necessary to restore natural order whereby freshmen did not prevail against sophomores. He decreed there would be a rematch and that he would be the referee. Remember, the guy wore an eye patch, but there was no doubt that Curran's vision of the court would rival any of us with two fully operational eyes. Sight might not have been an issue, but the absence of an impartial whistle was. As the controversial calls accumulated, the freshmen on the bench began to register their outrage. Curran's reaction—he sent the entire freshmen bench to the showers, thereby requiring the players remaining on the floor to continue without substitutes. A freshman left on the floor, Mike Vollmer still remembers his exhaustion and his relief to hear the final whistle, even if they lost!

The Curran I remember was aloof from both his fellow teachers and the greater community, including parents whom he viewed as potential threats to his turf. He was unmarried and not inclined towards small talk. These impressions, though, may have been incomplete or even inaccurate. His photos in the school yearbook reveal a warm smile on a handsome face. In talking with people who knew him in his pre-Anaconda years, I have heard that in his college days and early teaching career he was an avid partygoer. While not actively social in Anaconda, he would spend weekends with friends in Dillon and even Belgrade where there were races. He also had had a love in his life, which ended up, according to his referee friend Frog Hull, "breaking his heart." The relationship apparently dissolved over "the fact that he and she were of a different faith."

Curran was a masterful teacher, well-read in American and English literature and knowledgeable about the most intricate rules of grammar. We witnessed his pedagogical style as his freshmen students; standing imposingly erect with a leg on a chair to form a surface on the thigh for his open book, his gaze traveled the room and demanded full attention. His appearance in the gym to teach all 50 freshman boys PE was slightly looser with his jacket off and sleeves rolled up. Even in the more relaxed atmosphere of the gym, no one hazarded inattentiveness lest he find an accelerating basketball headed in his direction.

Curran acknowledged my competitive determination to shine by making me his foil when he wanted to demonstrate some technique in a particular sport or exercise. I remember vividly his volleyball demonstrations. I was the pawn attempting to block his vicious spikes, which seared through my hands. After I had put together a respectable defense against the spike based on his instructions, he then deftly tapped the ball to the left to avoid my outstretched arms aiming to stop the spike. Even then I recognized that by selecting me as his hapless opponent, he was signaling me that he thought I could "take it." His special acknowledgement to serve as his opponent in those demonstrations oddly felt like an expression of affection.

I will never forget our most remarkable moment with Curran, the morning in English class when he revealed to us the story of how he lost his eye. I don't recall what provoked the story, for it certainly wasn't his nature to talk about himself—especially about an event that was so life-altering. As he told it, he was an official at a meet where he was handling the starting line for the running events. When the starting gun malfunctioned at the beginning of a race, he turned the gun towards himself to inspect it. Accidentally he pulled the trigger while the gun was facing him, and the explosion from the blank destroyed his eye. The details on the accident were horrific, but we were more moved by the aftermath. He described his painful perception of his colleagues' attitude towards him after the accident. "I would be walking down the hall in school and I would wonder what they would be saying about me," he confided to us. His words revealed to us that post-accident he viewed people as defining him primarily with reference to that black patch, and he certainly was defining them by what he thought were their opinions regarding the patch. It was an emotionally-charged soliloquy and a soul-stirring several minutes for a group of freshmen to share with their teacher. Many of us had tears in our eyes.

We were not to share other similar moments with Curran as our life with him was cut short. On a Monday in late October shortly before the basketball season, we arrived at English class with no Curran standing at the front of the room. Instead we were greeted by Mrs. Walsh, our new English teacher. The prior Friday Curran had been fired by Father John McCoy, the Director of the school.

The firing of Curran stands out as one of the enduring Anaconda basketball stories of the era, and as with all things related to Curran, there remains an element of intrigue and controversy as to what actually happened. The official line and prevailing explanation at the time was that he and McCoy had a dispute over the use of the gym, with some reference to Curran objecting to the utilization of the gym for other events, such as dances. While plausible, it seems strange that Curran would have waited until his third year of coaching to raise the issue with sufficient rancor to prompt his dismissal. Another story is that Curran accused someone of stealing something from his locker. I also have heard that Curran had been involved in a physical altercation with a student ridiculing the patch. One person advanced the theory that Curran acted to precipitate the firing because he did not believe the season would be successful after losing so many talented seniors the prior year. If so, a late October confrontation seemed a rather peculiar exit strategy since he had many months to mull over the prospects for the season. Since both the protagonists are dead, we most likely will never know the full story.

Whatever the reason, the firing deprived me of the privilege of having Curran as a coach. The school also experienced the loss of an outstanding teacher. It may have required a few schools and a number of years for him to earn his teaching degree, but he did emerge with outstanding teaching skills. Jim Gransbery, a captain of the Saints my sophomore year, views his year with Curran as a seminal experience that led him to become one of Montana's most respected political journalists. Jim remembers well Curran leading the freshman class through a special program on writing. "I was inspired," Jim noted, "and never studied so hard for anything." An anecdote illustrates the individual attention to the concern of his students underneath that stiff and brusque exterior. When Jim received back his exam results, his heart sank as he looked with disbelief at the bold "75" written on the top of the page. Noticing his shocked and disappointed face, Curran walked down to Jim's desk and half-smilingly commented: "That is an A." It was the second highest grade in the class as Jim encountered grading on a curve for the first time.

Following his departure, various stories circulated as to where Curran landed. Many contended that he returned to Minnesota. Others reported he became the assistant basketball coach for the Gaels of St. Mary's College of California. A few years later I would be able to fill in some of the blanks when Curran re-entered my life for a brief but momentous period of time.

The Reverend John J. McCoy

Before proceeding, I should say a few words about the man who fired Curran, the Rev. John J. McCoy, Director at our school and Superintendent of Schools for the Diocese of Helena. Under no circumstances would McCoy be described as a basketball coach, mentor or role model. A sighting of him in a basketball gym was a rare event, but he played a critical role in the basketball affairs of the Saints during my years.

On first impression, one might regard this man with a roly-poly figure and a slightly delicate bearing as soft. To the contrary, he was "hard as nails." A man with an imperial and brusque manner of interacting, he was a petty and dictatorial person who wielded power in an arbitrary manner, often without any perceived need to justify his actions. His job as Superintendent frequently took him away from the school premises, an absence that may have contributed to his lack of rapport with students and faculty, including the coaches. In general, he did not associate with other priests, and he rarely attended school events. He lived alone in a small apartment at the school, and I've no idea how he spent his leisure time.

I acknowledge that no profile can be all negative. He must have handled the responsibilities of Superintendent competently because he held the position for many years. He also seemed adept at running an organization efficiently within a budget. According to my father, when McCoy arrived in the late

1950's, the school was in dire financial condition and through a plan of eliminating programs such as the band, speech and debate and the school lounge, he succeeded in righting the ship. In implementing the plan, he also demonstrated political adroitness in leaving untouched programs such as basketball whose constituency was more extensive than supporters of speech and debate.

As a matter of full disclosure, I should acknowledge that I had a number of run-ins with him during my four years at the school. The most serious occurred at the end of my junior year. I campaigned for Student Council President on a thinly veiled anti-McCoy platform that the school deserved a more participatory approach to decision-making, a position which won the enthusiastic support of the nuns teaching at the school. As I gave my speech to the student body, I noticed him appear briefly in the rear right doorway of the auditorium. As he departed, he told a student standing next to him that if I were elected, he would not deal with me. Following my election, I paid him the formal courtesy call, at which point he repeated to me the offhand remark in the auditorium. He held to that vow for the entirety of my term and would only speak to our vice president, Tom Callan, on Student Council matters.

That was the Rev. John J. McCoy. Regardless of whether you liked him or not, and I obviously was in the latter camp, you could not ignore his presence if you were associated in any manner with the school, particularly athletics. The firing of Curran was only the first of many actions by McCoy that would impact our basketball during those four years, although admittedly not all his actions could be faulted.

The Optimism of Eighth Grade and Freshman Year

The Curran saga was the backdrop for two successful seasons on the court—my eighth grade and freshman years. The eighth grade games were particularly thrilling since we played at the Memorial Gym on Saturday morning. It was a stimulating experience for an eighth grader—playing on the same floor as all those high school stars I had followed in the prior years. I fondly recall it as one of my favorite years of basketball, spending countless hours during the week at St. Paul's and playing Saturday morning at the Memorial.

I was in the midst of a growth spurt, reaching nearly 5'11" by the end of the season, and my upper body strength reflected a 14-year-old going through puberty. As throughout grade school, I continued to play the center position. With the increased physical strength, I had decidedly improved my rebounding skills. The jump shot from the top post position had become reasonably accurate, and I also developed an effective drive, mostly from the post position on the court. Physically I was primed to take advantage of all that I had learned from my Hagerman and Molendyke clinics. Projecting that my growth pattern of the past few years would continue, I optimistically saw myself as a 6'4" sophomore.

Our St. Paul team did not win the championship, but unlike the prior year we were in the mix. As I thought of my move in the fall to Anaconda Central, I nearly burst with excited anticipation of playing for the Saints.

Following Curran's departure, Mike Devitt, who had been the B squad coach, was promoted to the varsity position with little time to prepare for his unexpected responsibilities. My focus was making it to the B squad, and after the try-outs fellow freshman George Martin and I found ourselves on the team's roster posted outside the locker room. Devitt's promotion left the reins of our team in the hands of Dwayne Manson, new Carroll College grad and first year history teacher. Manson was hard working and personable, establishing a close rapport with us.

I won the job of starting forward, but our first game proved to be a disappointment. It involved a trip back to my father's territory to play the varsity team at the small town of Twin Bridges. Even at the age of 14, I had some sense of historical reference in playing ten years later against one of the Vigilante's more formidable opponents, a team that typically thrashed them. The game was tough, and I was a little intimidated with the age differential—a 14-year-old playing against players predominantly 17 or 18. We ended up in the loss column for the game but did fare better than the Vigilantes a dozen years earlier. Subsequently playing against other B squads, I gained my footing and became a consistent, and occasionally leading, scorer. Under Manson's guidance, we won most of our games.

I also played at times with the freshman team (when there was not a conflict with the B squad), and two of those games stand out in. The first was in Missoula against Hellgate High School, which was both a new and an old school. That year the Missoula County High School, the largest in the state, was split into two schools with Missoula Sentinel winning the basketball jackpot as nearly all the best varsity players entered its doors in the fall. Led by Mike Lewis, the later Duke star and ABA player, the Spartans went undefeated in winning the state championship the following year. While the varsity talent had remained at Sentinel, Hellgate was allocated most of the freshmen talent, including Gene Lewis, the younger brother of Mike, and Sid Rinehart, the first African-American I encountered on a basketball court. The Knights were a tough team, and we lost badly to them. The pain was eased since the inside scoop was this team would hoist the state championship trophy in three years. As things turned out, they came extremely close.

The other freshman game was against the Copperheads. When I was chosen for the B squad, a number of the guys from rival AHS had been gracious in congratulating me for securing a spot on the team. Of course, we all knew that a number of them would've qualified for their B squad if their school had had a policy of allowing freshmen to play at that level. The AHS frosh was a formidable foe with familiar faces—Dave Nielson pushing up close to the 6'4" that he would eventually reach, Paul Greenough, Charlie Spangler, Dave

Beatty, Bill Hill, Ken Boyer and others. What was most distinctive about the team, though, was the emergence of two guys who generally had not been prominent during our grade school days: my former teammate John Cheek and the guy who seemed to come out of nowhere, John Harold. They beat us handily. While I did not think they were quite as strong as Hellgate, it was clear that my friends at the Copperheads would be a force in the state when they reached the varsity.

At the end of my freshman year, I'd travelled an upward trajectory that had commenced in the seventh grade after the game in which I had scored no points. Brimming with optimism, I hoped to capitalize on my gains and looked forward to varsity play the next near—to truly join the ranks of the Saints. Slightly tempering that expectancy was one potentially looming cloud in the picture—I had grown only one inch since eighth grade. It was a fact that I tried to ignore and dismiss as an inconsequential and temporary plateau. In truth, as I was soon to learn, my vertical growth was done as I measured 1/16 of an inch below 6'0".

I also faced one critical uncertainty: who would be coaching us? While the Saints record that year was less than .500, I thought that Mike Devitt had done a good job. Admittedly, his basketball experience was limited, but the genial history teacher made an incredible effort under difficult circumstances, and we all had confidence in him. A career of high school history teaching and basketball coaching, though, were not Mike's career ambitions; rather he aspired to be an FBI agent, and in the spring he announced his resignation and that he was headed to Washington D.C. for training. The Saints were facing their second coaching change in less than a year.

Chapter Nine

The Big 32

Sophomore Year: A Bust

Several changes greeted me the fall of my sophomore year. Most critically, we were now in a new basketball conference, which combined all the AA, A and certain of the B schools into one super conference, to be known as the Big 32.[4] As one of the smaller schools, the bar had been raised considerably to reach our goal of qualifying for the state tournament. Our division included former AA stalwarts such as Bozeman, Butte High, Butte Central and Anaconda High as well as three of our stronger southwestern B opponents, Dillon, Deer Lodge and Hamilton. That's correct: for the first time in memory, the two Anaconda schools were in the same conference. While the schedule only included one game during the regular season, the city championship, there could be a second meeting in the tournament, leaving open the possibility of both schools coming out of a season with bragging rights for defeating their arch-rivals.

Our new basketball coach had been hired. Tracy Walsh was no stranger to Anaconda basketball fans. Graduating from Central in 1955, Buddy (as he then was known) starred for the Saints as a player known for his hustle and opportunistic play. Despite being undersized for college ball, he continued his basketball at the Carroll Saints, playing under the two Hunthausens: the future Archbishop and his younger brother Jack, also a priest. Remarkably, he was only 26 years old (young for such responsibilities) although physically he appeared older due to a prematurely balding and shaven head.

The final change was self-initiated. I made the decision not to spend afternoons that fall on the football practice field so I could concentrate on basketball. While I enjoyed playing football, I did not love the game as I did basketball. After the final school buzzer each day, I headed to the gym to play ball with Jim Gransbery and others who might be hanging around. A senior, Jim was to serve as one of the captains of the varsity that year and had enjoyed a very successful junior year. About 6'2", he was a strong rebounder and offen-

---

[4] As a technical matter, it actually was the Big 30 that year, the Big 31 the following year and the Big 32 thereafter.

sively had a powerful drive to the basket along the baseline where he used his body well to protect the ball as he vaulted up for a shot off the backboard. As a freshman, I had studied his under-the-basket offense and began to emulate some of his techniques—strong movement upwards with arms spread out so that any defender trying to reach for the ball was bound to commit a foul. Practicing with him was a valuable experience.

The pleasure of spending time with Jim was not limited to basketball. An excellent student and public speaker, Jim always had astute observations on a variety of subjects, particular political matters. Thus, it was of no surprise to me when he became the highly respected journalist for the *Billings Gazette* for decades. A few years ago I witnessed the respect Jim commanded in Montana political circles. I'd returned to Anaconda for the St. Patrick's Day celebration. Central to the festivities is a parade that draws many of the state's political figures. Standing outside the Ancient Order of Hibernians Hall where the parade commenced, Jim and I recognized each other after 40 years and chatted for a while about old times. While we were conversing, Brian Schweitzer, the popular governor of Montana caught sight of Jim and immediately left his spot leading the parade to greet him. Soon after, Jon Tester, Montana's U.S. Senator, whose next morning declaration of victory in 2006 tipped the Senate to the Democrats, similarly spied Jim and made the pilgrimage over to us. The impressive display of deference spoke volumes about Jim's stature as a leading political journalist.

That fall of my sophomore year Jim and I also undertook the responsibilities of refereeing the girls' intramural basketball games. I'm not entirely certain that blowing the whistle on their fouls, traveling and double dribbles was the best way to ingratiate myself with the girls or advance my social life. On the other hand, we certainly had ample opportunity to hang out with them. The refereeing also introduced me to the restrictive girls' basketball rules peculiar to the time—six players, three on defense and three on offense and the prohibition of players of either group crossing the center line.

That year I also had to face the reality that I'd stopped growing and I now possessed the body that I would have to build my game around. I was not to be a 6'4" center for the Saints. My disappointment was offset by the fact that I had exceptionally strong legs, and my leaping ability was far above average. Also, I had reasonably quick feet. With this genetic luck of the draw, I'd be able to competently guard guys up to 6'6" during my high school days despite my limited height.

Practice began in November and it soon became clear that Walsh's priorities as a coach mirrored his specialties as a player: defense and hustle. "The key to defense is the feet," he would bark, and we developed this through many drills, such as defending with hands behind our back. We practiced man to man and zone, full court presses, half-court traps and a variety of other schemes. Many hours were spent on techniques for stealing the ball. Most vivid in my memory was his mantra that on defense there was to be no switching. Everyone was responsible for their own man. We were to "fight through picks" and not rely on someone else to switch to pick up our guy. This early training has meant I've never become accustomed to playing a defense based on switching, To this day I'll yell out "Don't switch, I'll fight through the pick." if a teammate gallantly tries to help me out. Also, I may fail to switch when it is expected I will.

I was the only sophomore on the team, and as the youngest member was subjected to some mild hazing, which couldn't detract from the excitement of finally making it to the Saint's varsity bench. I recall entering the Memorial Gym floor for the first time in the Saint's warm-up jacket with my heart pounding as the fans stirringly sang our two school songs, the "Victory March" (based on the Notre Dame anthem) and "When the Saints Go Marching In."

Then disappointment set in. I had fully anticipated when practices began that I would see many minutes on the court that season. Granted this might be the expectation of every ambitious sophomore who becomes part of the varsity squad, but based on my year on the B squad and the development of my game that fall with Gransbery, I thought it was a reasonable belief. Moreover, I thought my performance at practices would lead to meaningful presence in the games. After the first couple of games, it became clear that my playing time was to be limited. The frustration was particularly acute at the city championship game in December I'd waited my life to play in. Disheartened, I sat on the bench during the game until there was about a minute of playing time remaining when I finally checked in at the scorer's table. The experience was particularly painful since my peers and rivals John Cheek, Dave Nielson and John Harold, fellow sophomores playing for the Copperheads, received noticeable amounts of playing time.

After a few games, a plan was devised for me to play the first half with the B squad and then join the varsity in the locker room. While it seemed a step down to be playing with the squad I had spent the entire previous season, the plan did work. I was quite productive with the B squad, which led to more quality varsity minutes as the season progressed, a trend I expected to continue until the end of the season.

Those ambitions came to a crashing halt in late January when the season ended for me. It began at the Montana School of Mines gym in a B squad game against Butte Central. We were playing a rare zone defense and their guy on the wing had hit a few. On the next possession, determined that he was not to make another, I surged out and leaped to block the shot (violating a Walsh cardinal rule that you never leave your feet if your guy can still dribble). He faked, and I came down on his back landing on my head. A quick trip to the emergency room yielded six stitches. Quite coincidentally I was hospitalized at St. Ann's Hospital in Anaconda four days later with appendicitis. A double whammy and my season was over.

My sophomore year was also distinguished by two incidents that put the Central basketball program in jeopardy. The first occurred at the Butte Central varsity game after my injury. I arrived back from the hospital with the game well into the second quarter, and it was a game of exceptionally soaring emotions, even by Montana high school basketball standards. The gym was of the same model as the Daly with an overhead track and had a similar modest capacity level, which was pushed to the limit for the game. The noise level was at a decibel point comparable to the city championship. In the second half, the gym exploded. A physical play led to an exchange of fists, followed by the emptying of the benches and the bleachers as the court was transformed into a free for all with the arms of players, coaches and fans swinging in all directions. After a short period of pugilism, the melee ended with everyone returning to their seats with no apparent serious injury to anyone. When I have told this story over the years, I always have been asked why it happened. The tightness of the gym partially explains it, but more importantly it was Anaconda vs. Butte, a roiling of the tribal rivalries. The two cities shared so much in ethnic heritage, religious loyalties and world outlook, but the competition was so impassioned, precisely because of that proximity in background and spirit.

Five weeks later, a similar incident erupted at Carroll College in Helena with another airtight gym and another Catholic high school as the opponent. As the game progressed, I sensed an emotional atmosphere much the same as that of the Butte Central game, and in the second half an incident triggered a scene duplicative to that in Butte. For some from Helena, further justice was required as they flattened the tires of the bus that was to transport us back to Anaconda. This incident is more surprising since there was not a traditional Anaconda/Helena tribal rivalry. The principal thing we shared was religion, and perhaps that was enough.

The following Monday an angry and upset McCoy called an assembly of all the students of Central to share with us his displeasure. These outbreaks between Catholic schools, with us the common protagonist, obviously were of great personal embarrassment to him as the Superintendent of the diocesan schools, and his ire was understandable. He flatly decreed that another such outbreak would result in the elimination of basketball at Central. No one present doubted his resolve in carrying out such a threat. Eliminating the popular basketball program would have been easier for him than terminating the band and speech with the malfeasance of all those involved in the melees. The message was heard; we had no further incidents during the rest of my high school years.

It is hard to argue with McCoy's actions on these incidents; others in his position certainly would have reacted similarly, although perhaps with not as extreme of a threat. That was not true, however, for so many other matters involving McCoy and basketball (or generally the school). Coaching in a McCoy-run school required not only mastering technical matters of play but also required a capacity to withstand indignities. Usually a coach's principal challenges are the players, the parents and the school board. At Central, foremost was contending with McCoy, as the firing of Pat Curran proved. As he did with the nuns and other teachers, McCoy treated the coaches as lowly subordinates and at times even as children. For example, Tracy Walsh did not have a key to the gym even though he was the varsity coach. If the gym was needed for a Saturday practice or game, he was required to call ahead and occasionally found himself waiting outdoors if prior to his arrival McCoy had not opened the door to the gym and locker rooms.

Walsh's tenure involved a number of incidents confronting the McCoy authoritarian and capricious style of governing. One in particular stands out since it occurred the same day as the Deer Lodge debacle. The organizers of the tournament sponsored a lunch for the players and coaches. Walsh was scheduled for certain minor administrative duties during the noon hour that day. When he approached McCoy about the conflict, he noted that as the coach he was expected to be there and his absence would catch the attention of other coaches and the organizers. McCoy informed him that he would miss the luncheon. McCoy further would not budge when Walsh indicated that he had lined up another teacher to swap duties with him. The proposal fell on deaf ears, and the team attended the luncheon without its coach.

The Junior Year Bounce Back

I remained committed to basketball as my first love, but I couldn't help being drawn down to the "green grass" at the east end of town for the first football practice. I thought that the football season would distract me from inflated expectations about basketball and that I would show up more relaxed for the first practice in November. I anticipated that I would be the back-up end to the two seniors. What I didn't expect is that I would become the team kicker since we lost Mike Vollmer to a broken collar bone at our first game of the season in Butte. (Butte played on a gravel surface!) I was called upon to assume the kick-off duties mid-point in the game, and it was a baptism by fire since I was asked to execute an onside kick later in the game. I remained the kicker for the rest of the season.

The basketball season did prove to be as I had hoped. That was the year I became a member of the starting five and consistently one of the top scorers, scoring 25 points against the powerful Missoula Hellgate team in their gym. It also was the year that my basketball style evolved to the form that characterized my play for many decades afterwards. It was an aggressive game of driving to the basket, rebounding at both ends, but particularly at the offensive. Although I did not completely pass up the jump shot, if given the option to drive, I usually took it. For me life was good on the basketball court. I felt I was a full-fledged member of the Saints, my aspiration since early grade school when I'd walked across the alley to mix with the Central stars.

We headed into the district tournament with a respectable but hardly overwhelming record of 11 wins and 8 losses, but a number of those losses had occurred early in the season. Also, we'd built up considerable momentum at the end as we tallied wins in six of the final seven games. Our team was confident that we could place high in the tournament. We generally viewed Bozeman as unassailable with its front line of Glen Smiley, Bill Monroe and Robin Stiff, each of whom measured 6'6". Other than the one concession to Bozeman as the likely champs, the sentiment was that it was wide open for the second slot for state qualification.

The tournament was to be held at the Butte Civic Center, a massive building built in 1952 which became the site for most of Southwestern Montana's headline-drawing events, athletic and non-athletic. I remember our family travelling the 23 miles to Butte in the late 1950's to the Center to attend a sermon by the rosary missionary Father Patrick Peyton, whose signature motto was "the family that prays together stays together." In more recent times, the Civic Center has been used to host the funeral of the daredevil king, Butte resident Evel Knievel. All the sports observers expected the Saturday night games to fill the seating capacity of nearly 7,000 spectators, and we wanted a shot at being Bozeman's opponent in the championship tilt that night.

We began with a victory over Butte High, setting up the semi-final game on Friday night where another victory would put us into the contention for that title. Our opponent was Hamilton, with whom we had traded wins during the season. Our frustrating loss to them in a game where we managed to score a paltry 38 points sent us back to the Civic Center the next morning to play Dillon. That game would determine who would play in the consolation game on Saturday night prior to the championship between Bozeman and Hamilton. We had prevailed over the Beavers twice during the season, and the Saturday morning game made it three in a row. With the victory in the morning, the stage was set for that rare second match of the season against the Copperheads. We were the clear underdogs. We'd lost to them earlier in the season, and our loss streak stretched back to 1959. But we were determined to end that.

Beating the Copperheads

To "rest" us for the evening game, rooms were booked at a cheap motel near the Berkeley Pit. Containing high school boys to their rooms isn't easy, and we escaped to view the fascinations of The Pit, probably a more effective preparation for the game than lying around in a motel room. A massive hole, at that time about two miles wide and a few thousand feet deep, the Berkeley Pit featured massive dump trucks filled with "dirt" snaking up its terraces from the bottom. It was a man-made mechanical marvel that gobbled large chunks of rocky soil streaked with copper. Commencing its open pit operations in 1955, its mission, as an early brochure of the Anaconda Company boasted, was to efficiently recover ore that "could not be economically mined by conventional underground methods." The Pit was devised and promoted as the savior of Butte and Anaconda's industry.

We shared that upbeat message as we looked with pride at the operations that afternoon. That optimism for the Pit proved to be short-lived as the demand for Butte copper declined in the 1970's with lower priced ores from Chile leading to lay-offs and finally a shut-down of the Pit. Following that, with no pumps operating, a new (and extremely toxic) discolored lake began to rise in the Pit. The lake received world-wide fame in the 1990's when 342 Canadian geese landed on the waters of the Pit and never rose to fly again with their dead carcasses destined to become part of the fabled Butte story. Today tourists flock to the observation platform to view the toxic waters.

That evening we became locked in a tight contest with the Copperheads before a near capacity crowd, surpassing the most aggressive estimates of the city championship attendance. The Copperheads had maintained a slight lead throughout, and late in the fourth quarter I looked up at the scoreboard, which indicated that we were down by six with .56 remaining. It had not been a great game for me as my point total was somewhere in the single digits, and I had four fouls. I decided I would go down fighting trying to do something, even if it would result in a fifth foul.

The Copperheads were inbounding underneath our basket, and I rushed in to successfully intercept the pass. Going up for the shot after the steal, I was fouled and made both free throws, which cut the differential to four. The next inbound pass came into John Cheek, who dribbled to the mid-court with me guarding him. I went in for the steal, got partial possession of the ball and the whistle blew. I figured I was out of the game with the fifth, but incredibly the play was ruled a steal by me and then a foul on him. Reflecting on this 45 years later, Cheek mused: "There was about 30 seconds left in the game, I had the ball and the foul was called on me." It was as favorable of a call as a defender could ever hope to get. I went to the line on a one and one, meaning that if I made the first shot I was rewarded with another free throw. At that time, the one and one was awarded when the foul was committed against someone not in the act of shooting. I made both the first and the bonus, making it a two-point game.

On the following play, the Copperheads moved the ball down the court and missed a shot. After rebounding the ball off the rim, I drove down the court and was fouled again as I went up for the lay-up. I made the first free shot, making it a one point game. We then headed to the bench as the wily Coach Cheek called a time-out to "ice" me. His strategy worked as I missed, failing to tie up the game. Severely disappointed with the miss, I knew I needed the ball again as the clock was winding down. The Copperheads again inbounded the ball to Cheek with me on him, and at midcourt I made another attempt to steal. The whistle blew. This time the infraction was assessed against me—now out of the game with less than 10 seconds left.

As I sat down on the bench, my emotions were mixed. I felt during the last 50 seconds I had made an effort that I could be proud of, but I also was convinced that it was all for naught since we were about to lose the game. Walking to the line for a one and one was Cheek, a 90% plus free throw shooter, probably the best in the state, who in an earlier tournament game had tallied 18 free throws. I didn't think he'd missed one the entire tourney. After he made both, we would be down three points, an insurmountable margin in those days before the three-pointer.

I watched with disbelief as he missed. We got the rebound, and Mike Vollmer hit a jump shot as the clock ran out. While the game wasn't the annual championship, it nevertheless was a long-awaited victory over the rival Copperheads and so was gratifying to us and our fans. As for the improbable Cheek miss, I like to view it as divine atonement for the final second exploits of Milt Smith and John Stipich and other Copperhead heroes who had tortured the Saints in by-gone years. Vollmer to this day relishes happy memories of his clutch shot.

John Cheek Jr.: "Quiet" Fifth Grader to Hall of Fame Coach

We might have won the battle against Cheek and the Copperheads in that game, but John did not lose many critical battles during his excellent high school career. The following year the Copperheads qualified for the state tournament, also held at the Butte Civic Center. In a spectacular display of offensive prowess, he scored 89 points over the four games, the highest scorer in the tournament, and earned all state selection. Yes, a healthy percentage of the points were thanks to his dead-on free throws.

As I look back on his high school career, I continue to be amazed at the extraordinary progression from the "quiet" grade school teammate to the leading scorer in the state tournament. In a recent conversation, John claimed that he did not score a single point during his fifth and sixth grade seasons. That may be hyperbole. What I remember most vividly was a quantum leap from his freshman to sophomore year, and I asked him what he attributed that to. His initial response was that he had grown considerably and gained body strength, which may be true but that doesn't explain his shooting touch. We talked about the importance of hand to eye coordination, and he credited his mother for playing catch with him tirelessly when he was young to help develop those skills critical to a shooter..

His scoring output was featured by that lopsided share of free throws, shooting over 200 in one of the seasons. "No one should get that many free throws," he commented. I agreed and asked him how he ended up getting fouled so frequently. It was here that the coaching of his ever crafty father was crucial—a little jab, a cross-over step and a lean into the defender who might be over-playing as he went up for the shot. It was advice which transformed the trip to the line into a well-traveled road. He also was a fiery competitor, which didn't always make him popular with opposing players and fans, but it was that same spirit that led to all those free throws.

John catapulted his high school success into a basketball scholarship at his father's alma mater, the Montana Grizzlies. He initially enjoyed success as he rose to the starting guard for most of the second half of the season of his sophomore year. However, the following year he lost the position to a quick junior college recruit. Disheartened (or, as he put it "my attitude sucked"), he declined the scholarship for his senior year and turned his energy to other things. By then he was married to his high school sweetheart, Debbie Kelly and had a daughter.

After graduation John accepted a position at Geyser High School to commence a coaching career that would lead to induction into the National High School Coaches Hall of Fame. His path began modestly at a school of 40 students where the scope of his responsibilities in the north central Montana town resembled those of my father in Virginia City. He was the sole basketball coach, the assistant football coach, coach of track and cross country and the advisor for the school annual and newspaper. The school also threw in the job of driving the school bus in the morning. For all these extracurricular responsibilities, he was paid an addition $600 to supplement his base salary of $6,000.

After spending several years at Geyser, a one year tenure at Class A Whitefish made him realize that he was a small school guy. The Whitefish experience was colored by his assignment as the assistant wrestling coach. "I knew nothing about wrestling," he remarked. Furthermore, "I had to wrestle the biggest guys at practice and they beat me up—a miserable year." He returned to Class C for about 20 years at Stanford and Cascade, small towns also in the Great Falls area.

While at Stanford, he began to develop a reputation for his skills as a track coach, which he eminently preferred to coaching basketball. As he described it, "if you walk into a bar with a basketball, everyone from ages 8 to 80 knows how to coach it; you walk in with a pole vault, and they ask you how far do you throw that thing." He also found the individual nature of the sport appealing, which permitted more opportunity to develop budding athletes. His niche in track is reflected by his being tied at fourth for the most state championships by a coach.

John's and Debbie's lives were to be changed forever in Stanford when they were approached by a high school boy who had lost his parents to live with them. After a family discussion with their daughters, they agreed to take him in and ultimately adopted him. His name was Harry Clark, and under John's tutelage he became one of the finest track stars in Montana history. He continues to hold numerous Montana records. Following high school, Harry was a national contender in the decathlon for the University of Houston and Montana State and currently is the head track coach at Carroll College. John and Debbie also are proud parents of two daughters, one of whom is a clinic director for a hospital and the other a neurologist.

When I visited John in 2011, he was coming off a few tough years on the health front. Despite these setbacks, his sense of humor was striking during our two and one-half hours of reminiscing, and he displayed a phenomenal memory of events long ago. When I asked him about playing basketball after the Grizzly days, his answered that "he could count on two hands the number of times" he had played since then. Even more remarkable was his declaration that "he never really liked basketball," obviously an issue growing up in a basketball family. I thought to myself—he was one helluva player for someone who really was not sold on the game!

John Harold: Consummate Team Player

If I were asked to list, from the thousands I have been on the court with through the years, the top ten that I would pick to be teammates, John Harold of the Copperheads would be on that list. He was the ultimate smart team player.

His rise was even more remarkable than Cheek's. Harold did not play on a team during those early years of grade school competition. When I first became aware of him in eighth or ninth grade, I thought he had moved recently to Anaconda. As it turns out, he always was there, but not visible to most of us. As a small child, John was afflicted with polio and had been rushed to the hospital in Butte. With an iron lung outside his room as a contingency, there was some concern as to whether he would survive. He did, but a few years later he suffered a kidney infection and in the process was diagnosed with a heart murmur. As a result, the doctor recommended that he not be permitted to play competitive athletics. Adding to his lower profile, as he describes it, "I was very shy and didn't talk to a lot of people." During those years of non-competition, he was working on his basketball skills—during recess at the Lincoln School and most significantly at the Jackson's garage. One of Anaconda's few African-American families, the Jacksons primarily played football, so I don't know how skilled basketball-wise they were. Their abilities must have been impressive if John Harold was a product of their hoop time together.

As eighth grade approached, John convinced his parents and the doctor to permit him to play. According to his narrative, because of his shyness, he failed to show up for a number of the games or practices. "When I did show up, they didn't know who I was so I didn't play much." He had a break-out game by scoring a number of points against St. Joseph, an achievement which in his typical humility he attributes to a guy "not very good" guarding him.

Shortly before the next season began, he was convinced by John Cheek in science class to try out for the freshman team. He made the team and within a short time became one of the starting five, which surprised him because "we had some really good players."

It was about this time the rest of us began to notice John Harold, and we were impressed with his steady skills. He had an excellent shot, particularly from the corner, and was an outstanding rebounder, defender and passer. Most tellingly, he had great basketball sense. He always made that right play or found the right position on the court. Those skills were to carry him through a very productive high school career, which was rewarded with an athletic scholarship for Western Montana in Dillon.

After college, John taught and coached at various levels in the Flathead Valley, both at Ronan, located on the Flathead Reservation, and then in Kalispell. He continued playing basketball in various leagues and pick-up games until his mid-40's when his knees forced him to quit the game.

Meeting with John, one is immediately impressed with his humility and lingering evidence of that youthful shyness. He's active and as trim as he was in high school. Talking about his high school years, he shared with me: "My mother kept all the clippings of my games," and in anticipation of our conversation he reviewed them. "According to the box scores," he continued, "I played 29 games during my senior year and in 22 of the 29 I scored in double figures, but my highest was 22 and I had no nights with 30." Statistics can be misleading, but in this instance I think they were on the mark in defining John as a basketball player: steady, never flashy, and always there to get the job done.

A Summer Interlude

Following our tournament, I was fired up and was looking forward to my senior season, hoping for a great season. Before the next season, however, there were to be a number of intervening events, including two detours that summer with lingering basketball-related memories.

That spring McCoy reversed one of his earlier cost-cutting measures, the virtual elimination of the speech and debate program. It had not been a total obliteration because each year we did participate in a tournament for Catholic schools held in the spring at Carroll College. Our failure to show up would have caused considerable embarrassment to him, the Superintendent. Considering it was our sole event of the year, we did okay but certainly were not going to excel against competitors who had travelled to meets all year. Shortly before the end of the school year, McCoy relented to the pleadings of students and faculty alike and reinstated the program.

I had participated at the Carroll event each year, primarily in declamation, an event defined by the delivery of a speech, either written by another (usually a famous person) or self-composed. I aspired, though, to the elite entries in the competition, debate and extemporaneous speaking. In late May I noticed that the University of Montana was holding its annual speech and debate camp in early July, and I decided to attend to get some training.

Distinct among this group was an African-American from Seattle with the evocative name of Franklin Delano Raines—distinct not only because he was the only black person but also because of his extraordinary talent as a speaker and debater. A friend of mine during those weeks, Judy Jones, told me that Raines was a legend in the Seattle debate circles even though he had just completed his sophomore year. In conversation, Frank was voluble, animated and singularly articulate. To the surprise of no one, Frank and his debate partner won the championship, and Frank took home the medal for extemporaneous speaking.

I became quite friendly with Frank not only because I competed against him but also because we stood next to each other during the rehearsals and performances for a group presentation of a dramatic poem about Lincoln's death, *The Lonesome Train*. We had been assigned solo parts for the poem with Frank being the black preacher and me the ballad singer. Since all our time was not consumed by the scheduled events, a few of us would head off to the playground for either basketball or touch football. Frank was an excellent athlete who played high school football, where he became a captain. As is true with all good things, the camp came to an end, and we went our separate ways.

That fall a few letters travelled between Anaconda and Seattle, mostly dealing with football and the new debate season, but after six months the correspondence petered out. Our paths were to cross twice, though, within the next ten years when we were both students at Harvard. Following his graduation from Harvard Law School, Frank had a storied career over a 30-year period as a member of the Carter White House staff, partner at the investment bank of Lazard Freres, head of the Office of Management and Budget in the Clinton administration and CEO and chairman of Federal National Mortgage Association, usually known as Fannie Mae. Then it all collapsed with problems at Fannie Mae. As I watched his rise (and then fall), I frequently was reminded of that young talented Frank who shared the debate floor and basketball court with me in Missoula when we were teenagers.

Frank's outstanding performance at that speech camp did whet my appetite to be a debater, and I became determined that winter I would both play ball and debate. As things turned out, I was to find that I would be faced with the same choice as Frank: it was either one or the other.

The American Legion-sponsored Boys State was my next stop on that summer's sojourn. In Montana, as in many other states, Boys State was a big deal. It numbers among its prestigious alumni Bill Clinton, Tom Brokaw, Phil Jackson and Michael Jordan. Each August representatives from virtually every high school in the state were selected by their schools and assembled at Western Montana College in Dillon as delegates. The number of delegates per school varied in accordance with the size of the school, ranging from one to the mid-teens with the aggregate number between 300 and 400. I was selected as one of several delegates from Anaconda Central and headed to Dillon in late August 1965. A few weeks earlier, Montana Girls State had completed its program in Bozeman.

Over a 10-day period, we divided our time at Boys State between education, consisting of lectures and training, and participation in political activities. The centerpiece of the political activity were a series of elections from the local level to the state level, culminating in the race for governor. I came to Boys State intent on running for governor, and my good friend Terry Callan, who had attended the prior year, provided me with a strategy. He advised me to win the following elections: any office at the local level, county party chairman and then state party chairman. The chairman presided over state party proceedings and hence would be given much exposure to all members of the party who determined the candidate for governor. I followed Terry's script and was elected the state party chairman of the Frontier Party.

Presiding over the state party meetings proved to be a mixed blessing. At the session the day before the primary, a gubernatorial opponent launched a series of objections and procedural motions in an attempt to undermine me. He succeeded. I didn't handle it well and looked frankly un-gubernatorial. To add to my woes, a new candidate emerged who was to swamp both of us in the primary. His was Glen Smiley, the best basketball player in the state, whose Bozeman team was widely expected to win the state championship our senior year. Glen was a tremendous basketball player, but he was not a "one trick pony" since he was an excellent student and had also served as a vice president of the state Key Club, affording him statewide recognition. Each of the candidates had to deliver a speech at the nomination assembly, and mine tended to be bombastic and overly-dramatic. In contrast, the 6'6" Smiley followed with a delivery that was low key and thoughtful. As he sat down, I knew the election was over.

The political activity was important, but Boys State included so much more. An "all-star" basketball game was featured, and the experience of playing with many of the best players in the state was an exhilarating one. The most rewarding part of the 10 days though were the Staters themselves, who made a lasting impression on me. I met an intriguing group of guys, and the existence of those friendships was to add an additional dimension to the following basketball season. It was not simply another game—it also was an opportunity to converse and even debate before and after the game with fellow Staters, whether they were players or fans.

With the glow of the summer detours still shining brightly in my mind, I was ready to move into my senior year.

Senior Year: A Respectable Regular Season Record

My senior year story began on the football field. That fall the football season represented one of those instances where Bill Matosich and I collaborated productively on the field. It was on the defensive side of the line that our effective teaming up occurred. I was the defensive end and he was the linebacker; however, the defensive scheme was that on each play one of us would maintain the outside and turn the runner inside into the hands of the other for the tackle. Similarly, on a pass play, the inside guy would rush the passer and the outside guy would cover any receiver in the flats. Throughout the season we were an effective duo and were selected, along with the very talented runner George Martin, to the All-Conference second team. With the end of football season, my attention shifted to the basketball court, where I was hopeful that our collaboration would continue.

Buoyed by the training and respectable showing at the Montana speech camp, I remained determined to squeeze into my schedule both basketball and debate. What I did not realize, or at least refused to acknowledge, is the near impossibility of doing that that because of the simultaneous schedules. As many friends I have met through the years learned, it is a choice of either debate or basketball. Nevertheless, I proceeded on and recruited early in the fall my good friend, Larry Jacobson, to be my debate partner, and we began preparations for the season. After a few tense conversations with Coach Walsh regarding my plans following my missing a couple of pre-season practices to attend a debate meet, the decision was rendered: debate was off the table during the basketball season. Walsh considered it to be detrimental to the spirit of the team for a captain to be missing practices. I was left to deliver the message to a disappointed Larry Jacobson.

Our young team included only three players with varsity experience: Matosich, point guard Tom Lovell, and myself, and the three of us were selected as co-captains. We began the season with one loss and two wins which brought us to mid-December and the game of the year—the city championship. In view of our surprise victory the previous spring, there was widespread anticipation of the game, and as usual no seats were available at the tip-off. After such a build-up, the game itself proved to be anticlimactic as we lost 64 to 50 in a game where the outcome never was in doubt. The Copperheads, who were to place fourth at the state tournament that year, were loaded—a squad with nine seniors. Four of them, Cheek, Dave Nielsen, John Harold and Paul Greenough, had been the stalwarts of the team throughout high school. In addition, there was 6'6" John Yeoman, who came into the season with limited experience. In his inimitable fashion, Coach Cheek had developed Yeoman into an imposing force around the basket.

I remember little about that city championship game except for one incident which has been etched in my memory these past 50 years. Towards the end of the game, I fouled out, which seemed to be my pattern in games against the Copperheads. I was to sit on the bench for the remainder of my last high school game against our city rivals and my childhood friends. As I headed to the bench, I turned around and to my astonishment was greeted by one of the Copperheads, either Cheek or Greenough, who had come over to shake my hand. Each of the other Copperheads players on the floor followed suit. It was an incredible and moving act of sportsmanship.

With all the dramatic moments of the city championships through the years, that event stands out to me as the highlight of the series. In fact, I consider it to be one of the poignant moments of my 60 years on the court. When I spoke with Cheek recently, he remembered the event, and I asked him: "did that gesture come from your father (the coach)?" He responded, "No, it came from us and it was a recognition of all the years we had spent together." In the case of Cheek and Greenough, that time had been spent as both teammates and rivals. In the case of others such as Charlie Spangler and Dave Nielson, we had been opponents in all the official games during the past eight years, but we had also been teammates—playing at St. Paul's and other playgrounds for countless hours.

Following the Copperheads loss, we cruised along for the next month mostly winning. Our most dominating win was against the Powell County Wardens of Deer Lodge, where I registered my highest scoring game for the Saints. I was able to exploit the weak Deer Lodge defense in the first half with 24 points. The defense tightened up the second half, and I ended up with 32 points in a game with a lopsided score of 78 to 49. That was my sole high school game piercing the 30-point barrier. Another player on our team was to exceed that mark more than once that year.

I'd received the lion's share of attention at the beginning of the season as the only returning starter, but the big story of my senior season was the emergence of Jim Meredith. I'd known Jim for many years since our mothers were good friends, and he and I had played a lot of ball together at McKittrick's and St. Paul's. We'd always been about the same height as kids though he was a year younger. In high school there was separation between us as he continued to grow to his 6'7" height and my growth spurt petered out. Jim had been put on the B squad as a sophomore, although he deserved a slot on the varsity. As a junior he became the starting center, providing a much needed presence underneath the basket even though his weight had not kept pace with the increase in his height. What really defined his game, though, was a deadly jump shot, particularly 20 feet from the wing, and it began to be reflected in the scorebooks. After the Deer Lodge game, he tallied 35 points, which was followed shortly by another game over 30.

As the season progressed, the primary focus of fan interest shifted from me to Jim. From the narrow perspective of an 18-year-old kid, I can't say I was always pleased about the trend. What I failed to understand was the combination of his incipient stardom and my continuing level of productivity was providing a linkage between us. In view of his subsequent basketball career, I today view it as a privilege to have been so linked.

As might be expected, while Jim and I were cooperating teammates in the games, there existed a healthy dose of competitiveness between us on the practice court. Utilizing the George Hagerman body techniques, I would contest every rebound if we were scrimmaging on opposite teams. In one of those encounters, I received a hefty elbow to the eye, which within a few hours was nearly shut. The incident occurred on a Wednesday. By the Friday night game it still appeared I couldn't see out of that eye while, if the truth be told, my eyesight was just fine. I ended up having one of my better scoring nights of the season. Following the game, I told Jim that if he gave me a black eye each week, it would do wonders for my scoring average! Eventually, the swelling receded and my scoring gravitated back down to the norm.

As the season wound down and we headed to the tournament, our record was 11 wins and 8 losses, identical to our previous season totals. On the minds of us and our fans was whether we could duplicate, or even improve upon, the performance of the prior year's tournament. To our dismay, it was to be a vastly different story, and the seeds of our collapse were planted several weeks earlier.

Chapter Ten

A Tale of Two Teams

The Anaconda Central Saints lost to the winless Powell County Wardens from Deer Lodge at our divisional tournament my senior year. How could this have happened? It was a bitter pill and one that stuck in my craw for many years. Our dream was to find ourselves at the Butte Civic Center two weeks later for the State, and we were bounced ignominiously with two losses. Looking back from this vantage point, I see a lesson in comparing the story of our team, one of the smallest in the Big 32, with the Libby Loggers, another of the small schools, who went on to win the State Championship. It is a tale of two teams.

The Captains' Meetings

Our tale began at a captains' meeting with Coach Walsh in late January. After we covered such mundane matters as the upcoming schedule and our recent performance, Bill Matosich raised the issue that there was some sentiment that the "offense was structured for two guys" (meaning Jim Meredith and myself). As a result, he continued, most of the "shooting and scoring was done by the two." In his view, the offense needed better "ball distribution" among the players. In a recent conversation in the dim light of a bar in Anaconda, Bill confirmed his position: "The team would have been better with more ball distribution."

I didn't see the logic of his position because we had two principal offenses: a weave for a man to man defense and a 1-3-1 for a zone. Both were designed to get everyone involved so that the ball on any possession could be touched by all five players on the court. I didn't believe they were designed to favor Meredith and myself. It was true that Jim and I were the top scorers, and there was no doubt that on any team the ones making the shots are the ones who get the most recognition. The passing and set-up that came before does not always get fully appreciated. There was more to Bill's complaint than offensive structures, though, but we didn't get close to those issues. We focused on the x and o's, and Coach Walsh made some changes to address Bill's complaints.

A few days later, Walsh called Meredith and myself into his office for a follow-up conversation to the captains' meeting. I believe his intended purpose was to mollify us for the changes in the offense. He had done his homework on us and had reviewed our statistics. He told us that we each were averaging about 8 and 10 rebounds a game and our respective scoring averages were about 17 for me and 22 for Jim. After expressing his appreciation for our efforts, he concluded with the compliment that "you guys are the best two players I have ever coached." At that time, perhaps still smarting from the captains' meeting, I don't remember being overly impressed and certainly not grateful. In hindsight, I appreciate it as a generous gesture on his part. He also must have discussed the issue of team harmony and chemistry, but I can't recall any of the details.

The issue of ball distribution surfaced again shortly before the divisional tournament at another captains' meeting. Matosich expressed the view that the offense had reverted back to its original pattern. My immediate rejoinder was that we had been winning recently, and it is true we had won five of the last seven games with the two losses coming at the hands of Bozeman, the acknowledged best team in the state, and Libby, the eventual state champion. While factually accurate, my comment probably was not the appropriate response. Our underlying issue was a weakness in team unity, and that problem was not addressed by any of us at the meeting. The professionals in the realm of sports or any other enterprise classically define team unity as the state of many acting as one. They also emphasize that a team cannot rise to the top if that unity is missing. The 1966 Saints lacked that team unity, and as I reflect back on it 50 years later the question is why.

Was it Matosich vs. Dowdall, a reprise of the battle over the trophy six years earlier? I think there was some element of that, if for no other reason we were the protagonists at the captains' meetings. But I think something else was going on. I have seen some experts reduce the components of team unity to two: (1) people care about their team's goal, and (2) people care about their teammates. Our captains' meetings should have been focused on the extent that these two ingredients existed in the Saints' uniforms that year. In particular, we should have explored whether we all cared about our teammates. I can't speak for others, but my own response to a request for recognition of the others revealed, I think, that I would have failed the test. As it was, we did not broach the topic, the meeting broke up with matters unresolved, and the consequences were momentous. Looking back at this incident, I think we all bear responsibility for the debacle that was to await us in the tournament when we faced the winless Wardens.

To repeat what was described in the opening paragraphs of my story, after a two quarter slow-down by the Wardens, we were frustrated. When the

Wardens finally lifted their stall, we responded with a total lack of discipline and team play. It seemed as if the ball was being thrown up from all directions as there was no pretense of any organized offense. We were the farthest removed from any semblance of team unity. We lost in double figures to a team that broke their thirty something winless streak over our heads.

As I was perched on a bench following that Deer Lodge upset waiting for a trainer to remove the tape on my ankles, I overheard Walsh confiding to Fr. Bill Stanaway, who served the dual role of McCoy's right hand man and un-official assistant coach: "This is it; I am finished with coaching." I thought it was a decision in response to the game. From his position, he certainly under-stood better than any of his teenage players the larger picture of the loss, the failure to cohere as a team. As the coach that failure was bound to weigh heavily on him. As I have learned, other circumstances also contributed to his resigna-tion. There was the rocky relationship with McCoy. Added to the difficulties of dealing with a dictatorial superior were other psychological pressures. Going back to Anaconda for his first varsity coaching job was not a great idea: "when you go back to where you grew up, everyone knows you," he recently told me. He also was quite young to assume the pressures of coaching in a town where basketball was so important. But the loss of that game had to be an overwhelm-ing factor in the calculus of his decision to resign.

That spring he left to teach and coach the junior varsity at Kalispell, positions that he held until he retired. As an assistant coach, he was part of an extremely successful basketball program which had been in the doldrums since the departure of Cheek in 1952. He never did venture back into the head coach-ing ranks. "I've had opportunities to go back to coaching," he disclosed to me, "but I've turned them down." I think that was a loss to Montana high school basketball with his strength in fundamentals and competitive spirit. On the oth-er hand, at 74 he struck me as one who has been very content with the progress of his life.

As for me, I have tried to suppress the memory of that game and the events leading up to it. Yet, the memory of that afternoon in the Memorial Gym (my final appearance on that floor) remains with me as if it occurred last week. Finally recognizing that it was a pebble in my shoe, I've allowed myself to reflect on it and recognize the valuable lesson that I absorbed from the loss. Whether it be a formal team competing in a league or a pick-up squad aiming to hold the playground court for a few games, you can't win without team unity, and the required building block of that unity is caring about your teammates.

As Phil Jackson succinctly sums it up, "more than anything else, what allowed the Bulls to sustain a high level of excellence was the players' compas-sion for each other." Jackson cites as the most dramatic example of this Scottie Pippin's returning after the funeral of his father. The Bulls were in the midst of a tough play-off series, and the indispensable Pippin was emotionally shaken. In the locker room, Phil called the players to form a circle around Scottie while he expressed their collective grief and love for Scottie. Upon the completion of his remarks, the team recited the Lord's Prayer and then departed through the tunnel to the court. Scottie responded with a 29-point game as the Bulls prevailed and moved on to the next round in the play-offs.

Nor are these lessons consigned solely to the realm of basketball, or any other sport for that matter. They apply to all phases of our life. In the business world and volunteer organizations, I have seen both the best and the worst. The best was exemplified by an eight-year experience with a start-up company. At our height, there were about 15 of us, and it was a group remarkably dedicated to the success of the venture. Most impressive was how everyone always was thinking about how we could do it better, how we could function more effectively as a team. The collective interest was elevated over the individual interests of the members of the team. What particularly stands out in my memory is our receptionist Ken, someone who in the business vernacular would be described at the lowest guy on the totem pole. Ken's official day began at 9:00, but he without fail arrived between 8:00 and 8:30 to polish the reception desk, check to see if anything else needed to be done around the office and fill his bowl of candy, which sat on the desk for the pleasure of clients and team members alike.

A Montana Hoosiers Story

Following the painful and disheartening loss, my interest in high school basketball plummeted. I felt robbed of a moment I'd spent my life to that point anticipating and confused about my role in it. Mired as I was, I did not attend the remaining divisional tournament games or the state tournament in Butte. What I missed was a story we had aspired to—one of the smaller schools among the Big 32, not part of the chatter of the odds makers, took home the trophy. The honors accrued to the Libby Loggers, coached by the colorful Bill Racicot, who hailed from a town of about 3,000 located in the far northwest corner of the state. Their path to the championship was a journey of luck, grit and, in contrast to us, a remarkable example of team unity.

The luck came out of our divisional tournament where it turned out our loss to Deer Lodge was not the major upset. Rather, that distinction belonged to the game in which the consensus pick as the best in the state, the Bozeman Hawks, were taken down by a scrappy Butte Central team. While the Hawks had incredible height, they could put on the floor only one guard, and consequently were, as Glen Smiley describes it, "bait" for the Maroons. Their aggressive defense was led by Mike and Pat Petrino, relatives of the football coach Bobby Petrino of Louisville, Arkansas and the Atlanta Falcons. Theirs was a defense that capitalized on steals and turnovers and rarely yielded an uncontested shot.

The Loggers' grit was demonstrated in their prevailing in a series of closely fought games. After narrowly losing to Missoula Hellgate in the divisional finals, the Loggers arrived in Butte relatively unknown among some circles, who at times referred to them as the Timberjacks or the Lumberjacks. After beating Lewistown by five and Billings West by one, they again faced in the final Missoula Hellgate. It was to be a game for the ages. The two teams slugged it out with the score tied 14 times and the Loggers on top 72-70 at the buzzer. The journey home the next day was a scene that could have been lifted out of the movie *Hoosiers*. About 50 miles outside town, the first of their enthusiastic fans joined their cavalcade. By the time they reached home, they were welcomed by 4,000 to 5,000 fans, exceeding the population of Libby and nearly equaling the county's total of 7,000. The victory ceremonies had to be held outdoors since there existed no building in Libby with sufficient capacity to seat all the welcoming fans.

Because of the size of Libby, the excitement generated by their winning the title has been compared to the similar run by the small Indiana town of Hickory in *Hoosiers*. For those knowledgeable about the Big 32, though, the rise of the Loggers to the top position in the state was not considered shocking—surprising but not shocking. The Loggers had a nucleus of five talented players who'd been playing together since grade school years and who as freshmen had defeated their varsity team in a scrimmage. Anchored by the 6'6" solidly built Agathar twins, Mark and Max, complemented by the shooting of Dean Leckrone and Ted Smart and coordinated by point guard and coach's son, Marc Racicot, the Loggers were a team to be reckoned with.

I knew of their prowess from personal experience. We played them four times over two years, losing three of them by double digits, with one being a deficit of 37 points. However, we did gain some respectability when we defeated them by three points in our intimate Anaconda Central Gym, where we rarely played varsity games. Marc Racicot remembers well that loss in what he describes as a "truly homer" gym—the tight confines enhanced by the presence of the nuns "with their rosary beads." It is true that the nuns were visible to all with their seats in a balcony area, but I do think Marc's reference to rosary beads is colorful but apocryphal.

The Loggers were talented, but that is not what led them to the top. They were the product of coach Bill Racicot's philosophy of team effort. A couple of years ago, I spent two hours with Marc, and a major topic was his father, whom he described as his best friend to the day of his father's death. Many of the stories about the hyper-competitive coach were humorous and charming, such as his mother getting upset because of his cussing (mildly) from the bench in the heat of the moment. What really came through was the love and care that Bill Racicot had for his players, and his players certainly responded with their own sentiments towards each other. There certainly was talent, but the essential element of team unity won the championship for the Loggers.

The Libby players dispersed to various Montana schools following graduation, but the most interesting journey was Marc's, which has had all the prints of the "team first" philosophy of his father. Marc's first choice was to attend Montana State in Bozeman, the home of the Bobcats, but his father had other plans. Bill was hired as the freshman coach at Carroll College and after a year took over the reins of the varsity team. A major compensation component of his move to Helena was free tuition for his children, and Marc was informed that he was to be the first in the family to receive that perk. While initially disappointed, Marc speaks euphorically about his experience at Carroll, where he played both football and basketball and was elected to the Carroll Athletic Hall of Fame.

He continued playing basketball during law school and three years in the military where he was a member of the Judge Advocate Corps. His playing days ended around age 40 when two successive sprained ankles and the aggravation of old football injuries convinced him that he was finished with basketball. In the meantime, he was elected for one term as attorney general and then two terms as governor of Montana as a Republican. With the election of George Bush in 2001, with whom he had formed a close friendship while governor, he moved to Washington where he served in a number of positions, including national chairman of the Republican Party. Today, living in the scenic Swan Valley, he keeps himself occupied with board activities and woodworking and looks back fondly to the weekend that Libby upended the Montana basketball world.

Marc also represents one of the best examples of the integration of the skills and lessons he learned from playing the game to the personal and professional challenges of the "real world." "When I was a freshman," Racicot related, "my dad [the high school coach] told me: 'Marc, you aren't big, but you are slow.' Therefore, my dad continued, 'you will need to do unselfish things to make the team. If you learn how to distribute well and provide inspiration and motivation without being obnoxious, you'll have a chance to play.'" In reflecting on his father's emphasis on providing a connection among players by helping them come together—to be an essential cog in forming that team oneness—Marc observed, "That has been my life's work. I have never been overly spectacular in any single endeavor, but I could be a good member of the team; that is what I have been for my whole time on the planet and it was his insight that provided that."

That coach's philosophy of teamwork inspired his undersized school to grab the state championship trophy and propelled his son into an impressively successful life on and off the court.

Chapter Eleven

Transitions

Moving on from the Saints

When I was about eight or nine, my parents took me to the movie, *Knute Rockne All-American*. Spellbound by the movie, particularly Rockne's celebrated "win one for the Gipper" speech, I exited from the theater announcing to my parents that Notre Dame was my choice for college. While I continued to harbor that dream, I realized the cost was beyond my family's resources, and I focused instead on Carroll College in Helena. Moreover, I hoped to play basketball at Carroll in the footsteps of Anacondans such as Jim Hogan, Tracy Walsh, Pat McKittrick, Bill Lowney, Tom Greenough and Bill Molendyke. With our strong family connections to Carroll, being the alma mater of my two priest uncles and the home of my uncle James Manion, the head of their excellent pre-med program, we knew many of the teachers at the college. I applied early to Carroll and was awarded a fine academic scholarship.

Several of the wonderful nuns who taught at my high school, however, had different ambitions as to how I should spend my college years. Dominican nuns based out of Sinsinawa Mound, Wisconsin and mostly Chicago area natives with a sophisticated view of the world, their message was that I would do well to "broaden my horizons." Inevitably, the conversation would turn to Notre Dame, the Midwest Catholics' Ivy League entrant. When I raised the issue of affordability, they responded that Notre Dame also had scholarships. With their firm encouragement, I submitted my applications for admission and scholarship by the January deadline.

Our phone rang one early evening in March, and the operator identified herself from South Bend, Indiana with a person to person call for me. Brother Raphael then introduced himself as the head of the Scholarship Committee at Notre Dame. Calling from their meeting, he informed me they were offering me a General Motors Scholarship in the amount of $2,000 per year, which he described as their best scholarship. At that time, the tuition, board and room at Notre Dame was $2,400. Before formally offering the scholarship, he continued, he wanted to confirm that Notre Dame was my first choice. The Anaconda boy thought it was a perfectly ridiculous question—of course it was!

The knowledge that I was on my way to Notre Dame in September partially eclipsed the painful memories of the Deer Lodge disaster.

Referee Frog Hull at the Moose Bar

Before heading to South Bend, I made another trip to Dillon for Boys State, this time in the role of a counselor. Traditionally previous Staters were invited to serve as "junior" counselors. Glen Smiley and Nick Fullerton from Hamilton also were among the counselors. Glen was on his way to Duke to follow the steps of Mike Lewis to play for the Blue Devils, and Nick was headed to Montana State. Our principal responsibilities were to assist the senior counselor assigned to each floor of the residence halls to monitor the activities of the Staters. In contrast to the prior year as a delegate, we had extensive contact with the senior counselors as we sat daily with them in meetings and helped to supervise activities.

My clear favorite among the senior counselors was Frank (Frog) Hull, a teacher at Dillon, but known to us as a referee in tandem with his brother, Richard (Toad) Hull. The brothers were a stocky 5'5" with remarkably similar features, resembling two sparkplugs running up and down the court. They were excellent at their craft. Whenever they were spotted emerging from the locker room tunnel, the unanimous verdict was that it would be a well-refereed game. Frog had a sharp tongue and a biting sense of humor as his laughter dominated the counselors' table. At times to emphasize his point, he would burst into song with that engaging tenor voice of his.

One evening we were privileged to hear those crooning skills highlighted at the colorful Moose Bar. At Frog's behest a group of us (mostly junior counselors) walked into the Moose, which perennially has been cited as one of Montana's most captivating watering holes. Frog and his accompanist, a banjo player, were sitting with beers on a modest platform which served as the stage. Close to the stage were a few scattered tables and chairs, and in the far corner was what put the Moose on the map, the famed "wino pit." That evening it was occupied by about five or six guys in various states of inebriation sitting on a bench abutting the wall. Some were asleep, and those awake passed down the line a bottle with each taking a swig before handing it to the next guy. I've heard that some of the "winos" were skilled musicians, but we didn't hear any music from them that night. That was left to Frog and the banjo player.

Frog had told us that he would meet us there so he could warm up for the concert, which entailed getting a few drinks under his belt. The warm-up had had its effect—he was even more gregarious than usual as he greeted us. He then proceeded to entertain us with a repertoire that included country and western and contemporary popular music as well as a few Frog originals, usually satiric lyrics adapted to well-recognized tunes. The skills of the banjo player were particularly impressive; according to Frog, he once had enjoyed a more illustrious career, which had been felled by drink. To the extent that they were alert, the winos seemed delighted with the special entertainment. After a few hours (and a few beers), we headed back to the campus with full knowledge that it would be a short night's sleep before our early wake-up call.

That next morning a group of us ran into Frog on the quad and thanked him for the concert. While acknowledging our compliments, his demeanor was a little sheepish, the only time I remember him not having a biting retort. He may have been suffering the effects of a hangover, but by afternoon a story was circulating that his wife had put him through the wringer when he arrived home late in high spirits from the Moose excursion.

I did not see Frog again until I visited him at his Dillon home 46 years later. He still retained the twinkle in his eye and that spark of energy at age 80 despite suffering a terrible family tragedy a number of years ago. Showing the old Frog spirit, he greeted me with two non-politically correct parodies of the Notre Dame fight song and some ditty about BYU. In the years following the Moose Bar concert, he enjoyed a full life of refereeing, teaching, acting and performing, but it all came to a screeching halt in the 1970's when his daughter was shot fatally by a former boyfriend. Despite the devastation wreaked upon his family, in a magnanimous gesture rarely seen by relatives of victims, Frog paid a visit to the prosecutor's office to successfully persuade them not to seek the death penalty. As he told me, "that man owes his life to me, but I didn't see what would be accomplished by the taking of another life."

The tragedy did drain his zest for teaching and refereeing, although he did return to the latter long enough to be inducted into the Montana Referee Hall of Fame. He then moved into a new career as a "toastmaster," referring to himself in his promotional brochure as a "giver of speeches, singer of songs." Describing the creation of his new business, Frog commented: "I used to give that stuff away for free and then I found out you could make money in it." Subsequently, he extended his scope of services to "teacher tune-ups," banquets, retirement parties, roasts and commencements. His appearance is mandatory for any funeral in Dillon. According to Frog, success in his field demands adherence to three rules: "Be loud, be good, be gone."

A Conversation with Pat Curran

When I was a delegate the prior year, one of the first guys I spotted after my arrival was Pat Curran, who was a counselor along with other teachers on their summer break. When I sought him out for a brief conversation, I found him to be his usual taciturn self but discovered he'd been tracking my school's basketball season despite his departure. In particular, he seemed to be fully informed about our victory over the Copperheads at the Civic Center. I also learned that he was an assistant coach for the St. Mary Gaels in California.

He was back as a counselor, and I again spoke briefly to him about the Saints. As expected, he was quite aware that our story was nowhere near as uplifting as the previous year. My principal memories of Curran from that summer of 1966, though, begin with a chance meeting at the Moose Bar.

Following a double date, friend and fellow counselor Terry Robinson (future star with the Mission Mountain Wood Band) and I stopped by for a beer at the Moose Bar. Now in those days the Moose Bar was the sort of joint that routinely served everyone unless they were in diapers. It was the site of our confab with Frog Hull a few nights earlier where at least a half dozen of the attendees were under 21. The common assumption of many Montanans was that even the young could be expected to "drink responsibly." In many places, the legal drinking age mostly was honored in the breach since bars were important centers of casual social interaction. We in Montana were not alone in those views since a number of states, including New York, had established a legal drinking age of 18. In sum, drinking among teenagers was common. I actually had been rather late to the game. It was on high school graduation night that I enjoyed my first "party."

Sitting at the bar when we walked in was Curran with one of his Dillon buddies. He nodded to us as we passed him to take a table. Terry and I left after our one sociable beer, greeting Curran as we headed to the exit. Early the next morning I was confronted by an angry Curran, who clearly had sought me out. He greeted me: "well, you think you're all grown up." After further expounding on what he viewed as my dissolute activities during the past week, he suggested that it was time for me to lay low and remain on campus. While he cornered me early, he already had contacted Jim Glover, the senior counselor who was my boss. Jim approached me to offer the same admonition as Curran—I should stay put during the evenings.

There was one person who thought the entire incident was a topic for unmitigated humor, Frog Hull. When I saw him later in the morning, he greeted me with a huge laugh and needled me: "I understand you ran into Curran at the Moose last night." Frog continued somewhat more seriously: "Well Curran gets upset when he thinks one of his athletes has gone off the path." I pointed out that technically I was not one of his athletes since he never coached me. As I reflected on the encounter later in the day, my ire at the injustice did not diminish, particularly since my companion Robinson did not suffer similar rebukes even though he also was under 21. Looking back, I can now see in this incident the traces of a protective connection he felt for me even if it was gruffly expressed—he still viewed me as one of "his" athletes for whom drinking underage was not conducive to advancing my game.

I don't recall speaking with him during the remaining Boy State days, and after I left I never saw him again. Like so many from Anaconda I wondered what happened to him. In my research during the last couple of years, I discovered that Curran's tenure with the Gaels lasted only another couple of more years. Under former Gael star Michael Cimino, Curran's principal responsibilities were coaching the frosh and recruiting. According to a former high school coach close to the program, the team's performance was weak as Cimino was not able to bring the magic to the Gaels that he showed as a player. Pat became a casualty of the lack of success when the Gaels decided to move beyond Cimino. In attempting to follow Curran's trail after that departure I located his 92-year-old "big brother" John in Minneapolis. He confirmed that Pat returned to Minneapolis after California and died at a relatively young age. He never married and never coached again. For many of us more than 50 years later, the image of that erect military stride with sleeves rolled up dominating the halls of Anaconda Central remains vivid.

An Assessment of My High School Years

Basketball was nearly a daily event for the counselors. Usually in the late afternoon when we had a break, a group of us would converge upon the gym to play some ball. Included among the group were Smiley, Fullerton, Robinson, Randy Davis and Jim Lodge from Dillon and Jim Corr, the coach at Dillon. Frog was there occasionally, and Pat Curran never was. The games were of high quality and competitive, the experience a fringe benefit of working as a counselor. It was the first time I had picked up a basketball since the Deer Lodge loss, and the outings led me to feeling a little more warmly about the game. While we were playing pick-up one day, someone raised the idea of a game between the counselors and an all-star team of delegates. The idea caught on, and a game was scheduled. Two incidents in connection with preparation for the game stand out.

While we were practicing one day, I drove successfully to the basket. Corr stopped the action and commented to one of the Dillon guys: "See what he does when he drives—he lowers the shoulder, puts the head down and gets a good first step…that's the way it's to be done." He then added something to the effect that he had been watching that move for the last couple of years. The second incident takes us back to our old friend Frog. In anticipation of the game, he wrote a piece in the daily newsletter providing an assessment of players on both sides. "Glen Smiley, best all-around player in the state, Nick Fullerton, best jump shooter from the corner." After mentioning a couple of others, he added: "Pat Dowdall, best garbage collector in the state," referring to the facility for grabbing offensive rebounds and putting the ball back up for a score.

I was somewhat taken aback by these comments. Both were intended to be complimentary. Nevertheless, as I considered that I had developed an impression among observers as being primarily a driver and a garbage collector, I was ambivalent as to whether I valued such a reputation. I candidly admitted to myself these were the things I had enjoyed the most in playing—driving along the baseline and banging bodies as I went up for the shot and positioning myself to grab the offensive rebound. It was a little jarring, though, to see others as viewing the two as signature traits. They didn't have the same elegant ring as "he shoots the lights out with his jumper."

For many years I tended to assess my high school career as mildly disappointing. Part of that may have been attributable to my comparisons with John Cheek, who had a great career, and Jim Meredith, who had an extraordinary career. Also, not having gotten to be that big and tall center I'd expected to become certainly was a consideration. The loss to Deer Lodge has had a lingering effect on coloring my views toward my high school ball. With the advantage of age and developing a benevolent perspective from coaching youth, I have reassessed it to put it in a more favorable light. Yet, to have been more effective, I probably should have pulled up more to hit that jumper.

Glen Smiley: On to Duke

Glen was one of the last of my fellow high school basketball players I saw before heading off to Notre Dame. He showed up in Anaconda in early September, attempting to ferret out the few existing Republicans in support of his father who was running for Congress. He joined us for dinner at our very Democratic house, but we had much to share in our mutual enthusiasm regarding the next stage of our lives: he facing the challenges of playing in the ever competitive Atlantic Coast Conference and me encountering a new type of life where daily practices and a full schedule of games were absent for the first time in many years.

I hadn't seen Glen since then and wondered what path his life took after his Duke years. Through the wonders of the Google search engine, I tracked him down in December, 2012. As always, he was the epitome of graciousness and indicated that he had often wondered what had happened to me. During the call, he casually mentioned that he had been diagnosed with Alzheimer's—it was so casual that I nearly missed the comment. We arranged a time to speak and I sent to him, as I frequently did with interviewees, an outline of questions. As we spoke, I was notably impressed with the detail of his discussion and was thinking that the Alzheimer's did not seem to have much impact. At one point, he was having difficulty retrieving someone's name and made reference to having problems with his memory. I told him that I was quite impressed with it. His response was "Pat, I spent seven hours reviewing your questions and taking notes." Following the call, he sent me several pages of those notes, concluding with "Thanks for doing all this Pat." I was humbled by the time he had expended on recollecting for my project!

One thing that impressed me particularly during that dinner with Glen in the late summer of 1966 was his tremendous admiration for his father, not a universal attitude of 18-year-old boys. Similar to my own, Glen's passion for the game came from his father's early career—in his case the broadcaster of the basketball games for the Bozeman Hawks and the Montana State Bobcats. As the son of the broadcaster, Glen was able to accompany his father to the booth for a special view of the game. His father soon purchased the radio station, which became a true "family business" with all the members of the Smiley family pitching in when the employees had the day off. The other formative experience for Glen was his close relationship with his brother Jim, a year behind him in school. Both played for Division I colleges, with Jim joining my former teammate Jim Meredith at Washington State. Their father was known to remark that the best investment he ever made was the cost of installing a basket on a pole outside the radio station, which yielded coverage of the full expense of two college educations.

While the Smiley brothers were always together, they were not indistinguishable. Glen was tall and slender while Jim, in his own words, "was the short and chubby one"—not reaching his 6'6" height until mid-high school years. Jim also lived in the shadow of an older brother who excelled on numerous fronts. He recalls a newspaper article citing one of his accomplishments, which began: "Glen Smiley's brother, Jim...." To this day, Jim, who has enjoyed considerable success in business, will tell you that Glen will always be his big brother and he continues to look up to him, figuratively if no longer literally.

With All-State selection his junior year and a number of games with a point total in the 30's, including a high of 39, Glen obviously had a number of memorable high school games. As is true in any endeavor, there were also the disappointments—a terrible ankle sprain towards the end of his sophomore year, which knocked him out for the remainder of the season, and at the state tournament his junior year he, Robin Stiff and Bill Monroe (the "big 3") all were felled by some form of chicken pox. And then there was his "most memorable game," the loss to Butte Central in his senior year. In his words, "you always remember best the ones that got away."

At Duke Glen enjoyed a good freshmen season, highlighted by an 18 point effort against the University of North Carolina coached by the peripatetic and Hall of Famer Larry Brown. The North Carolina team included the future NBA stalwart Charlie Scott, Jim Delaney, who ultimately became the Big 10 Commissioner, and Eddie Fogler, the assistant coach at UNC under Dean Smith for many years and then head coach at South Carolina. According to Glen, his playing time on the varsity was limited, but he enjoyed the experience and the opportunities for travel.

In recognition of his extraordinary interpersonal skills, Duke hired him as a coordinator at the Duke Alumni House and then as a development officer at the Duke Medical Center. What he most finds memorable about those seven years of employment at Duke, though, was the opportunity to follow in his father's footsteps as a broadcaster working with two legends, Jim Thacker and Billy Packer. Initially for $25 per game (later increased to $200), his primary gig was to serve as the "sidekick" to Thacker, long-time ACC broadcaster. On occasion he would be asked to team up with the noted Packer, who in later years was to gain wide prominence in national college broadcasting, particularly when he called the games for several years with the incomparable vocabulist Al McGuire. The broadcasting career abruptly ended in 1977 when he was recruited to assume a position at Baylor University Medical Center, which was followed by a number of other positions at various medical institutions.

My calls and correspondence with Glen have epitomized the pleasures of the journey of writing this book. As for Glen, we all hope that he has remaining many years of lucidity so that we may continue to have the pleasure of enjoying the company of a true gentleman.

The Emergence of Jim Meredith as a Star

I never saw Jim Meredith play after the Deer Lodge loss. What I missed, and was relegated to follow from afar as I was living 1,600 miles away in South Bend, was an extraordinary senior year and college career at Washington State. It was a basketball odyssey far beyond the dreams of any of us when we were playing at the St. Paul's court in our late grade school years.

In his senior year, which proved to be a bonanza year for the Saints, Jim enjoyed one of the great seasons in Montana basketball history. He scored 649 points and registered 379 rebounds, which averaged out to approximately 30 points and 18 rebounds per game. By the end of the season, the Saints, led by Jim and Jack Lowney, Bill's younger brother, were highly ranked in the Big 32 with an 18-1 record and expected to advance to the state championship game. For the second consecutive year, the divisional tournament was to produce a major upset of the Saints—this time at the hands of the Copperheads. At the city championship, the Saints had prevailed over the inexperienced Copperheads by a score of 61 to 50. After the loss, the cross-town rivals matured as a team, and John Cheek pulled off one of his tournament magic tricks as the Copperheads edged the Saints 71 to 69 in the first round despite 41 points by Meredith. The final shot with a few seconds to go, while not as dramatic as Milt Smith's mid-court "shot" a decade earlier, belongs in the annals of the historic rivalry. As Jim describes it, a "kid named [Ronald] Nicholas hit the edge of the backboard on a corner shot and it caromed in. Tough loss." This was to be only a temporary setback for Jim.

He originally was interested in playing for Montana State, but after receiving some interest from such schools as Notre Dame, Villanova and St. Joseph, he ended up at Washington State in the very competitive Pac Eight. His freshman coach was Jud Heathcote, who later was to win the national championship in 1979 coaching Michigan State with Magic Johnson in the title game that defeated Larry Bird and Indiana State. Under Heathcote's tutelage, the freshman team compiled a 26-1 record. Heathcote, whom Jim describes a "tough guy with a big heart," has remained a friend to this day.

Once he arrived on campus, a major objective of Jim and the WSU staff was to increase his weight through a combination of diet and work-outs. I saw the results of this training after his freshman year—he seemed to have gained 25 to 30 pounds, a body that clearly was prepared to withstand the rigors of the rugged competition. In those days, body conditioning for basketball at the high school level was rare, at least in Montana. We always were amazed to observe the results of what the college programs could do to craft the bodies for optimal performance. Several years earlier we had admired the new svelte Wayne Estes undergo a transformation. In the case of both Jim and Wayne, the coaches had success with their programs; they simply had moved in the opposite direction on the weight scale.

At WSU, Jim enjoyed an outstanding career. He was the leading scorer on the team his junior and senior years and the captain his senior year while he garnered All-Pac Eight honors in each year. Among the highlights were playing his sophomore year against Lew Alcindor (later Kareem Abdul-Jabaar), whom Jim guarded for part of a game. At the completion of his senior year, Jim was drafted by the Cleveland Cavaliers, who also had chosen as the first overall pick Austin Carr of Notre Dame. Jim started on the rookie team and was offered a contract at the standard base salary. A professional team in Belgium offered him more, and he headed to Europe to play and enjoy the life: "drove a Mercedes and got an apartment, etc." The enjoyment was short-lived when he "blew" his ACL, which effectively ended his basketball career. Following that he travelled around Europe and then headed back home.

Similar to many that I played with in Anaconda, Jim's educational career in the state of Washington combined coaching and high school administration. As to coaching, he found it more enjoyable at the lower levels where he coached earlier in his career. "Varsity coaching was more stressful," he admits. As is true for so many of us, although geographically he has not resided in Anaconda in decades, he's never left the Smelter City.

Anaconda's Tough Times

The way of life that Jim and I knew in Anaconda was to change radically within a few years after we left. Reflecting these changes, its population today is about 75% of what it was when I was shooting around at McKittrick's garage.

The first blow came in 1974 when the decision was made to close most of the Catholic schools in the Helena diocese because their continued operations were considered not economically sustainable. Both St. Paul School and Anaconda Central ceased to exist with the building for the latter housing the Fred Moodry Middle School. My grade school eventually was demolished. The Memorial Gym has not hosted the annual city championship ritual in over 40 years. The last game ended with a result similar to that of its origin in the early 1920's with the Copperheads prevailing 67 to 47.

Things were to get worse. In 1977 the Anaconda Company went out of existence when the Atlantic Richfield Company purchased it as part of a buying spree by major oil companies, flush with cash from the high oil prices caused by the Arab oil embargo. On September 29, 1981, ARCO stunned all current and former residents of Anaconda when it announced the smelter was to cease operations immediately as the copper mined in Butte was to be shipped to Japan for smelting. The official rationale for the closure was that it was not economically feasible to meet federal and state environmental regulations, in my view a ruse. As was apparent to those of us who spent any time working on the smelter, the Anaconda Company had failed to routinely upgrade the facility. Not surprisingly, its equipment, on the verge of obsolescence, could not compete with state of the art smelters. The zinc plant, where I worked after my freshman year, included no technology later that the 16th century other than the electricity that lighted the building. The virtually overnight disappearance of the smelter in a "one industry town" ravaged Anaconda's economy.

The economic climate and reduced population was bound to affect the basketball programs with a smaller pool of talent. In recent years, the high school enrollment has dropped to less than 300. By comparison, when I was in school approximately 400 matriculated at Anaconda Central with the four classes at AHS aggregating about 700 students for a total of 1,100. The Big 32 no longer exists, but if it did Anaconda would have no representation whereas in its heyday the city had two entrants. Commencing in 2015, the Copperheads moved down to compete in Class B against such opponents as Ronan, Three Forks and Corvallis in contrast to Great Falls, Billings and Missoula of our day.

Another sad loss to Anaconda basketball was the determination by the School Board that the Daly School had become "obsolete" due to aging structural problems. Now enclosed within a chain-link fence with all its windows boarded up and possibly facing the wrecking ball, the building housing the historic gym, with ties to Anaconda basketball stretching back to 1905, is in danger of becoming another vanquished Anaconda institution. The Daly stands as one of the two foundations of my basketball education. At McKittrick's garage I learned to play, and at the Daly I learned to compete in games with a whistle.

Anaconda's Mr. Basketball: Bill Hill

In the view of Tim McKeon, an old family friend, "no one sells Anaconda better than Bill Hill." My grade school basketball competitor, Bill has done this through tireless sponsorship of sports-related ventures. His fingerprints have been all over Anaconda basketball for the last 40 years, ranging from youth recreational director to his recently assuming the head coach of the Copperheads boys team as he approached the official retirement age. Most significant has been his involvement with the Wayne Estes Tournament.

The tournament has served as a bright light in the Anaconda basketball firmament. In 1984, Hill and a group of Anaconda basketball promoters launched the tourney in late March in Wayne's honor. Having competed its 31st year in 2015 and billed as the largest basketball tournament in the Northwest, it now features about 100 teams competing in nine divisions, ranging from Men's Open to Boy's and Girl's High School. The tournament regularly features some of the better players from such states as Washington, Oregon, Utah, Idaho and Montana. Between players and fans, 4,000 visitors are drawn to Anaconda, providing a healthy economic boost to the economy. The quality of play can be evidenced by a quick look at the rules regarding eligibility. For the men's open division, no current semi-professional or professional players are allowed, which opens up the possibility of including former players on the roster. The men's B division restricts each team to two current college players, including red shirt and JV players.

There is a double elimination format played over a four day period in the existing gyms in Anaconda. The 2015 tournament included $20,000 of prize money distributed to winners in the non-high school divisions. There also are slam-dunk and three-point contests, shots that were not part of the game when Wayne played, but certainly ones he would have mastered. A recent YouTube clip captured spectacular displays of dunks of all variety with the winning slam featuring a leap over two crouching players, reminiscent of the NBA dunk contest on All-Star weekend.

Hill served as the Estes tournament director until the late 1990's. After a short absence he re-assumed the position and also undertook an additional basketball role, that of coach. In 2007, the Big Sky Hoops, coached by Hill and two others, won the women's B division at the tournament. Formed the prior year as an AAU team, the Big Sky Hoops was a super AAU team comprised of a number of high school stars in Montana, including Hill's daughter Torry, who starred for the Lady Griz of the University of Montana. Over a period of three years, the team compiled an enviable winning record of more than 85%.

In the spring of 2012, Hill decided to undertake the greatest coaching challenge of his life. At age 64 he was hired as the head basketball coach for the Copperheads boys' team following a winless season. Upon his appointment, he expressed his ambitions, harkening back to the basketball of our youth: "I want to see that Memorial Gym full again." I sat down with him in Anaconda shortly after his appointment to talk about old times and his upcoming challenge. Demonstrating that ultimate self-confidence, verging on cockiness, that I remembered from the first time I met him on the baseball diamond more than 55 years earlier, he seemed unfazed about undertaking high school head coaching responsibilities at our age, his raspy voice betraying earlier bouts with throat cancer. When interviewing before the school board, he informed them in view of the limitations of his voice he planned to use cards to call out plays during the game. Despite the drawbacks of his age and a limited voice, the board was persuaded by his inspirational call to bring back to Anaconda a Memorial Gym with every seat filled.

In between fielding numerous calls on his cell, he confided that a substantial challenge did lie ahead. Taking over the reins of team that had gone winless would be no cakewalk, and he was under no illusions regarding the upcoming season. As it turned out, the team did enjoy a considerably better season. They had garnered a respectable number of victories while losing several close ones at the end of the season. Hill was pleased with the season but acknowledged a "ton of work to do."

A key injury in his second year led to a disappointing season. A shortage of talent and interest among upperclassmen in the third season also led to a disappointment. Bill remained bullish for the future in that two of his starters were freshmen and he had a number of talented sophomores. Moving down to Class B to more appropriately reflect the size of the school would help to realize that goal. A major obstacle to his ambitions surfaced in June 2015 when the school's athletic director submitted a recommendation that his contract not be renewed. At the subsequent board meeting held at the Memorial, Bill survived the challenge as the board voted four to two to retain him. At the meeting, a majority of the crowd of more than 100 who showed up were firmly in his corner.

Bill's efforts to promote Anaconda's economy through sports events is not limited to basketball. He also founded and currently runs the Goosetown Softball tournament. Over a three-day period in the summer, 180 teams from 10 states and Canada contend in the tourney. It's considered one of the three largest softball tournaments in the country and has been featured on Fox Sports. "It adds a million dollars to our local economies," he proudly reports to us, "it's the Woodstock of softball."

In sum, Bill Hill is a very busy man for someone who has entered the so-called "golden years". With his trademark spiritedness, he remains the same as that nine-year-old I met on the diamond so long ago at the Commons.

Farewell to Anaconda

As I headed eastward with my parents in the second week of September in 1966, I couldn't have realized that I was bidding farewell to my hometown. I did return the following summer to work in the zinc plant at the smelter, but two-thirds of my work days were either on the afternoon or night shifts, which had a dampening effect on socializing. The following summer was spent in construction in Minneapolis where my girlfriend lived, followed by jobs driving a bus for the Chicago Transportation Authority for two summers. In 1969 my parents sadly divorced. Married quite young, their interests had diverged. Their struggles largely occurred after my departure to college. My father moved to Helena and my mother to Missoula. My subsequent visits to Montana more often than not did not lead me to Anaconda with family members living in other parts of the state such as Missoula, Polson and Whitefish. For a while, my visits to Anaconda were limited to my high school reunions, usually five years apart with a couple stretching to ten.

Although I physically left Anaconda, I've never severed my emotional ties to the town. I've moved a number of times in my life but I will always be an Anacondan, and within 10 minutes of meeting someone they usually will learn that. I'm grateful for the privilege of having such a marvelous place to have grown up.

Chapter Twelve

Playing at the Rock

That 1,700 mile pilgrimage with my parents in our 1964 Ford was a leisurely journey, visiting along the way several nuns, my great-aunt and a close family friend. I was beside myself with excited anticipation and basking in my parents' pride. As the hours on the road progressed, the trip reminded me of how far from Anaconda I was being taken. Upon arriving at Notre Dame, we were sent to Stanford Hall, the northern-most residence hall located near the campus power plant. Stanford was a product of the glory days of drab cinderblock building construction. Except for a few upper classmen and graduate student RA's, the 300 or so residents were all freshmen—a housing scheme that no longer exists.

A Gym Filled with Terrific Players

The fourth floor housed a diverse group. Across the hall was Jim Brogan, who went on to be a highly regarded stand-up comedian, star of a couple of television shows and the lead writer for Jay Leno. Around the corner was Terry Shaughnessy, whose family name graced the liberal arts building. As is common among college freshmen, we all endeavored to establish our calling card among the group. I took the route of politics, getting elected to the hall council, and an Anacondan, posting on my door that it was the home of the highest smokestack in the world—a dubious, but relatively exotic distinction of which I was most proud. There also was basketball. The floor was filled with good athletes and, in particular, basketball enthusiasts so I had plenty of company when I was interested in scaring up a few games of hoops. Initially, we played at the outdoor courts in front of the campus' geodesic domed Stepan Center, then the premier all-purpose building on campus. As the weather turned cooler, we gravitated to the gym that became the center of my basketball existence for the next several years, the Rockne Memorial, known affectionately by all as "The Rock."

Standing at the far west end of the Main Quad, the massive brick building completed in 1938 in the Collegiate Gothic style then served a dual role on campus. It was, and remains, a shrine to legendary coach Knute Rockne, whose bronze bust sat in the first floor vestibule, and the principal student athletic center. The exterior of the building features numerous images of athletes representing various sports and closely neighboring statues of saints and other religious figures. This cozy association between saints and sneakers was familiar to me through my parochial school upbringing and was, and arguably still is, a distinguishing feature of the Notre Dame culture.

Considering the fact that we were at a school of 6,000 undergraduates plus a few thousand graduate students, many of whom were impressive athletes, the facilities were woefully inadequate for the demands placed on it by the student body. The basketball gym featured only two full courts. In addition, at the east end, there were two side courts of roughly 25 by 25 feet, which could comfortably support only a 3-on-3 game. At the west end were two other hoops, squeezed in between the line for the western full court and the wall. The distance was less than ten feet, barely permitting a little warming up or maybe a tight two-on-two game.

Our Friday night fall ritual for fourth floor Stanford Hall basketball players was to stroll 10 minutes across campus along the edges of St. Mary and St. Joseph Lakes, passing by the venerable Grotto, until we reached the Rock. Usually there were four or five of us with the regulars including Jack Farrell, Tom Rouse and Ed Traille. Jack, an engineering student from Mineville, New York, had played point guard in high school and was a major basketball enthusiast. He also had a successful career as a high school high jumper behind him. Rouse was a very smart ballplayer from the Chicago area who had played on a Catholic championship team while at Loyola Academy. Traille was a valued inside man from California.

We were typically greeted with a gym taxed beyond capacity. The prevailing rules were that the winner stayed on the court, to be challenged by the team next in line. With so many on the sidelines, one of our first tasks was to determine the identity of the teams that were waiting so we could establish our position in the queue. Occasionally our only games for the evening might be at the side courts, but for the most part we eventually did make it to one of the full courts. After our work-out, we reversed course as we headed back to Stanford Hall, vowing that next time we would show up earlier and perhaps even hold the court for a few games.

So why were all these college guys clamoring for court time on a weekend rather than showing up at a women's residence hall to meet a date? The answer lay in the discouraging male-female ratio at the school. Notre Dame's undergraduate population of 6,000 was all male then. On the other hand, only about 1,200 girls were residing at our sister school, St. Mary's. Freshmen lacked the cache of the upperclassmen, thereby reducing our chances even further. The effective ratio of men to women was for us, therefore, about eight to one. This translated into plenty of time for us freshmen to play basketball.

We soon figured out that there were more efficient times to get on a court, particularly between one and four p.m. on weekdays. For those of us whose classes were predominantly in the morning, this proved to be an ideal time to play. For others, particularly engineering and science students, whose afternoons usually were spent at labs for their science courses, it was a little more difficult to hang out at the Rock on an afternoon.

Regardless of when I played, the thing that impressed me about Rock ball was the high caliber of talent on the court. Notre Dame obviously was known as a football school. During that fall of our freshman year, the team on the gridiron did in fact win the National Championship. By contrast, the previous season the basketball team posted a 5-21 record. Things didn't start out much better by freshman year. By January the team had compiled an unimpressive 3-9 record, which included for me an embarrassing loss to the University of Montana during the Christmas vacation while I was home in Anaconda. A casual observer watching the action at the Rock would be quite surprised to learn that a school with such talent on that court fielded such a mediocre team. Some of the upperclassman we observed playing at the Rock struck us as better players than their classmates who would have been part of the 5-21 team. That was all about to change, though, as the aggressive recruiting program initiated by coach Johnny Dee two years prior to our arrival began to bear fruit.

As the fall progressed, the Rock chatter turned to the upcoming try-outs for the freshmen team. Dee tended to focus on recruiting in alternate years. Scholarships had been awarded to seven or eight players in the sophomore class. As for our class, Dee had limited the number to three: John Gallagher, Mike O'Connell and Bob Freeman. Freeman resided on my floor so I knew him well, and I did get an opportunity to play with him a couple of times. My path rarely crossed with O'Connell, a quick guard who enjoyed substantial playing time during his sophomore year, but was cut back somewhat with the arrival of Austin Carr on the varsity our junior year. Gallagher, an English major with an engaging personality and talented in many areas, was a 6'5" forward who had played for the highly-rated basketball program at Archbishop Malloy in Queens. He hailed from a basketball family with brothers playing at Princeton and Georgetown.

Since NCAA rules did not permit freshmen to play on the varsity, their basketball the first year traditionally was confined to practices. To promote the development of his young players, Dee decided to institute a new program whereby the freshmen would play a limited schedule. Since that would be difficult to achieve for a class with only three players, the decision was made to hold try-outs to fill out the roster. I briefly gave consideration to competing in the try-outs, but ultimately decided that even if by chance I were successful, I was not interested in attending practices under the supervision of a coach every day. More attractive to me was devoting that time to exploring the wonders of college life. As it turned out, the odds of success would have been very low. Only four guys were chosen from the try-outs, one of them being Tom McCloskey, a 6'4" outstanding shooting guard from Santa Monica. The remaining roster was filled in with football players.

Notre Dame also had vigorous intramural programs to showcase its basketball talent: the Intrahall Tournament, the Interhall League and the Club League. The first one up was the Stanford Intra-hall, the competition of teams from each of the four floors. With the nucleus of our weekend evening Rock group, our fourth floor team managed to come out on top. Our victory may or may not have been attributable to all those hours we had to strategize as we waited to get into a game at the Rock. Tom Rouse recalled that our championship "trophies" consisted of a free hamburger and coke at the 11 p.m. Stanford snack hour. My roommate Rick McDonough, who helped run the nightly operation, affirmed our legitimate claims to the chow.

Given Stanford's basketball talent, we were very fortunate to claim those hamburgers. Two of the best were Corky Sterling and Dick Reynolds. Corky, or more formally Con Francis Jr., had attained All-State status in Pennsylvania. He was a guard roughly my size who combined a strong drive with a deadly outside jump shot. I frequently found myself at the Rock paired up against him, and learned he also was a tenacious defender. Dick was one of those 6'4 guys of our generation who knew how to play the post or center position, something rarely found among similarly sized or taller guys who are 10 to 20 years younger. A tremendous rebounder who to this day still retains the Wisconsin high school single game record of 29 rebounds, Dick was one of those guys you wanted on your team. I was to spend many hours over the years at the Rock with Corky and Dick, two stalwarts who helped define the Rock experience.

I was not, however, to share the court with them for the Interhall League. With the abundance of talent and interest among the Stanford residents, we entered two teams in the Inter-hall League. I don't recall how the teams were determined nor can I recall everyone who was on our squad. Farrell, Traille, and Bob Campbell, our hall president, are ones I do remember. The other Stanford team was anchored by Reynolds and Sterling, who somehow managed to spirit away Tom Rouse from our fourth floor group. We played well, but not as well as the Reynolds/Sterling team, which won the intramural championship.

I never did play in the Club League, all of whose teams were sponsored by organizations recognized by the university. Apparently the rules were somewhat loose on qualification. Steve Effler, a fellow Government Department major, was unusually creative in engineering his entry into the league. Steve was a certain contender for the "Rock Jock" award of our class since he estimates today he was on the court at least six days a week. Belonging to no club with a team in the League, Steve approached the Notre Dame chapter of the Students for a Democratic Society, the radical 60's political group also known as SDS.

Their membership at Notre Dame was miniscule so they were in no position to recruit a basketball team from their ranks. Making no political commitments other than their basketball play would bring honor to the group challenging the Vietnam War, the draft and racism, Steve successfully won the SDS banner for his friends. SDS did contribute one member to the effort.

According to Steve, their games with the ROTC teams invariably drew an overflowing crowd to witness the Battle of Ideologies (at least on paper). I am sure that Steve provided great entertainment at those game with pithy remarks about the "political" stakes of the game. Gifted with a whimsical sense of humor, Steve would provide a running commentary during our games at the Rock, which could disarm his opponents or deflate a tense moment on the court. He remains convinced to this day that somewhere in the FBI files there is a paragraph or two noting his basketball efforts on behalf of the Notre Dame SDS.

Basketball in the Fieldhouse

About 100 yards from the entrance to my residence Hall and situated between the Library and the Student Center, the Notre Dame Fieldhouse was a formidable building that resembled a Midwestern agricultural storage facility or perhaps a riding arena. Earlier in the decade, *Sports Illustrated* had dubbed it the "South Bend reconstruction of a Roman ruin: an ill-stacked pile of yellow brick." It served as the home of the Notre Dame varsity basketball and myriad other athletic functions, including hosting indoor track meets.

With two intramural leagues, the other basketball court facilities were overworked so the Fieldhouse was drafted into service for our games. As we entered the building from the main entrance, we walked through a narrow hallway before we came into its cavernous interior. We then crossed a dirt-covered area to reach the retractable basketball court at the far end of the building. As we headed towards the court, we encountered to our right a massive wooden entrance, which reminded one of a large barn door. L:ooking around, it appeared that the seating accommodated no more than 4,000 fans for a game, probably fewer than Memorial Gym in Anaconda for the city championship. I remember the thrill of arriving my first game to play on the floor that the Irish had hosted such luminary teams as UCLA and Kentucky. The specialness of the experience soon evaporated when I realized that I had played in more impressive quarters in high school.

That first intramural game was not our introduction to the Fieldhouse. That fall we had crammed into the building with perhaps 10,000 others on several Friday nights for football pep rallies. Packed in like cattle at the Chicago Stockyards on the way to slaughter, those rallies exuded heat, not only from the passionate zeal for a team that continued to rise during the season but also from physical closeness. Dripping in perspiration after 45 minutes of what some in the student press irreverently referred to as "orgiastic energy," we would depart into the cool evening to continue on with our Friday night revelries.

By the end of November, we saw the last of the pep rallies. The main event at the Fieldhouse then turned to varsity basketball. While not attaining the mythical status of the gridiron and despite their recent woes, the basketball program had a celebrated past, particularly in the 1930's and 1940's. Moreover, the burgeoning program also was associated with Knute Rockne, who in his other role as athletic director hired in 1923 the legendary basketball coach George Keoghan. Until his death in 1946, Keoghan's teams were perennial contenders for the Helms Foundation National Championship, capturing it in 1927 and 1936. During the Keoghan years, the Irish basketball team featured a number of All-Americans including three who won the honor in three consecutive years—Edward "Moose" Krause, John Moir and Paul Nowak. The 1936 team had anticipated that they would represent the U.S. in the 1936 Olympics, whose star, Jesse Owens, so antagonized Hitler because of his successive victories over athletes of the Aryan race. Unfortunately for the team, the University vetoed the trip because it required too much time away from studies.

While there were no more national championships, the Irish continued to enjoy successful seasons until the mid-50's. One highlight was a 1950 upset of Kentucky, the defending national champion, by a score of 64 to 51. Following the game, Kentucky's renowned coach Adolph Krupp vowed that he would never play in the Fieldhouse again as he blamed the Notre Dame coach, Moose Krause, for placing the band immediately behind his bench. As one reviews Rupp's record at the Fieldhouse, it is surprising that he did not register a protest earlier since that loss was Kentucky's sixth straight at the venue, stretching back to 1936. The 1950's brought a few deep runs for Notre Dame into the NCAA tournament and featured two All-Americans, Dick Rosenthal and Tommy Hawkins. However, as with the football team, the latter part of that decade brought decline that extended into the 1960's.

The renaissance of the football team was to precede that of the basketball by a few years with the dramatic 1964 turn-around in Ara Parseghian's first season. Coaching changes also were made in basketball with the dismissal of long-time coach John Jordan and the hiring of Johnny Dee, who had played at the school in the 1940's. The diminutive Dee, also an attorney, was brought in to revive the program. The dismal 5-21 season prior to my freshman year revealed the warts of a rebuilding program. Despite this, at the Rock and in the dorm there was a low-level buzz about the basketball team, focused primarily on the sophomores. Dee had recruited three top players in that class: Bob Whitmore, the center at DeMatha High School in Washington, D.C., the team that had broken New York's Power Memorial 71 game winning streak during Lou Alcindor's reign; Bob Arntzen, a brawny forward from Kentucky who had a soft touch, and Dwight Murphy, a smooth guard adept at passing and shooting. Besides the talent of the three, a few other things stood out. Two of the three were African-American. Historically, there had been a dearth of black players at the school. Whitmore also represented the first significant DeMatha graduate to suit up for the Irish, a school which was to contribute mightily to Notre Dame basketball for the next 15 to 20 years.

In contrast to the football pep rallies, the basketball games rarely exuded heat in the Fieldhouse. The stands were at less than capacity for most of the games I attended (and I rarely missed one). That was not the case on Saturday afternoon, February 11, when an overflowing crowd crammed into the Fieldhouse to watch the Irish hoopsters confront Elvin Hayes' Houston Cougars, the only team that was to beat Lew Alcindor's UCLA during his three years. Besides Hayes, the Cougars also starred Don Chaney, who was to play many years with the Boston Celtics, and included a plethora of tall and talented role players who would have been stars on other teams. With some trepidation, a number of us from the fourth floor headed down the quad to the Fieldhouse where we expected to watch a blow-out. The team had recovered somewhat from its slow start, but Houston was a force, and the betting line in favor of the Cougars was well into the double digits.

We knew that the game would be popular so we arrived early, for which we were treated to the Houston pre-game warm-up show. And what a show it was—one-handed dunks, two-handed dunks, reverses of every variation. It seemed to us that every player on the Houston team was a flying acrobat soaring over the rim. With a mixture of awe and despair, we turned to each other and commiserated it was to be a long afternoon. Then the game started....

From the moment of the tip-off, the building rocked with the crescendo of the roaring and deafening sound of the crowd. The ghosts of the Fieldhouse had been re-awakened, as had happened 17 years earlier when Adolph Krupp objected so strenuously. The Houston stars were rattled as the scorebook recorded one missed shot after another, and their play was sprinkled with a number of critical turn-overs. My memory is that Notre Dame scored close to 20 points before the ball finally fell through the net for the Cougars. Houston eventually acclimated themselves to the crowd, but they never recovered from the early deficit as the game ended 87-78. Elvin Hayes could not break away from the stifling defense of Whitmore, who emerged as the winner of contests over both Alcindor and Hayes. Arntzen enjoyed one of the best offensive outings in his Notre Dame career. As loyally engaged fans, we never left our feet for over two hours with our voices never silent and were exhausted when the final buzzer sealed the victory. As we walked back to Stanford, incredulous and invigorated, we knew we had witnessed something remarkable. Through the years, the Irish have had their share of major upsets—UCLA twice, Ralph Sampson's Virginia, to name a few. To my mind, none exceeds Houston because of the colossal gap between expectations and performance.

That game represented the beginning of the revival of Notre Dame round ball, which was to become a major force in collegiate basketball for the next couple of decades. Ironically, the low point of our four years was to occur precisely two years later on February 11, 1969. The uproar over the game, however, was wholly unrelated to the score although the Irish did lose the game played at the newly opened double-domed Athletic and Convocation Center. The ACC had been built to house a reinvigorated basketball program, which had outpaced the capabilities of the Fieldhouse. The opponent was Michigan State, a team of middling distinction, and the game featured the return of Austin Carr after the healing of a broken foot. Carr, who was to become one of the college greats of all time, had created a sensation as a prolific scorer as a sophomore. Unfortunately, the Irish were not at their best on his return and were at the losing end of a 71-59 score. All this was to be relegated to the realm of insignificance because of a controversial incident towards the end of the game.

Dee pulled out a couple of players, including Arntzen, so the five players left on the court were all black—the first time that had occurred in Notre Dame history. Subsequently, boos arose from the student section. Generally everyone is in agreement with the narrative up to this point. What remains as a matter of debate is the cause of the Bronx cheers. On this issue there was, and continues to be, no consensus. One friend, for example, is fairly certain that the students were booing the presence of the five blacks on the floor. The word in the campus halls during the next couple of days attributed it to fans being upset with Dee and dissatisfaction over the less than mediocre play. Player John Gallagher, from the position of the floor, was not aware of any booing.

The account of the game the next day in the *Observer*, the student newspaper, makes no reference to the incident and focuses on the unexpected and disappointing loss. The following day was a different matter—the front page featured an article with the bold headline: "Black Players Protest Booing." The five players, it was noted, had issued a statement demanding an apology from the student body "for their booing when there were five black players in the game against Michigan State." The statement continued that without such an apology "we will no longer practice or play for the University." Gallagher credits Dee with a strategic decision to help defuse the crisis. Aided by his legal training, he diplomatically cancelled practice that day to avoid any unexcused absences. Richard Rossi, president of the student body, did issue an apology the same day, and the season continued without incident.

I had missed the game, but reading the accounts and engaging in subsequent discussions about the incident was a painful experience for me. I loved my school, but if the accusations were true, it was saddening. The reason for the booing probably will never be determined and those expressing their unhappiness most likely had differing motivations. Regardless, that evening inevitably is rooted in any history of Notre Dame basketball.

Austin Carr

The arrival of Austin Carr was far and away the milestone basketball event during my four years. Almost from the day he arrived as the highly touted star from the D.C. area, the mention of his name created a stir. Dee decided to showcase him as a freshman so he scheduled 13 freshman games. I remember showing up for a game after having missed the first two and sat down with Stanford Hall friend Tom Rouse, who pointed to Carr and instructed me, "All you need to do is keep your eye on that guy." It was good advice. The following year Carr's offensive skills were on full display as he commenced a varsity career that would compile 2,560 points, a stunning 34.5 points per game average in the pre-three-point era. The totals included 61 points in an NCAA tournament game, a record that still stands. A 6'4" shooting guard who could score from anywhere, he recently was named by ESPN as the 22nd greatest college player of all time. I would place him within the top ten. Austin Carr put Notre Dame back on the basketball map.

Everyone seems to have an Austin Carr story. John Gallagher remembers that 1970 NCAA Mideast regionals game in which Carr broke Bill Bradley's previous record of 58 with his 61 points. The game is special to John because he was selected to start as Dee was upset with a couple of the starting five for their performance in a prior game. It was a good night for John as he ratified Dee's confidence in him by scoring nine points. His performance has become the grist for one of his favorite stories—the night he and Austin scored 70 points.

Our classmate Tom McCloskey was playing at the Rock in September when newly arrived freshmen Austin Carr and Sid Catlett showed up. Tom ended up playing on the team opposing the two. On a fast break led by Carr, Tom retreated in a classic fashion to stop it at the key. As he set up his defense, Carr soared by him and dunked the ball. "That guy can play," Tom mentally noted. His embarrassment on the play did not prevent him a year or so later becoming part of the regular Carr game. Through the recommendation of John Gallagher, he was selected to scrimmage in the varsity off-season work-outs.

Dick Reynolds also had the opportunity to play with Carr. As he was wandering the halls in the ACC to find a game one day, he opened the door for one of the gyms and recognized a few of the varsity players, including Carr. Short one player, they invited Dick to join. As he describes it, "I didn't embarrass myself," and he came away from the game with the story for his grandchildren—about the day he played with Austin Carr. I never had the opportunity to play with Carr, but that hasn't prevented me from using his name in vain. From time to time, I have jokingly told people "no, I didn't play college ball; there was a guy named Austin Carr who took my position!"

While my playing with varsity basketball players was limited, I did find myself on the court with football players at the Rock. It turns out that football players love to play basketball. During the off-season, it was not uncommon to be in a game with one or two football players. I can recall one specific game that was predominantly football players, including my classmate Mike McCoy, the defensive tackle, and a mountain of a man who became the second selection after Terry Bradshaw in the 1970 draft.

I found the playing style of football players to be distinct from the typical Rock player. While the observation may be a cliché, theirs was a game of power rather than finesse, with more physical contact. It wasn't that they committed more fouls. Rather, the essence of their game, built upon their football mentality, was to occupy space. In football, the principal focus for each player is to establish and maintain control of a designated territory on the field, whether it is the offensive lineman creating a hole, the running back establishing his hegemony or the defensive lineman ridding himself of blockers to control his turf. In basketball these instincts carry over. Someone driving to the basket defended by a football player more than likely will find a body in his path. Conversely, a football player looking to move to the basket, with or without the ball, will be more adept than the rest of us in clearing the space. It isn't simply size, but rather leveraging the body, that contributes to the physicality.

The Decline of the Rock

The opening of the ACC in the fall of my junior year had profound implications for the role of both the Fieldhouse and the Rock in the Notre Dame basketball firmament. The impact on the Fieldhouse was obvious—no longer was it to be the sight of a monumental upset of a 1949 Kentucky or a 1967 Houston. All varsity games migrated to the new structure. The Rock story was more complex. Adjacent to the circular halls of the ACC, which funneled fans into the stands, were a number of gyms, not noticeable since they were entered through unmarked doors. While they contained rubberized floors and had limited natural lighting, they were generally available. Most importantly, by multiplying the number of courts on campus, the immediate effect was to relieve the pressure on the Rock, which had packed us all together jockeying for playing time. The opening of the ACC was the first step of several that left the Rock a marginalized ghost of its former self as the center of student athletics.

My loyalty to the Rock remained—at least for a while. For my sophomore year, I ended up living in Lyons Hall, and 50 paces from my room was the side door to the Rock. The proximity was fortuitous since it made it easy for me to sneak in an hour or so in the afternoons during the week and the periods of lesser demand on weekends. All of this was important for we were still a year away from the grand opening of the ACC. I worked to organize a team at Lyons to compete in the Interhall League, a challenging task. Unlike halls such as

Walsh, Dillon and Alumni, Lyons was not known for its athletic talent. It was widely viewed on campus as the home of intellectuals, radical politicos, art and cultural aficionados and "freaks," the latter term generally used to describe hippies and others inclined towards the counterculture (such as it was at Notre Dame). While I did manage to put together a team, it was considerably less successful than my Stanford Hall team despite the short commute to practice.

The next year I roomed in Badin Hall with pre-med student Bill Knapp, close to a full outdoor court behind the bookstore. It was an unremarkable court in only fair condition, but it served well enough to host play with Knapp and friends Dick Roddewig and Dean Hagan and was centrally located on campus. I was amazed when years later I read an article in the national press on the popularity of the Notre Dame Bookstore Tournament played on "our" court. Originating in 1972, two years after we graduated, the tournament was played on that same shabby court with a field of 52 while spectators arrayed themselves on the roof of the building. Today the tournament is a single elimination event open to anyone associated with the university. It began as a playful element of "An Tostal' (Gaelic for 'festival') event before finals. The tournament was given its name by former Stanford fourth floor buddy and then alumnus Jimmy Brogan—a master of fun—who went on to a career as comic and comedy writer. It's now morphed into a national phenomenon.

The Book Store Tournament attracts more than 700 entries, and over the forty plus years of its existence has featured future NBA and NFL players, a few Hall of Famers and about 50,000 other players. The tournament's attained a high profile in the press and has caught the fancy of basketball fans everywhere. While I missed the tournament, the Dowdall family was represented through the years by my sons, one of whom made it to the round of 16. Today it is played on state of the art courts outside of the enormous stone Gothic structure that is the new Notre Dame Bookstore. As a 60's hoopster at the old court, I continue to marvel that those modest grounds launched another storied tradition of sports at Notre Dame.

The Running Hook and the Fade Away

The Rock also remains close to my heart for on its floor I developed two of the shots I've relied on over the past 45 years. Nearly all players are defined by one or two signature shots, favorites that they employ repeatedly when they play. Perhaps the most famous and recognizable signature shot of all time was Kareem's sky hook. The signature shot, though, is not restricted to famous professional players because as nearly everyone who dons the sneakers knows, even those with the humblest talents possess a shot that defines their game. Through the years, my signatures have been the hook shot, particularly the running hook variety, and the fade-away jump shot. Both of these shots were the legacy of playing at the Rock. I do not know when or how they evolved, but by the time I left Notre Dame they'd become an important part of my offensive repertoire.

I had never used the hook shot in any of the Saints' game because of Coach Walsh's edict that we were not to employ "hot dog" or "fancy" shots. Freed from coaching dictums, I began experimenting at the Rock with certain hook shots, and my favorite became the running hook, a hook off the backboard after driving down the lane. I found it to be a shot that could rarely be blocked—between the ball and the defender was the width of my body and the length of my arm. In later years, I have heard guys shout out "Tommy Heinsohn" when I have taken the shot, suggesting that he was my inspiration. However, I don't recall ever seeing him play so I don't think he was the source. More likely the shot evolved from my memory of the hook shot demonstrated to me by Wayne Estes when he took me to the Memorial Gym in the summer of 1961.

Others have referred to my running hook as "patented" or "old school." With regard to "patented," maybe that's a euphemism for the fact that I stumbled into the shot and made it my own. I'm never quite certain as to how to react to "old school." Strong on fundamentals? Old-fashioned? Obsolescent? The latter may apply generally to the hook shot, which has fallen far from the glory days of Heinsohn and Kareem. As Heinsohn observed in 1988 in his book *Give 'em the Hook*, "it's as if there's a stigma attached to it, like it's a relic from the 1950's, which is ridiculous." The hook shot has not gained in popularity in the intervening years. Like Heinsohn, I am mystified as to why it is so infrequently utilized since it is such an effective shot vis-à-vis the defender. Also the aesthetic beauty of the hook shot is unparalleled; what can compare with the grace of a Kareem or Estes hook? Interestingly, Heinsohn blames the high school coaches, whom he claims stopped teaching it because it was a "showoff" shot.

The fade-away shot violated the high school maxim that we were always "to go up strong" when shooting around the basket. Similarly, I had to wait until college to experiment with it. I ultimately developed three variations of the fade-away; in the key, slightly to the left banking off the backboard and along the left baseline with no bank. Unlike the hook, the fade-away has remained a popular part of the modern game. Attributed usually to Wilt Chamberlain, the shot was mastered by Michael Jordan at about 15 feet and was the instrument of numerous Chicago Bulls wins at the buzzer. Similar to the hook, it is a shot difficult to defend.

I didn't hone these shots and make them my own until my Rock days. As I think back, it would have been nice to have them available in high school. On the other hand, part of the fun of this lifelong game is the continual process of creative discovery of what the mind and body can learn, even when we can't recall in detail the timeline of the discovery. What I do know is that the journey to master the game involves a trip over a long and wonderfully endless road.

Anyway, it is good to know it's true: you can teach an old dog new tricks.

As the controversy about the five black players at the ACC reflects, my college life occupied the second half of the tumultuous 1960's. The tenor of the era was to influence me, although my involvement was oriented more towards the arts rather than politics. Yet, as was true with anything in the 60's, frequently the two intersected. As it turns out, basketball forums or themes were the backdrop for several of these arts-related ventures.

PHOTOGRAPHS

Leading the Prom at age four (author's collection)

John and Mary Dowdall (author's collection)

Coach John Dowdall (Virginia City yearbook)

Virginia City Gym today (courtesy of Erin Dowdall)

At Virginia City Content Corner 1974, our home in 1951-52 (author's collection); Below, Devine Family store circa 1900 (author's collection)

Susanne at Virginia City Boot
Hill 1974 (author's collection)

First Grade photo (courtesy of Leo Berry)

Big Stack (author's
collection)

Sister Joseph Marie, Leo Berry, sister Mary Anne, Butch Prigge and me

,

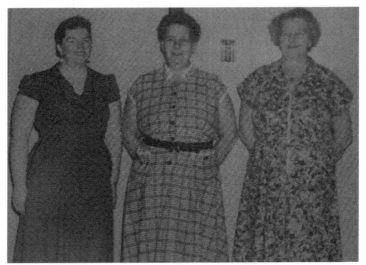

Above: Grandmother Kantack at work (right) (AHS yearbook); Below: McKittrick's garage today (author's collection).

Daly Gym (left) and Memorial Gym (right) today (author's collection)

Sixth grade championship team; me holding basketball, Bill Matosich to immediate right, Paul Greenough next, John Cheek second from left front row,
Coach Bill Shea in back (courtesy of Joe Furshong and Leo Berry)

Anaconda Coaches
John Cheek (left) and
Pat Curran (right) (An-
aconda High and Ana-
conda Central year-
books)

Senior year team (Anaconda Central yearbook)

A-Squad: BACK ROW: Manager Jim McDonald, Dean Leary, Ben Lovell, Bob Hogan, Mario Ramirez, Mick Ohman, Jim Meredith, Dan Walsh, Pat Dowdall, Jack Lowney, Dave Kloker, Bill Matosich, Tom Lovell, Mr. Walsh, Coach. FRONT ROW: Varsity Cheerleaders.

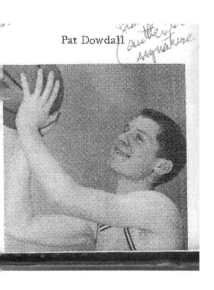

Pat Dowdall

Yearbook editors arrange remarkably similar poses for two sports.

Jim Meredith (42 in white) guarding Kareem (courtesy of Jim Meredith)

Glen Smiley modeling Duke
Uniform (courtesy of Glen
Smiley). Below left, Dick Reyn-
olds and author in front of the
Rockne Memorial (the Rock) at
class reunion 2015 (author's
collection). Below right, play at
Stepan Center courts circa
1960's (courtesy of Notre
Dame archives).

"Save Fieldhouse" banner on Fieldhouse (1969) (Notre Dame Archives)

Hemenway Gym today (Author's collection)

Upstarts: Law school intramural team members. Clockwise from right Dowdall, Dolian, Davis, Drooyan, Inlow, Powers (Harvard Law yearbook)

Dewey, Ballantine team: Greenberg, Mueller, Whelan (front row); Dowdall, Weiss, Blythe, Hilaire (back row) (courtesy of Paul Mueller)

Dewey Decimals vs. Firm game: referees Greenberg (underneath left basket (shirtless) and Dowdall (to right of number 8) (courtesy of Paul Mueller)

Edition of THE BULL when author started at Dewey, Ballantine

$\mathscr{C}he$ BULL

VOL. 56   SEPTEMBER 15, 1975   NO. 33

TRINITY INDUSTRIES, INC.

At a closing held June 17, 1975 in Dallas, Texas,
the firm represented ... ...ny, Teachers

OFFICE NOTES

On behalf of the office, the BULL wishes to welcome
the following new associates:

J. Patrick Dowdall, who was a
summer associate last year, was
born in Missoula, Montana and
raised in Anaconda, Montana.
After graduation from the University of Notre Dame in 1970
with a B.A. in Government, Pat
attended Harvard University from
which he received a M.A. in Gov-
ernment in 1972. He is a 1975 cum laude graduate of Harvard
Law School, where he was a member of the Board of Student Advisors. Pat is married and lives at 50 West 72nd Street, New
York, New York 10024. His telephone number is 787-0500, ext. 711.

i The North-
chases") in
ustries, Inc.
ember 1, 1990
of $25,000,000.
ions by the
ed by nine of
ubsidiaries
and the law
osidiary of
ubsidiary, which
in the guaranty,
ould have been

i the fabrica-
i recent years
il products,

Sonnenschein senior hoopsters:

Shelly Fink (L) Harold Shapiro (R) (Courtesy of
Shelly Fink and Sonnen-
schein)

Above, Coaching Mike's team (author's collection);

Below right, Mike, Brendan and Colin circa 1991 (author's collection)

Referee John Buckley (author's collection)

Above, Lenny Kesten (right) holding up Black Law Students Association (BLSA) trophy (courtesy of Lenny Kesten); below right, Lenny recently on the court (author's collection); below left, erection of FerryDome (courtesy of Jim Ferry)

Over the Hill 60th birthday collage (author's collection)

Family at one of last Celtics game in old Boston Garden (author's collection)

Upper left, shooting running hook at portable hoop in Falmouth; below left, with Geoffrey MacDonald at his Chatham court about a year before his death; below right, Colin shooting on Dowdall driveway court (all author's collection)

With the guys at Hall of Fame in 2014 (author's collection)

Lonnie Powell as
Galahad in Spa-
malot (courtesy
of Lonnie Pow-
ell)

Tom and Pat: basketball buddies for forty plus years.

Chapter Thirteen

Basketball and the Arts Under the Golden Dome

In early February of my freshman year I received an invitation that was to change my life. I was asked to attend an introductory meeting on the fourth floor of the Administration building for a discussion of a special freshman English class. The speaker was Donald P. Costello, a professor in his mid-30's with jet black hair, a little long in the back and slightly balding in the front. Dressed in a dark suit with all three buttons buttoned he began his address to about 25 of us with words that I remember well: "There are many Notre Dames, and one of those is that it is the home to some of the best students in the country." This class, he continued, "was to provide an opportunity for some of them to meet each other." We'd been chosen for this meeting, he continued, because each of us had attained at least a 3.75 grade point average the first semester.

As he spoke, I couldn't help but notice his ability to retrieve precisely the right word and the striking synchronization of his hand gestures with his diction. He proceeded with a description of the class, which included a continuation of our writing instruction based on his philosophy that "structure was the foundation of effective communication." As a bonus, the course was to be an exploration of the arts—literary, performing and visual. As part of that curriculum, we would attend live performances, films and art exhibits. Inevitably, the question was posed by a student about grading: was it be based on the "curve"? He cut short the question and abruptly replied "Don't worry about the grades." He then moved on to the next topic.

I decided to take the course primarily because it would introduce me to the arts, about which I then knew virtually nothing. Little did I suspect that they would became a dominating presence of my Notre Dame life. The course also introduced me to two people who were to become close friends and advisors during my college years and whose friendship I cherish to this day as they have moved into their mid-80's with exceptional grace: Professor Don Costello and his wife, Christine.

A Rugged Forward and a Scholar of J.D. Salinger

The first special program that Professor Costello assigned to our class was a public lecture by Thomas Lorch of the English Department titled "The

Decline of J.D. Salinger." To prepare, we read all of Salinger's works with a particular emphasis on *Catcher in the Rye*. I'd read his classic in high school but was wholly unfamiliar with his other works such as *Franny and Zooey* and *Raise High the Roof Beam, Carpenters*. The lecture was to take place at the Main Library (today the Hesburgh Library), unofficially known as the "Touchdown Jesus" Library for its distinctive mosaic of a gesturing Jesus on the library wall, visible to nearly all fans at the football stadium. When I entered the auditorium, I immediately recognized the speaker on the stage—a man in his 30's with longish light brown hair and an upper body that would rival any of the Notre Dame football players. I had seen him at the Rock a few times where he was known as an aggressive, physical player on both offense and defense. "An animal on the court," a friend describes him.

In fact, Professor Lorch had played football at Yale for some excellent teams in the 1950's and had been the assistant basketball coach at Groton Prep for a team that went undefeated. Lorch knew athletics, but as it became clear that night, he knew Salinger and other contemporary authors equally as well. A major theme of his talk was speculation as to where Salinger's literary career was headed from that point. In Lorch's view, his recent works had reflected a hesitation to communicate and a withdrawal from his audience, paralleled by an increasingly retreating pattern in his personal life. My notes indicate that as a group we disagreed with Lorch's pessimistic prognosis, but as we all know he was prescient in his analysis since Salinger was never to produce another literary work, his last published in 1965. He also became notorious for his reclusive behavior.

Following the lecture, Costello shuttled us to his home at 209 Wakewa in his classic VW bus—a vehicle with a distinctive history. It had been purchased by the University for them. It was not the norm for the Notre Dame administration to endow their young professors with automobiles, but a couple of years previously, the typically generous Costellos had loaned their car to students travelling South to participate in the Civil Rights movement. The locals apparently didn't take kindly to the Northern intruders and nearly destroyed the VW, leaving Don and Christine and six small children without transportation. When Father Hesburgh, the university's president and future Chairman of the Civil Rights Commission, learned of their plight, the new VW was purchased.

Upon arriving at his house, we comfortably found a place to sit in the modest living room, mostly on the floor, as we drank beer and munched on potato chips. For several hours, we engaged in a lively discussion on the past, present and future of Salinger. I was incredibly impressed with the sophistication and knowledge of the students in the class and wondered at times whether this kid five months removed from Anaconda could keep up with them. I returned to Stanford Hall at 1:30 or 2:00 a.m. challenged but also charged up. As Don had promised, his course went on to introduce us to films such as Michelangelo Antonioni's *Blow-Up* and performances of the inaugural season of the campus Contemporary Arts Festival. That semester we often gathered in the warmth of the Costello's home. It was dazzling to be introduced to a world of the arts at that point in my live, a priceless legacy of the Costellos.

Costello's class gave me another gift, a number of lifelong friends and fellow basketball players, including Dick Roddewig and Dean Hagan. Another member of the class was Jim O'Connell from Newport, Rhode Island, an excellent player who had starred on his high school team and a member of the track team. Jim had leading-man good looks and delivered his articulate remarks in class with an (exotic to me) New England accent. O'Connell was attached enough to the sport to briefly coach basketball in Hawaii before entering Harvard Medical School at the age of 30. He was persuaded to spend a year or two providing medical care for the homeless during his medical education and found the work compelling. Inspired by the need he recognized here in Boston, he formed Boston Healthcare for the Homeless, now one of the the the city's leading charities with O'Connell becoming one of Boston's luminaries. Described as a "saint" by our fellow classmate and varsity basketball player, John Gallagher, O'Connell's garnered more awards than can be enumerated, including the Albert Schweitzer Humanitarian Award in 2012. The sneakers, though, were left in his locker a few years ago.

As for Lorch, he soon left the world of Salinger and other modern writers. During the late 1960's, influenced by some of the "New Age" ideas coming out of the northern California Esalen Institute, he experimented with sensitivity training in the classroom, something I briefly experienced in a Lorch class until I decided to transfer out. His application of the techniques had an aggressiveness akin to his action underneath the boards, and I decided to keep that competition restricted to the basketball court. He subsequently and abruptly left Notre Dame for the Bay area, and I have no information as to what he's done since then. Nor do I know whether he kept playing basketball. I do know that on his way out Lorch stopped by a residence hall to see a friend and as a parting token gave his basketball to the friend.

How will the Chicago Symphony Sound in the ACC?

With Professor Costello guiding the way, I became a committed participant in all things arts-related on campus. By sophomore year, thanks to membership in the Blue Circle Honor Society, I got to share in holding the reins for the Contemporary Arts Festival. When the call went out for volunteers at a Circle meeting, senior John Leonardi and I raised our hands. While neither of us could claim depth of experience, we were armed with the confidence of youth and began the task of putting together a program. The first step was to send out letters to performing companies.

In late October, I received a call from a dance company in New York, to whom one of my letters had been forwarded. They told me that a young woman from their troupe, Twyla Tharp, was to be in South Bend the following Monday and inquired as to whether we would like to set up an interview. After quickly accepting, I arranged to meet the 26-year-old Tharp on campus to escort her to a meeting with John and Jay Schwartz, also a Blue Circle member who in contrast to John and myself knew something about dance. At the meeting I sat with my head spinning as Schwartz and Tharp engaged in a lively discussion of her views towards such contemporary notables as Martha Graham, Paul Taylor, Merce Cunningham, Erick Hawkins and the Joffrey Ballet. Personal knowledge informed most of her comments since she had had experience with nearly all these dancers despite the fact she could have passed for a cute undergraduate with her gamine face and pixie hair style. We also learned that her troupe, formed three years earlier, frequently performed without any music to highlight the pure nature of the dance.

Following the meeting, I accompanied her to the Notre Dame Circle where she waited for a ride. At that time, the Notre Dame football stadium could be viewed from that spot, and our conversation drifted towards sports. I mentioned to her that the word on campus was that one of the football stars, receiver Jim Seymour, had some ballet training. She indicated that her dream was to recruit basketball players to perform because of their height and grace. I told her I played but knew I wouldn't be much of an asset on the dance stage with her group.

Twyla and her four troupe members (minus any basketball player add-ons) arrived to perform at the venerable old Washington Hall in late April 1968. The dancers performed their movements without music and in silence punctuated only by Twyla's periodic commands—certainly unconventional and a challenge to an audience expecting a ballet. The turn-out was far from robust, which led the student magazine, *The Scholastic*, to run an editorial decrying the fact that the auditorium was half empty for an "outstanding group in the New York avant-garde." Another writer on campus suggested that the group should have performed on a gym floor, a more appropriate venue for their works. Coincidentally, their rehearsals and many of their programs were performed in gyms.

On the other hand, a gym might not have worked that night since the centerpiece of the program, the premiere of an 18-minute piece titled *Excess, Idle, Surplus*, required smoke through which a strobe-light was to penetrate. Since the school did not own a smoke machine, the impromptu solution was to have the stage hands blow their cigarette and cigar smoke onto the stage. Such a makeshift stage effect surely would have worked poorly in a spacious gym. (I don't recall any discussions as to conformity with fire code regulations.)

Despite our failure to fill Washington Hall, Twyla proceeded to enjoy a stellar career in the national dance world albeit without recruiting basketball players. Shortly after, she abandoned her music-free dance and became known for utilizing classical, jazz and pop music. Unsurprisingly, I've followed her career with great interest through the years as she climbed to the top of the dance world. As I watched her being honored by the President, official Washington and celebrities in the arts world at the Kennedy Center a few years back, I did fondly relive that afternoon in October 1967 when I got my chance to discuss basketball players and dance with a future star while we waited for her ride.

With the graduation of John Leonardi, I became the de facto head of the Festival and convinced student government that the Festival would do better as an independent organization. It would establish a more effective platform to recruit volunteers since our experience that year had taught us we needed 10 to 15 active members rather than two or three. My first step was to interest fellow Costello classmate Dick Roddewig to serve as vice-president.

As only 20-year-olds are apt to do, we thought "big," at times oblivious to the practical side. One of our ambitions was to bring the Chicago Symphony to campus, previously not feasible as no building on campus could accommodate them. The scheduled opening of the ACC basketball gym, with its rising seats and spacious capacity, provided a forum we thought would work. We wrote to the Symphony, and to our considerable surprise they accepted. The contract provided that the Symphony would perform on February 7, 1969 for the princely sum of $8,000 (about $60,000 in today's dollars). For better or for worse, I placed my signature on the contract.

Having secured a contract with the Symphony, we then had to figure out how to pay for it. Fortunately for us, we were the beneficiaries of a couple of lucky breaks. First, we convinced the local South Bend Symphony to be a co-sponsor. A meeting with the president of the Symphony led to Board approval of a sponsorship, but with an attached condition—namely, that the conductor of the South Bend Symphony conduct one of the pieces. When I raised potential logistic issues such as rehearsals, she suggested that perhaps his conducting the *Stars Spangled Banner*, traditional with the South Bend Symphony, at the beginning of the concert would satisfy the Board if one piece did not work.

Shortly thereafter, John Garvey, a member of the Committee and now president of Catholic University, and I set out for Chicago for a meeting with Irving Hoffman, the Acting Music Director. I could've probably been described at the time as confident if not downright brash. John lent our little delegation some urban sophistication. Together we headed into the offices of the Chicago Symphony aware we had the task of making an unconventional request. The program part of the meeting went smoothly: Stravinsky's *Firebird Suite*; a Chicago Symphony premiere of a recent work by the young composer, John Corigliano, *Concerto for Piano and Orchestra*; and Prokofiev's *Symphony No. 5*. With the program in place, we turned to the delicate issue of conducting. I explained to Hoffman the request of the South Bend Symphony Board, to which he responded with a disdainful laugh: "We frequently seek out visiting conductors, but this is the first time anyone has asked us to conduct." He then followed up with the remark that the South Bend conductor could conduct the entire program. Undaunted, we then raised the Board's suggestion of the national anthem, an unconventional first selection for a big city symphony. To our surprise, he agreed. Subsequently, upon hearing of his Board's no doubt embarrassing request on his behalf, the conductor declined the opportunity.

Our second major break came via a former member and coach of the Notre Dame basketball team. Jim Gibbons had played for the Fighting Irish in the early 1950's and later served as the top assistant coach. When he called me in mid-winter that year, he held a position in the Public Relations Department. He explained that the law school was celebrating its Centennial Observance concurrently with the appearance of the Symphony and was inquiring if sufficient tickets numbering in the hundreds could be made available. As I struggled to contain my excitement and relief over this windfall, I assured him that we could cover it. With one unexpected call, we were solvent and could show the world an "auditorium" filled to capacity!

With all the administrative and financial logistics in order, the only remaining concern was how the music would project in the basketball arena. One issue we had not discussed with Hofffman was the venue. The contract described the site of the performance as the "Convocation Center," which obscured that fact that the building served primarily as a basketball gym. In an article in the *Observer*, the student newspaper, I touted the ACC as conducive to symphony performances, a comment based on no real evidence but with the confidence of a college junior.

Opinions vary as to the quality of the acoustics. The musicians were placed on one side of the floor facing the audience seated on the floor and the rising stands. Behind the orchestra was a baffle set up to refract the music towards the audience. According to Dick Roddewig, several musicians were quite unhappy and had suggested at intermission that they not continue. As for Corigliano, he was ecstatic during the intermission as he had just listened to his work being inspiringly played by the CHICAGO SYMPHONY and the soloist Sheldon Shkolnik. I vividly remember him effusively greeting us, not much younger than he, as he stood triumphantly on the gym floor. The *South Bend Tribune* gave the performance mixed reviews. "The orchestra in the huge arena of the center came through in all its beautiful sound," the reviewer acknowledged. However, he also commented that "there is much to complain about," noting that the "center is not a concert hall and bright lights had to be used to enable the musicians to see the music." He also complained about seating some audience members on the floor and that it took until near intermission "for the audience to settle down." Nevertheless, he concluded, "with all the faults it was a magnificent evening of music and one a young composer will cherish."

Corigliano proceeded to have a brilliant career. He has composed more than a hundred works for which he has received numerous Grammy Awards, the Academy Award (for the score of *The Red Violin*) and the Pulitzer Prize. He currently stands, in the words of a friend, as the "dean of American composers." To this day he has fond memories of that night at the gym. In a recent note, he recalled: "Sheldon Shkolnik was the soloist--and I dedicated my 1st symphony to him [he died of AIDS]. It was a superb performance, and that's all I can say...." Through the years we have watched many Notre Dame home games televised from the ACC, and there have been some remarkable ones, including the ending of the UCLA 80 game winning streak in 1974. Yet to my mind, that February evening in 1969 when we "sponsored" the Chicago Symphony on the Athletic Center's floor ranks near the top of the celebrated triumphs those rafters have witnessed. One of my prized possessions is a copy of the evening's program, inscribed: "To Pat from John Corigliano."

The experiment was a success, but not to be repeated. Today a visiting orchestra can perform in the magnificent concert hall of the DeBartolo Center.

To See Faust or Be Faust

My college girlfriend Kathy Blunt shared my new-found enthusiasm for the arts, and that summer we explored theater together in her home town of Minneapolis where I'd found a job in construction. One of our favorite destinations was the Firehouse Theater. Located in an abandoned firehouse, the troupe had developed a national reputation as a platform for experimental and avant-garde theater, comparable to The Living Theater in New York. Enthused about the prospect of bringing them to campus, I pitched their brilliance to the other committee members. When we approached them, the troupe similarly was enthused about visiting the Golden Dome. Their acceptance did leave open which work they would chose to perform.

As we moved close to the performance date, the troupe selected what was alternatively described by them as a play or an improvisation with the unwieldy title *A Mass for Actors and Audience on the Passion and Birth of Dr. John Faustus According to the Spirit of the Times*. More commonly it was referred to as *Faust*. Learning a little something about their staging requirements, we debated the venue possibilities and settled on Stepan Center, whose use ranged broadly from concerts to Mardi-Gras festivals to major lectures. On occasion, portable basketball hoops were installed for either a tournament or a sports camp.

Shortly before the performance date, Kathy reported to me a Minneapolis newspaper headline story she'd read: St. John's University, a Catholic school in Collegeville, Minnesota, had cancelled the Firehouse's *Faust* production because of a nude scene. That action had led to a campus wide uproar with demonstrations and a class boycott. The St. John's administration finally did reverse its position and permit the play to be performed to "prevent physical violence on this campus." Recognizing what might be coming at us, I called Dick Roddewig, our vice president, to debate our options. On the one hand, the promise of a nude scene would likely have a salutary impact on ticket sales. Exploiting this fact, however, had the appearance of unseemliness running counter to the artistic objectives of the Festival. Furthermore, the tactic could backfire as the administration might react by cancelling the play altogether. We decided to commit a sin of omission and tell no one.

The morning of the scheduled performance dawned, and we woke secure in the belief we were beyond censure. Then I got a call summoning me to the office of Father McCarragher, Vice-President for Student Affairs. He greeted me with a memorandum from James Murphy, the Chief Public Relations Officer for the University. The St. John's story had been reported on the national Catholic news wire that very morning, and the ever-vigilant Murphy had recognized that the problematic performance was about to hit his campus. McCarragher categorically declared "The play is cancelled; Stepan's doors will be locked." Desperately trying to salvage the performance, I asked to make a direct appeal to President Father Hesburgh. With Hesburgh on the line, McCarragher handed the phone to me, and I pleaded my case to no avail. "Father McCarragher is to make the decision," I was admonished. The only card left for us to play was to request a meeting for a broader discussion of campus free speech, and to his credit McCarragher agreed to it.

A few words about our adversary across the table—Charles McCarragher had been at the university continuously since the late 1930's. Known as Charlie to his contemporaries, he was nearly universally referred to by the students as "Black Mac," reflecting his reputation for an iron-fisted approach to discipline that he had employed as Rector of Zahm Hall, Prefect of Discipline and Vice President for Student Affairs for 25 years. He had a gruff and raspy voice, and spoke out of the side of his mouth. McCarragher was tough, but he also was a shrewd calculator of risk who knew how to cut a deal or even fold if his hand was weak. He was a canny deal-maker and was rumored to be responsible for the investment decisions for the Province for the Holy Cross Priests, the order that governed and taught at Notre Dame. He would have been a splendid ward boss in the golden days of the Chicago political machine.

The high noon showdown on theatrical nudity saw Roddewig, myself, Student Body President Phil McKenna, Student Union President Denny Clark, other student government officials, two members from the Firehouse and, at the request of McCarragher, the head of the Theater Department, at the table. We made our case and there ensued a lively discussion. The Theater Department head, probably not eager to be a party to censorship, offered up the association with classic author Goethe but was met with the Firehouse Theater's admission "there was only an incidental relationship" between the two. After the discussion had exhausted itself, the deal-maker McCarragher turned to us and pronounced: "You can have your play, but no press is to be allowed." There was no discussion as to how such a restriction could be enforced. His second condition we readily accepted. Only Contemporary Arts Festival patrons could be admitted, which led to our most successful day for season pass sales.

After the doors opened, we made a half-hearted effort to exclude the press, but frankly we knew it was an unenforceable condition. With the day's brisk sales, we had a capacity crowd. The play itself was representative of those chaotic 60's participatory-style productions. As the audience streamed in to sit on the floor surrounding the "stage," they were approached by cast members quizzing them "are you here to see Faust or be Faust?" The "correct" answer of course was the latter. The performance featured much energetic scurrying and bounding about, in and out the audience and on and off two structural platforms. Loud music blared, and we experienced continually changing lighting patterns. I would like to say that the activity even included dribbling basketballs in a scene, but that was one of the few actions missing that evening. At the end of the production, I am sure the actors were as fatigued as any varsity basketball player after a game. As for the SCENE: it consisted of two men and two women writhing in pain for two minutes—the antithesis of anything remotely erotic.

The next morning the *Observer* had two front page articles on the play. The first titled "*'Faust* nearly cancelled…*'*" was a recounting of the day's events. The second filed under the double entendre headline "…but everything came off all right" was the personal reflections of a reporter who "eluded" our "security," accompanied by a somewhat blurry photo of the event. That day's editorial "Hide and Seek," criticized our agreement to the ban on the press.

Shortly after the circulation of the paper, I again was summoned by McCarragher. As I entered, he held up the paper exclaiming: "I said no reporters!" I assured him that we did the best we could and asked whether he had read the editorial describing the photographer hiding in the men's room. He quickly skimmed the editorial and seemed to be satisfied with our "enforcement" actions. As for McCarragher, if truth be told, I believe he knew the condition was unenforceable and that the critical editorial gave him cover suggesting his condition was violated only through "skullduggery." The incident also spotlighted the calculating McCarragher at his best—striking an imperfect deal that more or less satisfied both parties and avoiding a potentially volatile situation, in this case a campus uproar comparable to St. John's.

As for the Firehouse Theatre, the *Faust* tour was their last hurrah. A few months later they lost their lease in Minneapolis, and they moved to San Francisco to perform under a new name. For me the day's events were a lesson in how to strike a deal—and it launched a performance that undoubtedly would've astonished the Stepan Center builders (or for that matter me and my Stanford Hall friends who as freshmen were introduced to Notre Dame basketball playing on the courts outside the building).

Save the Fieldhouse!

With the opening of the ACC, the Fieldhouse became an antiquated and underutilized building residing in the center of campus. In the fall of our senior year, the University announced plans to demolish it and replace it with a mall. The impending destruction of the storied building linked to Notre Dame athletic history raised few dissenting voices, but within a few weeks opposition did develop from an unlikely group. The Art Department recognized an opportunity to find a home for offices and studio space. On October 10, Thomas Fern, head of the Department, met with the newly formed University Arts Council (UAC), chaired by my friend Thomas Kronk. There he unveiled detailed architectural drawings and a budget of $1.825 million to convert the Fieldhouse into an arts complex to address the "cultural vacuum that exists on campus." The Art Department's facilities, Fern emphasized, were spread over four cramped buildings, and some of the faculty members lacked studio facilities. The UAC voted to take action to halt the demolition, for which a contract had been awarded.

For the next several weeks, Kronk and Fern sought to build support for their cause. In early November, I joined their campaign and helped Kronk run a rally three days before the scheduled demise of the building during the Thanksgiving break. Tom was serious and quiet-spoken, and I think he hoped I'd be more willing to tell disrupters at the event to shut up and sit down.

The rally began about four p.m. on November 21 in the big upper floor room of the Fieldhouse and drew between 400 and 500 participants, substantially exceeding our estimates. It was a diverse group as a columnist from the *Observer* described it in a manner reminiscent of Chaucer's depiction of his Canterbury pilgrims. "Miracle of miracles! There was a rally and people came to it. Art freaks, student senators, drama people, student union bureaucrats, writers from the *Observer* and the *Scholastic*, radicals, conservatives and even a plain student or two." That diversity had some drawbacks as the meeting took on the overtones of a typical 60's rally. After speeches by Fern, Kronk, myself and of course my English professor Don Costello, a fixture at any arts-related event on campus, the "feel good" atmosphere dissipated.

One of the campus radicals stood up and accused us of being alternatively naïve and "liberal" in thinking that anything other than direct action would accomplish the goal of stopping the wrecking ball. For him, the strategy was clear—forego Thanksgiving vacation and occupy the building to prevent the bulldozers from moving in. He contemptuously ridiculed our alternative to meet with the Administration to discuss plans to save the building. This debate continued for about an hour, and a few in the crowd trickled out as they became bored with the repetitious arguments. Someone then showed up to report that he had just spotted Father Hesburgh at Keenan-Stanford Hall Chapel to celebrate Mass. After some discussion as to whether the entire group should march to the chapel, it was agreed that a couple of us would go to invite Hesburgh to join the rally. As I walked down the North Quad, I wasn't optimistic about the odds of our success. Since we had to wait for Mass to end, we were away from the Fieldhouse longer than anticipated. A surge within the impatient crowd to head down to the chapel was averted when someone arrived to announce that Hesburgh was accompanying us back to the Fieldhouse.

When Hesburgh arrived, he received a standing ovation by the crowd, whose number two to three hours into the meeting was reduced to about 200. Father Ted reciprocated the admiration of the gathered but emphasized the demolition was a financial decision. Hoping to avoid an impasse, I asked whether he would he give us six months to raise the funds for renovation and, to our considerable surprise, he agreed but emphasized his decision would need to be ratified by the Board of Trustees. As Kronk and I left the building, we felt vindicated that the tactics of the naïve liberals prevailed despite the dire predictions of the confrontational radicals. I also reflected on the special meaning to me of our actions—converting to the arts that old building that had housed so much Notre Dame basketball history and had been so central to my campus basketball life as a freshman. It represented the fusion of those two great loves of my Notre Dame life: basketball and the arts.

The rest of the story is anticlimactic: the Board gave us the extension, but with no prior experience in fund raising we couldn't find the money. Moreover, interest among the student body waned as events in the outside world intruded upon the campus, culminating in the Kent State shootings. Nonetheless, the Fieldhouse lived on for another 13 years as the Arts Center. I think the University kept the building because it presented them a good interim solution for the arts and related departments with a minimum infusion of cash. Bottom line, our meeting halted the demolition crew from tearing down that venerable old building, and I believe the administration ultimately was grateful.

The solution was only an interim one, albeit one that lasted nearly a generation. By our 15th reunion, the building was gone, and in 1986 the Fieldhouse Mall was completed, surrounding the massive Clarke Memorial Fountain memorializing 500 alumni killed in various wars. In a corner of the Mall is a plaque attached to bricks from the old building that commemorates the Fieldhouse. When plans were announced for demolition in 1983, petitions circulated to save the Fieldhouse again, but this time their argument was based on history and memory. The arts departments were ensconced in better quarters. No last minute rally was called this time. No last minute deal was struck.

The Long Goodbye to the Rock

By senior year, outside activities began to take a toll on my basketball game. My playing was reduced to once a week at best, and my game was suffering from the infrequent play. For my senior year, I had moved off campus to a house I shared with Knapp, Roddewig and three graduate students. On campus, my headquarters was at the Student Union offices in LaFortune Center, which was closer to the ACC than the Rock. What little time I spent on the court was split between the two, and the Rock became less of a presence in my life.

While as a senior my "Rock time" may have diminished, my years at the Rock were pivotal. Most significantly, I regained my fervor for playing, which had reach its nadir in that final high school game. I also began to play more on the outside as I worked to combine an effective inside/outside game. Nevertheless, whether inside or outside, I still retained the preference for the drive and always tried to be in motion. My friend Dick Reynolds told me, "Pat, you were like a whirling dervish, always moving." It is a style of play that I credit my high school coach Tracy Walsh for creating, one that he perfected in the mid-1950's as a player. Through the years I have retained those memories of the Rock. Whenever I return to the campus, I usually pay my respects to the west end of the Main Quad to visit a court that meant so much to me so many years ago.

As our senior year marched inexorably to June graduation, we increasingly were faced with the question of what was to be next. From the moment I'd arrived for freshman orientation, my goal was to attend law school. Law was a well-respected profession in my hometown and seemed like a good fit with my interest in government and politics. On the other hand, Notre Dame had provided me many academic mentors and excited my interest in scholarly pursuits. Just like the nuns who'd introduced me to a wider world beyond Anaconda in high school, the community and example of my Notre Dame teachers and their belief in me made me think I too could aspire to be a professor. I was painfully torn between the two possibilities and resolved it by hedging my bets and submitted applications to law school and graduate school. I had the good fortune to be accepted at Harvard and Yale law schools, and while debating between the two I received a letter from the Harvard Government Department offering me a Ford Foundation Fellowship and a stipend. I decided that it made sense to follow the route that would compensate me to determine if that was the profession I wanted to follow.

In looking back at life, we often speculate as to what would have happened if we'd made different decisions, or to borrow Robert Frost's brilliant imagery, "took the other fork in the road." In my case, I have often reflected on that other road since that relatively small Yale law school class entering in 1970 included two students by the name of Bill Clinton and Hillary Rodham, who undoubtedly would've made interesting classmates.

I considered many things in making that decision, but playing basketball was not one of them. That was to be the last move, however, where my calculations did not include at least some consideration about the prospects for playing.

Chapter Fourteen

Harvard Theorists vs. Yale Empiricists

I arrived in Cambridge, Massachusetts in a 1965 Dodge I'd purchased from earnings driving city buses for the Chicago Transit Authority. Leaving Missoula a week after Labor Day 1970, I travelled about 125 miles to Townsend to pick up Jim Ragen, who was entering his senior year at Harvard. He'd followed Glen Smiley as governor of Boys State. About 2,000 miles later, we made a stop in Sharon, PA to pick up John Garvey, my classmate and fellow negotiator with the Chicago Symphony, who was entering the Harvard Divinity School graduate program. John and I were to be sharing an as-yet unseen apartment with several other recent Notre Dame alumni, including my good friend, Denny Clark. Other than Denny, I did not know any of our housemates well, but he fortunately had managed to secure a few spots for us in the incredibly tight Boston student housing market.

As we drove into Boston on the Mass Pike at daybreak, the city's skyline was dominated by the newly erected 60 story John Hancock Tower, its glass exterior pock-marked with plywood replacing faulty windows that had detached and crashed to the ground. Before reaching the downtown, we exited the Pike to cross the Charles River in the direction of the elegant cupolas of the Harvard Houses, the undergraduate residences, where we unloaded Jim's luggage at Eliot House.

John and I arrived at our new home early in the morning. It was a "student" apartment building on St. Paul Street in Brookline, a block from the Boston city line and near the Boston University campus. We were greeted by an unfamiliar fellow N.D. graduate who pointed to the empty door-less parlor: "That's your bedroom." Our late arrival meant we'd drawn the short straw. I soon learned that Garvey, whom I had known primarily for his outstanding intellect and knowledge of music, also was quite handy with manual arts and a creative problem-solver. Before long, our room was enclosed by a pair of junkyard French doors that fit perfectly and, thanks to Morgan Memorial Goodwill, was furnished with mattresses, a portable closet, a small bookcase and a chair. Our final requirement was a chest of drawers, and that need was satisfied thanks to the lucky find of an abandoned four-drawer file cabinet from the parking lot (still giving service in my office today). The bedroom done after two days of toil, we were able to turn our attention to academic matters.

Searching for a Gym

While I anticipated spending a considerable amount of time devoted to my studies in political theory, I also wanted to carve out some time for hoops, particularly since I was rusty after a several months-long hiatus. Garvey, who had played his share of games in Sharon and at Notre Dame, particularly on the Bookstore courts, also was interested. Among our four housemates was a lanky 1969 Notre Dame graduate who was a very accomplished player, Tom Comerford. The question was where we could play. After all these years of having available courts handed to me, this was a new experience.

I looked around the Harvard campus, and all I could locate was the Indoor Athletic Building, a multi-story brick building, which had a couple of full courts and was the home of the varsity. I discovered there weren't many times free for pick-up. Similarly, Boston University's gym, which Denny Clark recommended, had limited availability. So we expanded our search and discovered the MIT gym, which was to become our favorite. Known popularly as the "Armory," the Massachusetts Avenue building in fact was originally constructed in 1902 to serve as an armory for the National Guard. It had been transferred to MIT in 1957 to anchor the school's athletic complex, and its conversion had been cited as an early example of "adaptive re-use" on the MIT campus. A brick building in the castellated architectural style common among urban military facilities built early in the century, it resembled a fortified medieval battlement. Free, available and not restricted to MIT students, it was welcoming to us. We typically were able to find a few others on the court to supplement the three of us for a game. It offered all we needed.

Harvard's Peabody Terrace was and is a complex of block-like high rises that serve as the residence for married graduate students. I had a few friends living there and had noticed the activity at the two full courts when visiting in the spring. On a typical day, most of the players were African-American, primarily in their late teens and early twenties. I had never represented a racial minority in a game nor had I played the classic inner-city playground basketball. Intrigued to see how the game would vary from what I'd played in Anaconda and at Notre Dame, whose black student population was miniscule, I convinced one of my graduate friends to accompany me one afternoon. The game was a little faster than I was accustomed to, and I was continually reminded to be diligent on blocking out on rebounds and releasing shots more quickly because the players were adept jumpers. Otherwise, the game basically was the same that I'd been playing the past decade. Overall, it was a novel experience, and of all the "gyms" I played in that year, this one was the most memorable.

That semester ended abruptly because I was called up for my four months of army basic training at Ft. Lewis. As an alternative to the draft, I'd joined the Montana National Guard and had been attending meetings with a unit in Cambridge. Hanging over me that year was the possibility of being called active, something beyond my control. Because of my positioning on the list, I had assumed I would be called up during the summer, which would have caused me to miss the first semester of my second year. I received a surprise call on a Tuesday in late May indicating a spot opened up because of an emergency cancellation. Those ahead of me on the list were not interested. "If you can be a Ft. Lewis by Saturday, you can be part of this cycle," I was advised. Seeing the chance to get my service done without interrupting school, I moved into high gear to make arrangements for late papers and delayed exams and managed to get myself to Ft. Lewis by Saturday afternoon. For the next four months, any basketball I played was in combat boots.

"Buck" Garvey

While I was spending my summer learning to become an infantry soldier, John Garvey was learning the ropes of being a cowboy in Montana. After our first semester, John decided that studying at the Divinity School was not for him and submitted his application to the Law School. Unsurprisingly, he was admitted. While employed the next semester in the Boston Public School System as a substitute teacher, he decided that his dream was to work on a ranch that summer. With my Montana background, he sought my advice. Explaining that I came from the mining, rather than the agricultural, part of Montana, I told him that I didn't have any ideas but that I'd check with my father. I was dubious this inquiry was going to bear any fruit, but to my considerable surprise, I received a call within a week to tell me that he had a ranching job for John, who was thrilled with the news and thereafter became "Buck" Garvey.

He later told me that he spent his first day on the crew branding cattle, which seemed an appropriate introduction to the cowboy life for an Eastern dude. Returning to Cambridge in September, he settled into the routine of the academics and activities of a first year law student. He probably spent more time on the basketball court than I did that year, which included competing in the Harvard Law School intramural league. The law school academic environment was accommodating to John's analytical mind, and he served as one of the editors of the prestigious Harvard Law Review in his third year.

After his graduation from law school, about 20 years elapsed before I saw John again. After a brief stop at a San Francisco law firm, he landed where I always expected him to, teaching law school, initially at the University of Kentucky. In the early 1990's he moved to South Bend to teach at Notre Dame. On a visit in the fall of 1994, I learned that his scholarship had focused on Constitutional Law, particularly on first amendment and religion issues, and he was in the process of writing *What Are Freedoms For?*

The next time I got to be with John was at our twenty-fifth college reunion in 1995. During that weekend I had the job of introducing Father Edward "Monk" Malloy, President of the University and former 60's N.D. basketball player at our luncheon. That gave me the enviable chance to be his seatmate, hear his recent basketball stories and learn that he continued to play. He was known to show up at the Rock in the evening for some pick-up. I mentioned in my remarks that Monk had many accomplishments, but he'd earned a place in my personal pantheon because at age 54 he continued to play basketball. Of course, that now sounds to me quite reasonable.

After lunch, classmate Jim Chandler, a Romantic literature scholar at the University of Chicago, asked if I'd brought my sneakers (I had) and suggested we recruit a few others to play some ball. We met at the outdoor courts near Grace Hall that faced Stepan Center—Chandler, Garvey, Dick Roddewig, and myself along with a couple of younger guys, including the son of a college friend. It was a nostalgic moment reminding me of freshman year 29 years earlier when my Stanford Hall friends and I wandered over to Stepan Center to play (and there was a brief recollection of our evening in Stepan with *Faust*). We were all changed, yet totally recognizable as our former selves—with a slower step. Lost in the moment, I forgot time and my promise to help at the five p.m. Mass where I was to be a reader. I arrived about 15 minutes late to the ire of the nun running the event. It was worth the lecture (at age 47) because that day I felt 18 again.

About six years later, John was selected to be the dean at the Boston College Law School, and in 2011 the announcement of his appointment as president of Catholic University was made. One of the highlights of his tenure has been the privilege of conferring an honorary doctorate upon a former Notre Dame basketball star with roots in his home town of Sharon. Dr. Carol Lally Shields is a world-renown ophthalmologist specializing in ocular oncology. While at Notre Dame, she played on the first women's team, for which she was the leading scorer and served as captain. Prior to graduation she was the first female to be the recipient of the award for excellence in athletics and academics. Honoring her had all the important elements for John: home-town roots, shared Notre Dame heritage, remarkable service to the world and, of course, basketball.

Playing Under Coach James Q. Wilson

Following my return from the army, that second year in graduate school rarely saw me in the gym and represented my least amount of basketball play (excepting injury years) since I first made a bucket at the old hoop in 1954. While the departure of friends Garvey and Comerford was a factor, I had to fight through a killer schedule that fall, including finishing papers and exams from the previous semester while beginning the new semester's courses. It was a dismal task. In addition to doubling up on course studies, I faced the formidable oral general examinations in the Government Department that spring—a requirement for the doctoral program. The general exams were a high-stakes two hour examination conducted by four professors, and preparation was a major undertaking.

I also had begun to come to grips with the evidence that the deteriorating job market for newly-minted Ph.D.'s was far from secure. I also envied the camaraderie I saw Garvey enjoying at the Law School. The life of a graduate student was lonelier than I'd reckoned as I spent countless hours at my carrel buried in the stacks of Widener library. I decided to go to law school with the intent of producing a doctoral dissertation based on some law school work. So the task of applying to law schools was added to my responsibilities. Basketball playing was pushed aside. In fact, the only game I remember occurred at the end of May when I managed to escape the fate my mother promised for all those who didn't practice enough.

Each spring the Government Department sponsored a picnic at Belmont Hill School, a private school where the sons of James Q. Wilson, our Department Chair, attended. The affair included all professors and graduate students, and typically featured one or another outdoor sport. After we played a few games of softball, Wilson, with his characteristic gusto, asked whether anyone was interested in heading over to the basketball gym. About eight to ten of us responded. I'd played only rarely for the past nine months, so I wasn't expecting much. As it turned out, I enjoyed a decent day on the court even when Wilson decided to double-team me. While admittedly the competition of graduate students and professors was not keen, I nevertheless was energized by the positive outing although I was not to pick up a basketball again until the fall.

Months later I saw Wilson at the Department's cocktail party. I was by then a full-time law student, while continuing as a doctoral candidate and teaching fellow in his department. Wilson remarked that he was surprised to see me at the party. My initial reaction was he was expressing mild disapproval that my path was diverging from the Government Department. "Yes," he added, "I would have thought that Red Auerbach would have given you a call and you would be practicing with the Celtics tonight." That was classic Jim Wilson—a scholar with masterful political skills, an engaging sense of humor and an excellent memory of a lowly graduate student's performance at a pick-up game several months earlier. Those social skills undoubtedly had helped elevate him to the position of department chair while still in his 30's.

Wilson wasn't a professor I saw often since his courses rarely overlapped my areas of study. My few discussions with him usually revolved around my Notre Dame friend and academic advisor, Edward Goerner, who had been a graduate school colleague of Wilson's at the University of Chicago and had written one of my letters of recommendation for Harvard. Following the pick-up game, we gained an additional topic to chat about—sports. Law School activities became my primary focus for the next couple of years although I periodically did stop by Littauer Center and the Government Department offices. On one of those visits, upon spying me in the hall, he issued an invitation to join in an upcoming touch football game scheduled between the Department and the Yale Political Science Department on the day of the Harvard-Yale game.

The impending game was a challenge not to be taken lightly. "Coach" Wilson scheduled practices for his team at the field near Harvard Stadium, and I vividly recall him clad in sweats with a clipboard tucked under his arm. I reverted to my familiar position of receiver to demonstrate that I could run a few routes and catch the ball. The quarterback responsibilities were to be shared by Wilson, a junior faculty member whose name I no longer remember and fellow graduate student Bill Kristol, (currently editor of the *Weekly Standard* and leading pundit of the neo-conservative movement).

The practices went well and we deemed ourselves ready to take on the Yalies. In the days leading up to the match-up, the game's significance began to take on a new dimension. The correspondence between the contending factions began to describe it as the battle between the Harvard Theorists and the Yale Empiricists, reflecting the well-known positions of each department regarding the proper approach to the study of politics. Harvard was very respectful to the value of the traditional mode placing emphasis on the perspective of history and political theory. While this orientation had been critiqued from time to time, it wasn't until the post-World War II era that a sustained challenge arose from the ranks of those who sought a more "modern" and "scientific" approach based on statistical analysis and the study of behavioral patterns. They looked to the methodology of the natural sciences as their model, and Yale was known for having embraced wholeheartedly the empirical method. It would be safe to say that the players that day half-believed the intellectual battles waged in the halls of the American Political Science Association meetings were to be settled on the football field.

The game of the Theorists vs. the Empiricists began about 10 a.m. on November 23, 1974, and on the first offensive play I knew this was to be a touch football game unlike any other I'd played. As I began to run my route, I was flattened by the Yale defender with the authority of an NFL cornerback. I immediately realized this "touch" game was going to call for less traditional tactics, with much strategic use of the hands. It was a struggle to move the ball every possession and the scoring the first half was minimal. Moving into the second half, Yale was ahead eight to six, the difference representing a safety against us, an unusual play for touch football. We had a significant drive in the second half when a major controversy erupted as we approached the goal line. At the end of the play, the entire Yale team, faculty members and graduate students, converged upon the official nearest the play, protesting loudly as they encircled him. The object of their derision incredibly enough was one of their own colleagues. Both officials were from Yale since Harvard didn't have any non-players available at the kick-off willing to officiate. At one point, I observed a Yale faculty member pick up the ball and suggest to his teammates they boycott the remainder of the game in protest. Cooler heads prevailed, and the game continued.

A reporter from *Sports Illustrated* witnessed the game and asked a friend my name after I scored the go-ahead touchdown after the disputed call. Eagerly awaiting the next issue, I read:

> **At adjacent Harvard Stadium the varsity football teams were scheduled to settle the small matter of an Ivy League title a few hours hence. But on an obscure touch football field a larger battle raged between the political science departments. It was, after all, a contest of philosophies as well as wills. Would the Harvard Theorists, weak on behavior but strong on vision, beat the Yale Empiricists?**
>
> **Early in the second half Harvard scored a go-ahead touchdown following a controversial interference penalty that set up a first down on the Yale two-yard line....Yale rallied to win 14-12 on an empirical plunge by Joe Morone. Not that any of the issues were settled. Some Yale players admitted Morone might have gone out of bounds before scoring.**

It goes without saying I was crushed to find no mention of my name. My one and only opportunity to appear on the pages of *SI* was pre-empted by a Yale player who scored the winning touchdown, perhaps illegally.

There was a re-match in New Haven the following year with another eruption by the Yale bench over a call by Harvey Mansfield of Harvard. It was another Yale victory. I had often heard it said that the academic world is the most competitive of all. I didn't pursue a career in the field, but if those games were indicative, I believe there is much truth in the maxim.

After that game, I didn't see Wilson again for about 35 years, but I followed his career through the media since he frequently appeared on television and in the newspapers. He established much of his reputation in the area of the study of crime and of bureaucracy. His "broken windows" thesis was known to be the model for law enforcement policies employed by former New York mayor, Rudolph Giuliani and others. He gained considerable stature within the political science profession, serving as president of the American Political Science Association and receiving its lifetime achievement award in 2001. He also became a noted commentator on the political right, reflecting a migration from his liberal stance as a graduate student. While descriptions of political identity can be slippery, I think most would describe him as a neoconservative.

In the fall of 2011, I attended a Wilson luncheon presentation at Harvard's Center for Constitutional Government, chaired by Harvey Mansfield, whose call during the second game had stirred the Yale team. At the luncheon, Wilson presented the argument for trying suspected American terrorists in military courts rather than the civil courts, a controversial topic which generated much debate. While it was an important topic, I was more interested in Wilson the man. He did display a humorous self-deprecation in a few instances. But I didn't see much of the politically adroit or the avuncular Wilson that I knew 35 years earlier. Also, he tired easily and ended the event about 20 minutes early.

After his remarks, I introduced myself and mentioned that I had played for the Theorists, which prompted a smile. I'd hoped for a chance to interview him about his obvious love for athletics, but observing him walking slowly towards the parking garage holding his wife's arm, it suddenly occurred to me: "he is not a well man." A few months later I opened the newspaper to read his obituary.

Hemenway Gym

When Comerford, Garvey and I were searching for a good gym during our first years in Boston, I failed to discover one literally "under my nose." I was unaware that Hemenway Gym, located in close proximity to the Government Department offices at Littauer Center, housed basketball courts. Hemenway stood as a three story brick structure resembling a Florentine palazzo with New England flair on the Law School campus. Similar to a palazzo, the building had no windows on the bottom two-thirds of the structure and was capped on the top third with several nearly full length vertical windows.[5] Atop the slightly pitched roof was a white cupola, so common on the Harvard campus. Built in the 1930's to succeed the "Old" Hemenway, a massive and glorious Victorian structure from the 1870's, then the largest gymnasium in America, Hemenway resided in an area steeped in history.

A modest granite marker about 50 yards from the gym noted that "here assembled on the night of June 16, 1775, 1,200 Continental Army troops under the command of General Prescott," who after a prayer led by the president of Harvard marched to Bunker Hill. Nearby was another marker memorializing the site of the birthplace of Oliver Wendell Holmes, the eminent jurist who served on the Supreme Court for 30 years from 1902 to 1932. Across the street was the Cambridge Commons, where General George Washington, stationed with his troops in 1776, assumed command of the Army under the "Washington Elm."

Based on my previous visits, I associated Hemenway with squash since on entering the building through a single door only squash courts were visible. If I'd continued down the hall and climbed up a narrow two flights of stairs, I

---

[5] Since then three small windows have been added on the first level to the left of the door

would have entered a rather bare exercise room with doors on each end, the entries into the basketball court.

The court itself was not a particularly attractive space with its brick walls a few feet from the out of bounds lines underneath each basket, anchored on square white backboards of 1940's vintage. It was a scene reminiscent of the photos of old gyms that you find at the Basketball Hall of Fame—in the words of the Harvard Crimson "an architectural nightmare—a large closet with two backboards." Actually there were six backboards. Dividing up the full court were cross courts of approximately 55 feet. in length and 45 feet in width, on which was played Hemenway pick-up ball so two games could be played on the crowded floor. On the plus side, the courts were showered with natural light since the windows extended to about 75% of the height of the walls. Despite its shortcomings, Hemenway became my cherished basketball home where I spent countless pleasurable hours during the next three years.

Chapter Fifteen

The Upstarts

Moving on to Harvard Law in the fall of '72 was the best thing for my basketball even though that might not have been the goal stated on my application. My class exemplified the prevalent cultural ethos of the time where "grade-grubbing" competition was considered uncool. Having a life, including playing sports and gathering at the weekly TGIF for talk and a beer on late Friday afternoons, was possible and even the norm. I was able to leave the lonely Widener Library carrel of graduate school and found friends who shared my interests, including incalculable hours of playing time at Hemenway with other Law School basketball junkies.

Meeting Tom Powers

I soon found myself making the trek through the law school tunnels five times a week to the gym with my Story Hall dorm-mate Bob Dolian, a Duke grad who'd just finished a stint in the Peace Corp. The objective was to get my game back to the level of a few years ago at the Rock. So committed was I to returning to a better form that I occasionally skipped Torts class to play, assured by upper classmen that one need only master the hornbook, *Prosser on Torts* to do well in Louis Jaffe's course. It turned out to be reliable advice.

The governing rules at Hemenway reflected a purely meritocratic view towards playing: the winners stayed on the court, and the challengers had to make free throws to qualify for the new team. One day in early October, I was standing on the sidelines waiting for a game to end when I recognized a member of my section, a tall slender guy with dark curly hair and black rimmed glasses. We formally introduced ourselves, made our free throws and played together that afternoon—the start of a 43 year-long hoops odyssey I've shared with Tom Powers. That day I noticed he was a strong player with an excellent jump shot, and I approached him after our games to see whether he wanted to join me in putting together a team to compete in the Law School league. Our four-decade hoops partnership began that afternoon when he agreed.

There were remarkable similarities in our background and basketball history. Although born in Boston, Tom grew up in Redfield, South Dakota, a town of about 3,000 residents where his step-father, whom his mother married following the death of Tom's father, became the pastor of a Congregational church. With the move, Tom gave up his dream of becoming a Red Sox player, but discovered basketball. With his athletic skills, he soon made up for lost time and became known as a good shooter. During his sophomore year, he worked his way up from eighth or ninth man on the varsity to a starting guard. It was a privileged position in town because, as in Anaconda, basketball was a big deal in Redfield. It was typical for all the 1,500 seats in the National Guard Armory to be occupied for home games. The highlight of his high school career was an upset of the defending champions, the Sisseton Redmen, a predominantly Native-American team. As Tom describes it, the Armory rocked during that game. For the most part, though, their record was comparable to ours. Although winning more than losing, they did not excel as they also competed as a relatively small school in the South Dakota Class A division, consisting of the same number of schools as Montana's Big 32.

Tom headed east for college to attend Oberlin and play sports. That may seem an unusual choice for a school known for its music and, in the 1960's, its radical politics. For Tom the rationale was simple—a school of its size afforded an excellent opportunity to play college-level sports. He sampled several, including football and track, before settling on varsity basketball. After playing a critical role in a number of games as reserve guard, Tom faced a dilemma his senior year. As a political science major, he was drawn to the opportunity to work for his Congressman in Washington for the month of January. That month also was the heart of the basketball season so that option deprived him of a chance to play on what turned out to be Oberlin's best team.

Tom entered law school following a brief career teaching school in Bloomfield, Connecticut, where he had temporarily dropped his basketball so law school also was giving him an opportunity to get his game back. He also arrived in Cambridge at his lowest weight in a dozen years from a diet, which had dropped him from the 195 of his football playing days to 155 pounds. As he acknowledges, "I got carried away with losing the weight."

After that day in the gym, Tom and I began assembling our team. He immediately told me that his roommate, Larry Inlow from southern Ohio, was a strong rebounder and defender who player taller than his 6'2 height. Also in his hall was Rick Drooyan, a quick point guard about 5'7", for whom Hemenway was a second home since he frequently could be found on its squash courts. I suggested that we invite my neighbor Bob Dolian and Scott Davis, who had played in the touch football league with me. With six players, we decided the roster was complete. We were highly confident that we'd identified a sufficiently rabid enough band of players that it would be rare for a no-show, a confidence that was borne out by our never forfeiting a game over three years of competition.

Our next task was to decide what league we would enter. At that time there were six leagues—A through E and a "Special" league defined by height.

Through "informal research," primarily bull sessions in the residence halls and at the adjacent cafeteria, Harkness Commons, we had developed some sense of the competency level of the respective leagues. Our playing with guys in the A League told us that our team members could be competitive with them. The issue was size; we were a relatively short team with no true center and me at 6'0' as the second rebounder. At the pinnacle of the A League were the Mashupee County Maulers, champions for the prior two years. I was quite familiar with their point guard, Carl Hawkinson, who lived down the hall and accompanied us a number of times to Hemenway. Carl had starred at North Park College, a school with ties to the Evangelical Covenant Church. His talents were not restricted to the court, however, as he was a member of the Harvard Law Review and would graduate magna cum laude. The team also featured scorers Tom Pfister from Stanford and Jerry Lopez from Southern California. Anchoring underneath was Willard Fraumann, a bruising rebounder who had played at Michigan. We knew that not every A team displayed the deep talent of the Maulers, but we decided it was prudent to go with the B League for that first year. After all, we had two more years to adjust, upwards or downwards, if our decision wasn't correct.

"Unsung Heroes" of the Intramurals

The final crucial decision was finding a name. With fifty or so teams each year, the league boasted an amazing array of creative names. They ranged from the suggestively obscene (Master Debaters, Folatio Alger's, Nocturnal Dribblers, F**k-Ups, which abandoned any veil of subtlety the following year as it became simply Fuck-Ups) to the legal (Strict Liabilities, Court Gestures, Elements of Style, Contingent Remainders) to the humorous (Beleaguered E-Leaguers, None of the Above, In re Scumbag, Crimson Swine) to the inexplicable, at least to the ordinary reader (Nada Mar Que Pendejos, But c.i.c.s.p.) and to the self-descriptive, both oblique and straightforward (Three/Fifths, Divinity Saints, Design School, Justus Blacks, Harvard Legal Aid Bureau). Eschewing any particular cleverness with parodying legal themes or otherwise, we took a much simpler approach. We looked for a name that would describe a group of unknowns who hopefully might surprise everyone—we became the Upstarts.

Our prescience on the underlying rationale of the name was borne out early in the season. After the initial week of play, it was noted in the *Harvard Law Record*, the student-run weekly newspaper, that the Nunc Pro Tunc, which had tied for the best record in the league the prior year, "was upset (50-35) by a group of newcomers appropriately named 'Upstarts.'" Other than that, we were ignored as the article focused primarily on two other B teams, Cert. Denied, the defending league champions and Little Big Men, described as "the team to beat." The message was clear: our upset was noted, but we were not considered a contender. In one of those seasons that I dreamed of as a young boy, we were to prove them wrong. At the end of two weeks, three teams were undefeated, and then we prevailed over One Buffalo One the following week in a squeaker, 50-48, which left two. In subsequent weeks, Little Big Men lost a couple and finished the season with three losses after we defeated them in the final week. The defending champions ended up winning only a couple of games, and in mid-season changed their name from Cert. Denied to Not Today to reflect their disappointing play. As for us, at season-end we stood undefeated with an 8-0 record.

We looked forward with great anticipation to the play-offs to test ourselves against the A league teams whom we had chosen to avoid in league play. As it turned out, we were not to be afforded that opportunity, at least not that year. In the play-offs, we faced again our B League's Little Big Men, the pre-season favorite who had ended up third or fourth in the standings, and we went down to a psychologically crushing defeat with a score of 42-40. Ironically, the loss gave us the press which had been lacking all season even though we had run the table in compiling our perfect regular season. We had watched as the weekly articles in the *Record* focused on teams below us in the standings or in other leagues. Our loss, it was reported, "brought an end to the season for the unsung heroes of the Law School Intramurals, the Upstarts." The team, "all ILs [first year law students] surprised many this year by capturing the B League championship." The article continued: "laboring under a height disadvantage in nearly every game of the regular season, the Upstarts employed a pressing man-to-man defense and fast breaking offense to wear teams down in the later stages of games."

All teams, successful or otherwise can recognize a certain chemistry that's more the sum of its parts—usually in retrospect. We'd put together a group of contributors who offset each other's weaknesses and augmented each other's strengths and took shared pleasure in doing so. Drooyan was an outstanding point guard who created chaos in the opposing side's defense which opened up opportunities for the rest of us. Defensively, he generated many turn-overs which enabled us to score on fast breaks. Tom Powers may have been the best pure jump shooter in the league. Larry Inlow had to shoulder the responsibilities of guarding the other team's center, who inevitably was taller than he, and formed the nucleus for our rebounding effort. Bob Dolian was a defensive specialist whose skills permitted him to face off against any opposing player from the point guard to one of the big men underneath. Scott Davis was one of those smart players who inevitably was at the right place to get that easy basket, the rebound of the ball coming off the board or the interception of an errant pass.

As for me, I did those things that I had been doing for years, getting my share of rebounds at both ends, guarding the center when Larry was taking a breather and offensively scoring under the basket and at the ends of drives, employing the shots developed in recent years—the hook and the fade-away.

And occasionally I would settle for the jump shot. As we have moved into our mid- to upper-60's, the Upstarts alumni continue to relive the season when six guys "surprised many" that first year of law school.

Commissioners and Referees

The booming success of the law school intramurals, which spanned 50 to 60 teams over six leagues, each playing eight games with an elaborate play-off schedule, was accomplished thanks to the extraordinary efforts of our Commissioners. During our three years, Xavier Suarez and Sheldon Solow stand out. In prior years the intramurals had been the source of controversy and discontent but began an upswing under the leadership of Bill Fraumann of the Mashupee County Maulers. He handed over the reins in 1972 to second year student Xavier Suarez, whom everyone called X. He was to find that navigating the political waters of running an intramural basketball league at Harvard Law School would be excellent preparation for his future challenges dealing with his diverse constituencies as mayor of Miami.

A Cuban refugee and a member of a family with 14 children, Suarez came from a basketball family, which included one brother who played for Jacksonville University. I got the chance to be on the court to witness the impressive skills of several of the Suarez brothers on one of their Cambridge visits. Previously the dean of Science and Technology at a major university in Cuba, Suarez' father was jailed for a period of time following the ascension into power by Castro. After the family's escape to the U.S., they settled in the D.C. area. One story that X liked to relate was that a few years after they arrived they won a contest whereby the family had 15 minutes to "shop for free" at a supermarket. When their 15 minutes elapsed, as reported by the *Washington Post*, groceries retailing for $11,249 ($85,000 today) sat on the check-out counters and adjoining aisles,

X's basketball playing began as a third grader at the courts near Villaneuva University in Havana. Similar to me at McKittrick's garage, he would hang around the courts, and the college students would invite him to play if they needed an extra player. In high school, he was captain of the high school team at St. Anselm's Abbey in D.C., which defeated the highly regarded Georgetown Prep for the championship of their invitational tourney. However, he ran into a major disappointment in his efforts to play basketball at the namesake of his father's school in Cuba, Villanova. Since the school had recruited only five scholarships players that year, an opening existed for another seven players for the freshmen team. According to X, he and 55 others showed up to try-out for the team in 1967. A lack of rapport with one of the assistant coaches, leading to a crippling misunderstanding, deprived him of his chance to realize his dream of playing college ball. This was particularly painful since Villanova in his senior year nearly defeated U.C.L.A. in the NCAA finals.

While he was deeply disappointed at the time, he now admits that one of the "unintended consequences" of the failure was that he focused more on academics, which led to his being awarded a scholarship to Harvard Law.

X was a great leaper. Although slightly shorter than me, he was able to get those critical inches above me (a decent jumper) as he went up for a rebound or finished up his signature drive with the ball above the rim. Shel Solow, who succeeded X as a Commissioner, describes his first game against him at Hemenway. Shel had made a couple of jump shots when X's teammate gave him some room to shoot. On the next shot, Shel suddenly found a pair of out-stretched arms over him. The leaping X then swatted the incipient shot away, dryly commenting, "on my court you can get two open shots, but not three." Not an outside shooter, X's offensive forte was the drive to the basket with a spinning release. He also had a jump hook, and of course the garbage shot off the offensive rebounds. There were some similarities in our games, which always made it an interesting match-up if I was playing against him. Facing off against him tested my physical skills to the limit.

After assuming the responsibilities of Commissioner with fellow 2L Charles Roybal, the two faced a crisis over the funding of the program. A one dollar refereeing fee per player was imposed by the sponsoring Dorm Council, but no one collected it with the Council threatening to pull referees. Michael Critelli, Treasurer of the Council and a future housemate of mine, described the impasse as "just a case of each one thinking the other would do it and nothing happened," demonstrating his diplomatic skills which were to serve him well as he rose through the ranks to become CEO and chairman of the Fortune 100 company, Pitney Bowes. The problem got fixed with a note to team captains, and the spigot providing referees to our games was kept open.

One of the referees was my teammate, Bob Dolian, who had begun his intramural refereeing career as an undergraduate at Duke. Based on his recollections today, one might conclude that the three dollars per hour was insufficient pay for the "pleasure" of refereeing fellow law students, particularly if the game involved 3L players and a 1L referee. Bob has vivid memories of A League games where ego-driven jockeying was on the line in games exploiting rivalries that had spilled over from prior years. Moreover, the rosters for a couple of the teams consisted of all African-Americans so some of the games could have a racial dimension, which was reflected in the crowds of opposing fans in the gym.

Any referee had to be prepared at all times for challenges to his calls, which as Bob points out, are "whistles blown upon split-second decisions." Particularly irksome to Bob was that a frequent challenger of his calls was a good friend. As he recalls, "off the court he was the nicest guy you would ever run into; during the game, he was challenging every call I make." Another 1L refereeing was future Commissioner Shel Solow, a relatively short guy with an irrepressible personality from Chicago, who began his officiating career while still an undergraduate at the University of Illinois. When we spoke recently, he fondly recalled some of the technical fouls he called against 3L's, which included one assessed against the mainstay of the champion Mashupee County and former Commissioner, Bill Fraumann. Now good friends in Chicago, they can laugh about the day that 1L Shel gave him the T.

Meeting my Future Wife

That first year of law school was not all about pick-up basketball at Hemenway and the Upstarts. There were classes in the core subjects of Torts, Criminal Law, Civil Procedure, Contracts and Property, and I was lucky to have an impressive group of professors. These included the noted author and celebrity lawyer Alan Dershowitz, then a relatively unknown criminal law and civil liberties specialist who had played high school basketball in Brooklyn; Abe Chayes, who was doing double duty that fall as a professor and chief foreign policy advisor for the McGovern campaign; and Clark Byse, who was widely rumored to be the model for the stern Professor Kingsfield in the novel *Paper Chase*, the movie version of which was being filmed during our first year. The most impressive of the group was Roberto Unger, a Brazilian native who was my age and a brilliant philosopher. At age 24 he had read EVERY-thing, all in its original language.

The most important event of the year for me, though, was meeting my future wife— even more significant than running the tables with the Upstarts. In mid-November, my friend and fellow Notre Dame "Domer," Mike Comiskey, arranged a mixer as part of his function as social commissioner of Holmes Hall. Mike assured me and others that there would be "plenty of girls there." Since organizers of social events often inflated the expected numbers from the opposite sex at these events, we were skeptical. Nevertheless, as a show of loyalty, I drifted over about eight on a Saturday evening with friends Tom Powers, John Gavin, a Holy Cross graduate and Navy veteran, and my old graduate school and Notre Dame buddy, David Toolan. To our happy surprise, we discovered that Comiskey hadn't over-sold the event.

I noticed a tall attractive young woman with long dark hair and brown eyes engaged in a lively conversation with a classmate—a short guy attired in a suit at a Saturday evening mixer who was holding a briefcase. He was notable in our class as an out-spoken conservative and outwardly religious, two attributes not common at the law school in 1972. Intrigued by this young woman who was talking to him and curious as to the subject of their animated conversation, I moved towards them to eavesdrop and discovered that they were hotly debating the merits of Richard Nixon. The 1972 election, in which Nixon had crushed the hopes of George McGovern followers, had occurred only ten days earlier. Despite his conservative credentials, her adversary was not wholly sold on Nixon since earlier he had confided in her that he had prayed to God before voting for him.

She called out to me and asked: "Who did you vote for?" With that irresistible invitation, I joined the conversation. She later admitted that she welcomed me into the discussion in hopes of pawning me off to the political debate as she escaped. Her plan misfired and soon I was left to flirt with Susanne Gossett, a college senior, on subjects other than Richard Nixon. That evening I wore my usual bell bottom pants, brown winged tip shoes, olive green army jacket and standard army issued black plastic glasses—a wholly different kind of sartorial challenge from the alternative suit-wearing, briefcase-toting suitor. Nonetheless, she says she decided I had a "great personality" and "showed some promise." We had our first date the following Saturday.

I can't remember whether the topic of basketball arose on that night we met. I did soon learn that while there were no basketball players in her family, she had brothers who were 6'4" and 6'6". At times she has claimed that those statistics are really what peaked my interest in her, an accusation which I of course will deny. Nevertheless, as the year progressed and the Upstarts season unfolded, she might've heard more about basketball than she signed on for. She had traveled from a world where balls and hoops were peripheral to one where she was spending her weekends with a guy who was a fanatic about playing the game. However, she was a good sport and even ventured out a time or two to stand on the sidelines of Hemenway to watch the Upstarts.

Playing the Jackson Five

When we returned for our second season, our ranks were reduced. Scott Davis, who had entered law school at the age of 20, had decided to take a one year sabbatical. With his loss, we were faced with the task of finding a sixth player since to attempt to play a full season with only five would have been a bold and reckless decision. We succeeded in finding a replacement for Scott, but for the most part the second (and for that matter third) seasons were a step down from the emotional highs of the first. There were no more undefeated seasons, although we won the conference each year with a loss or two. We were no longer "upstarts." There was one exception to this lack of drama, which all of us remember vividly—the game against the Jackson Five in the play-offs.

The Jackson Five was another of the A league powerhouses. The previous year they had been undefeated in regular season play, only to be upset by the Divinity Saints in the play-offs. They were the favorites to capture the championship with the graduation of the Mashupee County players. An all-black team, the Jackson Five was loaded with talent. Their big man was Greg Tillman, who had been a stalwart at Columbia. Complementing him were three excellent shooters in Jarobin Gilbert, one of the most talented players I saw on nearly a daily basis at Hemenway, Sherman Stimley, who had been on the roster at Kansas and Clint Burch, a fine outside jump shooter. In short, we were out-matched and going into the game our best hope was to avoid embarrassment. As it turned out, we were to play our finest game of the three seasons.

Shocking everyone in the building, including ourselves, we were sitting on a lead when the referee blew the whistle to end the first half—less than ten but more than respectable. Tom was shooting brilliantly, Larry held his own against Tillman, Rick was harassing them on the outside and I was able to connect on a number of shots around the basket. Bob Dolian, our defensive specialist, remembers that he made two out of three in the game, all in the first half. We entered the second half of play with hopes high, but their superior size and talent prevailed as they took control. Our upset bid was thwarted.

The second half also brought on foul trouble for me. At the end of the first half I had two fouls, not an uncomfortable position, but things were to change. I was called for two additional fouls within a few minutes of the second half. With four I headed to the bench and sat for a while. Shortly after returning to the court, I was whistled for another and was out of the game. Frustrated because I was prevented from contributing more, I fumed about it to teammate Rick Drooyan after the game. I have never forgotten his response: "With your style of play, if you don't get a few fouls, you're not playing a very good game." Those were wise words, and I always have applied the Drooyan maxim in assessing my performance. Playing "all in" means taking those risks of fouls, and if the scorebook shows me with two fouls or less, I haven't been "all in."

An enduring presence during that season we lost to the Jackson Five was Shel Solow, who was doing triple duty for the league: commissioner, referee and fellow competitor. His team was the Frankfurters, suggesting both the legendary former Harvard Law professor and Supreme Court justice and the "hot dog," which of course has a colloquial meaning on the basketball court. A Chicago guy to the core, he is pound for pound the most effervescent sports enthusiast I have ever met. He was one of the law school's sports trivia expert and was engaged by the *Record* to produce a weekly trivia quiz. In class, he was apt to invoke a sports analogy in analyzing a case involving some abstract principle of contracts or torts. When we were discussing a notable baseball case in Contracts class, the formidable Professor Byse called upon Shel to lead the class in our analysis of the legal (and baseball) principles the case presented. Competitor, commissioner, referee, sports trivia expert, dispenser of sports analogies in the classroom—Shel was one of those individuals who uniquely defined our law school experience.

Besides the Frankfurters, the other consistent B league opponent during those three years was the Nunc Pro Tunc, the team that we "upset" in our very first league game. Their name literally means "now for then" and is a legal term frequently used to describe a ruling that corrects on a retroactive basis an earlier ruling that was erroneous. The name may have been an oblique reference to that fact that their entire roster was composed of law school alumni who, under grandfathering rule, were permitted to continue playing after they graduated. One of the members of the team, in particular, made an impression on us—a hard-charging, muscular guard who had a crew-cut. This popular style of the 50's was rare and distinctive in college towns in the 70's.

Seven or eight years after we graduated, Tom Powers reminded me of the crew-cut guard. "His name is Scott Harshbarger," he informed me, "and it turns out he's a really good guy. He is running for district attorney of Middlesex County, and I've been helping him out." Scott, who played halfback for the Harvard football team, won that election and served for two terms before being elected Massachusetts Attorney General. In 1998 he secured the Democratic nomination for governor and lost in an extremely close election as he made a bid to unseat the sitting governor, Paul Cellucci—an election I have heard described as being one that would have gone the other way if it had been held two days later. Subsequently, he served a three-year term as president of Common Cause, the public interest organization that serves as a watchdog over the political process. I'll always remember him as the aggressive guard who with his teammates were able to enjoy "post-graduate education" through play in the intramural league.

Hemenway Pick-up from the Perspective of a Future Mayor

The remainder of those years at Harvard Law brought me to Hemenway four to five days a week mostly devoted to pick-up ball. I spent nearly as many hours practicing on the court as I did learning the essentials for the practice of law. Pick-up games afforded me an opportunity to experiment, including combining an outside and an inside game. "Mixing it up" clearly had the salutary effect of making me a more effective player (although if the instincts controlled, I headed underneath).

Pick-up ball at Hemenway also was so much more than simply basketball. It was one of our social centers—there always were familiar faces on the court, whether they were ones we met on the court, fellow students who listened to Archibald Cox in his first class following his being fired by Richard Nixon, long-time friends who reentered my life on the floor of Hemenway or housemates with whom I sat down for dinner each night.

I moved out of Story Hall my second and third years of school to share an apartment with Tom Powers and John Gavin at 52 Dana Street. We were joined by three 3L's, including Mike Critelli, who was most notable for his quotations of Humphrey Bogart. Our third year we were joined by three other law students, including X Suarez, who was finishing up a four-year joint Law School-Kennedy School of Government program. While no longer Commissioner, he continued to be very active at Hemenway. The previous year he had played on the Three-Fifths team, a previously all-black team anchored by a former Boston College player, Stafford Hilaire, who became a prominent part of my basketball life a few years later. As X describes it: "I asked them to integrate the team." He no longer was burdened with the responsibility of reporting regularly on the league activities in the *Record*, but he did pen an occasional piece that year, sharpening his communication skills for his future career as mayor of Miami. One of them, "'Lawyers' Game at Hemenway," featured a partially tongue in cheek analysis of the similarities, and more pointedly differences, between Hemenway ball and playground basketball.

X's observational humor was evident in his characterizing rebounding at Hemenway as a matter of "perseverance," with the ball often "slip[ing] through two or three player's hands before ending up in the surprised hands of the ultimate possessor." He also made a number of insightful observations regarding the nature of the competition at Hemenway. In contrast to playgrounds where methods of selecting teams results in games with "players of fairly similar expertise," he noted that at Hemenway most of the time the teams have one or two "skilled players." The others he describes as "generally in good shape by ABA (American Bar Association and not American Basketball Association) standards." This diversity of talent on the floor created "often a thing of beauty...involving human interactions." Moreover, while the dominant players certainly had a significant impact on the course of the game, more often the winner may be the team that "gets the most out of their less-than-expert members." This is a phenomenon that extends far beyond Hemenway, even to the outcomes of the NBA finals today.

X also had some interesting comments on how different types of players fare in Hemenway play. In contrast to playgrounds where players have to deal with bent rims, uneven backboards, wind, weather and other outdoor disadvantages, the outside shooter could distinguish himself at Hemenway. In contrast, he opined that driving was not as popular or effective at Hemenway, attributing it to the cramped quarters and the proximity of the out of bounce line to the wall. While in agreement with him on the outside shooter, I would disagree on the driving. He was a player who thrived on the drive at Hemenway.

He provided a good description of the ball being played at Hemenway, but inevitably the nature of the individual games was defined by the personality of the guys on the court. Hemenway offered a rich diversity of players, including a number who were not law students. A constant in the early afternoon games was Jarobin Gilbert, a Jackson Five star. An extremely talented 6'3" player, Jerry may have been the first person I ever saw wearing a rubber sweat suit on his upper body. Jerry was an asset on a team—both for his commanding presence and his skills. A student in another of Harvard's schools, he had an authoritative, stentorian voice which carried much weight in the event of disputes over calls and other contentious matters. He also did not suffer fools lightly, and anyone on the court slipping into that category could expect to hear from him up close. "Fast Freddie" was another memorable frequenter at Hemenway, who with his long hair looked like a street hippie who had somehow landed in Hemenway rather than a Harvard Square jam. Despite appearances, there was no mistaking that he belonged there. Extremely quick, he handled the ball like a magician as his flowing hair enhanced the picture of motion similar to a futuristic painting.

On many afternoons, we were joined by a shorter guy who had been a fellow graduate student. Tim O'Brien fit well Suarez's description of that role player who could be the difference between a win and a loss. He always hustled and could be counted on to hit the 10-foot shot from the baseline. Tim was a few years older than some of us since he had been in the Army, and we generally understood that he had spent some time in Vietnam. What we did not know was that while studying for his General Exams, he was writing a memoir about that Vietnam experience titled *If I Die in Combat, Box Me Up and Ship Me Home*.

As he recently described it, he studied until midnight and then turned to his other pursuit, writing. To fit some relaxation into the killer schedule, Tim discovered Hemenway. He literally learned the game since prior to that he had never shot a basketball. By the time I was playing with him he no longer resembled a player who had been a rookie a couple years earlier. I did not see Tim after I left law school, but I certainly read about him. A few years later, his Vietnam experiences were captured in *Going for Cacciato*, a highly acclaimed novel that won the National Book Award in 1979, edging out such writers as John Cheever and John Irving. That book became the launchpad for a stellar writing career. I'll always remember him as the guy with the sly talent for finding the spot along the baseline to put up the uncontested shot.

The essence of basketball at Hemenway was to win and hold the court. During our third year, the 52 Dana Street gang would on occasion travel en masse to Hemenway to play as a team. In addition to X, Tom and me, we had two rugged front court players with John Gavin and Jim Hitch, who snatched rebounds and held down opposing big guys. It was a competitive five, and we nearly always had a good run of several games before heading home to spend a little time on the books before our Sunday dinner. That was the best of Hemenway—camaraderie with friends and, of course, the satisfaction of winning some games.

A Copperhead a Long Way from Home

One early afternoon in the fall of 1973, I walked onto the court and immediately recognized the face of a guy attired in a blue and silver sweatshirt with "Copperheads" emblazoned across the chest. It was my boyhood friend Bart Campbell from Anaconda. As I walked up to greet him, I remarked that I bet I was the only person in the gym who could identify the insignia and would not mistake him for a refugee from the reptile house of a science lab.

A year younger than me, Bart and I had known each other for about 20 years. Our respective mothers had met in the mid 1940's working at the Intermountain Bus Station, and our fathers became good friends through the Anaconda school system. Hugh was the principal at the junior high. During our Anaconda days, Bart and I shared the lonely existence of being Yankee fans. In the late 1950's and early 1960's, when the Yankees appeared in nearly every world series, the entire town rooted for whoever was their Series opponent—Dodgers, Braves, Pirates…. As a result, every October Bart and I jointly faced the hostile allegiances of friends, schoolmates and family members. One of the most formidable of the contrary fans was Hugh. By nature studious and low-key, the only person I knew in Anaconda who had read James Joyce, Hugh could transform himself into a most effective needler of 11- and 12-year old boys on the subject of the Yankees. A Pittsburgh Pirates fan, he was insufferable when his hero, Bill Mazeroski, drilled the ball over the left field fence in the ninth inning to break a tie in the deciding game as the Pirates prevailed over the Yankees in 1960.

Bart and I were compatriots as Yankee fans, but otherwise we were fierce competitors. Since he was a year younger than I, this competition usually did not occur in organized leagues but rather erupted at more informal gatherings. One incident where it was on full display was an organization's summer picnic held at the Foster Creek grounds west of town when we were about 11 or 12. A staple of such events was a friendly, low-keyed volleyball game. On opposite sides of the net, Bart and I took it upon ourselves to see who could be more aggressive in spiking the ball. That meant that some players other than us would find a ball zooming towards their head or chest, and after they'd had a couple of beers, avoiding our spikes became an increasing challenge. We accompanied our spikes with loud and escalating mutual taunting. My dad, understandably upset and embarrassed, finally took me aside to explain the appropriate behavior expected for the afternoon's picnic competition. In short, Bart and I had shared much history when I walked into Hemenway that afternoon.

He had matriculated at Harvard the year after I did at Notre Dame. After his sophomore year, he took a sabbatical, a not uncommon practice during the 1960's. When he arrived after a four year break, he was a three-year army veteran and married with a three-year-old son, Bartley. I hadn't seen him in a few years since my family no longer lived in Anaconda, but the years of absence were to be more than made up on the floor of Hemenway. He typically arrived in the afternoon with his small son, who went off to find his snack-providing friends at the reception desk.

Bart and I almost always played as teammates rather than competitors on the court. In the early afternoon, teams were put together on an ad hoc basis when ten guys arrived so it was not necessary to shoot free throws. We usually finessed that selection process to end up on the same team, and I always found it a pleasure to have my old friend as a teammate. He had not played varsity basketball for the Copperheads since he opted for debate, but he had played much pick-up during the intervening ten years. From this he had developed into a very effective player—a smart one with great court sense. His offense featured a fine shot from about 15 feet, and the guy guarding him was well advised to not let him shoot unchallenged.

What Bart remembered best about his stint at Hemenway is that it was his introduction to play with African-Americans—something that had been unfamiliar to us both coming from Montana. In later years, particularly when he was living in Spokane, Washington, he played for extended periods in pick-up groups where he was the only non-black player. Today he continues to play in Helena, Montana as the oldest guy on the court. To the less seasoned participants, he is "gramps."

Inlow v. Inlow

Towards the end of March 1975, the Upstarts played their last intramural game, which would've been a loss, the fate of all participants except one in a post-season tournament. Unlike the Nunc Pro Tunc, the Upstarts would never play again as a team as we scattered in various directions across the country. Rick Drooyan headed back home to Southern California where he has had a distinguished career in litigation, including serving as Deputy U.S. Attorney for a period of time. I saw his name a few times in the *New York Times* when he was involved in the investigation of some jury tampering allegations in connection with the noted John DeLorean drug prosecution. Scott Davis, who graduated a year after us, returned to his home city of Chicago, where he clerked for Judge Luther Swigert, and following that spent his career at the firm of Mayer Brown as a merger and acquisitions specialist. Bob Dolian travelled about three hours from Cambridge to his hometown of Stamford, Connecticut where he became an associate and then a partner in the city's largest firm, Cummings and Lockwood. In his 35 plus years as a litigator at the firm, Bob was to participate in the explosive growth of the firm, paralleling the proliferation of corporate headquarters in southern Connecticut. Tom Powers was the sole one of the group to remain in Boston where he found the work that had inspired his original law school mission. He began his career as an environmental lawyer at the State's Attorney General's office.

Similarly the 52 Dana Street gang dispersed to all parts of the country. John Gavin clerked in San Francisco before taking a position with the Justice Department and then on to Chicago. Jim Hitch took his international law expertise to Baker and McKenzie, where he eventually served as a partner in their Russian and Ukraine offices. X moved to Miami with the intention of entering politics as a representative of the Cuban community. He ran unsuccessfully for a number of offices, but upon a defeat he would follow up by contending for a higher office. The formula worked as he was elected the first Cuban mayor of Miami in 1985, serving for eight years and then briefly in 1997. Now a commissioner of Miami-Dade, he occasionally puts on his sneakers for a game at one of Miami's playgrounds.

The most fascinating story, though, belongs to Larry Inlow. Similar to Tom and myself, Larry was raised in a small town located in southern Ohio with a population of less than 2,000. While the town was about 50 miles from Cincinnati, Larry decided not to practice in any of the large cities in Ohio and settled instead in Indianapolis. Tom and I lost touch with Larry and were unaware of his whereabouts until I noticed his name in the papers in the early 1990's. I reported to Tom: "I just read in the paper that Larry Inlow made more than $2 million last year, making him one of the highest paid corporate lawyers in the country." We were incredulous at this news, not only because it was a staggering amount of money at that time, but also because he was the recipient.

Larry was very much the small town guy, something that he shared with Tom and myself, and his mannerisms reflected that during our law school days. One would never mistake him (or us) for one of the more sophisticated in the class, but underneath that Midwestern rural exterior was a shrewd and sharp guy whose perceptive remarks were evident in our classes. Nonetheless, in law school he didn't seek a position at the New York or other big city firms where the potential monetary returns were the highest.

In the intervening years, he had become a partner at a mid-size Indianapolis firm, but left in 1986 to join an insurance company that was on the verge of entering stratospheric growth. Founded in 1979 by a former encyclopedia salesman, Stephen Hilbert, Conseco was managing $103 million in assets, a very modest amount by insurance company standards, when Larry joined the company in 1985. Twelve years later that amount had leaped geometrically to $27 billion. As the executive vice president, general counsel and secretary, Larry was a key figure in the phenomenal growth through numerous acquisitions. Its stock price averaged annual gains of 47% for ten years, and the company became a high-flying darling of Wall Street, generating much buzz in the trading rooms of lower Manhattan.

A couple of years later I was able to spend some time with Larry at a law school reunion, which he attended with his second wife. His comments at our class forum reflected an acute understanding of the inner workings of the business world, but fundamentally he was the same old Larry. As the reunion ended, we talked about the next one with plans to try to get all the Upstarts together again and make an appearance at Hemenway. There was not to be another reunion for Larry.

On May 21, 1997, less than two years later, Larry was killed as he exited a helicopter at the firm's hangar, struck by the moving blade. His family discovered that he hadn't executed a will, not an uncommon oversight by lawyers. Press reports speculated as to how much the government (via the estate tax) and attorneys would benefit from the absence of the will. As it has turned out, the lawyers have benefited mightily. The lack of a will, the strained relations between his wife and his children from his first marriage and other factors unleashed a rash of litigation extending over the next 12 years, echoing the long-lived testamentary controversies of *Jarndyce v. Jarndyce* in Charles Dickens' *Bleak House*.

The story of the Inlow litigation has been told and re-told in the Indiana press. To my mind, the most disheartening aspect of it was the conduct of the attorneys involved. Similar to Dickens' classic, they made out well from the whole affair, and their actions didn't reflect well on that legal profession that the Upstarts team members aspired to so long ago. Despite the admonitions and even sanctions from judges, the lawyers continued to file cases, even as the value of Larry's estate declined precipitously. At the time of his death, that estate was estimated to be worth about $180 million, the bulk of it attributable to the Conseco stock and options. In a dramatic reverse of fortune, after Larry's death things did not go well at Conseco. Due to rising indebtedness resulting from the acquisition spree and a less accommodating stock market, the company was compelled to file for bankruptcy. At that point, the stock was worth four cents per share. The final chapter of the family litigation revolved around who would bear the funeral expenses, of which the principal item related to the construction of a mausoleum to house Larry's remains.

I have no idea as to the amount of the legal bills generated by this litigation, but I would have to surmise it was well into the millions, perhaps even reaching five million dollars. Nor do I have any estimate as to what in the aggregate the heirs received from the estate in view of the bankruptcy. What I do know is that it is a very dispiriting story. As I have read over the articles and the legal decisions about the disputed estate of a prominent businessman, there is another image of Larry that keeps popping up in my mind—Larry at Hemenway with his blue collar hustle and effort in guarding these taller guys.

Chapter Sixteen

Winning One for the Governor

Returning to classes in the fall of our second year, we were faced with the challenge of navigating the shoals of the interviewing process for summer internships. These internships, referred to by firms as summer associate positions, were opportunities for "test runs" by both the firm and the intern. Getting selected by a large prestigious firm for an internship and making a favorable impression could put one on the road for future professional success to secure an attractive income. From the firms' standpoint, summer associate programs were important recruiting tools.

An Introduction to Wall Street

Wall Street was in no way a familiar world to me. It was light years from the routine and vernacular of the streets of Anaconda. In recent years I'd been cloistered in the academic world and now was comfortable in that universe, but that too was far removed. In short, a Wall Street law firm was, for this small-town Montana kid, another galaxy. I'd spent the previous summer working at a small law firm in Washington, Landis, Cohen, Singman, and Rauh, a delightful job with work assignments interesting and intellectually stimulating, but that firm, about the size of the largest firm in Montana, bore little resemblance to the behemoths of New York. Because of my unfamiliarity, I decided I wanted to get the experience of spending a summer at one of those storied firms. What I could not have anticipated was that those interviews were to set me down the path to enjoy my first basketball championship since sixth grade—at what would have appeared to be an unlikely place, a Wall Street law firm. I also was to have the good fortune to end up at a firm that took its dominance on the basketball court nearly as seriously as its domination of its opponents in the courtroom.

As I began thinking about the interviewing process, the firms generally were indistinguishable to me. My scant knowledge was based solely on fragments of unreliable information from law student chatter, describing firms as "stuffy," "sweatshop," "good atmosphere," "boring partners," or "progressive." My ignorance was alleviated somewhat with the publication that year of a book titled *Lions in the Street*, written by Paul Hoffman, a reporter who had covered the New York legal scene. The book purported to be an insider's view of the "Brahmins of the Bar" and was filled with history, stories, anecdotes and gossip concerning two dozen or so New York firms. With few other sources of wisdom and advice available, it became my "bible."

One firm that caught my attention was Dewey, Ballantine, Bushby, Palmer and Wood, listed as the second largest firm in New York with an attorney headcount of 174. The firm's storied past had included a number of high and low points. According to the "bible," in the 1930's and 1940's the firm, then known as Root Clark, had been a hotbed of superior legal talent, partly attributable to the fact that it was one of the few traditional Wall Street firms that readily welcomed Jewish attorneys. The firm then suffered an historic split in the late 1940's with a significant number of the younger, and nearly all the Jewish, partners exiting to form a new firm that became known as Cleary Gottlieb.

The Dewey in the name referred to Thomas Dewey, former governor of New York and twice Republican presidential nominee. Dewey was a perennial butt of jokes, both because he resembled a stiffly-posed groom on a wedding cake and because of the infamously presumptive *Chicago Tribune* headline the day after the 1948 election: "Dewey Beats Truman." But Dewey also was an excellent lawyer and businessman. During his 16-year tenure commencing in 1955, he was widely credited with restoring the firm to its earlier glory years. I also learned that, in addition to the illustrious history, the firm had a vibrant extracurricular calendar centered on an annual dinner where partners were satirized by the younger associates.

Despite the fact that I was an ardent Democrat and the stuffy Dewey had always been viewed with contempt by my family enamored with the earthiness of "Give 'em hell Harry" Truman, I decided to interview with the firm. After meeting with hiring partner Everett Jassy in Cambridge, the firm invited me to visit at 140 Broadway, New York, where an agreeable interview lead to an offer for a summer associate position, to begin the first week of June.

To my pleasant surprise, I soon discovered one aspect of the firm *Lions in the Street* had failed to mention was its athletic program. My introduction to it was through the softball team. After a couple of days at the firm, I was told that I was to assist senior associate Eric Mock with some "closings." I arrived at Mock's office to find a tall light-haired guy with his arm in a sling, which he promptly informed me housed a broken arm from sliding at a firm softball game. For the next few days, my job was to travel with him to Washington, Richmond and Philadelphia to carry his briefcase filled with documents for a low income housing transaction. In law school, there were anecdotes about the menial tasks that might be consigned to young attorneys at large firms, often derisively referred to as "carrying the bags" of the partners. In this instance, my assignment actually WAS to carry the bags. During the two day trip, Mock entertained me with stories about the Dewey athletic teams, leading me to conclude that the firm was a potent force in the New York lawyers' sports leagues.

I must've accomplished my bag-carrying tasks satisfactorily or been a sufficiently rapt listener to his stories of Dewey exploits. When we arrived back in New York in the early evening, Mock asked me if I wanted to accompany him to the firm's baseball game. We grabbed a cab at Penn Station and were deposited at a field on the East River near Houston Street where the game was in the middle innings. Mock prevailed upon the team's captain to insert me into the line-up, something the captain was reluctant to do. Mock cited summer associate recruitment, and I was penciled in to bat in the last inning. When I arrived at the plate, we were down by a run and the go-ahead run was on base. I am certain the other team members were nervous about a wholly untested summer associate batting at this critical point but were constrained from pulling me because of the recruiting rationale. Fortunately for all concerned, and to my own relief, I hit a single into right-center, which drove in two runs. My brief cameo audition earned me an invitation to join the softball team.

A Basketball Firm

In the ensuing weeks, I was to learn that while the softball team was a respectable perennial contender, Dewey Ballantine staked its athletic claim to fame on basketball. Firm lawyers had been prominent in the organization of the New York Lawyers' League a few years earlier, and the league's commissioners had all hailed from the firm. Everyone boasted of Ed Blythe, a lightening quick guard who had played at Southern Illinois with Walt Frazier, the legendary guard for the New York Knicks.

To promote the firm's basketball, a special summer associate game was arranged at the Downtown Athletic Club, known as the DAC. In mid-summer, about ten or so of us headed out the doors of 140 Broadway past the landmark orange cube in its plaza and down Church Street. We passed the American Stock Exchange and Harry's, the watering hole of the traders, and then the approximately 45 story Art Deco building faced us on the right. We were awed to gain entry to the DAC because it was the famed sponsor of the Heisman Trophy, and as I strolled down the first floor to the elevator, my imagination was captured by the scene before us—a hallway filled with photos, trophies and other memorabilia of the Heisman winners. I had followed their proceedings religiously since my Anaconda days when Notre Dame's Paul Hornung took home the trophy in 1956.

Since there were no other players on the court that day, we had the gym to ourselves. Among the attorneys were Blythe, Brad Race, who also played softball, George Pataki, whom I'd met through a mutual friend, and Barry O'Connor, who had arranged the game; on the summer associate side were Bob Dolian, my Upstarts teammate, Joe Angland, another Harvard classmate,

Peter Gold, a student from NYU, David Howorth and one or two others. The games clearly demonstrated that the firm had talented players, but in a class by himself was Blythe, who was as good, if not better, than advertised.

On our return walk, I caught up with Blythe, a soft-spoken African-American about 5' 7". When I mentioned the topic of Walt Frazier and Southern Illinois, he laughed with a hint of embarrassment and said the dimensions of the story had tended to outpace the reality. After playing with him that day, one could understand how the story might've taken on a life of its own.

Ed had grown up in Carbondale, Illinois, and his history had been one of over-achievement on the court in view of his size. His affinity for the game had begun at an early age playing at the hoop on a pole in his backyard, which was to become the epicenter of Carbondale black basketball during his school years. Drawing a mix of players from grade school through high school years, the Blythe backyard was the McKittrick's garage of black Carbondale. I speak in racial terms because although not officially segregated, in the 1950's Carbondale, geographically closer to Huntsville, Alabama than Chicago, did have distinct racial areas. Ed attended all black schools where he was a basketball standout. Despite the size of his high school, with his class graduating a paltry 31, their team enjoyed considerable success playing a schedule that included both black and white schools.

At Southern Illinois, Ed lettered three years for the Division II level school. Frazier was a freshman when Ed was a senior so their principal basketball experience together was on the practice court where the talented freshman team scrimmaged the varsity. Frazier was not the only future NBA player at SIU in those days since a roommate of Ed's was Charles (Chico) Vaughn, who enjoyed an extended professional career with the St. Louis Hawks, the Detroit Pistons and the ABA. While in law school at the University of Iowa, the "little guy," as he referred to himself, maintained his game playing with members of the Iowa basketball and football teams during the summer months. When Ed arrived at Dewey in 1968, the firm had no basketball team, but his talent positioned him well to become one of the stars in the Lawyers' League when its doors opened two years later.

Ed also held a unique position at the firm in that he was the senior African-American—he also may have been the first, having arrived in 1968 when the presence of black attorneys in Wall Street firms was negligible. A litigator with a prominent position on the sprawling AT&T antitrust case, the word was that Ed was in the running to become a partner in a couple of years when his class was to be considered.

Commissioner Farren

One person missing from the DAC game was the heart and soul of the Dewey basketball program, Richard Farren, a middle-level associate in the

Trusts and Estates Department. He was the dedicated commissioner of the League and the captain and administrator of the firm's basketball teams. He also was the firm's unofficial basketball historian, being the repository of knowledge of virtually every game the firm had played (and needless to say a very valuable resource for this book). Richard was absent from our DAC game because he was suffering from mononucleosis, caused in no small part by working 15-hour days for several months as he juggled his responsibilities to the League and the Governor (the insider's nickname for the firm).

As the commissioner, he solicited and approved rosters, organized the teams into divisions according to perceived strength, scheduled all games, handled the finances, contracted for the numerous gyms, hired the referees, collected the scores and monitored the records, ran the play-offs, handled all correspondence for such matters in pre-email days, enforced the rules and arbitrated challenges arising from disputes. The latter chore was one that couldn't be considered lightly in view of the fact that the parties involved were aggressive and overly competitive New York lawyers. After recovering, he found his salvation in building an organization and appointed six assistant commissioners to help shoulder the myriad taxing responsibilities he'd handled by himself for two years.

Farren's initial acquaintance with Dewey was intertwined with basketball (and politics). After he had graduated from Harvard Law, he was committed to a tour of duty with the army, which delayed his path to getting a job right out of school. Before reporting for basic training, he decided to interview some New York firms and casted about among his friends for advice. One of his calls was to his predecessor as president of the Republican Club at Harvard Law. A young associate at Dewey, he invited Richard to lunch and brought along another associate. Richard immediately recognized George Pataki, who had been a cohort at the Yale Conservative Club and a fellow player on the Yale intramural circuit. Pataki eagerly told Farren that he needed to interview at the firm because they had a great basketball team. Richard followed George's advice and, following his military tour of duty, joined George, Blythe, Race, O'Connor, former commissioner Don Robinson, and Tom Carroll, a member of the all-city team in the mid-1960's in the competition for those initial years of the League. The Dewey teams twice won the championship in the early 1970's, thus launching the legacy we inherited.

I was pleased to get an invitation to return as an associate and began my legal career in September 1975. When I first met Farren, he gave me the lowdown on how the personnel landscape had changed. Pataki and O'Connor had left the firm, and the class of 1974 included two new members of the team, Stafford Hilaire and Paul Mueller. A year ahead of me at Harvard, Staff was a veteran of the Boston College basketball program. Extremely agile at 6'5", he was a left-hander who could put the ball on the floor like a guard while creating the "big-man" presence under the basket. He had been described as a "crowd-pleaser" while at B.C. Originally from Antigua, where he was a member of a prominent family, he told me shortly after we met that his original sport was cricket. He did not pick up a basketball until he moved to the States in his mid-grade school years. Mueller hailed from Minnesota, where his athletic skills had been applied to tennis and golf as well as basketball. In addition, Paul possessed impressive journalistic skills, which were to be featured at the firm as he chronicled the exploits of Dewey basketball for the internal weekly rag, THE BULL.

Farren also explained that Dewey was not restricted to the sponsorship of one basketball team, but rather the firm had an entry in three divisions, the A, B and C. The A team was called the Terns, and to this day no one is certain as to the origin of the name. Most agree that it is an abbreviation of "interns," but beyond that there is little agreement. The B and C teams were respectively Team Bushby and Team Ballantine, names from the firm's letterhead, and again there is some uncertainty as to origins or rationale since Ballantine preceded Bushby in the firm's official name, so logically Team Ballantine should have been the B team.

Creating the league divisions according to the anticipated strength was the brainchild of Farren, who expanded the number of teams from 30 to 72 during his stewardship. The divisions were required, he told me, because "we were having games with scores of 80 to 20," evocative of my father's fate in Virginia City. In addition to the three divisions, which restricted participation on a team to attorneys and paralegals at the firm, an "open" league was introduced that year with the only criteria being that the player had to be an attorney. Farren put together a team called the Shysters, of which about half of the players were from Dewey. Finally, 1975 was the inaugural year for a women's league, with the firm's entry being the Dewey Decimals. The highly successful team was to be led by Fran Morris, the first point guard for Connecticut women's basketball team, and coached by Hilaire and Mueller. It's true—the firm was represented in five basketball leagues. By comparison, most firms in the city had one team with a few reaching two if they had a women's team.

Playing in Three Leagues

That year I got my first taste of the practice of law, but what I remember most was getting to play on three of the firm's teams with talented teammates—some of whom came with impressive athletic resumes and all of whom just happened to be legal colleagues. Those teams were the A team Terns, the B team Bushby and the Open League Shysters. Originally, my intention was to play on only the A team. After the first game, John Whelan, captain of the B team and one of the guys who migrated between the A and B teams, asked me to play with them when my scheduled permitted, which amazingly enough proved to be most games. Farren also invited me to play on the Shysters, which besides Blythe, Hilaire, Race, him and me included Grady O'Malley, who had played with the Atlanta Hawks, the former Dewey associate Tom Carroll and Bill Madden, who had captained the Yale basketball team where he received All-American honorable mention. The team was loaded with talent, but so were the four or five other teams in the league. I remember in particular one team anchored by Ed Hummer, who had starred at Princeton during Bill Bradley's era.

This was a hoopster's heaven—an amateur whose fondest dreams were being fulfilled by this chance to be surrounded by diverse and exciting talent. All of this was abetted by the fact that my wife Susanne was 300 miles north in Burlington, Vermont, completing a doctorate and blissfully unaware of my late night gym commitments.

The Dewey firms clearly had their share of victories during that era, but one in particular stands out among the firm annals. At the tip-off time in a game the previous season, the Terns could send only four players to the mid-court circle with nearly all their big men missing. The opposing captain approached Farren to offer him a forfeit. Echoing my father's words of over 20 years previously when reduced to four players and anticipating Coach Dale in *Hoosiers* a decade later, Farren defiantly responded: "No, we'll play with what we got." The fifth player, Pataki, who had a calendar conflict, showed up during the last minute of play to witness the demolition of Cahill Gordon by a score of 78 to 44. The game was memorialized in THE BULL, under the by-line of "Four Terns Victorious." It opened with an over-the-top declaration that "it is comforting to find amidst these troubled times a handful of loyalists whose hearts beat strong and true." Attributing the victory to a "stupefying 2-0-2 zone defense with poised perimeter shooting," the article continued by advising "THE BULL wishes to take this opportunity to chastise the five absent Terns over 6'4" who abandoned their shorter compatriots." This fine specimen of prose concluded with a plea for the firm's partners to exempt tall associates from Thursday evening meetings to preserve "the vitality and productivity of medium-sized associates."

A word should be said about THE BULL and its role as interpreter and reinforcer of Dewey culture. A typewritten newsletter that appeared every Monday on our desks, it purported to be a round-up of firm-related events during the previous week. It usually was headlined with a somewhat scholarly (and occasionally humorous) analysis of a recent legal matter in the office, but it was the rest of THE BULL that interested us most. These reports and notices included profiles of entering and departing attorneys, marriage and birth announcements, address changes, attorneys travelling on business, office vacationers, lost and found and of course the firm's athletic events.

With respect to the latter, a careful reader of any column in THE BULL would note the lack of any reference to a player's name. Paul Mueller recalls being instructed about the de facto policy of "no names" by senior associates Brad Race and George Pataki when he undertook the job of basketball scribe. As George explained it to Paul, "we never know what an associate has told a partner as to why he couldn't work that night." Accordingly, individual legendary performances never graced the pages of THE BULL. As an historical note, when Dewey arrived, he objected to the name and demanded that it be changed to THE BULLETIN. Upon his death the masthead reverted immediately to the original.

While there was no championship that prior year, the late season momentum propelled by the triumph of the four heroic (shorter-statured) guys was to carry over to my first season. What a spectacular season it was to be! We melded together well as a team; the starting five for the season were Blythe and Mueller at guard, Hilaire and myself at forward and usually Brad Race at center with Farren as the sixth man. Though Pataki had left the firm, he regularly returned to play and my N.D. classmate Mike Kelly was recruited to play when he could. Some of the regular B team players such as Ira Greenberg, Whelan and George Weiss also were part of the A team rotation. With Hilaire, Race, Pataki and Kelly, we had four players in the 6'4" to 6'6" range, but there was no doubt that the key to the team's success was the 5'7" Blythe.

My rosy memory burnished over 40 years was that under Ed's leadership and Staff's relentless rebounding and disruptive quickness we rolled up victory after victory with large margins. The recollection of the fabulous times we had is still tangible as we have exchanged emails over the last couple of years about a game or even a moment. Happily, thanks to the pack rat proclivities of teammate and BULL scribe Paul Mueller, his records bear out those memories. After two relatively easy games with victory margins in excess of 30, we faced a personnel shortage in early December at Friends Seminary against Donovan Leisure and were forced to play with only five men with Farren the tallest at 6'1". The final score was 91-51. And the game report in THE BULL crowed "a dazzling offensive display unequalled in the Terns' six-year history."

The game was most memorable to me for another reason, however. Towards the end of the second half, one of the Donovan players collapsed at midcourt. Play was suspended while medics carted off the injured player to an ambulance, with a diagnosis of a ruptured tendon. We noticed that he was clearly older than the rest of us and questioned among ourselves whether he should have been on the court. When the teams shook hands at the end of the game, the Donovan team disclosed that our injured opponent had been none other than the renowned lawyer John Doar, the chief counsel of the House Judiciary Committee Watergate investigation.

A methodical and quiet-spoken attorney, he had been a nightly presence on Walter Cronkite's CBS News as he systematically in that flat steady legal manner established the case for the various malfeasances of the Nixon administration. Described at the time as a "Kennedy Republican," Doar also had played a prominent role in the civil rights actions of the Justice Department during the 1960's. Most famously he had stared down Mississippi segregationist governor Ross Barnett on the campus of the University of Mississippi as the latter attempted to block James Meredith from becoming the first black student at Ole Miss.

As I subsequently learned, Doar did belong on the court that night, even at the age of 54, probably the oldest player in the league. He had a long and distinguished history with the game. Coming from a school in a small Wisconsin town that did not sponsor a team, he fulfilled his dream of playing college basketball when he earned a spot on the Princeton varsity team, whose roster included future NBA players Bud Palmer and Butch van Breda Kolff.

The following week the Terns met the always tough Townley and Updike team. Our victory was shared with the rest of the firm in the Christmas issue of THE BULL, which lyrics would not be mistaken for ones penned by T.S. Eliot or W.B. Yeats or for that matter Clement Clarke Moore, the author of the Christmas story which was so shamelessly parodied in this verse:

'Twas a cold wintry night—
　　And all through the gym
The Updikes were uptight
　　Their shots missed the rim.

The Terns started slowly
　　And built a small lead'
Then visions of victory
　　Brought baskets with greed.

The Terns' passes were missiles
　　That raised oohs and ows
So the refs blew their whistles
　　And called many fouls.

Rebound—pass and break—fast break
　　That's how the Terns played
Next stop and pop, then head fake
　　The Terns had it made.

The Terns' thoughts turned to steins
　　Of beer after beer
While still from the sidelines
　　Came cheer after cheer:

On Naughty! Oh Daughty!
The cheerleaders cried.
Go Peerless. Go Fearless
The benchwarmers sighed.

> Then the game ended. The Terns
> Had scored ninety-two
> While Townley's uptight Santas
> With forty were through.

As the score of these two games suggest, the Terns were racking up points in these games, a trend that continued throughout the season. After the sixth consecutive victory, THE BULL reported that the Terns and opposition's average scores during those games was a staggering 88-54.

That season and the succeeding two represent some of my most productive and satisfying years of basketball. After a practice at the DAC prior to the season, Hilaire and I chewed the fat about the upcoming season. In his diplomatic style, he admitted that his original impression was that my stature limited me to playing guard, but after seeing me play he predicted I'd be making my contributions underneath the basket, and that's what happened.

Many of these were scored in our one-three-one zone offense, which was used in most our games. Since virtually no one in the league could handle Blythe one on one, our opponents attempted to limit his production through a zone defense. Happily for me, we responded repeatedly with my favorite offense, the one-three-one—setting up the point guard on top, one guy on each wing, a player at the post and a baseline runner. As explained by Tracy Walsh, my high school coach, the objective of the offense is to create open shots through quick passes so that the ball moves quicker than the feet of the defenders. The baseline runner is the only player that moves as he alternates from one side to the other, attempting to create an offense "overload" on a side.

Ever since my high school days, I found that as the baseline runner I could get a number of relatively easy shots around the basket if I timed my movement across the paint properly. The optimal way to begin the offense is to pass to the wing opposite the baseline player. Typically, the zone will shift with a tendency on the part of the defenders on the ball side to overplay. On the other hand, the weak side defender playing low might not be inclined to shift as quickly, resulting in an opening around the basket for the baseline runner. After this was repeated a few times, the zone would tend to collapse down low, which would leave Hilaire and Mueller on the wings open for their high percentage shots. The collapsing of the zone also put the guy at the post in position for a shot. Blythe of course created shots for himself wherever he was located, frequently taking a dribble to the left or the right to evade the defender at the top.

A couple of times during those years, the opposing team responded by running a box and one,[6] which was complimentary but undeserved since my

---

[6] With a box and one, four members of the team run a zone and the remaining player guards the targeted player one on one.

offense was enhanced so much by the threat of Blythe and Hilaire. It goes without saying that the box and one didn't work; bottom line: it's effectiveness in shutting me down just created opportunities for the extraordinary shooting of the others, and it soon was abandoned. I think the one-three-one is a terrific offense, but it's rarely seen today in this era of the three-point shot.

A treasured personal best occurred when we were short players and missing our tall guys, including Hilaire. Blythe and I shared the scoring that led to a big win. When the game ended, firm basketball historian Farren walked over with a big smile to inform me that I had tied the firm's record of 44 points set by Don Robinson, the League's organizer and former captain.

As should be clear by now, basketball at Dewey was FUN! The game day began with a camaraderie-filled pre-game trip on the subway to our destination as we discussed recent gossip at the firm (and perhaps a little about our upcoming opponent). The game usually was a win and provided the grist for stories at the lunch table for the next couple of days. After that we would begin to strategize about the next game when we ran into each other in the halls. Needless to say, we were not hired to be basketball players but rather to practice law at 140 Broadway, and at times that aspect of the firm interposed itself into my life.

Life at the Firm When not Playing Basketball

My years as an apprentice on Wall Street coincided with the final days of an era that had begun many decades earlier. The partners at Dewey and other Wall Street firms viewed the practice of law as a profession and not a business. Collegiality among the partners was considered to be a value of the highest order, and the most obvious manifestation of this ethos was "lock-step" compensation. All partners of the same class were entitled to the same share of partnership profits regardless of the number of hours they billed or the amount of client receipts they were credited with. These values also were manifested conspicuously in the emphasis on the quality of the work product. Every legal document bearing the Dewey name was expected to reflect the highest level of craftsmanship, regardless of the time required to produce it. The firm was known for training new associates in meticulously careful draftsmanship, deemed essential to the culture. No document with a typo was to leave the offices of 140 Broadway, and the critique most associates faced in their first formal six month review was insufficient vigilance in catching those typos.

There were five departments at Dewey: litigation, corporate, tax, real estate and trusts and estates. After I spent the summer at the firm, I had decided to join the tax department. Well-respected throughout the city, the department featured a particularly large and diverse practice, which during my time at the firm listed 11 partners on the letterhead whereas most of their New York competitors probably had three or four partners. I also thought that practice promised more predictability of work schedules in a profession notoriously typified by unpredictability.

My mentor in that department was a young partner Fenton Burke, who devoted much of his time to international tax matters. Fenton represented all that was good of the old Wall Street practice of law. He had a nearly obsessive commitment to the craft, handling all matters in a thorough and careful manner, was hard-working (perhaps too hard), conducted himself at all times in a gracious manner and was thoroughly committed to the professional growth of young associates. Furthermore, he was tolerant of my departing temporarily to play a basketball game in the middle of a major matter.

One of my first assignments was to research and prepare a memorandum on some abstruse issue regarding international tax. I submitted to him what I thought was a good memo. As was his practice, he and I sat at a small table in his office as he went through the memo marking it up extensively—sentences and sometimes paragraphs were moved, sometimes my favorite phrases being replaced with language inserted in pencil-drawn balloons on the edges of the paper. As I sat watching this evisceration of my work product, my heart sank as I concluded that I had blown this assignment. When he finished, he turned to me with that gentlemanly and kind smile of his and quietly remarked: "That was a damn good memo." Whether or not it was, he was someone committed to the job of mentoring and understood the importance of encouragement as well as correction.

The firm also sponsored a number of social events, including monthly dinners referred to as Wranglers, but the social year clearly revolved around the Annual Dinner, held at either the Pierre or the Plaza Hotel. "The Dinner," as it was invariably referred to, was a lavish affair meant to help cement our collective pride in the Dewey culture rooted in old boy traditions. (Rumor had it that a grand piano had been jettisoned out an upper story window as part of the high-jinx of one of The Dinners in the 1920's). It also gave a bantering and fun-loving voice to the lower-echelons. They had the opportunity to lampoon with skits and songs the best-compensated who on a daily basis they served with their toil. It was an event which incidentally the humor-less Dewey boycotted after his first year. Through the prearrangement of The Dinner organizers, Dewey was the last to enter the dining room, at which point all the attendees turned towards him wearing the signature Dewey moustache as the band played "Hail to the Chief," spoofing his failed 1948 presidential bid. He was not amused and never returned.

The preeminence of The Dinner was underscored by the fact that a tremendous number of otherwise-billable hours were devoted to its creation by a committee comprised of a group of perennial Dinner organizers usually chaired by a senior partner. The committee relied upon all second year associates drafted to do the grunt work. When I attended my first meeting, we were informed that if there was a conflict between client work and Dinner work, the latter was to take precedence. Accordingly, my assignment to The Dinner committee was nearly full time over the next five weeks and largely involved aspects of theater production that were novel to me and certainly not features of my law school education. The Dinner experience taught me much about the firm and its people, but it also proved an education of the backstage haunts of Times Square that I never will forget.

The commitment to the profession, the devotion to craftsmanship, dedication to the weekly publication of THE BULL, the high priority given to social events—this was the firm the served as the incubator of as robust a basketball program as was to be found in any law firm.

A Firm that Wins Championships

The Terns continued to cruise through the regular season undefeated but met with disappointment in the play-offs at the hands of Hertzfeld and Rubin, a team we had handily defeated in the regular season. The upset prevented us from winning the trophy which we'd all anticipated after the undefeated regular season. Upsets were always stinging, of course, but certainly not new to me in my basketball life. Excepting that final game, it was an extremely successful season, a success that was to be shared by all the firm's teams. As reported in May, the cumulative record of the firm's teams was 41-6 with three divisional championships.

The winning ways of the Dewey teams were to continue in the following year. Prior to the season, we were greeted with more personnel changes. Farren, the mainstay of the program for several years, had left the firm the previous winter. In addition to the deleterious effects on his health, his commitment to basketball matters, he reckons, had hurt his standing within the firm. While he continued to play with us after his departure, he relinquished his administrative positions. I stepped up to assume the role of captain of the A team, and with Mueller took over the administrative responsibilities for the program. Fellow Harvard alumnus Joe Angland returned after completing his clerkship and became an active participant on the A and B teams. Upon his arrival, Joe was informed that his basketball responsibilities included coaching the women's team. He still remains uncertain as to whether that was a good thing or a bad thing. Another new associate was Fred Butler, also a veteran of the Harvard Law intramurals, who although only 6'2" played the post position as it should be played. From Iowa came Fred Hubbell who had decided to forego a career (at least for a while) with his family business, Equitable Life Insurance in Des Moines, to practice law in New York.

The new season also featured name changes. The A team dropped the Terns moniker and became Team Dewey, the B and C teams exchanged names so that they respectively became Team Ballantine and Team Bushby, the same order in the firm's name, and the open team co-opted the Terns name while discarding the unflattering Shysters. As for me, my basketball playing for the program was cut back somewhat since there was a substantial change in my living situation. Susanne had moved to New York the previous summer after spending her required residency for the Ph.D. program at the University of Vermont. We jointly decided that my spending three nights playing basketball probably was excessive. Also, I needed to spend some of those evenings on my Ph.D. dissertation if I was ever to finish it. The result was that I eliminated my participation with the Open Team and joined the B team for not more than half of their games.

Early in the season, we had the opportunity to demonstrate to the prior year champs who was the best team in the division. In the season opener, both Angland and Mueller made key shots within the last minute with Mueller's coming from half-court as time expired to provide us with a one point victory over Satterlee. A close score was an anomaly that season, though, as we continued to overpower most opponents, even with the strengthening of the schedule as Farren dropped the two weakest teams from the prior year and added the two strongest teams from the B division.

After we defeated the All Stars in a mid-April semi-finals contest by 10 points, THE BULL duly noted that we were advancing to the championship game with the date and the opponent still undetermined. Through a series of delays, the game was not to be played until May 18, nearly outlasting the then NBA play-off season. With a solid victory of 77-68 over the team we considered the crown pretenders of the prior season at the august DAC, we were successful in capturing for the Governor the third championship in the seven years of the League's existence. It was my first championship since my sixth grade team 17 years earlier. Reflecting his Dewey training, Mueller couldn't help noticing that the trophy we received has a typo with a misplaced apostrophe in the inscription, reading "Lawyer's League" rather than "Lawyers' League."

With the Open and Women teams' championships, the firm captured three of the five titles that year, which was to be the apogee of Dewey basketball. The most dominating team was the Dewey Decimals, the firm's entry in the Women's League, which won the championships in 1976 and 1977, suffering only one loss during that period. The defining force of the team was the center, Fran Morris, who had moved into the paint after her years of playing point guard.

Playing at Friends Gym with Referee Mickey Farber

Dewey teams skipped all over Manhattan Island and the Bronx to play games, and in my four years I was to run up and down the court in a diverse array of gyms. Friends Seminary Gym at 222 East 16th Street, though, was our favorite haunt. We held our formal practices and played the majority of our games there during my first regular season. Claiming to be the oldest coeducational school in New York, the Quaker institution was founded in 1786, and its oldest building dates back to 1860. As might be expected, the school has had a glorious history, with a stellar list of alumni, including Theodore Roosevelt, the author Caleb Carr, the actors Amanda Peet and Liev Schreiber and the designer Vera Wang. Somewhat at odds with its historic tradition, our basement gym was in a four story modernist building constructed in 1962, and that compact gym was less spacious than my father's in Virginia City. As one former Dewey player characterizes it, "it was a true cracker-box where a player finishing a fast break had better stop quickly." Nevertheless, it was our home and we thrived there, rarely losing a game on its floor.

Our second favorite was Power Memorial High Academy. Though lacking the nearly 200-year pedigree of Friends, the school had a 70-year close association with the rise of immigrant Irish Catholics in New York. While appreciating its history, we considered it a privilege to play there because it was the school where Lew Alcindor (now Kareem Abdul-Jabbar) had first reached national prominence when the purple and the gold dominated East Coast high school basketball. That included running up an astonishing 71-game winning streak. The gym entrance featured the "shrine," a trophy case solely dedicated to him with his photo and uniform and other memorabilia. The Power Memorial High gym was an upgrade from Friend's Academy, but it struck me as relatively modest considering its prominence in basketball history. There was no doubt in our mind, though, that the lingering specter of Alcindor returned to the court to inspire us when we played on its floor.

Our other gyms brought us all over the City and included Public School 33 in the Chelsea area, the prestigious New York Athletic Club across from Central Park, the School of Arts and Design on 57th Street, Trinity High School on the Upper West Side, Dalton School on the Upper East Side and Cardinal Hayes in the shadow of Yankee Stadium in the South Bronx. Invoking the spirit of the ballad, "East Side, West Side," it was an interesting way to get to know New York—through the single lens of "basketball friendly" spaces.

Each of those gyms required referees, and any discussion of referees of that era immediately brings to mind "Mickey." A retired worker in the garment district, Mickey Farber was a short, overweight, balding 50-something ball of energy. Some would claim that he had faulty eyesight, but all the free throws he awarded me during those years would put me in the opposing camp. He was a talker who would entertain us with stories before and after the game in that familiar New York idiom. He also had a knack for priceless comments during the game. Mickey knew he was refereeing lawyers, a profession that did not overly awe him, and he never let us forget that he knew.

I remember particularly the reactions of opposing players to certain fouls Mickey would call in my favor around the basket. Usually it was a drive along the baseline, followed by an attempt to power up the shot off the edge of the backboard. Inevitably there was contact, sometimes precipitated by me, but the call by Mickey invariably was a blocking foul on the defender. When the opposing team would attempt to claim that it was a charge, Mickey would scoff at them and instruct them to "keep their arguments in the court room." I was not the only Dewey beneficiary of Mickey's calls. All the former Dewey players to whom I have spoken agree that they shot more free throws when Mickey controlled the whistle. Some have attributed our disproportionately favorable calls to the fact that Farren, as commissioner, was the signatory on the checks handed out to Mickey. I prefer to think that we simply deserved the free throws.

Basketball night was not limited to the time on the court. Particularly if it was an early game, we would head to a local pub for a beer and perhaps some food "on the Governor." The latter phrase was the euphemism for charging an expense to the firm, and the wisdom passed down through generations of associates was that expenses in connection with firm-related athletics were appropriate items to be reimbursed by the firm. The tradition was that any reimbursable expense was to be paid by the junior attorney, who would then submit the request for reimbursement. As the junior member of the team, that responsibility fell upon me for that first year. Following the first meal of the season, I filled out the form at the disbursement window, recording account number 900000/16900, otherwise known as "Office-General," with the description of the dinner and a list of the participants. Nervously I handed it to the clerk at the window, who perfunctorily verified that the form had a correct account number and was signed, and then she promptly counted out the bills to me. A sense of relief came over me as I knew that I had passed one of the initiations of being an associate at the firm.

That form would have been one of many "Office-General" charges the clerk would have seen that day—dinner bills and cab fares home when working late, invoices for new shirts if one worked all night on a court case or a business deal, client entertainment and a host of other activities. The ready reimbursement of such items was indelibly ingrained into the DNA of the firm. In today's world of cut-throat "business-oriented" firms, some partners may view these types of expenditures as a wasteful indulgence of associates. At Dewey and other similar firms, they represented simply the way things were, and should be, done.

Refereeing Dewey Decimals vs. The Firm

Not surprisingly, the firm's culture spawned some special basketball events, including a game between the women's team and the partners at the firm, who, with the exception of one, were all male. The January 12, 1976 edition of THE BULL reported that the following legal document had been served upon the firm: "YOU ARE HEREBY SUMMONED to answer the challenge in this action by appearing in attire suitable for the carrying on of a basketball game to begin at 6:30 on Monday, January 19, 1976 at P.S. 33." The challenge was accepted.

On the night of the game, both teams arrived with full rosters—respectively 11 partners attired in t-shirts with "The Firm" emblazoned over the chest and 12 regular members of the Decimals plus their two valiant coaches, Hilaire and Mueller. The narrow sidelines of P.S. 33 were filled with spectators eager to witness the historical game although none seemed to have adhered to the dress code, which had been announced as "black tie." I was asked to referee the game with the always outspoken Ira Greenberg. Despite the efforts of the referees, as reported in THE BULL, the Firm "upset" the Decimals by a score of 60 to 34. The score remained relatively close the first half, but then the secret weapon of the Firm began to assert himself. The Decimals was not the only team fielding a former NCAA Division A player that evening. Joe Williams, a tax partner, had played for Iowa during the mid-50's after leading his high school team from Ames, Iowa to the state championship. Joe modestly summarized that championship game 60 years later: "I had a pretty good game." While he hadn't played much in the years preceding the firm contest, the latent talent asserted itself, and it was too much for the women players.

The game has been memorialized in a number of photos that have survived through the years. My own favorite is an action photo that includes the two referees, me backing off to avoid the action after throwing the ball up for a jump and Greenberg to the side with his hand raised and inexplicably without a shirt. According to Ira, there is an explanation. He discovered prior to the game that his shirt too closely resembled those being worn by the Firm and to assure that he would not be mistaken for a member of the team, he discarded it before the tip-off. He also had failed to pack a tuxedo in his bag. Following the game, the players, referees and spectators all reconnoitered at a local establishment to have drinks and a meal on the Governor.

In addition to anchoring the women's team, Fran Morris occasionally played on the firm's otherwise all-male C league team where she reverted to her traditional position of guard. She may have been the only woman to play in any of the men divisions. She and Ira tell about one game where Ira insisted that she play center while he took over the point guard responsibilities, not a natural for the lanky Greenberg, known more for his rebounding than ball handling. As always with Ira, there was a shrewd strategy behind his seemingly incongruous plan. He had anticipated that no one would take her seriously under the basket and that after a pass from him she would score underneath relatively uncontested. It worked a number of times until the opposing team figured out that Fran knew something about playing underneath.

Joining her at times at the other guard was Russell A. Beatie, Jr., the only partner who played consistently for the Governor. Cap, as he was called by everyone, was known for his signature cigar and his aggressive and irreverent attitude towards all matters relating to his practice, the firm and fellow partners.

Post-game dinners with Cap were not to be missed since he insisted on dining at a high quality restaurant while he entertained us with an evening of priceless repartee. He and Fran made an interesting duo on the court. As Joe Angland recently pictured it, the team had a unique backcourt with a woman and a guy with a cigar in his mouth.

Winding Down

With the championship season behind us, we moved into the next season with more personnel changes. Most significantly, Ed Blythe had left the firm to join AT&T. He was to play several games that year, but we were to miss his consistent presence on the hardwood. Similarly Hilaire's presence was not as dependable as in prior years as family and work matters began to impinge on his ability to make the games. The C team also was missing Cap Beatie, who organized and captained the firm's squash team in the inaugural season of the Council of Law Associates Squash League. A former college player, Cap led the team to win the downtown division, extending the firm's athletic success into squash. Despite these personnel losses, the firm continued forward with the basketball program, but the dominance of earlier years had evaporated. Team Dewey compiled an 8-6 record, but its season ended with a play-off loss to the powerhouse that season, Emmet Marvin.

My final season was for the most part a lost season. In September, my wife Susanne and I had decided to move to the Windy City. In contrast to past seasons, I was not a regular at the games and nowhere near top playing form. The distractions of looking for a new position, putting in additional hours to complete projects before I left and tending to various chores relating to buying a house all contributed to diminishing my time in the New York gyms. Departing at the end of March, shortly before the season's finale, I said farewell to the Governor's basketball.

As a final reflection on this extraordinary chapter of my basketball life, there were several ways in which one could garner attention within the firm: leading and especially winning a high profile case was perhaps the most glamourous, being the clever brains behind the Annual Dinner was another, and lastly contributing, and particularly winning, on one of the firm's athletic teams was a third. Of all the unlikely happenstances, I landed at a firm that considered its stable of winning amateur athletic teams to be a critical component in promoting its image. A poignant piece of evidence for this was the fact that in our second season when we fielded teams titled "Dewey," "Ballantine" and "Bushby" the 80-year-old aristocratic William Palmer sheepishly asked Fran Morris if there wasn't a team named for him—the next name on the firm's letterhead. The lowly level associate had to inform the disappointed Palmer there wasn't any such team.

I remain grateful to this day that I was able to play a game I've loved since childhood and to have it valued as a contribution to the culture of a firm that was singularly culture-conscious.

Chapter Seventeen

The Diaspora of the Dewey Alumni

Once you became a member of the Dewey family, privileges extended even beyond departure—and departure was a given for most of us since the narrowing hierarchical pyramid structure meant that most associates would not become partners. When I announced that I intended to move to Chicago, the placement machine in my department moved into action connecting me to partners' friends and contacts there. Of course this policy was not only generous and collegial but also reinforced loyalty to the Governor that served the firm well when the departees had reason to refer business back "home" again. My fellow associates similarly found their transitions elsewhere were smoothed by the firm, and we were always welcomed back to the top of Chase Tower for the annual Christmas party. This sponsorship served us all well—to paraphrase Garrison Keiller, we mostly have done "above average" in our post-Dewey life. Yet, as is always true in life, there were some winners and some losers among the people and institutions that we knew.

From Massachusetts to Arizona

Ed Blythe was not elected as the first African-American partner at Dewey, but as is the case for many who do not get the nod, the decision proved to be a blessing. When he left in 1977, he moved a few blocks up Broadway Street to AT&T or "Ma Bell," for the beginning of a very productive career in corporate American for the guy from Carbondale. Riding upon his instinctive corporate political skills and the Dewey-educated analytical skills, Ed held major positions in New York and Chicago, finishing his corporate career at an AT&T spin-off company, Lucent Technologies in 1996. He retired well in advance of the mythical 65 while the successful entrees into the Dewey partnership during his era continued to toil in an increasingly unsatisfying profession and, in the case of those who remained at Dewey, in the midst of a troubled firm. Basketball no longer is part of his athletic regimen with his skills being applied to tennis and golf. Settled in Roswell, Georgia, his comments on retirement are short and pithy: "I love it."

Paul Mueller left Dewey about six months after I did to take a position with the Houston office of Andrews and Kurth. Most importantly, he left with every copy of THE BULL for the approximately five years he worked at 140 Broadway. That archive has been an invaluable trove of information about our life of 40 years ago. Following his Houston years, he moved his practice to Phoenix, which most importantly offered a better climate for golf and tennis. Tennis soon followed basketball to the retirement bins. As he describes it, tennis is a "young man's game" with golf being more "age friendly." In November 2011 he notched his first-ever hole-in-one, "a swing that cost me lots of money" as he fulfilled the traditional duties of buying a round back at the clubhouse.

Mike Kelly was a Dewey teammate whose schedule at the firm prevented him from attending as many games as he would have liked, or perhaps he was less adept than the rest of us of coming up with stories for the supervising partner. Since leaving Dewey, Mike has been part of a team in corporate finance that has held out their shingle at a number of firms. The current one is the New York office of Greenberg Traurig. Mike's a fellow Notre Dame '70 grad, and we've continued to share stories through the years about playing at the Rock and attending games at the old Fieldhouse. Unlike the rest of us, Mike seems to grow taller as he ages.

Joe Angland is one player of our group who did rise to the partnership ranks at Dewey. Similar to a number of guys I have met, Joe was a debater and a basketball player in high school. Maybe it's because I know a lot of lawyers, or maybe there's something else going on here—but it's a curious correlation. Joe reached his current height of 6'2" in eighth grade and was looking towards a high school career in the Bronx.

After making the varsity team his junior year, he faced that choice of either debate or basketball. In his case, the pendulum was weighted heavily towards the debate side in that he was one of the best high school debaters in the country. He maintained that national ranking at the collegiate level while at MIT. Despite the debate choice, Joe never forgot basketball. When his debating schedule permitted, he participated in the very active MIT intramural league. At Harvard, his law school team had one of the more unusual rosters in that all the players had been top college debaters. Joe was a leading scorer for that team as the ball frequently found the net after being banked off the board with his trademark shot from the corner.

With his background in debate, litigation was the obvious choice for Joe. Those skills were transferred to the tax practice where he became the litigation partner in connection with some high profile tax cases. Joe also continued to play with the Dewey team until the early 1990's, thereby being the last of our group to play for the Governor. Joe left Dewey in 2004 at about the time that it merged with another firm, an event that was to have a profound effect on the future of the firm. Today he practices at the prestigious firm of White and Case as an anti-trust lawyer and is considered a leading lawyer in that area. While retired from competitive play, he sneaks in a little shooting around at a hoop to keep up the touch.

Connecticut Women's First Point Guard

Fran Morris is the only Dewey player who has ridden on a float in a parade celebrating an NCAA championship team. She is unique among us in that her basketball play has had an historical dimension—mirroring the rapidly changing landscape of women's basketball. When she began playing in junior high years, the rules still required each of the six players on the floor to play either defense or offense with members of each group not permitted to cross the center line. In 1962 the rules were changed to permit each team to have two "rovers" who could cross the line. With her quickness and athletic skills, Fran was chosen to be one of the rovers and excelled at the position during her high school years. Upon entering the University of Connecticut, she initially made a decision to not participate in sports and concentrate instead on her studies. When she came across the practice of the field hockey team in the fall, she felt the pull back to athletics and it became clear to her that she just couldn't stay away from the hardwood. She also figured that a respite from studies would invigorate her academic performance.

Fran showed up for the women's try-outs, and to no surprise her name ended up on the varsity roster. The rudimentary U-Conn women's basketball program in those days bore little resemblance to the perennial NCAA powerhouse that has accumulated eleven national titles since Fran's days. "If there was an away game, you would ask around to see if someone had a car and could give you a lift," she remembers. After a regular season of eight or so games, the team moved on to the Northeast tournament where the teams to be beat were now-forgotten Queens College, with a long tradition of women's basketball, and Southern Connecticut.

As it happened, Fran's playing years corresponded to rule changes that favored her style of play. While in high school, the limitation on dribbles to three, in existence since the origins of the women's game in the 1890's, was thrown out and replaced with the unlimited continuous dribble rule. The principal beneficiaries of the new regime were the rovers, who now could grab the ball at the defensive basket and dribble the entire length of the court to make a lay-up. Prior to her college sophomore year, the rules committee went one step further to convert the game to the men's model of five players playing full-court. For Fran it was a natural progression from rover to point guard, and hence she became Connecticut's first point guard.

While in law school, she officiated college women games and then coached the women's team at Mills College. Arriving at a firm with few females among its ranks in the fall of 1975, Fran's persona as an athlete gave her an easy confidence that fit her comfortably within the male-dominated environment of Dewey. Those basketball skills were to further enhance her status within the firm when she emerged as the dominant force not only of the Dewey Decimals

195

but also the emerging women's league. Fran's significance to the Decimals is well illustrated by the fact that after two consecutive championships, the team's record fell to four wins and eight losses the following year when she was pregnant. Reflecting her dogged commitment to the team, she didn't miss the entire season as she played while pregnant and returned two weeks after delivery.

Fran left Dewey when I did to practice law in the Bridgeport-Fairfield area, but she loyally made the trek to New York for the entirety of the following season to play with the team. After that, to the consternation of her fellow players, she retired from the Decimals. For the next ten years, Fran worked at a small firm and then became inside counsel for a real estate firm, after which she entered her first retirement. During the retirement, she discovered women's masters' basketball in Connecticut and spent the next five years raising children and playing basketball. After another legal stint partnering with an old friend, she took on her second retirement. To her dismay, knee replacement surgery knocked her out of basketball, but she's a constant presence on the golf course to employ her athletic skills. She has many unforgettable memories from the game, and among the best is riding on that alumni player float in the parade honoring the Connecticut 2004 national three-peat team.

Pataki and Farren

Our teammate George Pataki achieved significant political recognition by ascending to the office of Governor in New York in 1994 and serving for three terms. While we were aware he was a committed Republican and had been active in some campaigns, those of us who played ball with him wouldn't have predicted he'd seek the limelight as he did. In his book, *Pataki: An Autobiography*, George describes the thrill as a young lawyer at Dewey making the princely salary of $15,000, the incredible views from the 45th floor, and the "eye-popping" size of the deals he worked on. He admits, though, he discovered he had a lack of affinity for the practice of law at a large corporate law firm. Despite these misgivings, he remained at the firm for four years "in significant part because we had the best basketball team in the lawyers' league," confessing he was not prepared to "give up this form of competition just yet."

As it turned out, George didn't give up the competition after he left the firm. He continued to commute to games from his work, and then residence, in Peekskill, about 45 miles north of the city. He could be counted on to generously show up to play if we needed him. I remember one instance of being in danger of forfeiture with not enough players from the firm available. George answered my call to save Team Dewey, travelling in from his new home in rush hour traffic and topped it off by playing a "helluva" game.

George began his political career in 1981 by putting together a coalition of Republicans and some Democrats to win the mayor's seat in Peekskill. He continued that winning strategy to be elected to the NY Assembly for eight terms and moved to the State Senate in 1992. The decision to challenge seven-term incumbent Mary Goodhue, wife of Dewey tax partner Francis Goodhue, in the primary was a tough one. It also created a split within the Dewey family, undoubtedly generating much discussion over lunch among the partners at 150 Broadway. The Dewey partners were not the only ones dismayed by his challenge. According to George, he was not immediately accepted by many Republican colleagues in the Senate who were Goodhue's friends. The discomfiture was short-lived. George won over their support and secured the Republican nomination for governor, defeating the renowned Mario Cuomo, who was seeking a fourth term. George proceeded over the next twelve years to compile a distinctive record of Republican moderation—fiscally conservative and more liberal on social matters such as abortion, gay rights and environmentalism. It's a record that I would have expected in view of his early tutoring in Republican politics at Dewey, which inclined towards the so-called Rockefeller wing of the party.

Richard Farren, our tireless Lawyers' League commissioner, has been George's consistent advisor, political confidante and personal lawyer. After he left Dewey in 1976, he practiced for about five years with trusts and estates lawyer Charlie Korn, but over time his practice has expanded to encompass real estate, which was housed for many years at the firm of McLaughlin & Stern.

His basketball days ended in 1982, but ever the athletic enthusiast, Richard returned to a sport of his youth, speed skating. Employing that same fervor he demonstrated as commissioner and czar of the Dewey program, he keeps a busy schedule skating competitively in both short and long distance events. When we had lunch in December 2013, he had just competed in a half-marathon (13 miles) at Lake Placid where he placed 34 out of 58 and fifth in his age division.

Farren's passions extend beyond athletic competition: he's had a life-long interest in music—he enjoys opera and has sung in a glee club for many years and shares this interest with his pianist wife and composer/ singer son. Though our days of playing for the Governor are in the distant past, Richard retains the incredible ability to recount those seasons in great detail, including savoring our days with referee Mickey Farber on the court.

Lawyers Playing in Madison Square Garden

An undisputed winner of our post-Dewey days has been the New York Lawyers' League. In the early 1990's, I came across an article in the *New York Times* about the League titled "In court or on It, Lawyers are Lawyers." As I read it, a couple of items particularly caught my attention. The first was the statistical rundown—145 teams, five levels of play for male players plus the women's division, a separate league for corporate employees and a six-figure budget. The other was the notation that the commissioner, Peter Grean, had resigned his position as an administrative judge to work full-time as commissioner. I had remembered Peter from my days at Dewey since I'd played against him numerous times—a dedicated basketball junkie. Initially I was puzzled by Grean's career step, but as I learned more I concluded it was a brilliant move.

In our day, the League operated under the auspices of the Council of New York Law Associates, formed in 1969 as an organization for younger lawyers. As Farren began winding down his role, Grean became more active, initially as a co-commissioner and then as the sole commissioner. Around 1980 he and Farren negotiated the spin-off of the League from the Council as an independent entity, and then Grean began to devote his full time energies to the League. Applying his entrepreneurial skills, the League that began as a fledging operation run out of the offices of a couple Dewey associates expanded into the recreational athletic conglomerate I'd read about. The franchise value similarly increased so that Grean was in a position to realize a very respectable profit from the sale of a majority interest about fifteen years ago.

The purchaser of his majority interest was Steve Frenchman, another basketball junkie and astute entrepreneur. A non-lawyer who previously had a business in the garment district, Frenchman has presided over the expansion into other sports such as volleyball, dodgeball, soccer and softball and today governs an organization with three full-time employees and a budget that almost certainly reaches into seven figures.

His most remarkable achievement, though, has been securing Madison Square Garden as the site for championship games for the Winter League. While I was impressed with playing our game at the Downtown Athletic Club, that experience pales with the thrill it would have been to win our 1977 championship game at the Garden. When I met with him in the fall of 2011, I asked him the cost of renting the Garden. He responded "$25,000 and we paid the full freight for a couple of years." Employing his creative negotiating skills, he then convinced the Knicks to become the principal sponsor of the League. As part of the deal, the Knicks agreed to provide the Garden free of charge for a date in late March or early April and also threw in the perk of producing one of their former players to serve as the "honorary captain" for the game. That spring the captain was Knick legend Walt Frazier.

Running a sports league for lawyers is your classic good news/bad news scenario. It is good news to have lawyers as your clientale since they are competitive and love to play; it is bad news to have lawyers since they are competitive and love to complain, particularly on the application of the rules. As might be expected, the League is governed by a comprehensive set of rules that run six pages single-spaced, including procedures for "Storm/Snow Days." The critical ones though are Rule XII (Rosters and Eligibility) and Rule X (Officials and Protests) with the two being inextricably linked since most protests relate to purported violations of Rule XII. The non-lawyer Frenchman described to me the first protest he received—a painstakingly drafted three page document resembling a lawyer's brief. After years of experience of dealing with these protests, he has acquired those judicial skills that the players witness when performing on the other court—the court of law.

Not all grievances end up being resolved by the commissioner. A number of years ago, it was reported in the press that a law firm recruited a permissible ringer, Devone Stephenson, a 6'8" former college player who also had played in the CBA. The opposing players apparently did not appreciate Stephenson as they taunted him, fouled him on four consecutive plays and then punched him in the face resulting in a broken jaw. Remarkably the opposing team was the Food Bank for New York City. Since the person who delivered the punch was not an authorized player, Frenchman suspended the team. Stephenson decided to pursue the matter further and filed a lawsuit against the Food Bank and the League, contending that the latter was negligent in its supervision and operation of the game. The judge dismissed the case against the League on the basis that Stephenson had submitted on online waiver whereby he agreed to not sue. The only recourse left to him was to pursue the Food Bank, leaving him in an unenviable position since any recovery would be at the cost of delivering meals to New York's hungry. I haven't been able to ascertain how the matter was resolved.

Despite an occasional hiccup such as this lawsuit, the story of the League serves as a model of success, one that would be aspired to by any of the firms competing under its auspices.

Decline of Dewey Basketball; Decline of the Firm

A clear loser in the intervening years has been the Dewey basketball program. Never again was the firm to sponsor five teams and win three championships in a single year. Soon the number of men's team was reduced to one, and in many seasons that team competed in the B division. It is likely that no other firm will match the Dewey basketball of the 1970's since, according to Commissioner Frenchman, no firm sponsors teams in multiple divisions. The eight-year period from the origins of the League until 1978 witnessed an extraordinary number of basketball enthusiasts and some extremely talented players to produce all those champion and contending teams. All of us who played then consider it a privilege to be part of that success.

An even more significant loser has been the firm itself, whose decline was to lead to disastrous consequences 30 plus years later. From my perch in Chicago and later Boston, I followed closely the fortunes of Dewey. Not only had my professional career began there, but it also hosted some of the most memorable basketball of my life. I continued to maintain a strong sense of loyalty to and interest in the firm. I watched with dismay (as did other friends who had shared those years with me working and playing for the Governor) as the bad news trickled out over time, only to be replaced by a cascade of misfortune.

Most noticeable to me after I left was that other firms were growing in size while Dewey remained relatively static, an indication that they were losing the competition for new business. The firm suffered a major blow at the hands of our post-game raconteur, Cap Beatie, who emerged as a vocal dissident of firm policies. He departed in 1981 to set up his own firm, an almost unheard of step by a partner of a large firm. As reported in the *American Lawyer*, Beatie was rebuffed by Dewey when he demanded that the lockstep method be abandoned and "unproductive" partners be fired to "staunch declining profits." The article was accompanied by a photo of Cap lighting up that signature cigar. Cap's departure was not to be the last, or worst, embarrassment for the firm.

A troubling pattern began to emerge where some very talented lawyers were "passed over," apparently for not meeting the "Dewey mold." As one of my former teammates commented recently, "you needed to be a WASP; you could be a Jewish or Irish WASP, but definitely a WASP." Those "passed over" obviously moved on to new positions, often taking along a number of loyal clients to their new professional homes. The firm did experience a burst of energy in 1983 when Washington power-broker Joseph Califano joined the firm but then returned to another period of drifting after his departure.

Adding to their woes was a major embarrassment over a typographical error incident that generated widespread publicity in legal circles. In a 1986-drafted mortgage in favor of Dewey's long-time client, Prudential Insurance, the amount was stated to be $92,885 rather than $92,885,000. The error of dropping the three zeros was attributable to another firm, but no one at Dewey caught the typo. The error bore legal consequences since the obligor entered bankruptcy and the debtor claimed the amount owed to Prudential was only the $92,885. The courts dismissed this sleight of hand, but Prudential incurred substantial legal fees and costs, for which Dewey was sued. The case was a huge black eye for Dewey, and the story is replete with irony in view of the firm's emphasis on training us associates to be vigilant in spotting typos.

In 2007 the firm's existence as an independent entity came to a end when it merged with LeBoeuf, Lamb, Greene & MacRae. The new firm became Dewey LeBoeuf. Contrary to what the name might suggest, the dominant partner in the merger was LeBoeuf since it provided approximately 60% of the attorneys and most of the executives for the new firm. The Dewey name remained first solely because of Thomas Dewey's stipulation in his will that his name could continue to be used only if no other name preceded it. Essentially the transaction was a humiliating acquisition of the storied firm by an upstart—my 1973 "bible" on the Wall Street firms included no mention of LeBoeuf.

Bankruptcy!

The story of decline continued as things got worse—much worse. On March 17, 2012, an item in the *The Wall Street Journal* caught my eye. Titled

"More Partners to Leave Dewey & LeBoeuf," the article reported the departure of 12 partners in the insurance department and added that since the first of the year another 18 partners had left. The firm was described as "troubled by internal disputes about compensation." An ominous pattern of law firm collapse was occurring. After a critical mass of attorneys leave, the remaining typically prepare for flight as well, updating their resumes as primary attention shifts from matters such as billing hours and collecting revenue to strategizing how to land safely with a new firm.

The firm received a psychological reprieve from the prevailing gloom when at the end of the month basketball great Magic Johnson visited the offices to sign the papers to acquire the Dodgers. I doubt there was anyone around to tell Magic about the glory years of Dewey basketball in the 1970's.

The hiatus was short-lived; the unraveling was shocking in its speed and inevitability:

- By April 5, 46 partners were gone; two weeks later the number was 66.
- Over the next couple of weeks, the new management attempted to find a merger partner to save the firm. A number of the potential saviors were firms that once had been a fraction of Dewey's size while I was there.
- On April 29, it was announced that the prior chairman Steven Davis was ousted from the management committee and that the Manhattan district attorney, on the entreaties of certain partners at the firm, had commenced a criminal investigation.
- A day later, an internal memo encouraged partners to look for other positions.
- On May 2, one news outlet described "chaos" at the firm. One the same day, Dewey lawyers discovered their medical insurance was suspended because of nonpayment, described by management as an "administrative issue."
- On the same day, the prior chairman of Dewey Ballantine, Morton Pierce, walked down a few blocks to join White & Case.
- The firm lingered on for a couple more weeks and then died when it file for bankruptcy protection on May 29, the largest law firm bankruptcy in history.

The story of how the firm attained that rather dubious distinction, the prospect of which would not have entered my mind in my wildest speculations when I left 33 years earlier, is one of massive mismanagement and an incomprehensible disregard for the basic principles of psychology and economics. The seeds of destruction lay in the firm's policy of offering guaranteed contracts to certain partners, many of which were over-priced. Reportedly an astonishing 100 of the 300 partners were afforded such agreements. Those of us who follow professional sports are well aware of guaranteed contracts being offered to free agent stars, who are paid a substantial amount regardless of their performance. Sometimes the contracts work out well, and the player becomes the foundation of a championship team, but far too frequently the athlete's performance is a bust. Financially, a sports team may weather the lackluster performance of an overpaid star or two with their cable revenue and a loyal fan base. The law firm's profitability, though, is solely contingent on the efforts of its partners.

Dewey's management's response to the structural problems simply compounded them. It borrowed money to pay guarantees. When that band-aid was no longer available, the only solution left was to not honor the contracts, which led to the parade of defections. Many writing about the ill-fated Dewey system have commented on the inherent greed, the lack of partner camaraderie and the lapse of the mores of old. While I agree with these observations, what most struck me about the system was its stupidity!

On February 27, 2013, it was reported that the judge had approved the bankruptcy plan resulting in the dissolution of the firm. Noting the largest law firm bankruptcy had been resolved in record time, the lead bankruptcy attorney proclaimed to the court that "we are about to make history." Expressing his pleasure, the judge congratulated all the professionals involved in the proceeding. In contrast to the self-congratulatory discourse in the court, a spirit of gallows humor reigned among a group of us exchanging emails on the legal internment. Capturing the paradox of the moment, Fran Morris offered: "The firm may not be a model of how to run a firm, but they are a model of how to complete a bankruptcy," to which another responded "it was actually pretty efficient at the end. The firm did die well."

Following the bankruptcy, a number of articles and blogs appeared, some of which were written by Dewey alumni. One of the best was a blog posting on *Mortal Coil*, written by my former officemate, Keith McWalter, not a basketball player but the star of several Annual Dinners with performances by his band. Poignantly, Keith pointed out that in a generation we "had lived through one of the most extraordinary transformations in modern American business: the conversion of elite law firms from patrician men's clubs into loose confederations of opportunistic gunslingers." He acknowledges that the firm we knew had to change, was "hardly a lawyer's utopia" with its "absurdly sexist, exploitative, frequently inept" management of its talent. Nevertheless, he fills his page with fondness for the post-graduate education and social circuit afforded to us as young associates at an elite Wall Street firm.

If I had written the blog, I would have added to the litany that the firm sponsored five basketball teams and won three championships in one year. In words that rang home to me, a guy from Montana, he emphasized that it was a commodious institution which introduced him to a world that he was wholly unfamiliar with before he arrived for work as a summer associate. He spoke for many of us as he sadly grieved over the "extinction of our professional alma mater." In that bankruptcy court, a part of our youth had disappeared, and we all were reminded of the tenuousness of existence, whether of institutions or individuals.

The Sad Story of Stafford Hilaire

The message of the precariousness of life has been emphasized by the deaths of three of our fellow players. Barry O' Connor, who had been the organizer of the game at the DAC when I was a summer associate, left for the investment banking world shortly before I arrived. He did not permit the bruising schedule of that business to interfere with his passion for exotic travel before his untimely death at the age of 60.

Our wide body center Brad Race combined a career in law and politics. Also a committed adherent of the Rockefeller-inspired New York Republicanism, Brad enjoyed a political partnership with Pataki, for whom he was chief of staff. About a dozen years ago, I met him in the elevator of the Dewey offices as I was headed to a conference room to do a seminar for the real estate department. That chance meeting gave us an opportunity to trade old "basketball stories." In July, 2010 I received a call from Mike Kelly to tell me that Brad had died from prostate cancer, discovered at a relatively late stage. He decided to fight this affliction in a very private manner, telling virtually no one about his condition. Towards the end it became quite clear to his closest friends that something was grievously wrong, and Pataki did get an opportunity to visit Brad the evening before he died. George also delivered a deeply personal eulogy at the service.

No story is as tragic, though, as that of Stafford Hilaire. While at Dewey, I had developed a close friendship with Staff. The radically different environments of our youth, the Caribbean and the northern Rocky Mountains, was the grist for many debates on weather. These debates took place as we endured the cold while walking five minutes from the Union Square subway to Friends Gym or standing on the Grand Concourse in the Bronx waiting for a gypsy cab to finally emerge. The topic of our "scientific" discourse was whether it was worse for the weather to be too hot or too cold. His position always was that the cold was "painful," whereas my response was you could put clothes on to get warm, whereas in the heat there is no such respite since clothes could be shed feasibly only at the beach.

Staff also was a terrific singer with a wonderful tenor voice. That voice was on display when he sang several times with the Keith McWalter band at the Annual Dinners. My most vivid memory of his singing, though, was in the wee hours of one Dinner when he and I stood around the piano and sang many "old time" tunes.

After he left Dewey, Staff decided to leave behind the large corporate law practice and return to the Caribbean where he set up a practice in the Virgin

Islands. At some point thereafter he moved to Denver, where members of his family lived, and he became president of a mortgage company.

In 2000 he hired Warren Williams as a loan officer on the recommendation of a real estate agent. About three years later, Williams and a number of other individuals were criminally charged with various counts regarding mortgage fraud. In the case of Williams, this activity had been extensive and dated back several years before his association with Staff. Williams pled guilty to reduced charges and agreed to cooperate with the authorities in providing "evidence" against others. As a result of these proceedings, Hilaire became ensnarled in the matter and was indicted in 2005. The indictments covered two major categories: certain alleged acts and conspiracy to commit certain acts. Following the trial, the jury acquitted him of all the alleged specific acts but rendered a guilty verdict on conspiracy. The trial court judge then threw out the conspiracy convictions, primarily because the three alleged co-conspirators at trial did not know each other.

At this point, the non-legal reader may be scratching his head. Can someone be charged with conspiring with people he doesn't know? A little background will be helpful to get a better understanding of what Learned Hand, one of the most notable judges of the twentieth century, described as "that darling of the modern prosecutor's nursery." The legal definition of conspiracy is an agreement by two or more persons to commit an unlawful act, coupled with an intent to achieve the agreement's objective, and often includes action that furthers the agreement. The definition is vague and over-reaching and carries the potential for abuse and prejudicial results. If charged with conspiracy, it is difficult to extricate oneself from the web, but it appeared that Staff had managed.

The Denver U.S. Attorney's office had other thoughts. They could have let the matter die and concluded that it was a case that should not have been pursued to begin with. The jury had not believed the testimony of their witnesses regarding the specific acts alleged against Staff, and the trial judge listening to the evidence did not believe there was a conspiracy as alleged. Instead, the U.S. Attorney appealed the trial judge's decision to the Tenth Circuit Court of Appeals, whose resulting opinion is a curiosity of legal reasoning.

The decision started out well as the court concluded that as alleged in the indictment a conspiracy among the three defendants at trial could not exist since the defendants did not know each other. So far, so good. Then the opinion wandered into the sphere of Alice in Wonderland logic. According to the court, a jury conceivably could have determined there was a conspiracy between Staff and Williams. Of course he was not charged with such a conspiracy. If there was a possibility, one would expect the Appeals Court to send the case back to the trial court for a new trial. This would permit the defense to present evidence on this new alleged conspiracy and focus on the testimony of Williams, whom the jury previously had not believed.

Instead, the court made the decision itself and disregarded the objections that it was prejudicial to convict Staff on a conspiracy allegation not in the indictment and to put him in the court with two other defendants he did not know. Of course, it was prejudicial! His attorneys didn't get to address this new conspiracy, and somehow Staff had been sitting in a courtroom with two other "joint defendants" conceded not to have anything to do with him. The court wrapped up its dismissal of these objections under the rubic of the legal doctrine of permissible "variance" and cited all kinds of legal authority. What was lacking in the opinion was common sense and justice.

The bottom line is that the court reversed the trial court's action and reinstated the conviction for Hilaire. When it came time for the sentencing, he was given 32 months. By comparison, Williams, who had been falsifying documents since 1997, was sentenced to 18 months. This lesser sentence was the result of his "cooperation." This Kafkaesque rendering of justice results from another anomaly of our criminal justice system. Those individuals (like Staff) who believe they are innocent will usually go to trial. If for any reason they are convicted, rightly or wrongly, their sentences will be heavier that those who have pled guilty, even when the latter are truly the bad guys.

In addition to being convicted through a bizarre process and set of rules that had evolved to convict drug lords, Staff also was a victim of the political times. The circuit court's opinion was issued in 2009, at the height of the mortgage crisis when the media was filled with outrage over the lack of criminal accountability by lenders. The conviction of "small fry" mortgage officials in Denver was something for the government to offer up to the press even if the niceties of legal process and fairness were sacrificed.

Staff's attorney requested that he be sent to a prison close to his family in Colorado. The response was to send him to Duluth, Minnesota, not only some distance from Denver but also probably the coldest city in the country that hosts a federal penitentiary. The Feds did not appreciate the cruel irony of assigning someone who so detested the cold to Duluth.

A few months after his sentencing in May 2010, I was told by Mike Kelly that Staff was in prison. I immediately retrieved a number of Denver-based articles and the various court decisions to get a picture of what had happened. I then decided to check the Inmate Locator at the Bureau of Prisons website to see where he was held. After I entered his name and clicked on the Search button, up popped the message "Stafford A. Hilaire Deceased." Stunned, I re-entered the name and received the same message.

Staff died from a cerebral hemorrhage resulting from thrombotic thrombocytopenia purpura (TTP), a rare disorder of the blood-coagulation system that causes extensive microscopic clots to form. As to the cause of death and place of death, the hospital in Duluth to which he was admitted three days before he died, there is certainty. There is considerably less certainty regarding the events leading up to the death. I have been able to piece together the following. About ten days before his admittance he had a flu-like episode that was treated with Ibuprofen. A subsequent rash on his arms and legs apparently was misdiagnosed and not recognized as symptoms of TTP. Based on this, it is questionable whether he received proper treatment for his condition in prison, and he probably was sent to the hospital too late. According to medical authorities, with an effective plasma exchange, the fatality rate for TTP can be as low as 10% after 6 months and without it the rate is about 90%. While we will never know all the facts, all evidence points to the conclusion that it is a death that should've been avoided.

I've lost many friends and fellow players over the years, but the circumstances of Stafford's death stand out as uniquely sad and unfair. I'm left with a sense of outrage and feel we all bear responsibility since I believe it was our justice system that incarcerated him under questionable circumstances and then failed to provide him the required medical care. I particularly am saddened that I'll never again have the opportunity to hear that courtly voice of his debate the topic of weather or share memories of winning one for the Governor.

Chapter Eighteen

A Simple Game

Once we'd decided to leave New York, my wife Susanne offered to type my resume for application to Chicago firms. When she reached my notes for the typically brief "Interests and Hobbies" section, she suddenly burst into laughter and exclaimed: "'Captain of the New York Lawyers' A League Basketball Champion!' *Who* is going to care about that?" I defensively responded that "it was a conversation starter and that it might catch the attention of some firm." As it turned out, the tactic for distinguishing my application from the rest of the pile succeeded at bit too well. It was the first topic that virtually every firm in Chicago mentioned when they contacted me: "How is the jump shot doing?" "How has the game been recently?" When Sheldon Fink of Sonnenschein Carlin Nath and Rosenthal met me in New York, he greeted me with "in view of the basketball reference, I expected you to be taller."

"I Did Not Play Guard at Notre Dame"

After interviewing a number of firms, I decided to accept an offer from Sonnenchein, a firm about half the size of Dewey which had grown substantially in recent years. The firm also had the distinction of being one of the "highest" law firms in the world with offices sitting on the 80th and 81st floors of the Sears Tower. According to Dick Roddewig and Dean Hagan, my Notre Dame friends who had been playing in the Chicago Lawyers' League for about five years, the Sonnenschein team was a mediocre one that could "use some help." Shortly before the move, Dick repeated to me a conversation he'd overheard one evening at the gym. A Sonnenschein player had commented to a friend that "the team's going to be good next year," adding "we're getting a guy who had played guard at Notre Dame!" I realized my story was outsized, and if I didn't manage expectations my anticipated arrival could only disappoint. Since it was about two months before my first day, there seemed little I could do immediately—sending a memo to the firm to shrink the story didn't seem like a feasible solution.

Arriving at the firm on April 16, 1979, I was a little apprehensive about how I'd be welcomed, given the inflated proportions of the rumor. The first few visitors thankfully were not interested in the topic. These included the other three partners in the Tax Area, Lou Freeman, Steve Swibel and Abe Fishman, and associate Doug Fisher, another Dewey alumnus who had moved about a year earlier. In late morning, an unfamiliar face peeked into the office and introduced himself as Rob Mark, the captain of the basketball team. Somewhat sheepishly, undoubtedly because he knew the answer after looking at me, he posed the question: "Did you play for Notre Dame?" Prepared for the question, I told him that I hadn't, but that I was a decent player and thought I could help out the team. We chatted a little about the players and the prospects for next season. Since no one else asked me whether I had played at Notre Dame, I am sure that Rob spread the disappointing word that the team was not to field a hoopster magician on the court next fall.

I was not finished, though, with the topic of basketball. In early afternoon I was visited by Harold Shapiro, who occupied the corner office down the hall from me. One of the leading attorneys in the partnership who later served as the firm's first chairman, Harold was an engaging presence and, as I was to discover, a devoted player himself. Straddling the legal and academic worlds, he taught a course at Northwestern Law School on corporate finance when not practicing at Sonnenschein where he represented such clients as Allstate. Sporting his signature bow tie and his impish smile, Shapiro welcomed me to the firm, and soon the discussion moved to basketball. In his early 50's, Harold told me that he still played, primarily with an older crowd at the Standard Club, although occasionally he made it to a firm game. He concluded with an observation that I was to hear frequently through the years: "it's a simple game—you have a round ball and it goes through a hoop 10 feet high."

As I reflected on the day, it was clear that even if the rumor about playing at Notre Dame had been deflated, there nevertheless were expectations about what I might contribute. Frankly my relative neglect of the game during the past year didn't put me in great shape to meet those expectations. At age 31 I faced a re-start and looked around for a forum, preferably in Evanston where Susanne and I had bought a modest home, to get my game back.

The Oak Ave Pick-up Game

I wandered around to a couple of the neighborhood parks, but didn't find any games that seemed designed for someone 31. Thanks to a chance encounter at the local Y, I heard about an outdoor game nearby where the guys were generally my age.

I showed up promptly at 11 a.m. the following Saturday and found a group of about 10 guys warming up. Out on the court, I confirmed my suspicion that I had work ahead if I hoped to contribute next season. After we finished, a guy whom everyone called "Gov" came over to me and asked me if I had graduated from Notre Dame—I was wearing an ND shirt. He was John Govreau, Class of 1962, and my initial estimation of his strong skills multiplied as I calculated he was performing at the "advanced" age of 38 or 39. Gov then diplomatically commented: "Your timing seemed to be off today, but I can see that you can play." He effectively robbed me of any excuses for not returning to form. My search was over. The morning's session confirmed I'd found a new basketball home.

After that day I became a regular at the Oak Ave game. Situated at the end of a cul de sac, the court was part of the Larimer Park, which included children's play equipment and a baseball diamond. Our court was located in a parcel that jutted out from the main part of the park and was nestled against fences separating adjacent residences on two sides with the cul de sac forming a third side. The trees populating the three sides added to the sense of intimacy of the court. The court also had the advantage of offering a playing companion for my son Brendan, Dickie Gleason. Soon our Saturday mornings began with a father-son bicycle jaunt to the park.

The court rules were that winners remained on the court, and since there were frequently extra players, a premium attached to landing on a team that played well together. The first ten guys to arrive shot free throws to determine the initial teams. Not surprisingly, being among the first ten was a coveted position, resulting in a curious pattern over the course of the summer. On each successive week-end, guys would arrive slightly earlier so that by October ten guys would be shooting free throws at eight a.m. Next April we would return to an eleven a.m. starting time, and the pattern would be repeated.

The Oak Ave court returned me happily to an outdoor game with a gang just like I'd had at St. Paul School in Anaconda as a kid. But there was a difference from the St. Paul game or for that matter any other game I had played the previous 25 years. Up to that point, I shared certain bonds in my everyday life with the other guys on the court. We were from the same streets in my home town, fellow students at a university or colleagues in a law firm. In contrast, the Oak Ave gang's common bond was sharing a basketball court on weekend mornings. While a few knew each other outside the court, for the most part we were strangers in our everyday life. So common to pick-up basketball, we mostly knew each other by our first names. We didn't need to know last names or professional occupations to develop chemistry on the court. Over the next several decades, I was to experience again and again these central elements of pick-up basketball—strangers (or at least semi-strangers) coming together to play some hoops.

The core group was about 10 or 12 thirty-something guys, many with the sorts of quirks that build the loyalties and attachments turning a bunch of players into friends and loyal rivals. Besides myself, I was to add one more to the core when I convinced my old roommate John Gavin to make the Saturday trip from Chicago's lakefront to Evanston.

Any conversation about the group must begin with the unofficial commissioner John Herron, an advertising guy and oldster at 37 when I joined.

A long-time veteran of outdoor pick-up basketball in Evanston, John assumed numerous roles at our weekend morning outings: on-court arbiter of the rules, the voice that settled disputes (unless he was one of the protagonists), scheduler and most importantly czar of the court towel brigade. When rain caused the court to be too slippery, everyone was told to show up early with a towel (and John always brought several). Anyone wandering into the park on those mornings would be greeted with the sight of middle aged men on their hands and knees assiduously drying asphalt. The brigade assured that the slippery rain-soaked court was made bone dry when the first shot was taken. On the court, John displayed impressive offensive skills with a mid- to long-range jump shot that projected a high arc after release. He was no slacker on defense either, being well versed in the fundamentals as a result of growing up playing ball with several brothers in Michigan. Incidentally, commissioner Herron <u>did</u> know everyone's last name.

For the best shooter award of the group, however, John was aced out by Sam Ramenofsky, who taught econometrics at the Loyola Business School. Sam probably weighed in at 230 pounds or so, distributed over a 5'10" frame, and so at first impression he did not appear to be an on-court threat. Despite the poundage, he had a deadly set shot with a quick release from the 15 to 20 feet range and was remarkably mobile.

He reminds me of the character Billy Hoyle, played by Woody Harrelson, in *White Men Can't Jump*, whose appearance would lull an opponent into over-confidence. John Herron remembers playing with Sam in the corporate league where within a few minutes the opposing team would be jumping all over the player assigned to Sam to "guard that guy," the one they initially had dismissed as not being much of a threat. We regulars knew better, and it was always considered a bonus to end up on Sam's team. That required us to make our first free throw when we shot to determine the first two teams because Sam always made his.

I later learned that Sam had by far the most impressive athletic resume among us. Competing in three sports at the mammoth LaSalle Peru Township High School with its 3,000 students, he garnered first team selection in football playing center and honorable mention in basketball. Sam proceeded to play football at Iowa State where he was captain of the freshmen team and twice won Big Eight academic all-conference honors, combining excellence on the gridiron at offensive guard and defensive lineman and in the classroom as a math major. He left behind the football competition, but his basketball remained with him while pursuing his Ph.D. at Oklahoma State. His graduate school team, which won the university intramural league, defeated the school's freshman team.

As in all informal playground sports, our game had its share of contention. Occasionally it might be a withering criticisms of some action by a teammate, but in most instances it was a "debate" over calls in these referee-less contests. In the world of pick-up ball, the tradition is that a player has the right to call a foul or infraction committed against him, but the precept that the call is to be accepted by the offender truly is more honored in the breach than the observance. This was part of the experience, and memorable arguments were fondly rehashed for years by the participants. Moreover, as John Herron reminds us, the discord never endured as we always left the court friends.

In addition to me, Gov and Dick Gleason, known as "Mad Dog," were frequent participants in the disputes. My fellow ND alum Gov had a smooth drive from the top of the key through the paint and always managed to get the shot up in the midst of traffic without being blocked. Those who defended him insist to this day that an additional step, a lateral move, was part of the drive. Gov of course always denied the traveling call. We did not have the luxury of instant replay to settle the travelling allegations, and who would have wanted it since it would have deprived us of all the pleasure of arguing the point. Ironically, we also could not have foreseen how inconsequential travelling would become. In the NBA today, travelling is not an infraction unless the player flagrantly picks up the ball and walks down the court with it.

"Mad Dog" Gleason was a short, extremely quick guard, who seemed to be everywhere. One of the youngest among the core group, Dick had the easiest commute to our court—he lived across the street. The best ball hawker among us, Mad Dog frequently found himself in the middle of a dispute as to whether his steal was accompanied by a foul, an issue not easily resolved in view of the wildly differing perspectives of the principals. When not stealing the ball, Dick worked as a pipefitter. Acting upon his father's paternal career "counseling," Dick added night law school to his busy schedule of pipefitting, raising two children and playing basketball. A trial lawyer for the past 30 years, his exuberance about his practice is undeniable, a rare posture for lawyers these days and reflective of his spirit on the court. He continued on the basketball courts into his 50's when he decided to permanently restrict Mad Dog to his kennel.

Pathologist Dr. Melvin Schwartz, frequently referred to as Dr. Mel, was the only physician among us. To Sam's family he was Dr. Doom because of his specialty. Mel was built solidly and could be quite an obstacle to driving on the court. When not in the game, Mel in jest would "generously" provide diagnostic opinions of his fellow players, which became a source of amusement among us. Being deprived of the privilege of an undertaker as part of the group, Mel at times served as a suitable substitute.

Since the group was not particularly tall, I ended up playing most of that summer around the basket, particularly facing off against Frank Holmes. An inch or two taller than me with long arms and a canny sense of timing, he was an outstanding rebounder and defender. Frank was soft spoken, and I do not remember him ever being involved in arguments. His play rarely generated any questioning—he went straight up on defense, and all blocked shots were clean.

As my timing improved, my offense of inside play and drives began to resemble my New York days. Most satisfyingly, my rebounding returned to form, as I occasionally heard from someone on the opposing team as a game began what was music to my ears: "Keep Pat off the boards." As my conditioning improved, the intensity factor correspondingly notched up. I didn't realize how much the intense style was recognized by the others until Susanne showed up one day. A number of them went over to introduce themselves to meet the wife of the guy who was such a fanatic on the court!

Pick-up Basketball—a Social Game

All of us hoopsters have played in some form of organized league at one time or another. But what really has defined our basketball life has been the pick-up game. Nick Bogard, a friend who played on the Princeton freshman team during the Bill Bradley era, has commented that pick-up basketball is the game that other athletes choose to play in their leisure. Why did the Oak Ave gang (and thousands like them on courts around the world) so love this game? This popularity is not restricted to the U.S. as interest in playing the game has grown exponentially overseas. Friends who've lived abroad have described their relative ease in finding a game. Is there more to this than a "simple game," as Harold Shapiro described it?

We can start with the ball itself. The contemporary artist Jeff Koons famously constructed a mixed media structure that features three basketballs suspended in a water tank with 50% of each ball below the water level. According to Koons, he chose the basketballs for his tank because of their "inflatability," which he relates to the human experience of being alive. While his is the view of the artist and not necessarily of the player, the amount of air compressed in the 29 ½ inches circular frame provides the right level of buoyancy to enable us to do some of our favorite things with the ball such as dribbling, bounce passing and banking it off the back board. Additionally, the dimpled leather (or more commonly today synthetic leather) and grooves of the exterior enhance the functional control of the ball and provide an aesthetic feel as the ball slides through our fingers when we shoot or pass or momentarily rotate it in our hands.

The air, the size and the feel of the ball combine to establish a unique rapport with the player. As we dribble, pass or shoot, the ball becomes an extension of our body. Julius Irving observed that the ball seemed like a yo-yo in the hands of Pete Maravich, whom he considered the most remarkable player of his era. All of us similarly have aspired to transform that ball into a yo-yo.

A deft drive or a brilliant pass can bring great personal satisfaction, but fundamentally the game is about putting the ball in the basket. When the lofted ball drops through the net, the body and the mind savor the moment. Erica Jong, the author of the heavy breathing novel, *Fear of Flying*, has described it as a "visceral" experience, "something very satisfying about that ball going through the hole." While she retreats somewhat from her metaphor in stating that she "wouldn't go so far as to say it recreates the sexual experience," her comments do suggest a powerful satisfaction. What I think Jong attempted to capture is that feeling of sensuous gratification at the moment the ball goes through the hoop with "nothing but net," or, in the jargon of a previous generation, "as a swish," whether it occurs in a critical moment of a game or during a solitary shoot around.

While the ball has some unique characteristics, what truly attracts players worldwide is the game being played with that ball. The ease of putting a game together is a refrain heard often. As to the number of players, there is considerable flexibility in that any number between two and ten will work. Similarly, the amount of equipment is minimal—a ball, sneakers and simple attire allowing easy movement. A hoop is needed, but most players have access to that, whether it is a garage, a playground or a park. Finally, in contrast with many games, the amount of required physical space is modest.

Once the game begins, the most striking aspect of the play, though, is its social nature. For the entirety of the game, the players weave around in close proximity to each other. It's a game of considerable contact among the players, but not because physical contact is the essence of the game as in football. Rather, in such close quarters where there is driving, picking, defending and rebounding, players' bodies routinely meet or even collide. Other sports feature close personal interaction during the game, such as football and soccer. What distinguishes basketball is that the interaction is constant and involves everyone on the court at all times.

This proximity irresistibly leads to considerable chatter among the players. Some of it is functional as players endeavor to work together by calling out picks and switches, signaling openings in the defense and indicating to a teammate that he's in position to grab the rebound. Following a change in possessions, two or more players can discuss strategy as they saunter down the court towards the opposite basket. At a more elevated decibel level, there are the spontaneous outbursts. The group may erupt in applause for a particularly spectacular play; for the more mundane goal, there may be a teammate, or even the defender, congratulating the shooter for a "good shot." A bad play may lead to encouraging words by teammates, while too many bad plays or shots may lead to some audible questioning.

As happened occasionally at Oak Ave, tempers may flare over a hard foul or a disputed call, sometimes leading to an unscheduled stop in the action. Banter is common, including the feigned hostility of the trash talking. Sometimes the only voice heard is that coming from the frustrated player unhappy over his missed shot or bonehead play: "Pat, what are you doing?" "I might as well go home if I am not going to play this game." "Oh, George!" The ostensible audience for these comments is the person himself, but they are loud enough to inform others that he understands he's screwed up.

The communication may not always be verbal—it may be pointing to a position or waving to indicate there is an opening on the floor or even a nod or a wink. The conversation continues to flow during time-outs or breaks between games, usually focused on certain aspects of the game but it also might gravitate to other topics such as the recent Bulls game or even the hottest current political topic, local or national.

Whatever the form, communication is built into the fabric of the game, with the result that playing becomes a social experience as well as an athletic one, even if we don't know everyone's last name or where they spend their time Monday through Friday. That is why the Saturday morning pick-up game has become the satisfying highlight of the week for so many of us.

A Firm with a Great Art Collection and an Unremarkable Basketball Team

It had been a productive summer, so when October rolled around I felt ready to face my new Sonnenschein teammates—not as a former Notre Dame guard as they'd hoped—but a decent player ready to give them the best I had to offer. Our first practice at the Standard Club's smallish gym within the confines of the elegant club gave me a chance to size up my new team. It seemed to me that the nucleus of the team was Mark, Michael Guthrie, Jim Lourgos and myself. Mark, a veteran of the intramural leagues at Brown University and University of Chicago law school, was introduced to the game playing at a Jewish league in grade school in Des Moines, Iowa. Guthrie, an African-American from Gary Indiana and a classmate of mine at Harvard Law, was an accomplished point guard. Lourgos was our ringer—a 6'4" center sole practitioner who had been assigned by the League to us.

Harold Shapiro also showed up for the practice and held his own among a group 20 years younger. I had a conversation with him in the locker room after practice in which I complimented him for the 50-year-old body keeping up with the younger guys. Appreciating the comment, he did lament: "It's the legs, Pat, they're the first to go." He also confessed that he didn't intend to play during the season with the "younger guys."

Rob Mark summarized best the five seasons playing Sonnenschein basketball: "We were unremarkable." Unlike certain other firms, he continued, Sonnenschein could not be accused of recruiting good basketball players out of law school. "They were more interested in adding to their art collection," he deadpanned. And a fine art collection it was, hanging on the stark white walls of the firm so that a visitor had the sense of walking through an art gallery. Spearheaded by corporate partner Julius Lewis, who subsequently became a life trustee of the Chicago Art Institute, the collection was significant enough that the

214

firm published a catalog of its impressive holdings, today available on Amazon. While I think Rob's comments about the firm and basketball are accurate, I do think that coming to the firm with some basketball skills was a plus for me, if for no other reason than it was a basis for landing within Shapiro's orbit.

Our basketball record hovered around .500, and we routinely lost to the powerhouses of the league, which included Kirkland and Ellis and Ross Hardies. Playing against Kirkland took me back to my law school days seven years earlier since one of its stalwarts was Bill Fraumann, who had starred at Hemenway Gym. Only one game of those years sticks out in my memory. Our opponent was Ross Hardies, led by conceivably the best player in the league, Fred Mattlin. In one of his team's victories, he scored 34 of the team's 40 points. Amazingly, we were still in the game in the waning minutes and with about 15 seconds to go the score was tied with us in possession. After a time-out, I received the ball on the inbound pass and dribbled around at the three point line to kill the clock. It served us well that day, and thanks to a solid pick by Lourgos, the lane was open when I drove to the basket to convert just before the buzzer. With the team victory, the basketball squad made it into the pages of the firm's *Daily Bulletin*, a rare event. It also was nice to get a win against the team of my old N.D. housemate Dick Roddewig because frankly we suffered numerous losses against them during those years.

Virtually all our games for the Lawyers' League were played at the De Paul Settlement, located on Halsted Street at Webster in the DePaul area, named after the eponymous university that is the bedrock of the neighborhood. The DePaul Settlement and Day Nursery was founded in 1915 to provide childcare services for working mothers. Built in 1958, the gym housed two full courts that probably exceeded in quality any of the gyms I saw in New York, even those with the more prestigious addresses. With the close proximity to the Fullerton stop of the CTA El, which serviced the Howard (now Red) line and the Ravenswood (now Brown), the El was our mode of transportation to and from the games. Standing in the bitter cold on the Fullerton platform waiting for our post game evening ride home with fellow Evanston residents, Ralph Loomis and Pat Moran, is a scene that has not left my memory.

In addition, there was an Open Lawyers' League on Sundays with no restrictions as to firm affiliation. A group of Sonnenschein players combined with a few other attorneys, including Jim Dill, an outstanding player who worked at Allstate, to compete in that league. With more big guys underneath, I found the need to change up my role, setting up more on the outside at the top of the key. From there I did a considerable amount of driving, which could lead to a lay-up or an easy pass to a wide-open Dill or Lourgos if the drive was cut off through switching or double-teaming. Now in my early to mid-30's, I was realizing what older athletes already knew: to keep performing and enjoying a team sport you've got to adapt to the needs of your team, an observation that would later be modified and expanded to include adaptation to an aging body.

The Open League was played in a variety of venues, including the Settlement House as well as a couple in my neighborhood, the YMCA and Evanston's Robert Crown Recreation Center. To my mind, the most notable of our courts was the Angel Guardian Gym, located in the northern part of Chicago. It had once served as a gym for an orphanage that was in operation at the site from 1865 until the mid-1970's. It now served as the practice gym for the Chicago Bulls. Ignoring the fact that it was "old," "dingy," "darkened," "cramped," and "cold," according to various press accounts, we basked in the glory of sharing the gym with the Bulls. Admittedly, the typical Chicagoan would not have been impressed with this news in our early Chicago years, but then the Bulls picked Michael Jordan in the 1984 draft and things changed.

Of all my teammates during those Chicago years, my strongest recollections are of our "ringer," Jim Lourgos. A son of Chicago, he had grown up in or near the city in an interesting mix of environments. His high school basketball years were spread out over three schools. Sophomore year was spent at South Shore High School, once a highly regarded school in the midst of decline. That year coincided with the movement of gangs into the area so that some of their games at schools controlled by rival gangs were played before empty stands behind locked doors. For his junior year he played at West Morton High School in Berwyn, a district in which his parents had a residence, and his senior year was spent back in the city.

Besides playing basketball and practicing law as a sole practitioner in the Greektown part of Chicago, Jim invested in real estate. A particularly good investment was a building at 3639 North Sheffield Street, whose location faced the right field fence of the Cub's Wrigley Field. When the Cubs qualified for the play-offs in 1984 after a 40 year absence from post-season play, he and his partners were approached to rent out their roof for a relaxing and excellent view of the series being played across the street. Despite the difficult access to the roof through a narrow ladder, the party was thrilled with their "special seats," which led Jim to a terrific idea for a business opportunity. After an extensive renovation of the building, 3639 Wrigley Rooftop was launched with a capacity of more than 200 patrons. They were to be served exquisite meals and drink while they watched the game in intimate and friendly surroundings.

The business was extremely successful—too successful. As the Cubs management from their box seats in the ballpark peered over the right field fence, they saw potentially lost revenue. The situation grew contentious after the Cubs installed a sign atop the right field bleachers, which partially blocked the view for Jim's clientele. Litigation ensued. Jim faced further challenges in 2013 when the Cubs announced a renovation plan that included a major video scoreboard off that right field fence. Recognizing that continued ownership was to be a rocky road, Jim and his partners decided to accept an offer from the Cubs for a buy-out.

Two Special Partners

While Sonnenschein was tolerant but not particularly invested in the success of their team, two partners were the exception. One was Shapiro. The other was Shelley Fink, the head of the tax practice who had introduced me to the firm when we met in New York. They were proud of the art collection, but they probably would have concurred with a recruitment strategy that gave at least a little weight to hoops skills. Shelley was 48 when we met, personable and quite interested in sports. He'd had perhaps the most illustrious athletic career among the Sonnenschein partners, including playing basketball for one of the strongest Chicago area high school teams, followed by freshman basketball at the University of Wisconsin. One of his high school teammates was Leonard "Whitey" Pearson who went on to play for the University of Kentucky. Shelley's primary love, though, was baseball, and he made his mark on the diamond as a three year starter at Wisconsin. He played shortstop until the arrival of the future American League batting champion shortstop Harvey Kuenn, at which point Shelley was shifted to second base to be Kuenn's double play partner.

Growing up in Chicago's West Rogers Park area, still semi-rural in the late 1930's and early 1940's, Shelley played basketball in rather primitive conditions at various makeshift baskets until he entered Senn High School. At a coaches' clinic the prior summer, the high school coach had been taught a "scientific" approach to selecting players. The prospects had to undergo a battery of drills and tests, nearly all of which according to Shelley had nothing to do with basketball. Fortunately for him, he was adept at executing the tests and was selected. The process, however, was not without its tense moments. One test required running down the court with a crude peg and dropping it in three coffee cans. A miss meant test failure. One can wobbled with one of Shelley's drops and nearly toppled but it eventually righted itself. By that stroke of luck, he reckons, he was launched onto basketball for his high school varsity, Wisconsin freshman, and Army teams, as well as 30 years of Standard Club basketball until the age of 75.

One of Shelley's more interesting chapters of play was the armed services basketball. After college, he was assigned to the Fifth Army Headquarters Division located on the South Side of Chicago. Shortly after he arrived, he received a call from his fraternity brother, Ron Weisner, a star guard on the Wisconsin basketball team who had been drafted by the Milwaukee Hawks. Weisner was looking for an opening at Headquarters, and Shelley discovered that the recreational director post was vacant, primarily because the program was moribund. Most of the soldiers at Headquarters lived with their families so at the end of the day they headed home with no interest in participating in army-sponsored activities. As a result, the recreational account was growing nicely with regular deposits and few expenses. Newly appointed as Headquarter's recreational director, Weisner began to explore how he could put this windfall to good use.

He proposed the establishment of a basketball team to compete in the armed forces competition. As Montana coaches Pat Curran and George Scott had learned, this competition, with its origins in the early part of the century, commanded considerable attention in the 1940's and 1950's. It was an easy sell to the top brass. Director Weisner wasn't done; he wanted a team that could win and discovered that Headquarters had the roster of all the Fifth Division's new recruits. He scoured it for prominent basketball players who might be relocated to Headquarters, and with his company commander's consent, landed a trove of great players: Dick Rosenthal, former All-American from Notre Dame who had been playing for the NBA Fort Wayne Pistons, Boris Nachamkin, a New York University star who had been with the Rochester Royals and Don Lance from Rice, also an NBA draftee.

Weisner and these guys became the nucleus of the team, and the rest of the players, including Shelley, rotated to fill the fifth spot. As it turns out, they were not the only unit stockpiling basketball stars. In one of their first games, they found the opposing team was comprised principally of the members of the Kentucky team which had won the NCAA championship. Headquarters fell short of winning the championship, but for Shelley it was a memorable experience to find himself a teammate of such an illustrious group.

Harold Shapiro could not rival Shelley's basketball background, but he more than compensated for that deficit with passionate engagement. Since his office was just a few doors down from mine, he would frequently stop by to review some recent development in the Chicago sports scene, the fortunes of the firm's team or some incident from the Standard Club where he played three times a week. His insights were typically philosophical, and to no surprise, I always was reminded of his favorite maxim about the simple game.

Inspired by the annual firm touch football game he organized, he and I began to plan a Partners/Associates game, which was played at the Angel Guardian gym one Sunday afternoon in early 1981. Harold and Shelley were the oldest participants in the game. Aided by a number of younger partners with athletic skills who supplemented the experience of the two, the Partners kept the game close till the end. Capped off with a post-game lunch with wives and children, it epitomized the collegial spirit of the firm that not only valued its art but also could rally around its teams.

Introducing My Sons to the Game

My years in Chicago coincided with my young sons' introduction to the game. Our first, Brendan, arrived soon after we moved to Chicago. Susanne brought baby Brendan along to watch the team play at the Evanston Y where he mostly expressed his fan appreciation by riveting his attention on the bright ceiling lights above the floor. One day, his gaze settled on me just as I was readying a shot at the free throw line, and he erupted with a loud "Dah!" of recognition. What dad wouldn't be distracted? I can't quite recall if I made the shot, but my heart was melted by the inaugural cheer of a new family fan.

As he got older, Brendan came to many of my games without his mother and typically got itchy watching from his stroller on the sidelines. One day while coping with the dual tasks of his entertainment and running onto the floor to play, I inadvertently made him giggle while wiping my face with a towel. I initially was puzzled by his sudden laughter, but I discovered what most grandmothers and strangers in supermarkets know about kids—a good game of peek-a-boo goes a long way to charm a kid. By the time Brendan reached two, he'd happily sit on the bench to watch. A cute kid with a mop of light brown hair, he soon caught the attention of the young women who accompanied their boyfriends to watch. More often than not, when I would glance over at the bench to see if he was okay, he would be planted between two attractive young women drinking a can of Coke or eating some delicious snack they'd purchased for him at the vending machine.

Our gym excursion party increased to three with the arrival of Colin. Not reliably delighted to be included, he learned how to be a fan from his older brother, who at times could be seen pushing the stroller back and forth on the sidelines. Each of these guys now have kids whom they have brought to their own games so the beat goes on. Obviously, one can introduce a son or daughter to competitive sports by treating them to a professional game or a backyard tutorial, but I think there is something special about an introduction where they see their father (or mother) playing. As part of that introduction, the guys also saw me cope with injury from time to time—all part of the game.

Weekend Warrior Injuries

No one gets to play basketball forever injury-free. The clash of bodies, stops and starts, jumping, miscues and flailing arms mean eventually you're going to get sidelined. I have to admit that I still haven't made peace with that fact and always react by cursing the Fates. Learning the discipline and patience needed to do what it takes to recover was an unanticipated lesson about playing the game, and one I've had to learn over and over again.

One summer game in '81, I was guarding Dr. Mel a bit too overzealously and he moved in a direction I hadn't anticipated. We collided with my right leg above the knee suffering the brunt of the impact. I felt a sharp pain and went to the sidelines as it became clear to me that I was finished for the day. What did not enter my mind was that I was finished for the indefinite future. I managed to bicycle home, but over the course of the weekend the bump on my right leg ballooned to resemble a half-cantaloupe and I began to limp. After several days of no improvement, I began to confront the need to overcome my aversion to seeking medical help. A doctor's visit was unavoidable. Paul Miller, a partner a few doors down from me, came to my rescue with a recommendation of Dr. Leonard Weinstein, just five blocks from the office.

After signing in, I sat on a bed with my suit trousers off when he entered the room. A grandfatherly type about 65, his initial comment was: "What big legs you have! Do you play football?" He then proceeded to examine the multi-hued injury. "Hematoma" he pronounced, adding that it was one of the largest swellings he'd seen. He then proceeded with a medical explanation. What really caught my attention was his warning the injury could lead to calcification with the effect of bone-like tissue in the muscle. A half cast would be necessary. Susanne, home with one small boy, wasn't delighted to add me to her list of dependents. I was ordered to use crutches and couldn't drive.

Recovery entailed soaking the leg nightly while working on gradually bending it. As I entered the tub that first night with two-year-old Brendan as my cheering squad, I immediately knew after the first tortuous attempt that I had a long project ahead of me—I was at a measly 25 degrees. As I continued the nightly ritual with Brendan providing support, the swelling slowly decreased and the degrees increased. By early December I finally reached 90 degrees. When I visited Weinstein to show my progress, my immediate question was "when can I return to basketball." With a friendly scowl, he impatiently remarked "why don't you take up swimming?" But after another month employing his regimen of strengthening, he reluctantly gave me the green light to return to the basketball court for the first time in six months.

My first game back was at DePaul for a Sunday Open League contest. I was quite tentative and basically settled for jump shots as I was hesitant to put significant pressure on the leg. After the game, Jim Dill came up to me and asked how I felt, and I responded not badly since I had not pushed myself. "Yes," he added, "you were a ghost of your former self." Over the next couple of games, I gradually regained my confidence to get more involved in the mix of the game. The closing chapter on the injury occurred a couple of months later when I returned to the Saturday morning Evanston basketball. Dr. Mel came over to ask how I was doing and apologized for putting me out for such a long period. I assured him that the fault was 100% mine! After our last game he commented that I seemed to have recovered completely, but then cautioned: "Five years from now, you won't be able to recover from such an injury."

Weinstein's comments in his office about my calves lead me to a brief digression since I happen to have large calves (some might call them freakishly large), attracting comment since high school days. At their most robust, they measured 16 ½ inches. Years ago a proprietor at our health club suggested I enter a "leg profile contest." I'd never heard of such a contest, but the proposal caused much hilarity when reported to Susanne, primarily because we couldn't figure out what I would do with the rest of my body. Because I have springy legs and have always been a jumper, I had automatically assumed there was a causal relationship between the two. Moreover, I had thought that wearing those ankle weights in high school in emulation of Wayne Estes was related to the calf size and the jumping ability. As time has taken a toll on my jumping ability and muscle mass somewhat has waned, I've grown curious about the relationship. I've learned that calf size is an inconsistent predictor of jumping ability. I've seen plenty of skinny-legged players who can soar and well-muscled ones who are earth-bound. The available literature focuses on issues of the relative proportion of fast- and slow-twitch muscles rather than simple mass. The science also isn't clear whether ankle weights can add to vertical leap although I would like to think they do to vindicate all those hours wearing them (and embarrassing my sister and cousin).

My second injury confirmed that I'd learned nothing from the first incident. It was at a low-stakes volleyball game at a family reunion picnic with participants ranging in age from 10 to 70. I entered the game with a small voice in my head reminding me that heroics were not required and warning me the wet grass would be slippery. It didn't take me long to ignore that voice. Stretching to play a ball near the line, my feet skidded in opposite directions until I felt an intense pain on my left knee. I spent the remainder of the vacation on crutches, leaving the job of entertaining our guys to Susanne.

Back in Chicago, Dr. Weinstein informed me that I had a partial tear of the ligaments in the knee. Since it was a partial tear and being conservative on medical matters, he preferred to let it heal without surgery. As we drove away from Michael Reese that following day with another half cast and now with two boys in the back of the car, a disgruntled Susanne pronounced: "One more major injury, and I think that should be it for basketball." I didn't return to basketball for nine months and missed the entire season as the bathtub therapy (even with the cheerleading of two sons) moved more slowly.

The following April I headed over on the bike with Brendan to play with the beloved Oak Ave group. No one was there! I waited around for about 45 minutes and concluded that there was to be no game. Later I put in a call to John Herron to check on the status of the game. They had changed the venue, he told me: "the game had become too popular so at times one might have to sit through three games after losing." The new site at the Ridgeville Park on the corner of Ridge Avenue and South Boulevard had a safety valve since there were two courts. But it was not the same. With the lack of trees and buildings in close proximity, that sense of intimacy of the old court was missing. The days of our idyllic cul-de-sac games were over.

Goodbye Chicago

In mid-September 1984 I received a call from Fenton Burke, my old mentor at Dewey Ballantine, about a potential job opportunity at the Boston firm of Bingham, Dana & Gould. Because of the imminent departure of a tax partner, they were looking for someone whose credentials were similar to mine. Susanne and I made the decision to move back East when I was offered the position. Although we loved Chicago, the move made sense for a number of family reasons. After our decision, we found a house in Wellesley.

I was excited about the professional opportunities, but concerned that the camaraderie and sheer pleasure of Evanston could never be replicated. I wasn't even certain I would find a game. One afternoon I happened to run into a law school friend with ties to Boston as we both were waiting for the traffic light on Chicago's LaSalle Street. I told him about my move to Wellesley and, figuring I could use a suburban Boston basketball player's recommendation, Matt gave me the name of his brother-in-law Kevin Crowley. Kevin happened to live in our new town and played with a weekend gang. It took me several years to meet Kevin, but our meeting on the court was to be followed by nearly 10 years of weekly ball.

Shortly before I left, John Herron proposed that the group move "our" game on to racquetball, suggesting we were aging out of basketball. That proposal to retire from basketball was roundly ignored, and for the next 10 to 15 years the core of my Evanston group continued to play together at various outdoor courts. Then the retirements, voluntary and involuntary, began to reduce the group's numbers. One involuntary retiree was Sam Ramenosky, who played his last game in late 2000 before he underwent over a three-week period replacements of both his hips, undoubtedly casualties of all those years on the hard outdoor surfaces. Dick Gleason played at various courts until his mid-50's when in the middle of the game, exhibiting the old Mad Dog spirit, he found himself ready to go after a younger guy. In a decision that is difficult to place in either the voluntary or involuntary category, Dick decided it was time to leave the sneakers at home and keep the arguments confined to the courtroom. John Herron may have been the last leave the courts when at the age of 60 he looked around and didn't see any of the old gang around the hoops.

The awards for the most remarkable longevity, though, belong to Shelley Fink and Harold Shapiro. When in my late 50's, I was once called "heroic" by a 30-something friend for continuing to play, and my answer was "well let me tell you who my heroes are—there are these two guys in their 70's in Chicago…." The two continued to play two or three days a week at the Standard Club. The basketball was open to any of the Standard Club members and their guests, who included Barack Obama when he was running for the U.S. Senate, and Richard Dent, the former Hall of Famer defensive end for the Chicago Bears. Shelley recalls fondly the perfect half court bounce pass that Dent delivered to him, which he followed up with a text-book lay-up. The age of the players in the eight minute games generally ranged from 30 to 50, and on the court one could expect to find a number of the Chicago luminaries in the business, real estate and legal worlds.

As the years progressed and they entered their 70's, Shelley and Harold were the oldest left on the court and naturally ended up guarding each other. As might be expected, this intra-firm rivalry occasionally led to on-court spats. In particular, Shelley complained that Harold would grab his shirt or pants to slow him down as he tried to drive around him. Harold of course denied all such allegations. According to Shelley, his position was vindicated when at a firm event a video of a game shown to honor the two included footage showing Harold grabbing Shelley's shirt as he began to drive towards the basket. "There is the proof; that is what I have been talking about all along," declared Shelley expecting a concession from his old court rival. Harold just flashed him his engagingly mischievous grin.

These guys also served as both inspiration and deterrence whenever thoughts about quitting crossed my mind. After a bad day or evening at the gym, I might arrive home threatening to retire. My sons would then admonish me that I couldn't quit as long as "Uncle Shelley," their affectionate appellation for a man who with his wife Nellie had been important figures in their lives from birth, was still on the court. Meanwhile, neither Uncle Shelley nor Harold were inclined to retire as long as the other continued to play. Sadly, this conundrum was resolved on December 1, 2005 when Harold succumbed to a ruptured aneurism at the age of 78. He played basketball the day before he died. Shelley continued to play for a short while, but with his retirement from the firm at age 74, there were few reasons to continue to belong to the downtown Standard Club. His last noon time game occurred at the age of 75. As for me, although now free to retire with the two no longer on the court, I decided that if physically able it wouldn't be respectable for me to quit until I reached the retirement age of my two heroes.

Today, if you enter the gym in the upper levels of the Standard Club, you'll be greeted by a sign above the electronic scoreboard. In bold letters, it displays: "HAROLD D. SHAPIRO. HE WAS OUR FRIEND, OUR 'COMMISSIONER' AND A 'TRUE IRONMAN.' HE PLAYED BALL FOR 50 YEARS 1955 – 2005." Below the inscription is a photo of Harold in coat and tie with the American flag as the backdrop and the caption "A SIMPLE GAME."

Chapter Nineteen

Inspired by the Celtics

Reunited with Tom Powers

On the fourth Sunday in January 1985, I boarded a plane at O'Hare to head to Boston to begin my career the following morning at Bingham, Dana & Gould. It was a trip I made with considerably mixed emotions. We were leaving behind important ties to friends whom we knew were going to be irreplaceable. At the same time we were lured to the East by career opportunities and the chance to be closer to one of our families. The departure from the Finks was wrenching. Shelley had been a cherished mentor at the firm, navigating for me the at times bumpy road to achieving partnership. More importantly, the Finks had become close friends. Nellie and Susanne had established a close bond, and they'd been terrific "surrogate" grandparents to our children with my family in Montana and Susanne's in New York.

I also harbored a deep affection for Sonnenschein, where I'd matured as an attorney. The firm was more than generous in their acceptance of my decision to relocate as they bid me farewell with a splendid party. I also knew I was leaving a good basketball situation with the lawyers' leagues and John Herron's pick-up group. It remained to be seen what was going to be the substitute in Boston. Nevertheless, despite these reservations, there was the excitement of a new chapter in life, and I showed up at the firm the following morning energized with high hopes and ambitions.

While there was uncertainty as to where I would be playing, for someone who loved the game Boston was a marvelous basketball city in which to land—the home of the Boston Celtics. In early 1985, the Celtics were in the midst of their third iteration of greatness, referred to variously as the "Larry Bird era" or the "era of the Big 3," the formidable front line of Bird, Robert Parrish and Kevin McHale. The Celtics were the reigning champions of the NBA when I arrived and were to be perennial contenders for the next several years, capturing another title in 1986. Under the tutelage of coach Casey Jones, whom we occasionally noticed dining at our favorite Chinese restaurant in Wellesley, the team demonstrated a highly proficient commitment to the fundamentals of team basketball. It was a style upon which we veterans of the 50's and 60's had been tutored in our high school days and one that we by default incorporated, at an obvious considerably lesser skill level, in our pick-up and league games as the weekend warriors.

One aspect of our move that I happily anticipated was the chance to reunite on the court with my law school pal and Upstarts teammate Tom Powers. Since our Upstarts days, Tom had added some heft to his 6'1" frame as a result of training to run the Boston Marathon. He remained an outstanding shooter but now had added strong rebounding to his skills. Much slighter in law school where he acknowledged he'd get pushed around under the basket, he'd added significant weight and muscle mass while training for the 26.2 mile run. "When training, you are always hungry because of the energy being expended so that leads to more eating" and ironically to more weight, he told me. Tom had arrived at one of life's epiphanies: to be healthy, you had to support exercise with lots of good food.

Initially I participated in a game made up of Tom's fellow-workers at the state environmental agency. On a weekly basis, I would hop on the Red Line to the Alewife station and then complete the trip on a bus to a gym in Arlington. As time went on, Tom started making the trip more frequently from Arlington to Wellesley. Eventually, he and his wife moved to a house near us, and I can't help believing the proximity to basketball contributed to the decision. In fact, Tom scheduled the viewing of his future home around a game we were playing in a Wellesley outdoor league and did an efficient inspection decked out in his basketball attire. Following the game, he and his wife Pat met with the broker to submit their offer on the house and by midnight signed the contract. Tom still was wearing his basketball uniform.

Tom and I have enjoyed 43 years (and counting) playing together. In those pick-up games where we play on opposing teams we are just like old dance partners—we read the other's moves and know the other's strengths and weaknesses as if they were our own. When playing together, our extensive shared time on the court turns into a huge positive for each of us. We anticipate the other's next step, creating many opportunities for each of us that might not be there playing in tandem with a stranger or even someone we know well, albeit not for so many years.

A Shooter

After we closed on our house in Wellesley, I was left with the question that had lingered ever since I had decided to move to Boston—where am I going find a game?

The answer to the question arrived through a rather indirect, and surprising, route. Within a few days after the move, a neighbor knocked on the door and asked Susanne to attend a neighborhood meeting about the impending closing of the Warren Elementary School, located about two blocks from us. When she returned from the meeting smiling, she told me she had a surprise for me—she'd found a basketball game. At the end of the meeting, the women were checking their calendars for the next meeting, and the following Thursday was suggested. Joan Eastman, who lived around the corner from us, interjected that the evening would be problematic since her husband Dan played basketball on Thursdays. Susanne jumped on the comment and asked for details on the basketball. I called Dan, and we arranged to drive to the gym together on the following week.

In our eight minute ride to the Wellesley Middle School, I learned a little about Dan and the Wellesley basketball group that I was to play with for the next six years. Dan was a native of Ithaca, New York, where his father taught at Cornell University. Although about 6'3", he primarily had played guard in high school. About a year ago he'd joined this group, which offered open adult basketball on Mondays and Thursdays with a starting time of 7:00 p.m. When we arrived at the gym, there were between 25 and 30 guys shooting around, nearly all of whom seemed to be younger than me. Shortly after seven, the organizers Joey Fortini and Bob Hine, known as Hino, whistled and everyone retreated to the first row of the bleachers. After we paid our three bucks, six captains were selected to pick the teams, and they stretched out along the length of the court facing us in the stands. As names of various players were called out, they ambled to the vicinity of the captain who had selected them until the process was completed. Being a wholly unknown quantity, I was apprehensive that I faced the humiliating spectacle of being the last seated on the benches. Dan came to my rescue when he suggested to his captain that he pick "Pat." With the teams determined, four remained in the gym and two headed out the door to the level below to play in the "lower gym."

The game was considerably different than any previous pick-up ball I had played. Most surprisingly, all the teams played a zone defense. Because typically three of the players on my team were taller than me, I was assigned one of the two guard positions in the zone, a wholly unfamiliar position. A zone defense typically will restrict the advantages of athleticism, and there was plenty of that on the court. What remained as an option for the younger legs was the fast break, and many of these were not your normal break with three players occupying the lanes. Rather, a more common sight was a guy heaving the ball nearly full court to someone streaking to the basket. There obviously were former high school quarterbacks and baseball pitchers among their ranks.

I also was impressed as to how well organized the group was, considering there were about thirty guys. After the first game, the two losing teams upstairs headed downstairs with the winning teams playing the teams that came up from the lower gym game. For the third games, the two that had not played downstairs headed down. The system had the advantage of maximizing the diversity of competition on any given night and regulating who would play at what was perceived to be the inferior downstairs gym. As for the scoring, the rules were fairly conventional—one point for each basket to eleven with the proviso that is was necessary to win by two subject to a cap of 13 points. After three games, nearly half of the group left with those remaining informally putting together teams to finish off the evening.

After that first night, I knew I'd found the game that I was searching for. It was convenient to my house, well organized and certainly competitive. It wasn't clear that I would develop the same fondness that I'd had for the more intimate group of players proximate to my age that I'd left in Chicago, but I was confident it would satisfy my need for a good game. That evening also introduced me to a neighbor with whom I was to play pick-up and league basketball for the next twenty years, Dan Eastman.

The Monday/Thursday group did present a couple of challenges to my game. With the average age about ten years younger than me and a healthy number in their early 20's, I clearly was one of the older guys at 37. That age differential, and the quickness that accompanied it, was bound to have some negative impact on certain parts of my game such as driving and maneuvering around the basket. The zone defense accentuated those limitations. My "inside game" wouldn't work. I had to retreat to playing on the wings, and the jump shot became my primary offensive weapon for the first time in memory. I worked on developing the shot and soon became reasonably accurate shooting from the 15 to 18 feet range. I also discovered that I probably was a more valuable player on that court if I focused on the jump shot, something that had been emphasized to me over the years by coaches and friends to little avail. Most often I had foregone the jumper for the drive. Now at age 37 playing with younger guys, I was becoming known primarily as an outside shooter, a novel experience.

Part of my basketball DNA, the offensive rebound continued to attract me, and being positioned on the wing actually provided an advantage. From that position, I had a terrific view of where the ball would land after hitting the rim. In chasing the offensive board, inevitably I would encounter some of the big men underneath. Since I was moving in from the wing, the odds of banging bodies would increase as we contended for the rebound. The additional contact created by my presence was not always appreciated by those underneath. Thus I was faced with another project—how to move in from the wing with a little more finesse.

While I occasionally ran into some of the guys on the street, I saw them primarily at the gym. I did develop a number of friendships from the group, but for most of the players it was never entirely clear to me where they hailed from, particularly the younger ones. We were reminded from time to time, particularly if there was a large turn-out, the game was open only to Wellesley residents and those who worked for the town of Wellesley. I'm not sure how many fell into the latter category, but I did encounter a fellow player behind the wheel of a town snow plow which came awfully close to meeting the rear end of my car one snowy day. I had the sense that a number of the guys had played for the Wellesley High School team in the 1970's.

As with any group, certain players stand out. There were the Tracy brothers, Tom and Billy. Tom was an outstanding shooter at about 6'3". At about 250 pounds, Bill (who later would coach a couple of my sons in baseball and football) was one whom you would not immediately identify as a basketball player, but he had incredibly quick feet and maneuvered deftly around the basket. "Fred" Perry had a deadly eye with a jump shot from the corner. Peter Chamberlain at about 5'9" was a terrific all-around player who had great leaping ability—a real challenge to guard. Mike Buckley (Buck) was the classic shooting guard scoring machine. Rich Carolan was an outstanding post player who knew how to play with his back to the basket. All in all—a very talented group.

The Wellesley Monday/Thursday basketball group served me well in many ways. It provided an introduction to the town, pushed me to an aspect of the game I hadn't emphasized all these years and helped me balance the time demands of life as I squeezed in the basketball while maintaining a full load at work and parenting three small children. A game I played between the ages of 37 and 43, it provided a path to transition me from a young man's game to a more mature middle age game, and some of the older guys from the Monday/Thursday later were to join me in that middle age game.

Another Lawyers' League

When I arrived at Bingham, Dana, I didn't make any inquiries about the firm's basketball team as I figured my law firm league days were over. Everett Parker, the managing partner who'd captained the Dartmouth baseball team in his youth, was the first to mention the firm's team. He'd given up play due to bad knees but still loved the game. Word must've spread about my interest in the game because I was approached in the fall by Charlie Janes, a litigator a few years junior to me, inviting me to play. Even though it would require driving to (and find a parking space at) several gyms in the Boston area after work, I realized it was my chance to open up my game a dozen times a year after the restrictions of the zone defense at the Wellesley pick-up. My first game was at Martin Luther King School in Cambridge where I put in a mediocre performance, but my appetite was whetted and I returned the next week and for the succeeding several years. I was faithfully on the court with Bingham colleagues at South Boston High School, the Boston Medical Center, the Park School, Beaver Country Day and the Wellesley Middle School, to name a few.

The Bingham team had originated several years earlier, and one of the founding members was Dick Harter, who continued to play with the team in his early 50's. An expert in executive compensation and pension matters, Dick was one of the most personable and approachable among the partners and in excellent physical condition. Shortly after I arrived, he'd stopped by to welcome me, but I didn't get a chance truly to meet him until four weeks later. My first partners' luncheon was dominated by a heated debate over a proposal regarding the minimum number of years of employment required for an associate to be considered for partner status. The background for the exchange was that about six months previously the firm had adopted a two-tiered partnership structure with the youngest partners (referred to as income or limited partners), not having the right to vote. As recompense, some senior associates had lobbied to lower the requirement from seven to five years for the entry level. The debate at the meeting was heated at times, and as a novice to firm politics I was bewildered.

The next morning Dick stopped by to see if I was free for lunch. After we sat down at the Federal Club, it was clear that a principal purpose of the invitation was to provide me with some context for the previous day's luncheon debate. In his precise and articulate manner, Dick gave me a helpful profile of the main protagonists in terms of whether they were liberal or conservative, both in relation to firm matters and generally politically. From the conversation, I quickly discerned that he fell into the liberal spectrum on both counts. Other anecdotal information about the firm's history, recent and not so recent, helped to advance my understanding of the institution to which I had recently committed. I felt deeply indebted to Dick for his generosity and candor during the luncheon in recognizing that this new firm member needed an introduction to the playbook. Through the years, we followed up periodically with equally candid and illuminating lunches.

About 5'10" of average build, Dick was known around the firm as an avid cyclist, and it was not unusual for him to commute from his home in Cambridge to Boston by bicycle. He also was a major basketball enthusiast as the game had played a central role in his life. When he failed to make the varsity at his high school in suburban Columbus Ohio, his father installed a backboard on his garage in 1951, the same time that the basket went up at McKittrick's garage in Anaconda. With a favorable flat surface, the ample driveway became the mecca for all the other boys who similarly had been cut from the varsity. Playing daily at the Harter garage, the guys discovered the social network aspects of the game—the dynamics of seeking entry into the group and the unwritten rules of maintaining the good graces of others, all lessons readily transferrable to any group.

After playing intramural ball at Yale, Dick headed to the University of Chicago for law school where he similarly found a superb intramural league. After his first year, his closest friend was ranked first in the class while Dick was second. As he admits, "he also was a better basketball player," thereby supporting the notion there may be a positive correlation between performance at sports and in the classroom. The correlation further was validated, Dick suggests, after the friend was forced to quit basketball following a diagnosis of asthma. The involuntary absence from the hardwood was accompanied by the slight depression of his grades, enabling Dick to move to number one.

Dick defines his game as a defensive specialist, and that is my striking memory of him. At least twenty years older than many on the court, he would assume the classic defensive crouch with legs bent and spread to enable quick lateral movement while his eyes were singularly focused on his man. His playing days ended as he approached 60 when he concluded that he no longer could play defense without fouling the younger guys.

His most endearing basketball memory, though, relates to his son. Despite Dick's valiant efforts, the son opted to play hockey rather than basketball while in school, not an uncommon decision in Massachusetts. "I was thinking," Dick told me, "how have I failed?" He nevertheless did continue to tutor his son in basketball. Following college, his son's first job was teaching in Hong Kong, where his boss recruited him to play basketball in a league predominantly Chinese. As a result of the paternal mentoring, he brought valued skills to the court for his hosts, and the league play became one of his most valued experiences of his Southeast Asia assignment. One day Dick received a letter with the type of message that all fathers love to receive: "Thanks dad for making me learn the game."

When I began playing with the team, the captain was Rick Metzinger, a classic forward, graceful and adept at all aspects of the game. Within a couple of years, Rick moved on to Philadelphia to become a member of the U.S. Attorney's office, and the organizational and leadership responsibilities were assumed by Bob Miley, another litigator from Boston College and Georgetown who at 6'4 was our center. As was true of our two captains, many of our players were litigators in their late twenties to early thirties. Included among them was Jim Schwartz, whose father Edward Schwartz was a noted trial lawyer and a nationally prominent product safety advocate. He annually published a list of the most dangerous children's toys and was a frequent guest on national talk shows promoting his lists. Bill Dailey was the son of another noted Boston litigator, who in contrast specialized in defense representation. Nearly all the basketball litigator associates moved on, but a number of the business attorneys remained to become partners, including Julio Vega, Rick Toelke and Jack Concannon.

Because of work demands, the prevailing assumption was that none of us would have a perfect attendance record. The closest we had to a reliable "yes" when the weekly memos were returned to the captain was Charlie Janes, who initially had approached me to play. Charlie was nearly always there despite living in Newport, R. I. with his family. Considering he had a 100-mile commute that could take between two and three hours to travel, it might seem unlikely that Charlie would make a detour to a gym before heading home. He didn't. Charlie slept in his office two or three nights during the week to avoid the daily commute, and one of those nights usually coincided with our game. Charlie also had the most compelling athletic CV among us—although in baseball rather than basketball. A star pitcher for Dartmouth in the early 70's, he was drafted by the Pirates organization and played a couple of years in the minors. A smart, solid forward with a perpetual smile, Charlie was a true pleasure to share the court with.

The Boston Lawyers' League had three divisions, and we played in the lowest one, where we usually compiled a .500 record. The League had loose rules, or at least they were so enforced, about who could play for a team. As Bob Miley recently commented, "our team was composed of the firm's attorneys (and occasional paralegal) with no ringers. Some of the other teams were filled with ringers." Our suspicions certainly were aroused when at the opening tip-off the opposing team fielded three guys 6'4" and above, and we all knew the firm had a total of 15 lawyers in its practice. I remember a game played at South Boston, where another guard and I were pressed full court for nearly the entire game by two guys about 19 years old.

One year our won-loss record was seriously deflated through a failed experiment. We were approached by a few women in the office about playing with the team, and one associate in particular was quite firm in her belief that they should play. Over the course of the year we had about a half dozen women who played with the result that at times we might have two or three women on the court. Since none of the other teams had female players and none of the women were of the skill level of Fran Morris of my Dewey days, the season did not go well as we lost nearly all our games. The following year there was mutual agreement that it made more sense for the women to enter a team in the newly formed women's lawyers' league with the expectation that both teams could be competitive in their respective leagues.

As is always the case with a .500 team, we had our share of high and low points, the resounding upset offset by the blow-out loss. For me the highlight of the Bingham years occurred in the spring of 1990 when Bob Miley asked me whether I would like to represent the team in the all-star game, an honor I readily accepted. As I was warming up in the classy Boston Medical Center gym for the mid-April contest, I noticed that I was the oldest player at 42, probably ten years older than any of the others. I was determined, nevertheless, to demonstrate my "youthful" legs and keep up with the younger guys. Thrillingly, though briefly, I did just that. I took heart in a good first half performance, even though it was followed by the inevitable decline. I headed home that late April evening happily anticipating returning to the court in the fall. As things turned out, an injury sidelined me so there was no next year, and my representation of the team at the all-star game marked the end of my full time playing for Bingham.

A Referee's Thought-Provoking Comment

The most unforgettable moment of my Bingham playing days occurred during a friendly interchange with a referee at the Park School. I had played an aggressive game with a few steals, some drives and offensive rebounds. During a break in the action, the referee complimented my play that evening and then commented: "You must be the managing partner of the firm." As I was driving home after the game, my thoughts returned to his remark. I believed he was mistaken in equating an aggressive style, which I had demonstrated on the court, with the qualities of a managing partner. Most managing partners I knew were consensus builders with superior organizational and management skills. His comments, though, did raise a broader issue that I was left to ponder for the remainder of the trip. In truth, there was little resemblance between the aggressive player I'd been that night and the role of the highly analytical, low key tax lawyer I fulfilled at work. There certainly had been a well thought-out rationale for my career choice fifteen years earlier, but the referee's comments jarred me into thinking about whether I should change and find a career that aligned better with my on court persona.

The interchange with the referee also raises the broader question of whether you can discern anything about the character of a person through his basketball play. My Notre Dame classmate Dick Reynolds volunteered: "It's true, Pat, through playing basketball with a guy I definitely can learn much about him." Certainly the basketball court will reveal the inclination of a player towards team effort and a sense of fair play.

Menno Verhave, with whom I have been playing for nearly 25 years, is such a believer in that measuring standard that he thinks a reliable tool in evaluating a guy who is a potential hire is to get on the court with him (assuming the guy plays the game). What Menno is looking for is how he fits into the group, his level of awareness of people around him and his trustworthiness—does he call "ticky-tacky" fouls? These all are qualities that we look for in valued employees. And as we all know, President Barack Obama was subject to that basketball interview by his future brother-in-law for the ultimate hire, to be wedded to his wife.

A good case can be made, therefore, that the true character of an individual can be discerned from his behavior on the court, but I am not convinced that it has universal application. I am reminded of a comment made to me a couple of years ago by Bob Matosich, whom I began playing ball with in early grade school: "You were never physically aggressive," he asserted "until you had a ball in your hand, particularly a basketball." His observation was that on the court I was intense, physical and hyper-aggressive. Yet, in Bob's view, that would not describe me in other aspects of my life. Bob's observations about me may or may not be accurate, but his comments suggest that a different persona might be exhibited on the court or the field. Actually, that is a phenomenon not limited to athletics. I have known a few professors who in routine conversation are unassuming and mild-mannered, but at the podium or behind the pen a bolder spirit emerges. The Irish poet William B. Yeats posited a theory of the man and the mask whereby a person may adopt a pose, an anti-self or mask, when confronting the world, suggesting that there is an ongoing distinction between the identity of one's self and others' perception of that person. Could the theory of the self and an anti-self be applied to action on the hardwood? If so, is our persona on the court the man or the mask?

A related issue is what skills or lessons one can learn from playing the game that could be carried over to confront the personal and professional challenges of the "real world." Some of the textbook answers to this would include teamwork, commitment to perfecting a skill, a sense of competitiveness as well as fair play, dedication and learning to deal with setbacks.

Some might consider this discussion, on the other hand, as simply hogwash. We play the game, they might emphasize, because it's fun! We're not trying to learn anything about anyone or about life from the game. Rather, they'd say, it just gives us an opportunity to escape everyday life with its stresses and disappointments. I don't know where the truth lies—and maybe there is a little on both sides.

I do know that for the next few years as I approached mid-life the questions arising about my career from that referee's comments kept tugging at my brain. More on that in a later chapter.

Gabriel and the International Game

We live in a college town, and a couple of years after moving to Wellesley, we heard of a program at Babson College that sought to place foreign students in homes to give them practical experience with English. Our home is a rambling old Victorian with plenty of room, and we figured it would be interesting and enjoyable to share our home and family with a foreign student. Gabriel appeared at our door dressed in blazer and tie, carrying a bottle of wine. He scooped up our very surprised toddler Mike and announced himself as our envoy from Spain. That scene in the doorway was the beginning of six months that none of us have forgotten.

Over the dinner table, we learned that Gabriel was from Madrid and that his father, now retired, had been a general in the Spanish army. Only about a dozen years had elapsed since the death of Francisco Franco, the long-time dictator of Spain and a major political non-favorite of mine, so I readily concluded that his father was a military man of the Franco regime. I gingerly raised the topic with Gabriel, who confirmed my assumptions. Furthermore, despite his generally liberal political leanings, he expressed his admiration for the Generalissimo. A rehashing of the merits of the Franco regime subsequently became a principal conversational topic between Gabriel and me. Our other favorite topic was the Celtics.

One day Gabriel spotted a Celtics shirt on one of our sons. The Celtics," he told me in his passable English, "they are very popular in Spain— the most popular team." Taken completely by surprise, I told him I was not aware that basketball was a sport followed in Spain, which I identified with bull-fighting and soccer. For that matter, I knew little about basketball in Europe other than that my high school teammate Jim Meredith, Notre Dame classmate John Gallagher and fellow Wellesleyan Terry Driscoll had played in European leagues. Our conversation around the table preceded by several years the NBA draft night featuring several first round picks of European-bred players. Gabriel filled in some gaps of my knowledge about the international game as he detailed how closely Spaniards followed the NBA and the game's growing popularity among the young.

In addition to being a fan, Gabriel loved to play. When we moved to Wellesley, one of the first family projects undertaken was to install a hoop. Our six-year-old Brendan and I shouldered the excavation work as we completed the last several inches digging with our hands through the rocky New England soil, and Susanne helped set the pole in the concrete. So Gabriel gained not only a family to practice his English on, but he also enjoyed the bonus of a driveway basketball hoop to play his adopted game. Weather permitting, it became nearly a nightly ritual to head out the back door to play some hoops—Gabriel, Brendan, myself and occasionally Colin, who was just reaching the stage where he could loft the ball up to the rim. The nightly recreation included HORSE, 21 and games with Colin and me against Gabriel and Brendan. Gabriel's enthusiasm was infectious and more than compensated for his skill level, proving what an international language sports can be.

Fellow players John Doerr and Charlie Brown have had first-hand experience of the popularity of the American game while living in Europe. I have not, but I've noticed games and hoops seemingly wherever I have travelled. On a visit to the Greek island of Santorini, I noticed a bunch of high school students playing at a schoolyard basket. Watching them, I couldn't help noticing that they could benefit from a few tips from a 50-year veteran: their drives weren't compact as arms and legs were flailing in different directions, their shooting techniques needed improvement and the defense lacked the fundamentals. Better judgment (and my lack of sneakers) ultimately prevailed, and I realized a group of Greek teenagers might not recognize the instructional contribution I was so eager to provide.

Other images come to mind. There was the older woman in a small town in Ireland shooting around by herself at a dilapidated basket. In Bilboa, Spain, center of the Basque country, we watched teams of middle school girls playing in an indoor gym. My attention aroused by the sound of a referee's whistle, I peered into the gym windows to witness a scene similar to home—girls in uniforms contending on the court, coaches yelling out instructions and parents sitting in the stands cheering. Were they speculating as to whether their daughters had any hopes of one day playing in the WNBA? On a trip to Paris, I spotted a well-maintained hoop in the Luxembourg Gardens, the center of so much literary and artistic history of the city. On weekends, I was told, the court hosted some of the best pick-up games in Paris.

In later years, when I watched numerous European players drafted in the first round and saw some of these draft picks such as Dirk Nowitzki, Tony Parker and Spain's Pau Gasol become NBA stars, I would think back to Gabriel, who introduced me to the notion that basketball is international.

Richie Balsbaugh's Game

Some of the more interesting pick-up games I found in Boston were those sponsored by one of Bingham's clients, Richard Balsbaugh, CEO of Pyramid Media, which owned 16 radio stations from Chicago to Boston, including the popular KISS 108 in Boston, Rich, or Richie to many of his friends, was one of Boston's more charismatic personalities when I met him. With legions of friends in both the media and the sports world, he was one whose name frequently appeared in both the business and society pages of the newspapers.

Raised in Harrisburg, Pennsylvania, Rich began playing, like so many of us, at garages in towns with northern winters. He affectionately recalls shoveling snow off the driveway and playing with a frozen ball that barely could be dribbled. While much of his playing was in the neighborhood, he became "good at the game" when he started to travel a little farther from his house to Reservoir Park, which was at the edge of the black area in Harrisburg. He soon became a basketball junkie and played guard on his high school team. He also played quarterback on a football team that included future NFL coach Dennis Green in the backfield. At Penn State he qualified for the freshman basketball team and thereafter played on a champion fraternity team that included a few ballplayers who by his estimate were better than most on the varsity.

Following the four years at Penn State, Rich was given that opportunity that many of us dream of—a brief foray on a professional team. Living in the Kew Gardens section of New York, he frequented a pub that was owned by a couple of players from the New York Nets. The Nets were a charter member of the American Basketball Association, more commonly referred to as the ABA and distinguished by its colorful red, white and blue ball. The ABA also introduced the three-point shot and a shot clock to promote its distinctive emphasis on offense. In the fall of 1970, the ABA was in its fourth season and through lucrative contracts had managed to recruit some stars, but most players opted to remain with the NBA. That meant the rosters could be thin. The owners of the pub encouraged Rich to try out for the team, and he spent two weeks with them before he was cut. From those two weeks, he acquired lifelong memories of scrimmaging with the pros and also learned that there is a difference between "good and GOOD."

In his recent induction speech for the Massachusetts Broadcasters Hall of Fame, Rich attributed the success of his next 15 years "more to luck than being smart." What his modest assessment does not reveal is the incredible entrepreneurship that he brought to the radio business. His career began slowly and far from broadcasting as he left the Nets to become involved in the paper business as an employee for Scott Paper in New York and Boston. Attracted by his sales skills, a Boston-based radio broadcasting firm with about a half dozen stations recruited him as a sales representative, and within a short period of time he rose to the position of general sales manager.

Then that unforeseen break occurred. He received a call one day in 1978 from a Hawaii congressman, Cecil Heftel, who owned a number of stations throughout the country and asked Rich to be the general manager of a well-known station he was planning to purchase in Boston. Rich was thrilled with that proposal, but the plan was derailed when he received another call from Heftel. The deal fell through, but as a consolation Heftel offered the same position for a small marginal station in Medford, a suburb of Boston. Teaming up with program director Sonny Jo White, Rich took control of the station, renaming it KISS-108. Through a change in format to disco and the adoption of media favored promotions such as the extraordinarily popular annual KISS concert, they propelled the station to the top of the Boston radio industry.

A couple of years later, Heftel called again. Wanting to reduce the size of his media empire, the Congressman offered his star station manager an opportunity to buy several stations. With the aid of his chief financial officer, Ken O'Keefe, Rich put together a group of investors to finance the acquisitions, which closed a few years before I moved to Boston. I was introduced to the company through a meeting with Ken and Ed Smith of our office to discuss alternatives available to buy out the investors.

Ken, a tall handsome Brown graduate, was my principal contact with the company, and one day he commented that his schedule that evening involved playing basketball at a gym rented by Rich. He invited me to join them. The game was played at the Natick Sports Club at 10 p.m.—too late for this suburban dad so I played there once in the spirit of client relations. Rich did find a more civilized hour to play—at the Fessenden school in neighboring Newton. It was invariably a treat to show up and be part of the very eclectic mix he could draw to the courts.

On any night there could be current and former pro and college athletes from basketball, football and hockey, radio personalities, night club guys, comedians, Boston cops and an occasional lawyer seeking refuge from playing other lawyers in a league. Rich had a long history of friendships with members of the Boston Celtics, going back to the 1970's with such stalwarts as Dave Cowens and Henry Finkel. At the time I was playing with him, M.L. Carr, Danny Ainge, Jerry Sichting and Dennis Johnson had been brought into his circle. In particular, I remember Carr showing up for Richie's game. The personable M.L. was the spiritual leader of the Celtics with his waving that white towel from the bench at the Boston Garden being a popular image captured by the cameras. As might be expected, the games were competitive, featuring a high quality of play. I generally shied away from the inside game because of the size of many of the guys playing on the front court. Driving and fast breaks I found to be my best way to contribute something. As for Rich, his specialty was the jump shot slightly shy of the three-point line from somewhat to the right or left of center. And he took it frequently; as he says, "I like to shoot."

Rich is the consummate impresario and has excelled at entertaining friends, business associates and celebrities. When he decided to get married a number of years ago, it was done on a grand scale. Several hundred guests celebrated with him at the Wang Center Theater with an array of musical presentations, including a rock band, a gospel choir of about 40 members and a couple classical music quartets. The guest list was sprinkled with glamorous luminaries from his worlds of sports and entertainment. Through the years he also has amassed an amazing collection of memorabilia from the entertainment and sports world, including over 200 guitars signed by various performers, jackets from Madonna and others stars and a wide assortment of jerseys from the likes of Larry Bird, Michael Jordan and Tom Brady, all of which were displayed in his conference room. When a nephew from Montana visited, he took in many of Boston's historical sites, but the highlight was a chance to linger in Rich's conference room. At one point, Rich was profiled in Robin Leach's television show *Lives of the Rich and Famous*, which chronicled his business and social activities. The producers kept the most important aspect of his life to the end when they included footage of Rich playing with his high-profile posse at his outdoor regulation-size full court.

While Rich can charm, fundamentally he's a steely businessman with an unfailing attention to detail. Many years ago I represented his company in a protracted dispute with the IRS, who were bent on scrutinizing extremely abstruse tax aspects of the original acquisition and perfunctory operational matters such as travel and entertainment expenses and compensation. Ken O'Keefe and I had no success at convincing Rich to run through a practice dress rehearsal to prepare him for the IRS meeting. On the appointed day, Rich arrived wearing a jumpsuit and sporting a pony-tail to greet the conservatively attired IRS agents. Whatever his initial impression was on them, their parting conclusion was that this was an executive who knew his company inside and out as he absolutely destroyed any attempt to build their case. Whether the questions dealt with esoteric matters such as allocation of acquired intangible assets or minor expenses for some promotional event, his responses were a masterful performance.

The agents saved what they believed to be their best shot for the end. "During 1984," they pointedly noted, "your compensation was... (I no longer recall the amount, but they obviously thought it was a very generous amount). Turning to them with that penetrating Balsbaugh beam, he parried: "Is that what they paid me that year?! Boy, did they get a bargain!!" End of interview. The final IRS report did not include any challenges to his compensation level.

Chapter Twenty

Coaching Youth Basketball

Thanks to my father, coaching was in my blood every bit as much as playing, and I got the nod early in life—at an age when I was not much older than the players I coached. Following the example of my grade school coaches, I coached every winter in high school for St. Peter's eighth grade team. I loved firing up the players, pacing the floor, and going to the mat for them with the referees. Getting to play the role of instructor, guide and team builder and discovering how to inspire effort was a thrill.

My youthful zeal occasionally tipped to the extreme, and I needed to be reminded of mature decorum. One of our games was played with a new and unfamiliar ref who shared his displeasure at my sideline antics after our game. The dress down somewhat dimmed the glow from our victory that day, but I learned not to burn bridges, and it was good to learn it young. The following week I approached the offended referee, and we soon became good friends. In fact, I think it's not a bad idea for anyone making basketball their lifelong sport to spend some time coaching AND refereeing. It helps expand the notion of "participants in the game."

Drawing upon what my high school coaches were teaching me, my coaching emphasized an aggressive defense. My teams employed a half court press with a liberal use of the trap, resulting in a number of turn-overs, usually followed by relatively easy lay-ups. While we did not win any championships, we were always towards the top, and I learned much about how to teach coordinated effort that leads to points scored and winning games. I loved coaching from the start.

The other perk of being at the Memorial Gym on Saturday mornings, incidentally, was I had a reason to hang out in the vicinity of the cheerleaders. Not a small advantage for a high schooler—it gave me a slight edge among my fellow classmen just by learning their names.

[Re]learning the Ropes

My return to basketball coaching happened 22 years later and extended for about a dozen years. I cherished the opportunity because it provided me a chance to spend time together with my guys doing something we enjoyed and drew me into the fabric of the larger Wellesley community. I also was to find coaching as a dad in a community where youth competitive sports was highly prized considerably more complex than being a teenage high school player on the sidelines on Saturday morning on a court where the previous night I'd played before fans. Being away from coaching for so many years, I was a little rusty, and I struggled at times to find the proper stance for my new role. As might be expected, there were some miscues.

My basketball coaching began in 1988 when I volunteered to coach my oldest son Brendan's third grade team in the Wellesley "Town League." A brainchild of Jack Hayes, who was looking to establish a competition that was instructionally-oriented, the Town League had an unusual format in that coaches were to divide their ten players into strong and developing categories. The latter played in the first and third quarters and the former in the second and fourth. The objective was that players of roughly the same ability would be playing against each other. At the beginning of the season, he provided a two-hour tutorial on practice techniques and game strategies. While most of the drills were elementary and resembled ones I employed for my eighth grade teams, it was good to be reminded because I had forgotten much.

My first task was to recruit an assistant and was lucky to get a yes from Larry Ingrassia. I'd met Larry a couple of years earlier after he had moved to Wellesley to become the Boston Bureau Chief for the *Wall Street Journal*. While our acquaintance stretched back only a couple of years, it seemed that I had known him much longer. When living in New York and Chicago, I had noticed a number of articles in the *WSJ* about Montana, including at least one on the bars of Butte and Anaconda. I was delighted to meet the author of those articles.

Larry was a natural choice to assist me. He and I had coached baseball the previous spring. A big plus was that Larry was an engaging presence on the bench. I am sure that when he was in grade school, he was one of those students whom the teachers commented "he's very verbal." Larry can talk, and he brings to his conversations enormous vitality and energy, a combination which I am sure is a formidable asset in chasing down a story. On the sideline, he was a source of continual encouragement and support for the players. From my standpoint, he was an enormously positive addition to the bench since I was still trying to figure out my "game-day voice," recognizing that my antics of 25 years ago weren't going to fly.

Coaching third graders presents a unique set of challenges that I didn't experience with the eighth graders. It's a level at which there exists great disparity of skills and interest among the players. Some can barely reach the rim with their shots whereas others may be prolific scorers from all points within 12 feet. Similarly there may be considerable variation in their focus and maturity with some there because their parents dropped them off at the gym while others have hectored their parents to drive them early so they could shoot around before practice. Energy may be expended by the coaches simply to make sure there are ten players on the court and that no one's wandered off to hide in the bleachers.

The theory of the strong and developing squads was designed to address these disparities. While ideal in theory, at times it was flawed in execution, reflecting differing views of coaches as to the spirit of the rules. The problems became most apparent when a team's headcount was fewer than ten. Who should play in the first and third quarters? One approach would be to put on the court players five through nine in the first quarter with player five returning for the second quarter. A different approach is to take anyone from the strong team, even player one, as the fifth player for the first and third quarters. I thought the first approach was most consistent with the program's objectives, but there were times when I looked out at the court at the opening tip-off to find the best player for the other team ready to play with the developing players. It was my view, shared by others, that sending the best player to compete against the developing players of the other team to secure a "win" for a third grade team was hardly consistent with the purpose of the Hayes scheme. In my Anaconda days, I would have confronted the coach, but letting go and moving on seemed to be the better choice. I understand the culture of volunteer parent coaches continues to be rife with these difficulties to this day, nearly 30 years later.

During the brief six weeks of the Town League from early March to mid-April, I learned the CYO program had long dominated youth basketball in Wellesley. Nearly all the best players in the third grade league had played CYO, which in contrast to the incipient Town League extended for four months—from early November to the end of February. When Brendan and I followed all his classmates and their parents to sign up for the St. John CYO the following fall, I didn't expect that the CYO was to become a central part of my life during the winter months for the next 10 years or so.

Prior to moving to Wellesley, I was only vaguely familiar with the CYO, the acronym for the Catholic Youth Organization. There was no such program in Anaconda since all schools, public and parochial, participated in the town's athletic activities. I mainly identified the CYO with Bing Crosby playing Father O'Malley in the popular 40's movie, *Going My Way*.

A Midwestern creation, the CYO was founded in 1930 by the fervent advocate for the poor, Bishop Bernard J. Shell (who later incurred the wrath of many Catholics for his outspoken opposition to the fanatical anti-Communist crusader Senator Joseph McCarthy). The CYO evolved from Cardinal Mundelein's charge to the Bishop to undertake the task of getting Catholic youth off the streets into activities that would further their spiritual development. Athletic events were introduced to entice the youth to abandon the unsavory alleys and passage ways, but soon sports dominated the CYO. In the early days, boxing was the main feature, but basketball soon surpassed it with 10,000 playing under the CYO banner in Chicago.

The movement spread to other archdioceses with the CYO soon becoming the outlet for high school students who didn't qualify for the school teams. Eventually the program expanded from the grit of the cities to the suburbs so that by the mid-1980's the vicariate comprised of the Boston suburbs of Wellesley, Weston, Wayland, Sudbury and Framingham sponsored a vibrant program that dominated pre-high school competitive basketball. Each CYO program was sponsored by a parish open to all regardless of creed. When we entered the program, Wellesley had two sponsoring parishes in St. Paul's and St. John's.

Following the sign-up, I showed up for the first practice of the 60-odd players in the 9-10 age group, named in the pre-politically correct era the "Midgets," to audition for a coaching position. Paul Daoust, Wellesley father, Parish CYO Commissioner and executive with a human resources company, invited me to help with preliminary drills and scrimmages to get some assessment of the players' skill level. With the exception of a couple, including one ten-year-old girl who was arguably the best player of the bunch, the players were all boys. After a couple of weeks, Dauost asked me to take a team.

Being somewhat absorbed in the instructional part of the practices, I failed to understand that the coaches were to select their teams through a draft process and the practices provided the chance to assess the kids' skills. The draft did not begin well for me as I drew the shortest straw and hence picked last. Then my failure to pay close attention to evaluation caught up with me. I made a couple of excellent selections of players that I'd coached the previous spring in the Town League, but I was unsteady on judging those not personally familiar to me, passing over a few, particularly older ones, who would have brought maturity to the team.

Despite my shortcomings in the draft, we had a respectable record as our young team continued to improve over the season. I also successfully recruited Larry Ingrassia again to the coaching bench—our fourth to date. Our practices were squeezed with three other teams in the cramped basement gym of the Middle School, which afforded each team a tiny half court for an hour on Friday evenings. With 40 players and eight coaches in the gym, the conditions can only be described as chaotic.

As many a suburban commuter dad has discovered, getting out early enough for practices was always fraught. For Larry, it was a singularly hectic time at the *WSJ* as the real estate crisis in New England was in its early stages, leading to the downward spiral of a number of financial institutions, including the Bank of New England. From a journalist's perspective, such crises represent both good and bad news—his articles frequently landed on the front page of the publication, but the prominence translated into many late evenings in the office. His son Nick sometimes showed up at practice to inform me that Larry either would be late or not make it, followed with the terse "Bank of New England."

On the first day of the next season, our new commissioner Jay Civetti invited me to take the Midgets A team, which would compete against the best teams of the other parishes. With this responsibility, I was forced to focus on the players because my decisions for the coveted slots would be subject to the closest scrutiny by players and parents alike. Our A Team roster reflected the strongest ten year-old players, but, as often happens, the course of growth and development is unpredictable. Only one member of the team ended up playing varsity basketball, and at least two that I overlooked did play varsity basketball with one leading the Wellesley high school team as captain. The late bloomer phenomenon, so familiar to me from my Anaconda days, blossomed again.

Our first practice began in the company of six dads, their presence suggesting at least curiosity, if not doubts, about my basketball knowledge since I was an unknown quantity. I felt I was being auditioned to determine whether I was the right one to guide their sons through the competitive schedule. Most of those dads evaporated by the second practice, so I must've passed muster.

As the first game approached, I had to make a decision as to the strategy for playing time. I settled on the policy of equal playing time even though there was not an equal distribution of talent. My rationale was that each of the players would have been a star on a B team, and I was determined to not have any such ten-year-old players spend most of their time on the bench. To maximize our competitive position, we fielded two squads of approximate equal strength. While I think the approach was approved by most parents, the decision led to my first coaching challenge of managing the strong opinions of parents. One father deemed my approach as "coaching to lose," and was not shy about letting others know his assessment. When I learned of his views, my initial reaction was anger, but then I came to appreciate the irony of the accusation—I probably was one of the poorest losers around!!

As it turned out, we had a very successful season, losing two games, one to a team that we would not have beaten under any circumstances and the other in a nail-biter. In the latter game, our system might have put us at a slight disadvantage since the other team didn't employ a comparable substitution rule and kept the two best players in for most of the game. Even if that were the case, would one additional victory ever be worth not providing all the ten year-olds the experience of being a full member of the A team?

Buck the Referee

Everyone who has even the remotest familiarity with basketball in Boston's Metro West knows referee John Buckley, or "Buck" as he is called by so many. Standing about 6'4" with fading freckles on a face that is continually lit up and strands of red among his predominantly white hair, he looks and sounds for all the world like a quintessential Boston Irishman. The truth of the matter is that he is not Irish; he is 25% Jewish with the remainder of his ancestors descended from the islands east of Scotland, most likely the Orkney Islands. When asked whether he is Scottish, he demurs and emphasizes that his ancestors were the ones who "raped and pillaged" the monasteries before the Scots conquered them.

I first encountered Buck at a small gym in Framingham at my CYO coaching debut. Since that first game with him more than 25 years ago, I've seen him referee third graders and guys in their forties and fifties, and virtually every age in between. Each game illustrates the Buckley philosophy that the skill of the players defines how the games are to be called. He is a master of dexterously applying the right touch to the right situation. "We're there to manage the game, not referee," he explains. And manage it he does. A principal tool of that management is a constant stream of commentary—instructive, comical and sometimes stern interchange with the players, coaches and occasionally the fans.

At the third grade level, for example, different standards are applied to various players, depending upon their level of development. As he summarizes his approach, "I'm not going to send a kid home in tears because he doesn't understand the rules for the pivot foot." He believes that 98% of the fans and the coaches have "bought into" his philosophy, but not everyone. In reaction to a coach or fan pointing out that a player with an uncertain command of the dribble takes an extra step or two, he'll nod to his critic with a smile and a shrug of the shoulders—his signal that "I know but I am not going to make the call on the kid." He recalls one incident when a coach yelled out in a third grade game "What's a travel?," and his disarming response was "about two or three more steps." With the senior guys, the complaint usually is that Buck missed a call when the complainant has been fouled. Quite aware that he is dealing with lawyers, executives, stock brokers and the like, accustomed to having their grievances attended to, he's well able to deflate egos and elicit grudging laughs even in the heat of competition. Without realizing it, they've been disarmed by the Buckley charm.

He's probably at his finest, though when the guys on the court are at the junior high level, his favorite clientele. He good-naturedly rides herd over their unruliness while making his pedagogical points, reflecting his 39 years of experience with adolescents as a math teacher. Buckley's calls are made with humor and a dramatic flair that guarantees their acceptance. At typical Buckley game may include the following:

- "That was a Kobe call," he yells out to a defender who claims that in setting up for the jumper the shooter took an extra half-step.
- Whistle in his mouth, he counts out the seconds for the benefit of the center sitting in the middle of the lane; it usually will take five seconds for him to invoke the three-second penalty.

- Following a nice lay-up in which there is some inconsequential contact, "Freddie, you are supposed to add 'and one'," but no foul is called.
- Later Freddie is standing ready to shoot two free throws: "We got you to the line this time, Freddie."
- Before he hands the ball to be put it in play after a score, he compliments the scoring team: "That was a nice pick and roll."
- When the action under the basket is getting a little physical, "watch those hands" he admonishes.
- When one of the coaches complains "what does it take to get a foul?" his deadpan response: "I saw more contact in the communion line this morning."
- When not dispensing this commentary, he jogs forward and backwards up and down the court maintaining 100% focus on the game—at the age of 70 plus.

Buck was raised in Chelsea, one of Boston's working class suburbs north of the city where he excelled in football, basketball and baseball. In a junior high championship competition at the Boston Garden, his Chelsea team defeated one led by Jim Calhoun, the future coach of the Connecticut men's team that won multiple national championships. He and Calhoun later were to play together on a semi-pro team, Shock's Auto Body. His football skills almost won him a slot at Yale, but the need for some verbal remediation kept him out. He returned to Chelsea High to do a "PG" program in two subjects but also registered as a freshman at Boston State College without sharing that information with his family. His mother didn't learn that he was enrolled at the college until she read in the newspaper that he had scored 16 points in a basketball game for the school. The team qualified for the NAIA tournament, but lost to Winston-Salem, whose star guard was future NBA star Earl (the Pearl) Monroe. As Buckley loves to tell us, "I held Earl to 29 points and then the second half began." For a kid who started off slowly, he gained momentum going on to earn a masters at Boston College and a Ph.D. at Boston University in education. He interrupted his teaching tenure at Natick High School in 1979 to co-teach a course at Harvard School of Education. In his words, "not bad for a boy from Chelsea with 400 on his verbal SAT."

In view of my identification of him as embodying the CYO program because of his ubiquitous presence, I was surprised to learn that he had never played CYO and that his involvement with CYO began as a coach and not a referee. His early officiating career actually was devoted principally to soccer, since the scheduling of the games enabled him to meet his wife's edict that his refereeing should not interfere with his being home for dinner.

For the first couple of years of my coaching, Buck probably recognized me and more than likely did his research on me since part of his management of the games is to know the coaches. But I don't recall having any conversations of note with him. All that changed in the summer of 1992 in rather unusual circumstances at an outdoor league game. He and his buddy Jimmy were refereeing our game, and I got clobbered on the head by an opposing player. Jimmy, who was near the play, did not blow the whistle, and I exploded in outrage at him. Incredibly, no technical was called! Buck came out to the top of the key and exchanged places with Jimmy. He continued to be his usually chatty self as if there had been no incident. Towards the end of the game, as I was standing on the sidelines to take a breather, Jimmy came over and asked how my head was. I told him that there was a lump. He responded in a conciliatory manner "well maybe I missed a call" and then added "but you shouldn't have yelled at me like that!" He was right, of course, and I apologized for the outburst. For whatever reason, as a result of the incident I secured a spot on Buck's radar screen. We spoke frequently at games the next season, and a friendship developed.

Notre Dame became an additional basis for our bonding. During warm-ups one summer evening, Buck came up to me and said "Patrick, I saw your name in the Notre Dame Boston Club newsletter." At that time, his oldest son was a recent graduate of the school and his youngest son soon was to enter as a freshman. Our conversations took on a new dimension—the vicissitudes of the uneven performance of Notre Dame's football and basketball teams. He is a frequent visitor to the campus during the football season, and occasionally in winter is in the seats at the ACC for a basketball game. He also has been called upon from time to time to referee their soccer games. During football weekends, he can be located either holding court at the LaFortune Student Center or chatting at the Athletic Department, where he seems to be on a first name basis with everyone.

My official association with Buckley ended about 15 years ago when I retired both from the CYO program and the outdoor basketball league. To keep in touch, I make a pilgrimage to the Wellesley Middle School in December to catch a game or two he is officiating (or rather managing). When he spots me standing near the door, he greets me with his eyes. At the first break, he will head in my direction, his face wreathed with that winning smile and with his charming Boston accent calling out: "Patrick, time for the annual check-up!" Despite his age and having survived three bouts of cancer, he shows absolutely no signs of slowing down. On the contrary, he has accelerated his blistering pace of refereeing as he estimates that he does at least 250 games a year, and I am certain that he always makes it home for dinner.

Equipment Manager

After a few years of coaching, I volunteered to help manage the St. John CYO. Jay Civetti wore the crown of "High Commissioner" at the time and John Bonsall, an attorney who was steeped in the CYO tradition in Milton

Massachusetts, was designated the "Low Commissioner." My first assignment was to coordinate the pre-season practices, which included the drills and scrimmages. Somewhat ironically in view of my shaky inaugural a couple years earlier in selecting talent, I became actively involved in team selection. Since my initial mediocre foray at drafting was not unique, we decided that a better system would be to have the teams designated by "management."

After a couple of years, Civetti retired, and the position of High Commissioner and Low Commissioner merged into the person of John Bonsall. I have jokingly reminded John that the merger was akin to the unification of the crowns of Upper Egypt and Lower Egypt six thousand years ago! I became the Commissioner's principal assistant, which meant "Equipment Manager." An essential qualification of this role was possession of significant storage space for 30 boxes of uniforms, 100 basketballs and such miscellaneous paraphernalia as scorebooks and pumps. From March to November, a portion of our basement was stacked from floor to ceiling with the CYO equipment. The duties, however, were more extensive than just storage. Hunting down errant uniforms, fumigating ones returned dirty, and fitting the hard-to-fit into our collection also was required. Every early November, appreciation flowers arrived for Susanne from John Bonsall, based on the Commissioner's accurate estimation of whose tolerance was routinely tested by this storage arrangement.

During the Equipment Manager years, my two younger sons, Colin and Mike, went through the program. In each instance, my pattern of coaching was the same—Midget B, Midget A and Bantam B (the level for 11 and 12 year olds). Following that, I would peel away from the coaching since I wanted someone other than their father coaching for part of their pre-high school years. In making such a decision, I had in mind the marvelous mentoring I'd received from so many during my grade school days.

Each of them were fortunate to have similar experiences. For Brendan's seventh grade year, our neighbor Marty Ford stepped in as a coach. A veteran of the superb St. Joseph (PA) teams of the mid 60's, the lanky Ford applied a patient and instructional approach to the middle schoolers, and Brendan thrived under his system. For Colin the moment I remember best was on the baseball diamond. Pitching in a game while in the fourth grade, he hit two consecutive batters. I might've been inclined to pull him, but the coach stayed with him. He pitched himself out of the inning, and from there it was an upward spiral for him on the mound, culminating as a high school varsity pitcher. Mike had the good fortune to be coached by two outstanding high school athletes, Justin Gaither and J. P. Comella. Their youthful inspiration led the sixth graders to the championship, a feat which had eluded the team under my coaching two years earlier.

After about eight years at the helm, my days of Equipment Manager ended in 1999 when I made my last appearance before the coaches to distribute the uniforms and balls. At the end of the season, I was awarded the John Bonsall trophy, originated a couple of years earlier in his honor to recognize John's prodigious efforts for the program. My selection most likely reflected that old adage that if you show up long enough you'll win something. I left the ceremony with a 30-inch trophy! It took me a couple of years to break the habit of heading over to the Middle School to hang out for that first day of practice. I guess it eased the transition away from a program that had meant so much to me all those years.

Coaches' Game: Terry Driscoll and Chris Stevens

The CYO program spawned the tradition of a friendly game, begun in 1981, between the coaches for the two town parishes. I should probably amend that to say "mostly friendly" because the competition was intense among the battling coaches. At stake was possession of the "Cup." This tarnished spittoon mounted on a pedestal with the winning team's name and date etched on a brass plaque was awarded to the winner of the coaches' game held in March. St. John had prevailed in most of the contests, and a major reason for their dominance was the presence of former college star and NBA player Terry Driscoll.

Terry is one of the greats among Boston College basketball players. In 1969 he captained the Eagles to a second place finish in the National Invitational Tournament, where he was named the most valuable player of the tournament. Bolstered by his 1071 career rebounds, still a BC record, and his All-American honors, he was the fourth overall pick in the 1969 draft. The first selection that year was the then Lew Alcindor. Over the next 11 years, Terry played in the NBA for four years, with the remainder of the time spent in Italy where he played and then coached the professional team in Bologna. At 6'7" with a solid frame, Terry was a dominating force around the boards. Even observing him in his middle-aged years, I could well understand why he had scooped down all those rebounds even though his height was not extraordinary, even by 1969 standards.

With these credentials, one might've concluded he'd been groomed for basketball from the start, but that wasn't so. His primary athletic interests were baseball and hockey. As he entered Boston College High School at 5'10", few would have predicted that he would play varsity high school basketball, let alone the NBA. Two developments changed the trajectory of his athletic curve. The first was that very shortly his shoe size mushroomed to a size 14, requiring special hockey skates, which would have pressured his family budget. Relatedly, he enjoyed a spectacular growth spurt so that by senior year he was 6'5", followed by two more inches in college. After gravitating to basketball, he was a highly recruited player following a spectacular high school career at B.C. High. Despite many entreaties from afar, he remained with the Boston College brand to enjoy the privilege of being coached by the legendary Bob Cousy.

Terry, though, was not St. John's tallest coach/player. That distinction was held by Paul Waickowski, a lanky 6'10" lawyer and future judge who had played at Harvard. As I assessed the two teams while warming up in the Wellesley High School Gym for my first appearance, I thought it would be a cakewalk with both Driscoll and Waickowski on our team. To my surprise, the resilient St. Paul team kept it close for most of the game until the superior talent ultimately made its presence felt in the final minutes. The game featured a fair amount of physical contact as mature bodies are not as adept at evading oncoming bodies, but Buckley "managed" this game by letting everyone play. My own contribution was undistinguished. After the final buzzer, the St. John team reconvened at Comella's, a local Italian pasta café, where the Cup was prominently displayed.

When I arrived at the Middle School for the game in the following year, the scene seemed familiar since most of the personnel on both sides were the same. There were some absences, mostly guys no longer coaching, and some additions, including Larry Ingrassia. This game proved to be vastly different for me—and happily so. As we did the previous year, we allocated playing time via three platoons for our squad of 15.

During a time-out at the beginning of the second half, Jim Ferry, a fine shooter from the corner, took me aside and suggested: "let's try to run; I will get the pass off the rebound and you break for the basket." On the first rebound, we executed it and I scored an easy lay-up. On the next opportunity, as I approached the basket, there was a defender near the basket so I evaded his outstretched arms with a running hook. By this point I was energized and the game developed into one of those rare middle-aged breakaway moments when the stars aligned on a middle school court. After our victory, we again retired to Comella's. Terry Driscoll was gracious in his comments on the game: "You'll be on the highlights tonight, Pat; it was a Dominique [Wilkins] performance." Coming from a former All-American and NBA player, that's about as good as it could get for a 40-plus player still trying to play the game.

Driscoll, Daoust, Ferry, Waikowski and others departed in the early 1990's as their sons and daughters graduated from the CYO program. With the departure of the old guard, the St. John ranks were replenished with new talent, particularly Chris Stevens and Mike Dowling.

Chris had been a three year letterman at Notre Dame from 1972 through 1974, but his path to that lofty basketball achievement was hardly idyllic. Much of his youth was spent in foster homes, an itinerary that included stops in Texas, upstate New York, Virginia and finally Washington, where his life attained some level of stability. During these years, his principal athletic interests were football and baseball. Despite these early inclinations, his tremendous growth spurt to 6'6" made the logic of turning to basketball in high school irresistible. It became the center of his life as he starred at St. John College High School as the "Hawk," reflecting his imposing wing-span. As he describes it, his life had been somewhat "hoody," and "basketball saved me." He excelled and received 125 scholarship offers, all of which he rejected except Notre Dame, "because I fell in love with the place."

At ND, he was a starter for the team in his sophomore year as an under-sized center who had to move from his natural forward position. Notably he scored the first two points of the Coach Digger Phelps era. That season was not a happy one for the Irish who went 6-20. The following two years his playing time declined as Digger adopted a youth movement with the recruiting of such players as future Hall of Famer Adrian Dantley and All-American John Shumate. Chris did experience the thrill of being a member of the team that ended UCLA's 88-game win streak when the Irish most improbably engineered a comeback from a deficit of 11 points with 3:32 remaining in one of the most famous college games of all time.

Fifteen years after graduation, he had lost little of his collegiate skills. I had seen these in a number of games where Chris always held his own, regardless of his competition. Also, I always thought that Chris was one of our best coaches among the CYO ranks. With his Notre Dame pedigree and his towering height, he was bound to maintain the attention of the players, and he was an excellent teacher. What really impressed me, though, was the positive attitude he brought to the job. He was a coach where the praise and encouragement far outweighed the criticism, and he never was he to be heard belittling a player. Cloaked in charisma, he was a master of the inspirational pep talks. His love of coaching was utterly transparent.

Mike Dowling is a member of a notable athletic family. His brother Brian was the star quarterback for the 1968 Yale football team that went undefeated with one notable tie at the end of the season in the Harvard/Yale game. The character B.D. in the Doonesbury cartoon was based on Brian. About eight years younger, Mike attended B.Y.U. where he played basketball. Since he was the sportscaster for the local ABC affiliate, his face was a familiar one. His visibility in Wellesley was enhanced further by his annual volunteering as the moderator for the Wellesley Spelling Bee, a major fundraiser for the town's school system. At one point, Mike had three boys in the CYO program, one of whom I coached. In his own last coaching gig for CYO, Mike teamed up with Celtic great and current President Danny Ainge to coach eighth and ninth graders. He too was a constant presence at the coaches' game.

In March 1998, the ninth anniversary of my first game, we experienced our first press coverage, thanks to the journalistic skills of Stevens. For a number of years Chris had been the unofficial scribe of the St. John CYO as he regularly penned the *Wellesley Townsmen's* roundups of recent action. Combining factual reportage, humor and reflection, he did a wonderful piece for the paper titled "CYO Practices its Preaching: Coaches Meet in Leagues Annual Clash." Excerpts from the article follow with my commentary.

While many of the town's hoop fanatics were home Sunday watching URI battle Stanford in the NCAA tournament, a game of equally-great proportions was played at the Wellesley Middle School. The CYO basketball coaches squared off in the umpteenth match-up between the rivals of two well-run CYO programs.

Chris says it all.

Each year seems to produce some surprises, a new star and invariably at least one injury. The star this year was a young athletic newcomer from St. Paul's who helped coach two teams for the parish (young by this game's standards meaning just north of 30). If Rick Pitino were in the stands Sunday, Mike Hornbuckle would have a new job as a free agent with the Celtics. Hornbuckle was simply a shooting machine. He drained his initial 3 and just about everything else he cranked up en route to 25 points – in the first half.

At the time Hornbuckle actually was just shy of 40, but with his ever youthful face and energy one could have mistaken him for 30, and his play would have furthered that misconception. Hornbuckle had starred for the University of Redlands, which won the Southern California Intercollegiate Athletic Conference in 1981. Contemporary accounts of his college years describe him as a "sharpshooter." Those skills were on display at the CYO game.

With his team down 27-11, Hornbuckle and Bill Peterson took control, pumping in jumpers from all over the court. By halftime, the rejuvenated team from uptown had knotted the contest at 38. There isn't much pride when you're trapped inside a slowly sinking ship. So St. John's decided to throw caution to the wind and play man-to-man. The strategy worked and St. John's regained control of the game. (Admittedly they got a little rough on Hornbuckle, but St. John's knew that as a rookie the sharpshooter would get few calls from veteran referees like John Buckley).

Of course Buckley was managing the game, and in doing so he was applying the typical Buckley standard for the old guys—blow the whistle only when there's significant contact.

While Mike Dowling and Chris Stevens dogged "The Buck" everywhere, the ageless Pat Dowdall provided much of the offense. While Dowdall--nearing 50 with gray hair and a gimpy knee—kept scoring underneath, the youthful legs of high schoolers Justin Gaither, Colin Dowdall and J.P. Comella began to make a difference.

As to the offense, we had devised a strategy during half-time that Stevens and Dowling would play outside to keep their big men, particularly Hornbuckle, away from the key. With the big men pulled out, that would open it up for me underneath. It worked well, but most of the credit goes to the fine passing of Stevens and Dowling and frankly to the willingness of these two outstanding players to sacrifice some of their own offensive opportunities. Yes, my son Colin had joined the coaching ranks, and this was the first time we played together in an "official" game.

Hornbuckle ended the game with 35 points though St. John's eventually prevailed and reclaimed the Cup. For St. John's "Lower Falls Leapers," the venerable Dowdall scored 21, Stevens 17, Comella 16, Gaither 12 and the irrepressible Dowling, just back from a blown Achilles tendon injury, 11."

Venerable? You hang around long enough and you get tagged as "venerable." As the senior member of the team, I took the Cup home to be held until the following year's contest. Stevens had referred to the Cup as a "weathered old piece of tin." Susanne agreed and sent it out for a scrubbing and polish and located a bookshelf corner for it.

The satisfaction of Sunday's contest was not in the final score, but rather in the friendly competition itself. Coaching is about teaching and inspiring, and kids appreciate it when coaches are willing to "walk the walk" after "talking the talk." While the mind often makes promises the body can't keep, basketball is a sport that helps keep even the oldest of bodies young at heart."

This well reflects Steven's motivational and inspirational self, which made him such a terrific coach.

A Coach's Reflection

Reflecting on my dozen years of coaching, what most stands out is spending the time with my guys. During those years, my work schedule at a law firm and entrepreneurial companies made heavy demands on me so time at home was relatively limited. Coaching required that time slots for basketball be inserted into the weekly schedule along with conferences, travel and meetings. That meant that barring something extraordinary I regularly would be participating in an activity with them. Moreover, being a group activity enhanced our time together since we were part of an endeavor larger than ourselves. I think our success can be affirmed by the fact they are now looking forward to coaching their own children.

Coaching one's offspring, though, is a situation that inevitably can create tensions since you inhabit two roles, coach and father, and the two may not always be harmonious. I think the most poignant comment on this dual relationship came from one who was coached by his father at the high school level, fellow Anacondan John Cheek. "I hated it," he exclaimed when I asked him about being the coach's son. "For other guys, if it was a bad practice, they could go home and complain to their dad about the coach. In my case, my dad was the coach."

Another aspect of the dual father-coach role is that the coach might have more of a vested interested in the success of one player, his son or daughter. To baldly pursue that agenda obviously would be ruinous for the team. A good coaching father will strive to avoid playing favorites. Many might go even a step further and be tougher on their sons or daughters, and I have heard many stories to that effect. I am not certain if I was tougher; only my sons can answer that question. My goal was to be even-handed, although I never could be certain I achieved that. I was reassured to hear from time to time that parents were pleased to learn I'd be coaching their kid, so at least they felt I aimed for fairness.

Whether dads are the best candidates for coaches or whether high school students who exclusively coached me in my early years do a better job remains an open question in my mind. Student athletes' fervor and proximity to the age of the players are distinct assets. We did have some teenagers as coaches, including two of my sons, Colin and Mike, but the majority were dads. I have to admit a bias that I think it would be ideal if all our coaches for youth sports would be teenagers of the fair, mature and dedicated variety.

Recent history, unfortunately, does not support that as the likely trend in the future. When I was coaching, I worried that we had veered too far from the McKittrick's garage model where self-motivation was preeminent and the younger guys were mentored informally by the older. When I finished up coaching, we were beginning to see multiple leagues for all sports, concentration in only one sport and proliferation of camps with the result that kids were playing these games nearly year-round under the constant supervision of coaches.

Today we are learning that youth sports has become big business, rife with the potential for corruption. This phenomenon was movingly chronicled in George Dohrmann's *Play Their Hearts Out*. Based on eight years following a group of players in Southern California in the so-called "grassroots game," the book details a web of ambitious youth coaches seeking contracts with shoe companies, players whose youth is robbed of them as they spend virtually all their waking hours preparing for and participating in year-round tournaments held all over the country and parents who so insidiously have lost sight of their priorities. This travesty is orchestrated by shoe companies willing to sacrifice the innocence of youth to secure earlier market penetration.

The tragic story focuses on an extremely talented young black player over-sized as a ten-year-old and a coach in his 30's who proves to be more adept at public relations than basketball fundamentals. All seems to going swimmingly when at the age of 14 the player is featured on the cover of *Sports Illustrated*, but then the story darkens. On the backs of his players, the coach gets his contract and a basketball camp. He becomes rich. In contrast, the young player struggles because he is deficient in the fundamentals needed (which the coach failed to teach) when he no longer towers over everyone on the court. He ultimately bounces around three college teams before finally being dismissed with no degree.

Coach Tom Powers

In sharp contrast to the unscrupulous coaches portrayed in that book, there is the story of Coach Tom Powers.

In the early to mid-90's another program purporting to be a higher level than CYO emerged in Wellesley. Metro West featured a single team from each town that competed against about a dozen other teams. When my son Mike was about to enter sixth grade, I was asked by the local Metro West leaders to coach the boys team. From the start, I had been skeptical about the Metro West program since I thought it contributed towards monopolizing the free time of kids with organized activities. I was uncertain about whether I wanted to get involved. Despite this ambivalence, I decided to accept the invitation after being encouraged by some parents to do so.

The first major task was to decide upon the assistant coaches. A little background is necessary. The usual practice of administrators of these elite programs is to seek out a dad whose son would be expected to make the team on a competitive basis. Assistant coaches similarly were selected by the head coach on this basis. I decided to take a different approach—to seek out an assistant who had no sons in the sixth grade, but who loved the game. I asked Tom, my basketball comrade since the first year in law school. Tom hadn't coached youth before by virtue of his being a busy environmental attorney suburbanite who happened to not have kids, but everything I knew about him told me he'd be terrific at it.

From that initial practice where we ran drills and scrimmages to evaluate the players until the final whistle of the last game a couple of years later, Tom proved me right. There was no special agenda. He loved the game, and he loved to teach. He brought a clear objective eye to the selection process and his instructional skills, acquired through two years of teaching high school, repeatedly were evident, whether at our weekly practice or during a time-out in a close contest. He often could be seen in a quiet one-on-one consultation, demonstrating how a guy's shooting could be improved or in the heat of the game patiently diagramming to someone how he could better contain the guy he was guarding who had scored a few baskets right before the break.

What was most impressive and admirable was his interaction with the guys, whom he knew, with the exception of Mike, only through the basketball. That extended to those situations that demanded a critical remark. One incident in particular comes to mind. Our tallest and physically strongest player, someone we'll call Joey, could lose his temper during the game. In one close game, frustrated over a call or non-call, Joey treated the referee to an expletive-filled outburst, which led to a technical. Fortunately, we managed to salvage a victory. At the following practice, Tom gathered the players in a circle and with a controlled and concerned voice said: "Joey, you need to control your temper on the floor. That technical could have cost us the game, and that would not have been fair to your teammates." Tom's kindness and concern allowed Joey to accept the feedback, and I don't recall another incident. It was something that needed to be said, but the rest of us might have hesitated to do so because we were parents. Tom's only interest was the welfare of the team, and the message came through to Joey.

Tom found coaching a "ton of fun" and was sorry when it came to an end. As he recently told me, "the teaching part of it is what I really enjoyed. I have thought that when I retire, I might look around to see if there is a team I could coach." He also continued to maintain an interest in the guys as he showed up periodically for games during their high school years. As a coach of youth basketball, Tom's selfless generosity and wisdom stands at the polar opposite of the gold-seekers we read about in *Play Their Hearts Out*. There is no doubt the game would be immeasurably better off if there were more Tom Powers in Southern California and other destinations of high-powered AAU basketball shaping the destinies of talented youngsters.

Chapter Twenty-one

Over the Hill Basketball

I wasn't playing any basketball on January 1, 1991. In fact, because of a mysterious orthopedic affliction, I couldn't run and was pessimistic about ever being able to again play. Forty-three years old and mired in depression over the situation, I couldn't have possibly imagined that when the new millennium emerged ten years later I would be completing the most remarkable and satisfying chapter of my basketball life—Over the Hill.

Will I Ever Play Again (Redux)?

This story of the descent into depression over my prospects of any future play and the subsequent ascent to reach new heights of personal satisfaction began in the summer of 1990. A few weeks after my second coaches' game, I was included in a memo from CYO coaching czar Paul Daoust to create an outdoor basketball team. When it became clear that other coaches' game veterans such as Terry Driscoll, Jim Ferry and Nick Bogard also were included, I leaped at the opportunity to spend more than one afternoon a year on the court with these guys. I looked forward to getting to know them better.

The outdoor league was made possible by the dogged efforts of George Snelling, a regular at the Wellesley Monday/Thursday basketball. Recognizing a need to have NBA-quality outdoor courts, George had raised the funds from local businesses and town-wide basketball enthusiasts and had prevailed over red-tape and NIMBY objections. The result of George's labors were two beautiful courts near the high school for the use of all.

We felt good enough (perhaps cocky enough) about our collective talent to accept the challenge posed by our first scheduled opponents, members of the Wellesley High school team of about five years earlier. While they had placed high in the state tournament during their senior year, we had among our ranks a former NBA player and were ready to discount the importance of the age differential of about 20 years. Before the game was five minutes old, they ran up a score of something like 22-4. Buckley, our trusty ref, couldn't help but quip at half-time on the advantage of young legs—and, of course, quickness: "not the same as playing the old guys from St. Paul's." I took those words personally when I suffered a couple of picks off my dribble as I attempted to drive. We lost. Not an auspicious start to the season.

Unfortunately, things went downhill for me as I didn't make it beyond the middle of the season. In mid-drive, I experienced an incredibly sharp pain in the groin area. This sent me to the doctor's office again for the first of several visits with an older orthopedic specialist not much interested in the medical needs of aging part-time athletes. His first question: why was I playing basketball "at my age?" He didn't seem to have a solution to alleviate the variable and shifting pain. After months with no improvement, I decided to venture into the office of a chiropractor, despite my orthopedist's remark that the undertaking would do no more than "help out the economy" with my spent dollars.

The practice was a husband-wife team, and I was assigned to the latter. I explained to her the circumstances of the injury, the symptoms and my goal to at least run again. "I think we will get you back to playing basketball," she assured me. At that initial visit, she did some measurements, made some chiropractic "adjustments" to my back, gave me exercises to do at home and proposed a long-term plan. I committed to it since there wasn't any other alternative. Rewarded by incremental improvements, I was running and shooting a basketball within months. As in the case of all interventions, it's impossible to know if time or treatment were the key elements in recovery. I didn't care—I was so relieved to return to playing form after worries that I was finished.

By late August I was ready to compete in the Wellesley Monday/Thursday game—after more than a year's hiatus. Another addition to their group was my coaching partner Larry Ingrassia. After the CYO coaches' game a year and a half earlier, Larry had decided to shake off the rustiness of his game, and the continuous playing and practicing had returned him to the form of his earlier playing days in Illinois. He was in excellent shape and displayed a great shot from the 12 to 15 feet range.

One evening after playing, Larry and I were ruminating on the pace of the game at the Middle School, figuring that the age differential would become starker as time went on since anyone over 21 could play. My recent extended injury reinforced the fact that playing with our contemporaries, 35-45 year-olds, made a lot of sense. We considered the feasibility of organizing such a group. As it turned out, there was a group in Wellesley that fit that bill. I had played with many of them in the summer league and had made a mental note before my injury to take up their invitation and spend a Sunday afternoon with Jim Ferry and his band of merry FerryDomers.

The FerryDome Gang

Since the early 80's, Jim had been sponsoring a basketball game in his backyard court, christened affectionately as the "FerryDome." The "Dome" was a spacious driveway court with a state of the art curved playground pole

256

and lines drawn to differentiate the three-point zone. An early 1980's photo captures the collaborative effort of five guys hoisting the entire structure and guiding it into place, lodged by stones and stabilized concrete. A public relations specialist who spent much of the week on the road, Jim is an affably engaging forward with a sharp left-handed jump shot. Despite our limited time together, I soon felt as if he'd been a close friend forever.

There were many similarities between the FerryDome gang and my Oak Ave comrades in Evanston. It consisted of a core group of about eight with a revolving cast of about a half dozen others. In contrast to many pick-up games, though, everyone knew the last names and the professions of everyone else. They were a close-knit group playing within the confines of an intimate court.

Original member and an ADP payroll specialist, Les Goldstein was a neighbor of Jim. About 5'8" and an excellent tennis player in outstanding physical condition, he was one of those guards who would never let his opponent rest. Another original member was Gene Comella, who owned the pasta shop where we congregated after the coaches' game. Gene probably is best known as the father of three outstanding athletes, including Greg, who played several years in the NFL. He was the starting fullback for the New York Giants 2001 Super Bowl team.

Through the FerryDome, I finally met Kevin Crowley five years after I first heard mention of his name as belonging to a good basketball group in Wellesley. His brother-in-law had casually passed it on to me while we stood waiting for a light on LaSalle Street in Chicago. His nickname among the Domers was "Strawberry Thunder," reflecting his size and his then reddish blonde hair. When he received this name, the NBA world was habitually abuzz with the backboard shattering antics of "Chocolate Thunder," the inimitable Daryl Dawkins.

Not an original but a faithful member after he moved to the neighborhood was Nick Bogard. A member of the Princeton freshman team, Nick remembers fondly the day early in his freshman year when he walked into the Princeton gym for some pick-up ball and was approached by a 6'5" guy with a familiar face to ask him whether he wanted to join their game. The invitation came from Bill Bradley. Other FerryDomers included Paul Daoust and Terry Driscoll.

The spirit of hotly contested games and friendly banter, which had so much dominated my experience in Evanston, prevailed at the Dome. And that spirit continues to this date even though the last appearances at the Dome occurred 25 years ago. When recently asked to reminisce about their play of long ago, the ex-Domers chose to provide an "assessment" of each other's style: Comella "never met a shot he didn't like"; Ferry "pretty boy of the group who played like it and didn't like contact"; Crowley "his accuracy improved with

Budweiser in his system"; Bogard "could shoot the eyes out when not guarded (by me)"; Daoust "rugby player playing basketball."

Birth of Over the Hill

So when Larry and I decided to put out feelers to 40-something guys to play, the FerryDome gang was at the top of the list. Not only could they deliver bodies, but they also brought a crucial intangible—a ten-year history of fostering friendship through competition. Also prominent on our list were CYO coaches Mark Mullaney, John Keefe, Scott Guild, Jay Civetti, Russ Meekins, George Kidder and Tom Shields. All were guys we had spent much time with on the sidelines in the gym. A call also was put into Dan Eastman, who had introduced me to Wellesley basketball six years earlier.

We decided first to do a trial run, a fall of outdoor play at the Snelling courts. For our first outing in mid-September, we ended up with eight for a vigorous half-court game, but on subsequent Sundays our numbers usually were ten so we were able to play regulation full court. The games continued for the next couple of months until the thermometer dropped in late November. The experiment was an undeniable success. There was something special about playing with guys exclusively in our age bracket, and Larry and I moved on to phase two of our planning.

We both agreed it would be a shame to permit the group to disband after the momentum of the fall. One day on the train, Larry threw out an idea: "I think if we could get sixteen guys to sign up and we charged $65, we could rent a gym for the winter." We suggested it to Jim and the other fall participants, all of whom were enthused about reconvening in a gym over the winter months. In the meantime, Larry and I donned our recruiting caps as we approached more players. I gave a call to Chris Doyle to see if his driveway group, including Charlie Brown, would be interested. At a holiday party in early December, I was talking about our proposed basketball, and an interested Dennis Chevalier jumped on the bandwagon. As the positive results of our activity continued over the next month, we became confident that we would reach that critical mass of sixteen, maybe more.

We found an open Middle School gym on Sunday afternoons and settled on a minimum age of 35. With those matters decided upon, we agreed to pay a visit to the gym coordinator to take care of required administrative matters. As it turned out, Larry made the trip alone. On Christmas Eve, we received the news of the death of my uncle Father Bill, whose early life-defining influence had inspired my childhood interest in sports, politics and many other matters. I was on the plane the day after Christmas with my son Colin for the funeral (Brendan was too ill to come also).

When I returned, I found Larry had booked the gym for the following Sunday, January 5, 1992. When informed that only organizations could rent the gym, his quick-witted journalistic skills kicked in and "Over the Hill Basketball" instantly became an organization recognized by the Wellesley Schools' administration. On the spot, he'd also unilaterally assigned a slate of officers naming himself president, me vice president and Russ Meekins, a member of the Wellesley School Board, treasurer. That was how Over the Hill (or OTH as it became universally and affectionately known) was born.

Having committed ourselves to the organization's creation, we were anxious to see if it would fly. We were relieved to find the gym doors unlocked that first Sunday, and happier still to turn the corner from the school's entrance into the gym to find a few already warming up. Soon they were joined by others as guys streamed in, a few cracking jokes about this being the old timers' game. By the time we began putting the teams together, we were astounded by our count. Twenty-three were warming up and chatting, nearly 50% more than our original goal. Our inaugural game of heroic combatants deserve to be enumerated in the tradition of the ancient Irish bards: Bogard, Brown, Chevalier, Civetti, Crowley, Daoust, Donovan, Dowdall, Doyle, Eastman, Falwell, Ferry, Goldstein, Guild, Ingrassia, Keefe, Kidder, Loomis, Meekins, Mullaney, Savage, Shields and Trussell. I still reserve special affection for them for heeding our call.

Since we had two reasonably good-sized courts going cross-way, we formed four teams with three having a sixth man. Following the format of the Monday/Thursday game, the two winners and losers played each other for the second game and for the third the teams who had not played each other contended. With this system, we all had an opportunity to be in a game with every person who showed up that afternoon.

The first day was a hit with all the weekend athletes gracing the floor, and loose banter ensued. Paul Daoust came over to tell me that he would cover the sharp shooting Ferry, his fellow FerryDomer. "I'll stop him" he promised, "I'll foul him every time." Of the twenty-three, all but two returned on subsequent Sundays, and many became regulars for ten to twenty years. Of the two single day veterans, one had a weak knee and another was reminded why he'd turned to golf. Not a bad attrition rate, and those dues paying players put us in the black. It looked like the goal Larry and I expressed, to play the game with like-minded and like-aged fellows, was shared by others.

The next Sunday I again rounded the bend to the Middle School to a rare sight in mid-January Wellesley—a large number of middle-aged guys in gym shorts milling around outside the school entrance. I was greeted with "door's locked," and banging on the door could do nothing to rouse the janitor at his desk deep in the bowels of the building. As we fumbled through a number of makeshift solutions, including pulling out a then rare cell phone with no number to call, I became concerned that some would drift away. Thanks to the ever-resourceful Jay Civetti, figuring out which window to ping on the lower levels, the janitor was alerted. We finally gained entry with our determined band only to discover that we had met unanticipated success with recruitment and had more players than the gym could comfortably accommodate. Fortunately, the lower gym was available, and Larry tracked down the janitor to open those doors as well. With that, OTH had successfully survived the first two crises of its infancy.

After two weeks we had proven we could satisfy a need on Sunday—middle-aged guys wanting to play basketball! That need blossomed in the subsequent weeks as word spread and attendance continued to climb. Larry and I watched in utter amazement each week as 30, 35, 40 and ultimately in late March 44 guys walked through the doors. Guys from Wellesley and nearby towns had somehow heard there was a game on Sunday afternoon for those who no longer were young bucks. I discovered that many acquaintances that I never associated with basketball loved to play and relished the opportunity to return to the court they had thought was no longer for them. It became common for me to hear from guys (and occasionally their wives) that Sunday afternoon basketball was the highlight of their week.

The word was spreading, but we continued our efforts of recruiting. One of my prize recruits was Bob Savage. A native of Pennsylvania, Bob had been an excellent football and basketball player in high school. He opted to attend Wesleyan rather than Notre Dame, unlike a couple of brothers, so our conversations about Notre Dame football and basketball were always colored by the dynamics of his sibling rivalry. For a number of years, I'd endeavored to persuade Bob to play, but he had always resisted because of a concern about injuring his hands. For him, such an injury did not fall into the category of a painful nuisance, but rather as an impediment to his practice as a plastic surgeon. Despite the concern, I finally succeeded when he said he would try it out our first Sunday. He returned and returned. Each Sunday we could reliably expect Bob to be on the court. Sometime in those years that followed, I was told that Bob dislocated his finger, but promptly and no doubt expertly he readjusted it and returned to the court to resume play.

That Magical First Season

As we brainstormed how to make our Over the Hill Sunday get-togethers fun for all, Larry and I hit on a couple of strategies to insure fair teams and promote overall camaraderie. Our first decision was to eliminate open floor picking by captains. No one coming to the gym would suffer through the indignity of being the last pick. During warm-ups, we sat on a bleacher and filled out a legal pad. We began with the centers and followed with the point guards. Our usual modus operandi was to pair the strongest guard with the weakest center and then proceed down the list. The remaining strongest players were then allocated among the teams, followed by the completion of the rosters with the remaining players. The success of this process required that we'd used our best judgment to put everyone on a balanced team with an even chance to compete. For the most part, I think we did a good job, but occasionally there might be a friendly ribbing: "That was the J.V. squad you put me on" or something comparable. The final organizational feature was the continuation of our first day precedent of changing opponents after each game to ensure that each of us was in at least one game with everyone who'd shown up. Larry and I were unwaveringly of the view that the team switching reinforced camaraderie and cultivated new friendships.

The procedures were important, but the critical ingredients of our success were the nature of the guys, their approach to the game and their genuine affection for each other. In a typical pick-up game, there exists a wide variation of talent on the court, but the OTH games seemed to integrate these disparities into a seamless whole. Probably because of their maturity and the lessons learned through the years on and off the court, OTH players seemed to appreciate that winning requires full team effort. It was not uncommon to find a critical shot, or several consecutive ones, sunk by the fifth guy on the team— similar to what my former housemate Xavier Suarez had observed about Hemenway 17 years earlier. This attitude led to an extraordinary esprit de corps on the court, reflected by spontaneous huzzahs (as often as not for an opposing team member) when someone made a spectacular, and probably unexpected, shot or steal. Team morale-deflating actions such as ball hogging were virtually non-existent.

What made OTH so successful and entertaining, though, was something even more fundamental. It permitted us for a couple of hours during the week to relive our youth. We were playing a kid's game with a bunch of middle-aged guys in a spirit we associated with that time in our life that preceded the responsibilities of family and professions. It made a little more tolerable the ticking of the clock that was moving us into middle age. As Rick Killigrew so eloquently expressed it a couple years later: "Where else can you get two hours of therapy for $10?" and "Where else can you be 16 years old for two hours and get away with it?" Those thoughts resonated with dozens of us. On the therapy theme, Scott Guild insightfully has added "and you get the full 60 minutes."

Membership in OTH also created a shared experience that connected us to our larger community. Whether it be a chance encounter at the grocery store or standing together on the sidelines for a Little League game, seeing a familiar face gave us a feeling of belonging in a town where our daily work hours typically required us to be away. Besides the usual chatter about the game, recent events at the school or broader matters regarding Boston or national political issues, our conversation would drift to the latest happenings at OTH— who had the hot hand the last week, a humorous dig at me for "the terrible team you put me on" or a lament for a bad injury that a fallen comrade had suffered recently on the court. No less than any club where members join in

261

"play," OTH reinforced a profound sense of belonging to a brotherhood that we could take with us outside of our time together two hours on the court.

As our numbers swelled, Larry and I soon dropped last names in calling out teams and began to use short-hand and even nicknames to refer to fellow players. This could lead to some amusing anomalies. I remember in particular "Big Steve" and "Little Steve." Contrary to what one would anticipate, Little Steve was about 6'3", but Big Steve was 6'6". One day I half-heartedly apologized to Little Steve for so referring to him, but he delightedly told me he loved the name, an ironic one since he was an effective "big man" player. There was an additional advantage to use of only first names. As I discovered years earlier with my Evanston Oak Ave group, a benefit of identifying each other largely by first name was that we could leave behind our identity in the larger world.

Yet, if you are together long enough on the hardwood, those identities do come to the fore. Among the ranks of the OTH players were a variety of professions—lawyers, teachers, business executives, entrepreneurs, bankers and accountants, to name a few, but the medical profession seemed to be particularly well-represented. By the end of the second year we claimed practitioners in a variety of medical specialties: cardiology (Mike Mendelsohn), urology (Chris Doyle), oncology (Phil Kantoff), cancer research (Myles Brown), gastroenterology (Menno Verhave), plastic surgery (Bob Savage) dentistry (Barry Spiro) and most importantly orthopedics (Charlie Brown and Leo Troy). The latter two considered their OTH fee a well-spent business development expense as they received many calls from our ranks to treat basketball injuries.

After Phil Kantoff joined us, I asked him about his specialty, to which he responded "you don't want to see me—cancer." Phil, who at times (not always) makes brilliant passes on the court, is a leading expert in testicular and prostate cancer, a matter which today catches our attention much more than it did twenty years ago when we were in our 40's. About 15 years ago, Phil (now the chief medical officer at Memorial Sloan Kettering Cancer Center in New York) was featured in an article in the *Boston Globe*, pictured in front of a display of x-rays of dozens of sets of testicles. He was mirthfully greeted by the guys at the next OTH.

From a personal standpoint, that first year of OTH took on a special meaning besides the pride and satisfaction of starting the whole thing with Larry. I was at my best playing level in years, bringing back memories of the New York Lawyers' League, and I felt renewed after 14 inactive months. In fact, for the next several years I found my legs were strong for the rebounding and driving and my shots were thriving, including the fade-away, the running hook and the jump shot. On a good day, my mind tried to convince me I was in my 20's, but in the recovery the next couple of days, my body was persuasive with its argument that I was in my mid-40's.

Based on my appearance, though, one would not guess I was doing so well. Depending upon the state of injuries, at times my on-court presentation was near-comical. Nick Bogard remarked at my entrance one day, "Pat, you look like you just came off the battlefield." Each of my legs had some form of protective gear—a brace on one and a rubberized support on the other, remnants of the Chicago injuries. One of my arms had a band around the elbow for reasons I no longer remember. Shortly into the season, I managed to sprain a finger and a thumb. The resolution for the finger was the standard taping it to the next finger for support. The thumb, proved to be more of a challenge. Since I hadn't previously sprained it, I had to experiment. I tried a couple of splints and braces from the pharmacy, but they either didn't work or resulted in too sharp of an instrument on the court. Finally, I devised my own splint with tape wrapped around two halves of a popsicle stick, which proved to be surprisingly effective.

Summer Play Followed by the Second Season

Summer brought us a wealth of basketball opportunity in Wellesley. Chris Doyle brought his Sunday garage game with OTH recruits to the newly opened outdoor court at my local elementary school, Warren. Other OTH-ers started a late afternoon game at Wellesley High School, where those who'd spent the morning golfing could further batter their bodies on the courts. The weekday evening games at the High School outdoor courts, organized by Commissioner George Snelling, provided us a senior league for the first time. Larry and I filled half of their ranks with our new OTH members as we formed three teams. For my own team, I again solicited Tom Powers to hit the court to compete in one more league. I then added a stealth marquee recruit whom I'd met through town sports, Gary Walters.

As fellow Princetonian Nick Bogard has commented, Gary was the only athlete in Wellesley who could claim a portrait on the cover of *Sports Illustrated*. He'd been the point guard for the 1965 Princeton team led by Bill Bradley, which made it to the Final Four and placed third in the tournament. Following graduation, Gary became the head coach at Union College, Dartmouth and Providence and served as a coach for the U.S. Olympic team. After 14 years of the pressure of collegiate coaching, he moved into the financial world and was then a managing director of the investment firm Seaward Management.

Prior to meeting him, I became aware of Gary through the CYO management. When we were absent a coach for the Cadet A team, Jay Civetti informed me that he asked Gary to coach the team. Not being from the East and only vaguely aware of the Bradley teammates, I queried Jay as to who he was. Jay recited the litany of his achievements, adding tongue in cheek that he "probably" met the minimum criteria for a CYO coach. I subsequently shared the sidelines with Gary at our sons' soccer game when we struck up a conversation. Finding out he was open to playing with us, I got my chance to snag him for the summer league.

Most striking about Gary's game was his passing, where there was plenty of evidence of the former star guard for Princeton even though he had not played in about eight years. I was particularly impressed with his distinctive wrist snaps on the two-handed pass. In executing this pass, which has two variations, the bounce and chest passes, the ball is raised to the midriff area with the elbows extended out. This creates a tension which is released as the arms push forward with the snapping wrists, providing momentum as the ball leaves the hands. Gary's wrist action produced energy that could have driven a motor. Apparently we saw too much of the wrist action in those early games for after the second game he called to indicate that he wouldn't be playing the next game because of a tenderness in one of his wrists and lower arms. Upon the advice of a doctor and a desire to not ruin his arm for tennis, he bowed out for the rest of the season although he did return for the championship game to give us moral support and to periodically don his coaching hat as he offered us suggestions on strategy.

I never got to play with Gary again although we stayed in touch through town youth sports and a shared interest in stock market analysis—he as the professional and me as the amateur investor. Then the call arrived in the spring of 1994 to offer him his "dream job," to return to Princeton as the athletic director, a position he recently retired from after a terrific 20-year run.

As the summer weeks wound down, Larry and I met to deliberate about the next season. We thought we could sustain that interest for a longer season (and be financially solvent if we raised our rates a bit). After the first couple of Sundays in late September and early October, we questioned our decision as attendance dipped significantly below what we'd seen the prior March and April. Competing with youth sports and other fall activities during that early Sunday afternoon time slot took a toll—our numbers were sufficient for only two games, if that. Within a few weeks, more regulars returned, and by January we were soaring again with forty or more playing upstairs and downstairs.

That second season also brought a few innovative changes. By midwinter, we managed to add a weeknight of play to our regular Sunday game since we'd whetted the appetites of our players who now wanted more. The added gym rental was a bit of a financial gamble, but we put to work Scott Guild passing the hat at the Wednesday games. Employing his distinctive style of friendly aggressiveness, we made budget since no one was going to turn down a former Harvard halfback.

The season also featured the arrival of the two best players in OTH history, Terry Driscoll and Chris Stevens. We felt privileged to have as fellow-OTH-ers a former NBA player and a member of the Notre Dame team that ended the UCLA streak. Other than the once a year CYO coaches' game, the one summer outdoor league and the light duty playing at the Ferry Dome, Terry had been reluctant to play much basketball because of persistent back problems. He eventually decided, probably contrary to his wife Susan's advice, to put on the sneakers again and became a relatively consistent presence at the gym for a year or two. In the case of Chris, the situation was the converse—he was playing a considerable amount of basketball, but in a number of different games, including Richie Balsbaugh's game. He soon included OTH as part of that schedule.

Their presence on the court added immeasurably to the OTH experience for the rest of us as their play demonstrated how the game is played at a higher level. Each had remarkable skills, whether it was Terry's superb play around the basket or the Hawk's magnificent inside and outside play. Most notably, they were the consummate team players. I remember well Terry coming up to the top of the key to set a pick for my drive and Chris passing off to the least skilled player on the team who was wide open as a result of Chris being double-teamed.

Departure of Larry Ingrassia to London

Larry truly was the spiritual leader of OTH. His high energy and exuberance were present everywhere—during warm-ups, on the court, on the bench taking a breather. I remember well one incident where a guy, one whom was not ordinarily regarded as an offensive threat, made an incredibly unlikely shot, released as he crossed the paint with his back to the basket. Off the court at the time, Larry was seen waving a towel and hooting in delight. He never passed up an opportunity for a cheer.

As the second season wound down, he and Vicki invited us out to dinner and partway through the meal glanced at each other. Finally, Vicki said: "Do you want to do it or should I?" A portentous remark if there ever was one. Larry said he would and then blurted out: "We are moving to London." He had been appointed the London bureau chief for the *Wall Street Journal*. Shocked by the news, and acutely aware of how important he'd become as my partner in the OTH endeavor, my immediate response was "what about basketball—where will you play?" Crushed with the loss of my fellow coach and fellow founder, the final weeks of that season were played with a heavy heart. Our first OTH social occasion, a goodbye party for Larry, was made doubly sad when charter member Jim Ferry indicated he too would be departing that fall—for Atlanta.

Larry's move to London was a personal and professional success. During his five-year stint, he oversaw the coverage of European affairs during a tumultuous and interesting time. He and Vicki traveled extensively throughout Europe and enjoyed being part of the social scene at the American Embassy, but he admits he could not find the climate of fellow-feeling he helped create at OTH in London. Once beyond the small pond that Boston represented and with the successes he'd created across the pond in London, Larry moved to the NYC headquarters offices of the *WSJ*. In lower Manhattan, he successively coordinated the Olympics coverage, led the planning group that established a Saturday edition, helped put together the 9/11 next day edition in makeshift facilities in New Jersey and then assumed the duties of editor of the Money and Investment section of the paper, sometimes referred to as the third section. Having become familiar with the Ingrassia style evident in all that he touched, we recognized it over and over again as the third section became a considerably more engaging read as analyses and insights of the stories behind the ticker tape headlines began to appear on a regular basis.

He was eventually recruited by the *New York Times* to assume the position of Business Editor, where again his efforts led to a substantial upgrade in the quality of the business news. During 2008, with both the presidential election and the financial crisis converging, the front pages of the *Times* usually were dominated by articles from his group dealing with the crisis while the political coverage that usually was featured had to settle for a secondary position. After serving as Business Editor for many years, he recently relinquished the position to become Assistant Managing Editor for the *Times* and then decided to move cross country to the *Los Angeles Times* as the Deputy Managing Editor.

As the years progressed, my unofficial title at OTH has become the "founder," but on every opportunity I've corrected that by reminding everyone the correct title is "co-founder," a title wholly inadequate to describe what Larry brought to OTH in those early years.

President of OTC in its Maturing Years

With Larry in London, it was a measured joy to return to OTH for the third season. Our immediate task was to take care of administrative matters. I assumed the presidency as Russ Meekins moved up on the "corporate" books to the office of vice president. Mark Mullaney was prevailed upon to serve as treasurer. Another issue we faced was the minimum qualifying age as our original minimum of 35 seemed too young. Mark Mullaney had the statesmanlike demeanor and respect of the group, so I informed our members that the minimum age now was "between 35 and 40" and that Mark would be the arbiter when questions arose. Mark did an outstanding job, but we eased his burden a year later when the minimum of 40 became writ in stone. With a few grandfathering and other special exceptions, it has remained 40.

Personally the most pressing issue for that third season was whether I would be on the court for the first afternoon. While playing the proverbial last game of the summer season, I landed lopsided on my foot after a drive to the hoop. Just six weeks before our season opened I found myself sprawled on the asphalt at Warren School. OTH member, friend willing to help on a Sunday afternoon and orthopedist Leo Troy X-rayed it and declared it a fracture. Of all my various basketball injuries, I happily discovered that a fracture was the best diagnosis if you had to suffer any injury. Bones heal faster than muscles and tendons. Thanks to a boot and six weeks of rest at Leo's insistence, I was on the court ready to play the first Sunday of that third season.

I count myself lucky having had Leo, fellow weekend warrior, as my sympathetic, if at times blunt, physician. A graduate of West Point and a veteran of the Army for a number of years where he first practiced medicine, Leo's basketball game was nurtured at army facilities and the halls of Harvard Medical School. He has a nice jump shot from the 15 to 18 feet range, usually towards the top of the key, but he is unrelentingly unforgiving of himself if he misses. An errant shot usually is punctuated with his own "Oh, Leo!!" To his considerable disappointment, he no longer is able to fire off that shot at OTH and enjoy its social amenities since a back problem sidelined him several years ago. At a recent office visit, I detailed the litany of my various leg injuries. Leo looked at me and unsympathetically remarked: "You know, if you didn't play basketball, you wouldn't be here." When I responded with feigned outrage and surprise that he wasn't "solving my problems," he countered "I can't solve my own problem; I can't play because of my back."

While blunt, Leo is also solicitous as he's proven over and over again, generously accompanying me through crowded waiting rooms and resetting a dislocated finger or two mid-game. I also have learned a valuable lesson from Leo—if you need to go to the emergency room, find a doctor to accompany you. It is amazing how quickly you'll be in and out.

Changing Careers

On Lincoln's birthday in 1988, I attended a business meeting in my role as tax attorney where I met Geoffrey A. MacDonald, someone who made an immediate and indelible impression on me—probably on everyone he met. While the meeting was to discuss the acquisition of a 75% stake in his company by Chicago-based (and former client) VMS Partners, Geoff managed also to treat us to a wide ranging commentary on Michael Dukakis, the relative latitude of cities in Europe and America, training for mountain climbing and a host of other matters, effortlessly retrieving obscure factual data in the process. Forceful and deeply entertaining, the conversation revealed that Geoff was a master at sales.

Geoff's company, American Finance Group, soon became my client, which led to us spending many hours together. Despite our substantial differences in personality, relative strengths and weaknesses and various opinions on matters, including politics, from the day we met until his premature death in December 2012 at the age of 64, our friendship was marked by tremendous mutual affection. Geoff was a "can do" type of guy, characterized by his over the top positive attitude towards any endeavor. One of his endearing traits was to respond to mundane questions like "how are you today, Geoff?" with "if I was any higher, you would have to pull me off the ceiling" or his trademark retort, delivered at bellow pitch, "I'm doing GREAT, thanks for asking."

Needless to say, Geoff's aggressively positive attitude was readily apparent in his approach to physical challenges and sports. In the midst of the VMS negotiations, an issue arose as to whether he was physically fit enough to qualify for the $15 million key man life insurance required by the lenders. Pointing to the conference table top, Geoff in coat and tie inquired: "How many push-ups do you want me to do?" His confidence was bolstered by the fact that he was training to climb Mt. Rainier that summer.

Soon after meeting Geoff, I invited him to our Monday/Thursday game, where he ended up being hit in the mouth. The next morning I received a call from him informing me that he had just returned from the orthodontist to deal with his cracked tooth. As I put the phone down after expressing my apologies, I commented to myself that this outing to further client relationships obviously had backfired. To the contrary—in true indomitable MacDonald form, Geoff returned to play with us and invited me to moonlight on his AFG team in the corporate league. His impassioned dedication to the game probably was best expressed by the court he installed at his Chatham summer home—NBA quality hoops and a massive AFG corporate logo painted at center court.

When Geoff committed to an idea or a project, you could expect 110% "buy-in," whether it be personal or business. In his mid-50's he and his wife Jane decided on adoption—a project that ultimately filled their home with five small children, all close in age. One would be pressed to find another more dedicated and happily engaged father, and all of us marveled at the reservoir of energy possessed by someone our age. Those five children born into such troubled circumstances hit the jackpot in winning Geoff as their adopted father.

Keeping up with the physical demands that Geoff regularly imposed on himself was a challenge and required a strong belief in mind over matter. One of our joint efforts was a client development trip to London and Norway. Arriving early morning at London's Heathrow after an all-night flight with little sleep, Geoff informed me that we were headed across the terminal to the Hilton hotel to work out and shower. "That's the only way to start the day after such a flight," he assured me. The day was to include a series of meetings: a shipping company client, lunch with representatives of British Air, a cab ride into central London where we met with Sea Containers and dinner with a London-based banker. "A full schedule was the best way to break jet lag" served as his motto. I also was admonished to drink plenty of water and eat little food during the day. "You won't fall asleep if you continually feel the need to visit the bathroom and if you are hungry," he advised. When I met him the next morning at breakfast, Ironman Geoff informed me that he had been up early to do a run through the streets of London.

My initial meeting with Geoff in 1988 took place shortly after my conversation with the referee whose chance remark that my intense, competitive play meant I must be the managing partner. This set into play some mid-career reflection. My professional role at that time could've best been described as a client-servicing consiglieri—not the originator of deals, but as a technical advisor and servicer of the transactions. I had begun to recognize that this role, although well compensated, brought me little satisfaction and was far from the thundering risk-taking persona I indulged on the courts. Working with Geoff opened my eyes to the possibility of taking that persona along to work as he had as the highly-charged and dominating executive of an entrepreneurial finance company. I became convinced that I should find a career where there would be a similar harmony between basketball playing and working.

Shortly before the third season opened, Geoff and his partner Gary Engle made a proposal that was to be life-changing. Would I be interested in joining them as a partner at American Finance Group? There were some risks, but Susanne and I concluded that it probably was the right moment in our lives to take risks. I joined AFG to become the client served by other lawyers and left behind my years of being that legal servicer.

My move to AFG required a good deal of travel, including several to London where I had the opportunity to rendezvous with the Ingrassias. While it was fascinating and exciting to have my work life change so radically, it did mean that I missed more OTH games after being a faithful attendee for those early years. The organization continued to percolate along with one notable change. After the fourth season, we decided to rent the gym during the summer so we became a year-round operation. The catalyst for this final evolution of OTH was a particularly windy day in late May when all our shots were errant with the unpredictable wind patterns. "Pat, why don't we just move inside for the summer, rather than deal with this?" one suggested, and that was the end of our outdoor summer pick-up.

I rarely played during the summer because we'd purchased a house in Falmouth on Cape Cod so my basketball on the weekends was enjoyed with my sons at a local court. During that summer, I also began to consider how much longer I wanted to continue running OTH. I'd invested a lot of time and effort to get the organization going those first years, and it seemed time for someone else to assume the mantle. Also, my absences during the summer and at other times due to travel obligations for AFG had some negative impact on the finances because it wasn't always clear who should collect from the non-season holders in my absence. The summer experiment had resulted in a loss, but the surplus from the regular season was sufficient to cover it. I took a lot of pride in what we'd managed to build, but felt the moment had arrived to hand off the torch as I approached my 49th birthday. It was handed off, and Peter DeNatale, who had been with us since the first year, became the third president of OTH..

Chapter Twenty-two

OTH: Succeeding Generations

Over the Hill continued to meet a community need and prospered for the next fifteen years. During that time I was lucky enough to keep playing and in doing so I witnessed a continual process of turnover, inevitable in a sport that takes such a physical toll. Some players were fortunate as I was to remain for years while others left after a season or two. Tallying the growing list of former players was a disheartening exercise for me since I considered them all friends. I continued playing with a terrific group of guys, many new recruits, but the thinning ranks of the first day players did impress upon me the passing of an era, the dimming of that magical first year. It also was a not so subtle reminder that I was getting older.

Back Problems, Sore Knees, Torn Ligaments, Aging Joints

In our third year, we scheduled basketball for the night before Thanksgiving. Shortly before we began, Terry Driscoll walked in with a big grin and yelled out: "This is the hard core!" Since it was a relatively small crowd, we only had enough players for two games. I ended up in the game with Terry, and part way through I glanced over to see him lying on the ground. As I approached him, he looked up and declared despondently: "Pat, I'm finished." Watching him walk gingerly towards the door, I interpreted his declaration as a verdict on the evening's play, but we never saw Terry at OTH again. I also think that was the end of his competitive playing as his back ailments, which had afflicted him for years, finally caught up with him. His departure also ended our ties to the NBA.

The slow but steady war of attrition that made many other friends hang up their basketball sneakers ticked on. Valued player around the post, Kevin Crowley also hit the floor with a back problem in another game. He took a five year break, but his brief return only confirmed his original decision. Dennis Chevalier concluded he was done because of back problems but today always begins our conversations with "I miss it." Bob Savage the surgeon had to listen to the report from his bum knee and leave us, as well.

Others such as Les Goldstein concluded when approaching 50 he'd had a great ride all these years and decided not to press his luck on debilitating injuries. For those who did not leave hobbling off the court, a decision usually was made before the opening of a new season. Sometimes I was warned they would be missing, while others simply were not there that first date in September. I might run into them around town and would comment "I haven't seen you at the gym recently." I'd then learn they were finished.

As we approached the tenth anniversary of OTH, there were five of us left from the 23 who'd shown up on the cold day in January 1992: Dan Eastman, Mark Mullaney, Nick Bogard, Charlie Brown and myself. Dan was the first of the survivors to retire as he found his knees so sore after playing that he was in great pain as he walked the next morning to the train. "I wanted to be able to walk at age 70," he recently explained to me. Nick was the next to depart as he approached his 60th birthday. A golf enthusiast for many years, he was advised by his doctor to quit basketball if he wanted to preserve his golf, so he reluctantly left the courts.

Of the remaining trio, Mark Mullaney was next. Two years older than me, Mark had taken a quixotic path to basketball. Raised in Concord, Massachusetts where he competed in football, hockey and baseball, Mark liked to entertain us with the story of his (very) brief high school basketball career. As he recounts, he was hanging around the basketball gym his freshman year when the coach shouted out to him, "Mullaney, let's see what you can do?" After he did a few drives and took some shots, the coach then told him he "was free to go." Mark then proceeded to Boston College where his solid 6'2" body served him well as a defensive end for B.C.

Mark's high school coach may have not been impressed with his basketball skills, but we at OTH certainly were. From the opening day, Mark was a sought-after teammate. When Larry Ingrassia and I would plot out the teams on the yellow legal pad, we frequently would have to "draft" Mark to fill in one of the center positions if we were short on centers that day. He had an uncanny ability to hold his ground against guys who had several inches on him. A body developed through those years of football and hockey, he knew how to occupy space and was not likely to be pushed around. On the offensive end, he had one of the most unusual and talked-about shots among the OTH faithful—a one handed set shot, which brought us back generations to the pre-jump shot era of the 1940's. From about 15 feet, he would launch the shot with a perfect arc and an impressive conversion rate. We did not completely lose the spectacle of that one handed shot since Mark did make a few "cameo" appearances after he ceased to be a regular.

Despite those cameo appearances, I didn't see Mark nearly as regularly as when we would be at the gym together once or twice a week. In 2013 I learned that he had cancer and that it was "bad." Specifically, he had been diagnosed with stage 4 lung cancer. To get a sense of its seriousness, websites will speak in terms of months for longevity and refer to 1% or 2% rates of survival beyond five years. Mark describes receiving this news as akin to being hit across the head with a two by four. Aggressive chemotherapy consisting of a punishing six cycles in three-week intervals reduced the malignancy by more than 80%. Then came the really good news. Additional tests revealed that the cancer was a mutation that matched the genetic code of a recognized type of cancer. With this knowledge, his treatment was reduced to a Tarceva pill a day

When I met with him after 16 months of the pill therapy, Mark looked fabulous. When he asked his physician to give him a rating between one and ten, the response was far beyond ten. The Tarceva also had the youthening effect of darkening his hair so he has been able to rid himself of those grayish white strands without any Grecian Formula. He has bought new golf clubs, competed in the seven mile Falmouth Road Race and threatened to make another cameo appearance at OTH.

Throughout this ordeal, Mark remained fully engaged in his professional life, mostly medical administration. In recent years his professional life has moved in a much different direction. Early on he became involved with the Voice of the Faithful, the organization formed in the wake of the exposure of the clergy abuse mishandlings by Cardinal Bernard Law in Boston and many other members of the Catholic hierarchy. From its humble origins in the basement of our parish, VOTF has grown rapidly to where its membership numbers in the tens of thousands with members spread over all 50 states and about 20 countries. The organization has focused both on actions that provide support to victims of clergy abuse and lobbying to make the Church hierarchy more accountable on financial and related matters. After serving on numerous committees and as acting executive director, Mark is currently the President and Chair of the Board of Trustees.

At our breakfast in late January, 2015, he'd just returned from a trip to Florida to provide assistance to a local affiliate that's been battling an autocratic bishop in Naples. Mark also managed to get in a round or two of golf while escaping the New England snows but didn't find a suitable basketball game for a cameo appearance.

I will always remember Charlie Brown's final game. With his "sweet" jump shot and incredibly team-focused mentality, Charlie was one of the more popular players. That high regard was further enhanced by the fact that he had treated a number of OTH-ers for their injuries. Tom Powers tells the story of being referred to a highly recommended "Dr. Brown" to evaluate the need for surgery. To his surprise, Charlie walked into the room in his lab coat—again another example of our knowing players by their first name and usually nothing else. Charlie quickly diagnosed the need for surgery and proposed doing it in a surprisingly speedy three days. As a fellow hoopster, Dr. Brown could appreciate the need not to "keep you off the court too long!"

An African-American, Charlie spent his early years in Tuskagee, Alabama. Although his father was not a member of the unit, many of his close friends were enrolled in the Tuskagee Airmen, the all black unit of pilots during

World War II who played an historical role in the integration of the armed forces and recently was memorialized in the movie, *Red Tails*. Charlie subsequently moved to Chicago where he played ball until high school, at which point he too was forced to choose between debate and basketball and opted for the former. Similar to Joe Angland, the champion debater whom I played with at Dewey, Charlie ended up at MIT, followed by medical school at Stanford. As a noted orthopedist in Boston and professor at Harvard Medical School, he became an internationally recognized authority on the treatment of knee ligament injuries. One of his notable achievements was to pioneer the use of hamstring grafts in repairing damaged ACLs.

About fifteen years ago, Charlie acquired the distinction of becoming the OTH player with the longest commute—from Abu Dhabi. In the 90's he had periodically travelled there for limited engagements of treating patients. Eventually, the government built a clinic for him to supervise. He and his wife decided that the family would remain in Wellesley so he commenced a rigorous routine of working two weeks in Abu Dhabi and then returning to Wellesley for several days rest. Thereafter we usually saw Charlie two or three times a month. One night he showed up in a tee-shirt commemorating the "Ramadan Basketball Tournament," an exotic addition to all the OTH gear on the court.

When I faced off against Charlie, I always felt that the key to guarding him was to focus on his jump shot because as the years progressed he drove less. Ironically, it was a drive that was his last move at OTH. I was not guarding him that day, but I did notice his first step for a drive from the left corner. My attention temporarily was diverted away from Charlie to check on the movements of my man, and when my eyes returned in his direction he was lying on the floor. No contact had occurred on the play, just an unanticipated leg twist, common enough for us mature players. Charlie then sat up and his focus, as well as ours, was on the knee, or more accurately, where the knee should have been. In place of the kneecap there was a depression. While the rest of us coped with our squeamishness, Charlie went about examining the area.

An ambulance was called, and Charlie left the gym on a stretcher. A few days later we received an email from him confirming his on-the-spot self-diagnosis was accurate and he soon would be undergoing surgery to correct the problem. He also announced that his basketball days were over and sentimentally recalled many of the memories of OTH he would miss. Besides losing the pleasure of sharing the court with Charlie, his retirement from OTH carried considerable symbolic meaning for me—I was the lone survivor of the 23 on our first day.

In contrast, Chris Stevens didn't leave the OTH court in agony after a bad injury. His story was one of frequent business travel and getting in on the ground floor of a wildly successful start-up. A good story and maybe even a good reason to miss our games. In 1996 Chris mentioned he'd be a no-show for the next game because he was traveling to California in connection with "a coffee company." He'd mentioned earlier in the season that he had joined three others in a start-up. When I asked him whether the business was similar to Starbucks or Dunkin' Donuts, he explained their product involved a machine that brewed individual cups of coffee. They thought it could be popular in offices—no one would need to make the coffee. "The name of the company is Keurig," he continued. Following that summer, Chris began to phase out his active playing with the time pressures of the startup.

When we ran into each other at Wellesley high school games, I'd get reports that the coffee company was making steady progress. The company received a considerable boost when a coffee manufacturer, Green Mountain Coffee Roasters, provided an infusion of cash for a 35% stake in the company. For about ten years, Chris lived the life of a start-up entrepreneur on the road or at an office in a warehouse space. After those ten years, the company made its first profit, and the following year Green Mountain acquired its remaining stake at an astonishing multiple of 100 times earnings. As it turned out, the price was a bargain for Green Mountain. The combined company, which recently was renamed Keurig Green Mountain to reflect the predominance of the Keurig products, has had a market capitalization as high as 25 billion dollars with its stock price at times experiencing meteoric rises.

Chris retired as the vice president of corporate relations a few years ago and turned his energies to teaching. He returned to South Bend to assume the position of an adjunct professor in the Mendoza Business School at our alma mater. There he's taught several courses, including the popular Business Problem Solving. In only his fourth year of teaching, Chris has received three prestigious awards for his teaching: the Business School's Moreau Outstanding Undergraduate Teaching Award, the Frank O'Malley Award, a university wide distinction awarded to the faculty member who demonstrates a commitment to excellence in undergraduate teaching, and the Harvey G. Foster Award for contributions to Notre Dame and the community at large. On occasion he has the opportunity to lunch with head basketball coach, Mike Brey, who was a camper at a basketball camp where Chris was a counselor many years ago. It has been quite a run for the guy who describes himself as a "hood" who was saved by basketball.

Strategic Recruits

The OTH story in those years was not simply one of departures; it also was the story of valuable recruits. We were joined be a number of guys who were to become the mainstay of OTH for many years. Some of them such as David Rosenblatt, known universally as "Rosie," can trace their OTH roots back to the first year. About 5'7", Rosie may be the quickest player we've had over the years with his signature move being a drive from the left for a lay-up slipping through the arms of the defender that always seems to get the right bounce off the backboard.

I was fortunate to meet Rick Killigrew during one of son Colin's CYO seasons as the father of Mike, an excellent player and our team's "big man." Rick always volunteered to be the scorekeeper of the game. One day I described OTH to him, he showed up the following Sunday and he's been treating us to his "rainbow" three-pointer ever since. His most critical role, though, has been as OTH's chief diplomat in residence. I first observed his skills during an incident at a CYO game where adult behavior was not always "adult." While minding the clock, Rick was harangued by an opposing coach without any basis. Rick sat calmly listening to this rant, held his tongue and when it concluded he made a respectful remark without actually conceding anything. In the more than twenty years I've played with him, I've never seen him involved in a dispute over a call, a remarkable achievement among guys who've grown increasingly cranky with age. My own affection for his style has been reinforced by his granting my on-court assertions, regardless of merit. "Founders Call," he pronounces with a playful twinkle in his eye.

Mike Holownia was another CYO coach recruited to OTH, which he's helped lead in a variety of positions, including president. Our shared court interchanges have been marked by an attraction between his shoulder and my jaw. Numerous times when we've been paired off in a game, my jaw has collided with his shoulder. We've subjected this phenomenon to close scientific scrutiny, but explanations have proven elusive. It's funny how basketball can sometimes parody dance—apparently our favored moves just guarantee jangling clashes instead of glides.

Another early recruit was Myles Brown, recently elected to the National Academy of Science for his work in cancer research. Describing himself as one who would rather pass than shoot, he is tenacious on defense, having been dubbed "Dr. D." Like many of the other strategic recruits of the next generation, Myles has been a mainstay of the OTH administration over the years.

I hit a goldmine the evening we attended a neighborhood caroling party. That night I discovered to my delight Lonnie Powell, John Doerr and Scot Wilson, all living within doors of each other and all proving susceptible to my recruiting speech. John and Scot succumbed immediately, but, as we will see, Lonnie required a second prompting. Scot played with us for a number of years, but John was the real keeper. Except for a three year sabbatical in Belgium, John became one of our most reliable (fanatical?) attendees, abetted by his remarkable ability to avoid injuries. John also faithfully has served in a number of roles, including Treasurer, to help run OTH.

My second triple thrill came in the form of a conversation with Menno Verhave, father of son Colin's friend Alex. Menno mentioned to me one day that he and two friends had been playing together, and all three made a great addition to our group. Mike Mendelsohn became our resident cardiologist, and

Irwin Grossman, a 6'7" veteran of the University of Rochester basketball program, became a teammate when we entered the senior games circuit. Menno has been dazzling us with his across court drive to the left followed by an unstoppable scoop. Every once in a while he surprises us with a move to the right, a skill nurtured during his OTH days.

Lonnie and Lenny

Lonnie Powell is a Hoosier through and through. His Midwestern warmth, gentle humor and friendliness tell you that even before you learn he was born in Indiana and attended the University of Indiana to study music. Lonnie's talents as a singer and performer and his bearish 6'3" shape don't immediately bring to mind a spry ball handler, and he required extra coaxing to try one of our games. I finally did convince him to give it a try, and when I showed up one Sunday I found him at the gym early practicing his shots. He greeted me with "We'll see how this goes today, Pat." It turned out that Lonnie was modest. He proceeded to shoot the lights out that day—and for the next 20 years.

Lonnie is a formidable force on the court: he plays excellent defense, uses his body efficiently under the boards and running the court—and is he a shooter! A jump shooter from the mid-range at any point on the court, he will make that shot if underestimated and left wide open and will frustrate many a defender who watches as the ball sails over his outstretched arms and into the basket. A shot from the wing frequently will be a bank off the boards. A drive into the area of the basket might be finished off with a fade away. Lonnie also can put those developed vocal chords to use on the court as well as the stage. In a typical game he can be heard above the general fray shouting out a compliment or complaint, the latter usually leveled at himself. No one can miss play commentary like: "ROSIE! What a shot!" as Rosie manages to maneuver around three players and miraculously sneaks the ball up to the backboard and through the net.

He's the sort any group would welcome. He has helped solidify friendships beyond the court, hosting barbecues and joining in OTH poker games. The OTH card games introduced Lonnie to poker and he's risen to the top with his newly acquired skills sufficiently to qualify him recently for a Las Vegas tournament. While he's proven to be a key component in the camaraderie of the group, he's further enriched it by bringing us to an appreciation of his other gifts, singing and performing. On-court hints that he's readying for another role in a production can be detected by a new configuration of facial hair or his absence from the Thursday game, a rehearsal night. OTH'ers have always been invited to his enjoyable productions. One that stands out was *Kiss Me Kate*, the mid-20th century rendition of Shakespeare's *The Taming of the Shrew* story set to lyrics. Lonnie enjoyed being cast as the romantic male lead—a role played on Broadway by handsome leading men.

Lonnie also played Dennis Galahad in *Spamalot*, a rustic character with ragged and matted hair mouthing 1960's era leftist slogans who is transformed into Sir Galahad. The play calls for Lonnie's character to engage in some serious dance moves. As we watched Lonnie perform a number of vigorous and complex routines, Susanne commented that the OTH basketball obviously gave Lonnie the training to maintain his form on stage. When he lifted his legs high for those chorus line kicks, he wasn't quite as aerial as the young women in the cast, but for someone in his late 50's, it was impressive. The play ends with Lonnie/Galahad being knocked in the head with a shovel. Lonnie's backwards fall after the blow was worthy of comparison to any of the dramatic "NBA flops" that have received so much attention recently.[7]

The Polish-born Lenny Kesten arrived at OTH in our second year and changed it forever. While Lenny's an excellent player, it's his personality that dominates the court. While others are stretching or shooting around, Lenny's warm-up typically occurs from the neck up—trading stories, anecdotes and opinions with others. Since introduced to it in high school, basketball's always held center stage in his life. On his first date with future-wife Vivian, he excused himself part way through as he informed his nonplussed companion that he had a basketball game to play. She forgave him, but she's never forgotten and still sends him off with a "to play with your bums" as he walks out of the front door in sneakers and shorts.

Lenny has one of the most extraordinary biographies among the OTH hundreds. He was born of Jewish parents in Poland in 1949, a mere couple of years after the end of World War II, which devastated, and nearly erased, the Jewish population of that country. His father had been a member of the Polish army and was captured after its collapse upon the Nazi invasion in 1939. Similar to many other Jewish soldiers, he eventually was released and sent back to a Polish ghetto where the risk of transportation to a death camp loomed. Foreseeing his fate, Lenny's father escaped to the forest where he and several others survived through foraging while saving many endangered targets of the Nazis. Lenny's mother was able to secure fake identification to pass as a Catholic, but those papers didn't save her from being shipped by the German authorities to the Reich where she was assigned to work in a munitions factory. The Kestens met and married at the end of the war but, unhappily, were soon living in Communist Poland. The family immigrated to Israel in 1956 and soon thereaf-

---

[7] A "flop" is an intentional fall by a player after little or no physical contact by an opposing player in order to draw a personal foul call against the opposing player. The flop has gained some notoriety through its effective use by some NBA players. In response, a couple of years ago the NBA issued regulations to penalize the more flagrant use of the flop.

ter made it to America where his father established a successful egg business in Connecticut.

Lenny enjoyed an All-American boyhood in Connecticut. His first sport was soccer so he was a little late to the game when introduced to basketball in high school. He's more than made up lost ground for the late start with his avid engagement for the next 50 years. This included his graduate school years at Harvard where he reports spending lots of time at "our" beloved Hemenway Gym. We've concluded we must've intersected during my law school days before we crossed paths a second time at OTH.

About this time Lenny went through his "African-American" phase. Adding about three inches to his 6'4" frame by displaying an impressive halo of Afro-like hair, he began to hang out with the Harvard Law School Black Lawyers Association, frequently referred to by its acronym BLSA, pronounced 'Balsa.' This got him a spot on the Harvard "B" team for a national BLSA basketball tournament. In wreaking revenge for their lack of respect by the "A team" guys, his team proceeded to win the tournament, and Lenny treasures his photo holding a trophy measuring nearly three feet in height. In those days, Lenny recalls, because of that Afro and his friends, he generally was perceived as African-American, an impression he did nothing to alter.

If he was interviewing for a job, for example, he could sense that the interviewer so considered him. Of course the topic never came up since no interviewer was going to cross the boundary of racial identification lest it appear to influence job selection. One of his jobs was as an assistant to the superintendent for a prison in Massachusetts. After he left the position, there was some discontent among the inmates at the prison. One of the grievances was the lack of African-Americans on the staff. During negotiations, one of the prisoners complained that "we haven't had any blacks in the administration since Lenny left." The superintendent then had to explain that Lenny was Jewish. Perhaps the most humorous story relating to that issue was that while in law school Lenny began dating a young blonde who thought he was black. When she learned that he was Caucasian, she dropped him.

I first met Lenny when he was playing for the tough Arlington team during our Wellesley summer league. His teammates included a number of future OTH regulars: George Harris, a challenging force on the court who had played at Georgetown, Lenny's long-time friend and former Hemenway player, O.J. Santana, Bobbie Phelan, an aggressive guard with a shot from downtown and Ralph Martin, who was to become District Attorney for Suffolk County, Boston office managing partner at my old firm Bingham and general counsel at Northeastern University.

Lenny's a strong shooter with a good eye from the corner or the wing in the vicinity of the three-point line—on the inside of the line these days. He also became known for the NBA "two step" dribble with the shot released about five feet from the basket and off the board. Similar to Lonnie, he likes to

278

drive into the key and then do a fade-away shot. Lenny also has a penchant for directing plays. One favorite is to hold the ball at the wing looking for someone to cut. If the movement is not to his satisfaction, he yells out "Go!." He also was the prime mover behind the introduction of "Lenny ball" to the OTH courts. Early in the evening, the games go to 11 with each basket counting for one point but late in the night, the number of players dwindles down to 10 or 12, enough to support only one game, played on the main full court floor. One evening, with the clock pushing 10 p.m., Lenny proposed a game to 30 with each basket registering two or three points depending where the shot was taken in relation to the three point line. Hence was born "Lenny Ball." I must confess that those of us who are not three-pointer shooters consider this to be a dubious innovation..

In sum, Lenny commands attention. Apparently, that presence is carried over to the other court in his life—the court of law. Lenny's a litigator whose cases principally are municipal-related controversies, and one of his specialties is the representation of police officers who've been accused of misdeeds. These controversial and highly-charged cases frequently draw media attention, and Lenny enjoys the role of a lightning rod, which can take the form of run-ins with opposing counsel or judges. He proudly circulates to us the latest press coverage of his most recent incident. One stands out in my mind.

The *Massachusetts Lawyers Weekly* chronicled a heated exchange in a court sidebar conference. An opposing attorney accused Lenny of physically pushing him. The judge disagreed although she did suggest that as a "big man" Lenny did "invade space." Further attempting to quell the argument, she explained to Lenny that his behavior could be interpreted as aggressive "because you move like a panther." "I'm not particularly graceful," he complained and suggested that he was unfairly targeted and "being blamed for being big." A clever court rebuttal which had the ring of truth to his fellow OTH members: a panther he is not.

Evolution of OTH Under Montalbano

After my departure, Over the Hill was run by Peter DeNatale for five or six years until he was sidelined by medical issues, including a blown Achilles tendon suffered on the court. Leadership then was assumed by Mike Montalbano, a relative newcomer to the group, who became its fourth president.

A Chicago native in his mid-forties, Mike was in semi-retirement after a successful business career. He'd heeded Lenny Kesten's invitation to OTH even though, by his own admission, Mike wasn't a skilled basketball player when he joined. What he lacked in skills he more than made up for in hustle. As he describes it, he sought to make his contribution to the team "by doing those things that nobody else wanted to do—chasing balls down before they went out of bounds, diving for loose balls...." He didn't shoot much because "no one would want me to shoot." One shot he did take was off the fast break. After his team's defensive boards, he would rely on his excellent conditioning to sprint full speed down the court and be alone to receive a pass and then put up a lay-up. Initially the lay-ups were often missed because he was travelling at such speed, but over time those fast break lay-ups became almost automatic conversions. Defense, rebounding, fast breaks and loose balls defined the aggressiveness by the newcomer. Today he remains aggressive, albeit a bit slower. He's also grown to become a very respectable shooter, particularly with a low arch jump shot from the top of the key, which spikes through the net with authority. He's a prime example of a counterintuitive phenomenon I've observed: as OTH players commit to the game, their playing regularly results in skill improvement despite their increasing age. It's reasonable to expect improvement for skills like shooting even into our 50's. We've disproved the conventional wisdom that skill development for the game tops out in the mid-30's.

Mike also brought his business acumen to the organization and running of OTH. He officially incorporated the league, created a structure with a board of directors and regularized communication. Recognizing an opportunity to reinforce the friendships we'd forged on-court, he began by soliciting our full names and collected interesting and entertaining facts about us, including not only our occupations and education but also trivia such as the highest level of organized basketball we'd played.

Some interesting information emerged—Rochester, New York was the birthplace of five OTH players and while we had a number of former college players, many respondents listed OTH as their highest level of organized basketball. Mike went further to personalize us as a group by creating a website with our photo, dubbed us with nicknames and associated us with a "signature shot." The revealing (and at times amusing) addition of "signature shots" helped remind us all of how we were seen by our teammates. It was a virtual clubhouse, and it served to bring us closer as fellow players and friends by recognizing each member's unique qualities.

Mike's investment in creating cohesion among us went further. He took on the tasks of arranging post-game beer gatherings locally, poker games at his home and bowling for those who wished to participate. These informal gatherings led to more formal events such as the fall barbecue and the holiday party. In the past, we'd had intermittent get-togethers to mark our co-founder Larry Ingrassia's departure or to celebrate Lonnie Powell's role in *Les Cages aux Folles*, but under Mike social gatherings became a reliable highlight on our shared calendar. Slowly the mission of OTH began to expand to include more and more time spent outside of the gym.

While we never had a secret handshake, we could identify each other by our sports clothing. It all began one year when Barry Lipsett, president of Charles River Apparel, offered to place the OTH logo on some surplus dark blue pull-over jackets. That initial dispersal to the OTH members was followed by twice a year distributions of OTH logo-laden apparel, which we proudly sported both at the gym and elsewhere. That insignia, a large orange basketball, encircled by the inscription "Over the Hill Basketball", often elicited comment. (Not everyone chooses to mark their advancing age on their apparel). Accompanying the comment was usually a smile, whether it be from the TSA official at the airport, a fellow subway rider or the pretty young woman at the bookstore checkout.

The OTH Split

The next part of my story is still a painful one, but it's an important chapter in my basketball tale. Mining it for wisdom has been a late-career task. I suspect that the dynamics of this saga have more to do with human group behavior than basketball.

As OTH passed its fifteenth anniversary, the organization began to experience some internal conflicts, which led me to question whether the twentieth would be celebrated. Ironically, I think the ultimate source of the division was an outgrowth of one of the remarkable successes of recent years, the evolution of the social club through the leadership and efforts of Mike Montalbano. Within the core of that social club were many who had joined me in carrying the torch of OTH's mission for those fifteen years. That mission was tacit, but to my mind and that of my co-founder Larry Ingrassia, it was to gather a group of basketball players who all wanted to play with each other. The precipitating event and challenge to the group's cohesiveness was the influx of an unusually large number of new players over a relatively short period (caused principally by the dissolution of the Monday/Thursday basketball), most of whom were younger. Some also have cited a problematic player or two. The battleground became the procedure for selecting members of teams.

The original system for playing games drawn up by Larry and myself had long been abandoned. The system of switching opponents after every game had the advantage of enabling each of us at some point in the day to play in a game with everyone who showed up. Its Achilles heel was that not all games ended at the same time. Not wanting to wait around, the teams would continue to play against each other. Inevitably it reached the point where there was no switching of opponents. The new normal was that on that day we would play only with the same guys. Whom we played with, therefore, depended solely upon team selection.

Team selection was always a challenge to create balance and fairness. The methodology was subject over time to a number of experiments, none of which had sustaining power. These included: the first ten to arrive would form a game, then the next ten and so on; or the first twenty would be placed on four teams by the president with the latecomers sent to the lower gym to form a game. There even was a short stint of naming captains. We never did get to the free throw shooting contest. The final iteration was the selection by a board member, usually the president, of ten players for the lower gym with the remaining players left to organize their own teams.

Theoretically this method appears to be as suitable as any of the previous experiments. The implementation of this method, though, coincided with the blossoming of the social club, and that confluence impacted the original mission (yes, tacit and, perhaps, mine alone) of playing with all OTH members. The deep friendships forged through the extracurricular social events among some but not all of the players meant they wanted to continue their mutual fraternization on the court. Once teams were no longer selected by transparent criteria such as time of arrival or player positions, rumblings of discontent among those excluded began.

Much can be said favorably about the emergence of this social club. In many respects, it represented the crown jewel of the OTH evolution. But it was operating within the confines of the larger organization. The dynamics of this arrangement were inherently unstable, and it seemed inevitable that something was bound to erupt. It did not occur immediately. Over the next couple of years, OTH continued to operate effectively as two organizations. On the surface, the duality might not have been readily evident. As guys were warming up, members of the two groups mingled freely, joking and otherwise seemingly part of one unit. The warning signals blinked, though, after the downstairs guys left. An atmosphere of gallows humor frequently permeated the air among those remaining.

The discontent coalesced around a Board election in 2011 and frustrations erupted. While the elections changed little as to who was on the board, the election process wrought considerable damage to the organization, and it led to the departure of the friendship-based group (many of whom I had been playing with for 15 years) to another venue. I was torn and saddened by the rupture and concerned that the organization I so enjoyed couldn't remain viable—that we'd lack the numbers to go on. Thanks to an aggressive recruitment campaign led by Angus McQuilken, the OTH games included about 15 new guys as regular players by the end of the year.

OTH would survive, but it was a different looking OTH with the departures and the infusion of new blood. I previously had not known any of the new players, but as we had discovered through the years, those who found their way to the Middle School on Thursday evenings and Sunday mornings were good guys to play with and chat with during breaks. My only problem was they were predominantly younger, and I became increasingly aware of the vast difference between me in my mid-60's and those in their early 40's.

I remained steadfastly, perhaps stubbornly, loyal to OTH, and the lingering sting of the split made it difficult for me to reconcile myself to the changes. I sorely missed having all the group, newcomers and veterans alike, together in one place. Over the next couple of years, Susanne encouraged me to loosen my stance and recognize I was denying myself the pleasure of the company of old friends in order to stand by a principle. Finally, in the fall of 2013 I showed up to play one Thursday evening with the old crowd. It proved to be an immensely enjoyable evening.

After so many years of being exclusively dedicated to OTH, my basketball time now is divided among three groups, with each offering different things for me. I am not certain how long I will remain competitive at OTH as I approach 70 and the infusion of more guys in their 40's continue. After all, when we founded OTH in our 40's, "over the hill" didn't quite describe us.

Regardless of how long I remain with the group, as I have repeatedly told friends, my dream is to wander down to the Middle School when I'm 80 to watch the play of a group of guys who've become friends through basketball. As I now view the events of five years ago from a longer perspective, I recognize the split, resulting in the infusion of many new players, has increased the odds of OTH being around then. I'll walk in, with a slower gait but hopefully without a cane, and tell them I was in at the start 40 years earlier.

OTH at 20

On January 5, 2012, OTH celebrated its 20th anniversary, albeit with its ranks reduced. As the date approached, I speculated as to how many guys had come through the doors over those two decades. By the measure of all who'd ever come to play, we were easily over a 1,000. By the measure of those who'd stayed for a season, the number probably was around 350. Regardless of how it was computed, we'd enjoyed basketball with a lot of guys.

I have much in my life for which I am grateful: forty years of a wonderful marriage, attending our three son's graduations, the birth of three grandsons with a granddaughter on the way, and a career that included starting a company from scratch and growing it. The founding and nurturing of OTH belongs on that list. Larry and I would have been astounded if we'd known we were creating something so sturdy that it would last all these years (and hopefully another 20 years). From a modest vision, we set the stage where fellow players came to grace us with their singular personalities and willingness to share in a mutual love of our sport. Body, heart and soul, even if "Over the Hill".

Chapter Twenty-three

"Geezer Jocks" of the Senior Games

My introduction to the Senior Games[8] was thanks to a nostalgic trip back home to Anaconda in 1997 and a chance encounter with old hometown friend and former Hemenway devotee Bart Campbell. I hadn't been in Anaconda on St Patrick's Day in more than 30 years. It was a holiday my father considered holy—perhaps the most important on the calendar. During the intervening years, I had attended parades and otherwise celebrated the day in Boston, New York and Chicago, but I'd concluded that none of them could deliver the experience of Montana's sibling Irish cities, Anaconda and Butte. My father made the long trek from Polson annually, and for years he'd been urging me to return. That year my son Brendan and I were joined in our pilgrimage by two uncles, two aunts, my sister Mary Anne and her daughter Tara to help him celebrate.

Since St. Patrick's Day fell on a weekend that year, the celebration was a three-day affair, which called for a full schedule: a Mass, breakfast-roast at the Ancient Order of Hibernians Hall, a parade featuring both the local Hibernian Pipe and Drum Corps and the Washer Women Drill Team and a ceremonial visit to the "sick" at the city's nursing home, which included treating the residents to drinks and song. Attendance at the home of the McCarthy's was particularly treasured. Bea represented Anaconda in the State Legislature and Eddie was a ubiquitous mailman whose passion for life and hearty friendliness to all made him the unofficial King of Anaconda. Virtually the entire town was invited, and the McCarthy's modest ranch home overflowed with hundreds of guests occupying the main floor, the basement and den and bursting out onto the front and back yards. It afforded me a chance to see and catch up with people I hadn't seen in decades, including most of the parents of my classmates.

Two people I hadn't expected to find there were Bart and his mother Sally who, like so many of us, no longer lived in Anaconda but was returning to her adopted roots. My conversation with Bart drifted back to our days at Hemenway at Harvard as we discovered that we both were still playing basket-

---

[8] The history of the term "geezer jocks" is explained in the **Notes**.

ball. Bart casually remarked that there "were tournaments for guys 50 and older." Nine months from my 50th birthday, that caught my attention. He didn't have any further information other than he knew someone who travelled around to play in these tournaments, and I vowed to find out more.

Looking for a Tournament

Finding a tournament proved a more elusive task than I'd anticipated. After a few futile attempts on the internet, I briefly gave up the quest, but in a moment of boredom on a long flight, Susanne thumbed through an inflight magazine and found mention of a "Master's Basketball Tournament" to be held in Jacksonville, Florida. When I returned home, I contacted them and soon received a call from the CEO of a Cleveland-based company, who was putting together a 50 to 54 age team although he was 56. One of his first questions was my height, and my answer clearly disappointed him. I tried to assure him I was a strong rebounder against taller players, but a few weeks later he called to tell me that he had found two 57-year-old Australian guys 6'7". He had decided to enter a team in the upper age group, which left me out. Thus ended my first effort to play in a senior tournament.

After telling him about this senior tournament, Tom Powers and I became invested in finding a way to participate. Not long thereafter a notice for a half court 3-on-3 tournament appeared for the "Massachusetts Senior Games." At that time, the MSG had been around for a mere eight years. In contrast to the intense competitiveness that faced us by the time of our first trip to Springfield, one participant described that first tournament in 1992 as an event with an inclusive, relaxed and "festive atmosphere." For the inaugural tournament, participants showed up as individuals from which the organizers put together teams. The championship honors were earned by the NECCO Old Timers, who were the only intact team to register (and were permitted to compete as such). Lest one assume they were loaded with "ringers," the team led by Carl Beal, who was to become a major force in New England senior games, registered a roster of guys measuring 5'8" to 5'10". We were to face a few players fully a foot taller in our introduction to the MSG.

What immediately attracted us to the MSG was the 3-on-3 format, doable in terms of recruiting enough players. Tom suggested Steve Leonard, an environmental lawyer he'd known for nearly 25 years who was a great defender and rebounder. We had to miss that first year because of my injury which was just as well since it gave us the chance to add a fourth player and insurance against game injuries. Rick Dana, a dentist and aggressive guard with whom Tom had played at the Jewish Community Center in Needham, decided to join us in our pursuit of glory in the senior circuit. Tom and I then got a second chance thirty years after the first to name our squad. "The New Kids" struck us as having just enough hopefulness combined with irony to stick.

One early Saturday morning the following June, the four "New Kids" rallied at Quebrada Bakery in Wellesley to head west 80 miles to Springfield College. As we entered the Blake Arena, we were greeted by a maroon sign with bold letters in white: "Springfield College: Birthplace of Basketball." It reminded us that in 1891 Dr. James Naismith, a Canadian-American teacher at what was then called the YMCA International Training School, invented the game to channel the aggressiveness of its male students into an enterprise that would bring out Christian values. The Blake Arena, constructed long after 1891, was not the site of the first game (that was the YMCA downtown), but playing on the courts still gave us a sense of participating in basketball history.

Unfortunately, our performance was not worthy of historical note. We had zero experience with the 3-on-3 format, and that deficiency cost us on the court. To begin with, we'd underestimated the intensity of the highly competitive game, which I'd always associated with a leisurely game of six friends in a backyard. What we faced was a game of continual motion that blew our energy reserves. There simply was no opportunity to catch our breath as is possible in a full court game where there's the possibility to opt out of a series to rest. Moreover, the 3-on-3 favored the team who understood all the strategies to exploit the rules, and to our dismay we knew none of them. We felt (and looked) foolish at times.

Under the rules, after a goal is scored, the ball needs to be passed beyond the three-point line, known as "clearing," before it can be put in play. In other words, the ball needs to be in possession of someone beyond the arc who must pass it to at least one person inside the line before the ball can be shot. A favorite tactic of the experienced teams was for the big guy underneath to grab the ball as it came through the net and whip it out to a guard who had sprinted to the three-point line. He immediately hurled the ball back to the big guy, who scored an easy basket. The elapsed time for this sequence of was about five seconds and was executed on us several times while we were scrambling to position our defense. Another unfamiliar rule to us was that the ball didn't need to be "checked"—the standard pick-up ball rule that the defender of the guy inbounding holds the ball until his team is ready. Once when I passed the ball to the defender "to check," to my embarrassment he turned around and dribbled to the basket to score an uncontested lay-up. Two points for them!

Not only were we caught flat-footed playing the unfamiliar version of the game, we soon were down a man when we lost Tom to injury in the first game. This forced the rest of us to remain on court longer than ideal, particularly taxing in view of the unusually high June mercury in the 90's. After the first two, which we lost badly, we reached the third game with tired legs. Despite our fatigue, we'd learned something from the previous drubbings. We made this game competitive with the lead alternating back and forth. With about 10 seconds remaining, I drove strongly to the basket and made a running hook, which put us ahead by two. As soon as I drove around him, my man conceded the basket and raced out to the three-point line to receive a pass from the rebounder as my shot went through the net. He cleared it, the teammate passed it back to him wide open and he lofted up the three-pointer. As for me, his defender, the momentum from the drive had landed me about seven feet beyond the basket. I attempted to recover as I scrambled back to guard him— only to helplessly watch him release the ball that went through the net with time running out. We returned home to lick our wounds both literal and figural— three losses, no wins, one injury and multiple humbling moments.

We were determined to learn from our long list of mistakes. We began by recruiting two more players so we wouldn't be caught short by exhaustion and injury. One of the additions was Irwin Grossman, a "big man" who had just turned 50. A ten year veteran of OTH known for his sharp outside shot from the corner as well as his inside play, Irwin at 6'7" provided that presence under the basket that we had been lacking even with Steve Leonard's terrific play considerably above his height. The other recruit was Bob Fierman, an attorney who had been a year ahead of Irwin in high school. Bob provided us another strong rebounder at 6'2" and a smart player with a nice drive from the left and a keen eye for finding for the open man.

We also focused on the basics for the 3-on-3 game, which we had failed so miserably the prior year. With the bulked-up roster, we headed to Springfield the following June and emerged undefeated in the 50 to 54 age division. Part of our success was due to luck: a couple of our strong opponents of the prior year had moved up to the next age division, 55 to 59. Regardless of how we got there, we were happily on our way to play at the National Senior Games the following summer.

The presence of a big man definitely was a plus for us. Similar to several others I've known, Irwin did not grow up dribbling a basketball at every opportunity. Swimming was his sport as he describes himself, "a little on the short side and somewhat overweight." Between his eight grade and freshman years, he grew six inches to stand as a 6'4" freshman (and slimmed down). The new Irwin caught the attention of the basketball coach, and for the next 40 years basketball was his game. Following his service to the University of Rochester's basketball team, which included a stretch as a starting forward, Irwin enjoyed a number of intramural and industrial league championships prior to taking up residence in Boston in the early 1980's.

A management consultant by profession, Irwin ventured into the coaching ranks in the late 1990's when he accepted the position of varsity high school basketball coach for Weston, a neighboring suburb. As with all his pursuits, Irwin grasped the coaching reins with intense commitment and determination. He and I had many lively conversations about the prospects of the team and the exploits of a scoring superstar on the team. After two years, Irwin decided that his "second job" was stealing too much time from his day job so he reluctantly walked away from coaching. The two years were a valuable and insightful education into the nature of youth athletics, including dealing with parents—confirming that the experience of today's coaches in suburban Boston is fundamentally the same as those of the young university graduates in Montana in the early 1950's.

In recent years we've seen less of Irwin on the basketball court. After a foot injury sidelined him for more than a year, his interest turned towards cycling, highlighted by his participation in the annual Pan Mass Challenge two-day 109 miles event. Having now "caught up" with us in the 65-69 age bracket, Irwin has promised to join us again. In addition to his contributions on the court, Irwin networks on the sidelines during the down time of the tournaments. Always ready to engage in trading stories, the affable Irwin has introduced the New Kids to numerous intriguing competitors through the years.

The Nationals in Hampton Roads

Determined to make a mark at the Nationals, we spent several months preparing for the competition. Fortuitously, we also had the opportunity to compete in another tournament in mid-March when we were invited to The New England Invitational Senior Basketball Tournament held at the Northern Essex Community College in Haverhill. Organized by Carl Beal, whose team won the gold at the inaugural MSG in 1992, the tournament was offered the following year as a warm-up for the Nationals. We accepted the "invitation" and headed out on a snowy day to Haverhill, about an hour's drive. Most of the 20 teams were headed to the Nationals in Virginia. As had been true at the Springfield games, I spent my free time watching the entertaining and inspirational games in the 70+ divisions. Then in my mid-50's, I once again marveled at these guys 20 years my senior still competing so skillfully on the court.

We played three games and won two. The team that we lost to, the Jumbos of New Hampshire, had a perfect profile of players for 3-on-3. Their offense was spearheaded by a powerfully charging guard, a challenge to defend. If you gave him room, he would put up the three and yet because of his drive it always was dangerous to guard him too closely at the top of the key. Underneath was a bruiser at 6'5" and about 235 pounds who was a force offensively and defensively. Complementing the two on the wing was a 6'4" shooter who also could muscle in around the basket. We've played the team numerous times through the years, and while a couple of the games were close, we've never been able to come out on top. Despite the loss, we were pleased with our performance and looked forward to Hampton Roads.

One Monday in June, we set aside our day jobs and headed for the Providence Airport in hopes of defending Massachusetts' honor at the Senior Games in Hampton Roads. As it turns out, Hampton Roads is a region consisting of Norfolk, Virginia Beach and Newport News, known for its military bases. Because of the strategic position of the harbor formed at the mouth of the

James River, the area has been a military center since Revolutionary War times. The events for the games were spread throughout the area, but for basketball only two were relevant: a practice gym at a school and a nearby military base that hosted all our games.

That Monday evening Tom and Irwin returned from the captains' meeting with disappointing news. We were scheduled a game on Wednesday and then didn't play again until Friday when we had two games in the morning. We hadn't expected so much downtime. Irwin then delivered scouting intelligence he'd obtained by schmoozing among the attendees—the expected favorites, the one or two former NBA players in the competition and a wealth of information about the other teams, all of which would prove to be invaluable as we navigated through the tourney.

The next day we showed up for our scheduled practice at a gym we shared with the shuffleboard players. Breaking down into two squads, we scrimmaged for nearly two hours and did we ever look sharp—shooting collectively well over 50%, crisp ball movement and energetic rebounding! When we met our first opponent, a team from New Jersey, there was no surviving evidence of that practice form. After the endless wait for our first game, we were wound up so tightly that offensively our shots were continually long, short or skewed. Defensively we managed to give them many opportunities at the free throw line. At the end of the first half, our collective offense had generated fewer than 15 points. We recovered a bit in the second half but fell short by eight points. As we walked out of the gym, I took notice of the bowling alley adjacent to the gym and commented: "Our best preparation for the game would've been to spend the morning bowling."

We then faced the prospect of not being able to gain redemption for two days, giving us plenty of time to obsess about how things should've gone better. One decision was to alter the allocation of playing time. In the first game, our platoons of three split the playing time for each half. With ten minute running halves (except for the last two minutes), we each played five minutes per half. We found that by the time we'd warmed up to get into the flow of the game we had to head to the bench. We decided that each platoon would play a full half.

On Friday morning we had an early game against a team considerably better than our first opponent. We played well, not well enough to win but certainly at a level that would have snared us a victory in the first game. A few hours later we faced one of the best teams of our age bracket, a team from Tennessee that featured two guys who, according to Irwin's intelligence, ran a basketball shooting camp. Playing with the best upped our game further, and we enjoyed by far our best of the tournament. Our shooting percentage approached our performance at the practice earlier in the week. The problem was that their percentage was equally high, and nearly all their shots were three-pointers. There was a reason these guys ran a shooting camp—they could execute! Unbelievably, they threw up one successful and demoralizing three-pointer after another. In one instance I was as tight on the shooter as I could have been without fouling him, but the ball still went through the net. We ended up scoring more than 60 points, but they had about ten more so we went down for our third loss.

The consolation was that it was a game we could be proud of. This point was brought home to us following the game when one of the sharp shooters told us we'd played them tougher than any of their prior opponents. Having lost the three games, we were out of the tournament, and we headed to the airport for post-tournament analysis.

Was that the "Hot Hand"?

During the intervening years, the New Kids made it to most of the Springfield games and nearly all the New England Invitational tournaments in early March, but ill-timed injuries have meant we've never returned to the Nationals. More than once, a last-minute decision was made to scratch the Nationals. While I always enjoy returning to Springfield to play under Dr. James Naismith's plaque, the New England Invitational became a favorite of ours, perhaps because it was such a welcome event heralding spring for us. The tournament also had a friendly intimate feeling, inspired to a large part by the organizer, Carl Beal. A genial man in his early 70's during those years, he managed to always include a short personal note on the flyers he would mail in January. He could be counted on to greet us warmly by name at the registration table.

Those tournaments always acknowledged our shared connections by including memorial services for our "fallen brethren." From the start, I'd always been drawn to watching the "old guys" play—the 70+ and 75+ age divisions. A few distinct images stand out: someone falls to the floor only to be surrounded by brother players to make sure he's okay, rebounds ending up in the lap of whomever happens to be closest to the ball and most vividly a wide variety of colorful shooting styles. Nearly all the shots of the 1940's and 1950's seemed to be represented: the one handed set, the two handed chest, the two handed over the head, the Rick Barry underhanded and my favorite, the one handed scoop. The latter, being the trademark of James Caselden, resembled the pitch of a softball and was a sight to behold when lofted. He had surprising accuracy with the shot, usually taken from beyond the three-point line.

I soon learned that the guys I watched play might be making their final appearance. It made the memory of their performances all the more precious. Retirement might explain some absences the following year, but often enough it was death. Carl always conducted a brief memorial service before he moved on to the nuts and bolts issues regarding the court rules for the day. These services usually consisted of a few remarks by him or one of the players about the deceased, whose photo was prominently stationed at the registration table and on the tee shirts we received. In 2005 it was Jerry O'Brien, a member of the first Massachusetts team to attend the Nationals. One year later the service was for two deceased veterans, Chuck Hughes and Harvey Lewis, honored by eulogizer Caselden. The speech was short but moving as he spoke about the two guys he'd shared the court with for so many years. He was obviously not accustomed to speaking to a large crowd, but his short speech was eloquent and touching. Regarding one of them, he remarked: "I don't know. I was really surprised. I thought he was in good shape and took care of himself." The following year the photo of Caselden was sitting on the registration table when we walked over to greet Carl.

As the years progressed, we moved up into older age divisions, Steve Leonard and me moving up a year before Tom. One advantage of moving up was that we landed a brief reprieve from the formidable New Hampshire team that always prevails against us. Our highlight tournament occurred in 2008 when we were all on the "young" side of the 60 to 64 division. With others having conflicting schedules, we drove to North Andover after our rendezvous at Quebrada with a squad of three, Tom, Steve and me. We were a little hesitant to commit to play with no substitutes. We convince ourselves that with the strategic use of time-outs and the avoidance of high risk playing we could pull it off. Also, we knew we had to conserve energy in the first game, something I always found difficult to do because of the temptation to fully utilize fresh legs.

For the first game, we started a little slowly, but as Tom and I took off and found our groove, we alternated on converting jump shots. It was one of those moments of being sublimely in sync with a teammate and the basket. Our understanding was perfect, our shots felt effortless until the scoreboard read 86 for us and 45 for the other team at the sound of the buzzer. After we shook hands with our opponents, Steve, who had done a masterful job controlling the boards and holding down their big guy, came over to us with a grin: "You guys just scored 84 points since I only had two." We were surprised, but while that first game felt good, we still had two more to play, and neither of us thought we could keep up the pace.

Our concerns initially were confirmed as we again started sluggishly and it took nearly the entire first half to establish some distance between us and our opponents. A strong second half enabled us to score 65 points as we prevailed again by a wide margin. In the third game we kept it going and scored in the mid 80's and won another game by about 40 points. Looking back, it was as good as it gets. It was one of those days that could've led to happy retirement from the game. And maybe we should've. Three months later when we arrived in Springfield flush with confidence from North Andover, everything fell to pieces.

As for our shooting that day, some might describe us as benefiting from the "hot hand" phenomenon. Many fans and players believe that a player who makes several shots in a row (or at least a high percentage of them) is more likely to make the next shot. Similar beliefs on success breeding success have been applied to hitters in baseball, golfers and even gamblers. This belief has been steadfastly held even though a ground-breaking article in 1985 concluded that the "hot hand" theory is a fallacy. In their widely-read study "The Hot Hand in Basketball: On the Misperception of Random Sequences," Stanford researchers Thomas Gilovich and Amos Tversky contended there was no statistical evidence to prove that there was a higher percentage of converting a shot if the previous one was successful. The scientific papers did not silence the "hot hand" believers, mostly players and fans, and a debate has raged for the past 30 years between the two camps.

Very recently the "hot hand" camp has begun to muster support from the academic community providing favorable studies by economists, finance professors and recent Harvard graduates. Based on my own experience and what I've observed over the last 60 years, I'm a believer in the "hot hand." I certainly can point to countless examples where a player simply has been on fire, but what is most persuasive to me is the evidence to prove the converse— if several shots have been missed, the odds are the next one will bounce off the rim as well. Personal experience verifies the truth of both legs of this theorem!

Despite our success in scoring that day, Steve was undeniably our most valuable player at that tournament. He controlled the boards and provided a defensive presence in the middle that none of the big guys could penetrate. By so doing he afforded Tom and me the luxury and the energy to take all those shots. With long arms, impressive jumping ability, a terrific sense of body position and a unique understanding of the court action at all times, Steve has impressed coaches, fellow players and opponents since he began playing the game relatively late as a freshman in his native San Francisco. That year he began his career of effectively playing taller guys when he was positioned as a center on the freshman team at 5'7." His maturing basketball game, the product of his private high school experience, was temporarily put on hold when he entered college. Those years were spent at Berkeley, where his attention was focused on free speech and other campus issues championed by the redoubtable Mario Savio.

Similar to Tom and myself, basketball became central again when he entered Harvard Law School a couple of years ahead of us, where in his words "I played too much." In 1967 the Vietnam War and the draft hung threateningly over his class as the deferment for graduate and law students was eliminated. During the three years, his class was decimated with a full one-third not around to graduate in the spring of 1970.

In the midst of the general disaffection, Steve found solace at Hemenway. Reflecting on those years, he credits his development as a player primarily to his Hemenway days. He played in both the A and B leagues for the intramural competition and recalls a humorous incident involving his team and the Justus Black team, comprised as one might guess solely of African-

Americans. His team was sporting dark jerseys while the Justus Blacks were attired in white. On a call where it was clear that ball should be with the Justus Blacks, the referee called out "white." For a few moments, action stopped with everyone temporarily puzzled by the call. Then collectively everyone realized that call was based on their uniforms.

Following law school, Steve played with a couple of legal-related teams, including one where he was the small forward and another with the Attorney General's office led by Scott Harshbarger. At that time, the crew-cut Harshbarger was merely a staff attorney in the office that he eventually would head as Attorney General. Following up with various pick-up games over the next 15 years, the amiable "big man" was well prepared to challenge the Senior Games circuit with us.

The Senior Games Fraternity

What began as games against a pool of strangers has slowly become competition among a circle of familiar faces. As we have become acquainted through play and chatting on the sideline during breaks, friendships have developed. There even has become somewhat of a flexible line between rosters so that an opponent one tournament may be a teammate a few weeks later. This fluidity frequently is dictated by whose available to play after all injuries have been taken into account. In the process, I've felt that I've joined a fraternity. There are a number of fascinating individuals who are part of this fraternity in New England, but three stand out in my mind: Ed Conway, Hank (Cowboy) Philbrick and Tom Winters.

Without a doubt, Ed is the leader and chief cheerleader of the New England senior basketball fraternity. Every year he sets himself the job of making sure we sign up, show up, have fun and stick together to do it again—no excuses—and he approaches that task with missionary zeal. Today there are at least seven annual tournaments in the region, and Ed has a principal role in administering and marketing six of them. He is indefatigable in his efforts.

The year reliably begins with an e-mail from Ed informing us of the tournament schedule extending from May until September. He keeps the drum beating with reminders and cajoling messages, sometimes specifically targeting the missing: "What about the New Kids, where are you on this tournament?" or "We don't have many among the 50's; where are you young guys?" Sometimes he issues challenges: "Bennett and Walsh said they'd be interested if there was going to be a good turnout. Every day that is delayed increases the chance of players making other plans." "The more that are coming the more that want to come so let's start acting." Post-tournament missives always list results, express his gratitude and conclude with the traditional Conroy sign-off: "keep hitting the 20-footer."

Occasionally, there is a note of sadness in his email as when he has to announce the cancellation of a tournament because of insufficient interest:. "Unfortunately NH has had to cancel this year's games. There was just too few teams committed to playing." Leaving us with no doubts as to his disappointment at the cancellation, he laments "it appears to be a sign of the times." For Ed the cancellation of a tournament is a tragic omen of a possible future—a world in which no senior games exist. For the present, though, the games are to be cherished both on an individual and a collective level. For some of the tournaments, Ed is the master of ceremonies who gathers the entire group in a circle to read out the rules. Before he begins the formal program, he reminds each of us that "we should thank God that we are able to come out and compete" at our ages. To remind us of our privilege and to drive home his point, he frequently will cite a former player who through an illness such as A.L.S or through death cannot be with us that day.

Having grown up in Roslindale in a typical 1950's Boston neighborhood filled with kids to field any sport, Ed is a product of the CYO basketball program. After various leagues and pick-up games for a number of years, he started a pick-up group at a high school in Roslindale, which lasts to this day— now well in excess of 30 years of hoops action. He was a relative latecomer to the senior games, being introduced to it about 2002 through another tournament that he organized. Soon after that introduction, Ed threw himself into the midst of the senior games administration. What else could be expected of one so inspired by his love of the game and his thrill to be able to play competitively against guys his age?

Over the last 12 years, I primarily have played against his team. A couple of years older than me, Ed is a guard who plays "all in." Cowboy Philbrick remembers his first outing on the court with Ed, who took a lot of physical punishment as he was mixing it up inside. Cowboy was impressed with the "tough guy" and decided this was someone he needed to know. Today he typically avoids the drive and looks to position himself for the open spot to launch his high arc set shot, particularly beyond the three-point line where, as I've learned to my detriment, he will hit "the 20-footer." Ed and I have shared the good and the bad. One memorable event was when he accidentally poked me in the eye at a tournament in Springfield, for which he was most apologetic. In the spirit of psychological warfare, I have found it convenient to remind him of the incident if he is guarding me—if I am successful with my tactics, I end up with a few inches of breathing room for taking the jumper.

Every Thanksgiving all the senior players receive a greeting from Ed. The following sent out in 2014 is typical:

No tournament news updates. Just a quick note to wish you all a Happy Thanksgiving. I have many things in my life to be thankful for and on that list is the opportunity to have met all of you and played (and continue to play) the game that we grew up loving. My wife is always amazed that there are so many other "idiots" (she says that in a loving way obviously) around who will drive 1, 2, 3 hours to play basketball. To that I reply "Thank God."

To which I respond, there are about 150 guys who thank God that we have Ed Conway.

Cowboy Philbrick is Mr. Massachusetts Senior Basketball. His business card says it all—in a bold green color, it includes his name, phone number, email address and SENIOR BASKETBALL as his line of work, a gift from his wife when he retired from his prior career as a shipping dock foreman. Cowboy takes his new "job" seriously, filling his time five days a week at various Boston-area gyms, including Everett, Newton and Roslindale and rarely missing a tournament in the New England area, whether it be in Massachusetts, Maine, New Hampshire, Rhode Island or Connecticut. Now in the 70+ division, he has been playing in Springfield on a variety of teams for more than 20 years, including the inaugural 1992 tournament. Everyone knows Cowboy. Most remarkable about his "addiction" to the game is that the Texan-raised Cowboy didn't touch a basketball until he was in his early 30's.

I began playing against Cowboy at our first or second tournament in Springfield. He was an aggressive player, particularly at the defensive end. Leg injuries impacting his mobility have slowed him somewhat, but his quick hands still can execute a stealthy block when we least expect it. Offensively, he typically will take a dribble or two and then release the ball from his side for a low arc shot that has extraordinary accuracy. The combination of the position of the ball plus the quick release make it difficult to defend, even in traffic, despite the fact that he barely leaves his feet in shooting.

Cowboy has suffered all manner of ailments in the service of the game and is generous and eager to share medical advice borne of this experience. At one of the MSG tournaments, he saw me benched from a strained calf muscle and sat down to solicitously inquire about my health. Cowboy then chronicled his own extensive history of leg injuries and ended by providing some useful advice about general leg exercises and proper methods of warm-up. On another occasion, he spotted me wearing a leg brace and he showed me his own with a strap for the patella, which he declared to be superior. Recently Cowboy sought me out to sing the praises of a massage as he explained that a massage on the right arm could paradoxically have beneficial impact on the left side of the body.

In short, one simply can't grow old in this sport without some war stories to tell, and Cowboy views his mission as a part of the senior fraternity to share solutions for our aches and pains so we can all strive to stay on the court just a little longer. I fully expect it to be more than a little longer for Cowboy. I'm willing to wager that ten years from now his 6'1" frame will be walking with that slight limp, legs and arms covered with all sorts of braces and bands, onto the court to join his fellow octogenarian teammates.

Tom Winters is the New England senior basketball gym rat. A fixed presence at tournaments, the 5'10" Winters with his brushy mustache and cocky stride also is very active on the Massachusetts pick-up circuit. His basketball history reflects his trademark hustle and assertiveness on the court. A fellow Montanan, Tom was a member of the Great Falls Bisons team which won the high school state championship my junior senior. Not being recruited, Tom secured a walk-on spot for the Montana State Bobcats freshman team by impressing the coach with his hustle and scrappiness. Despite this achievement, he was not fated to have a long career with the Bobcats.

Tom then moved his game nearly 1,000 miles east to pursue pre-med studies at the University of North Dakota. Shortly after arriving at the campus, he met a tall, gangly player who was leading the Fighting Sioux (nickname now retired) to national prominence. His name was Phil Jackson. Tom has remained a close friend of Jackson's through his years playing for the Knicks and coaching Albany and Puerto Rico before he rose to prominence as the coach for the Chicago Bulls and the Los Angeles Lakers. Sitting down with Tom at the tournaments nearly always elicits a story about a visit to Coach's "cabin" on Flathead Lake in Montana or his most recent career developments.

On the court I've contended frequently with Dr. Tom's scrappiness on both offense and defense. Offensively, he combines a powerful drive with a dangerous mid-level shot that can destroy the opposition. "Used to have a three-point shot, but no longer—legs," he muses. On defense, he gives little ground, and I've found that attempting to drive against him can be a slog. He never concedes a rebound. In sum, going against Tom is a competitive and exhausting ordeal. As we tug and pull for every inch of space on the floor, I sometimes have to remind myself that though our heads are competing in the 25-29 age bracket, our bodies have weighed in for the 65-69 division.

At age 68, Tom is a magnificent physical specimen. After our most recent tournament, I walked out with him—I was headed to my car while Tom, dressed in cycling gear, was planning to bike home after playing three grueling games. This summer he'll be making his annual sojourn to Montana to do some mountain climbing in Glacier Park. In his sight is the 10,500-foot Mt. Cleveland, the highest in the Park and just shy of the Canadian border. With this cross-training, his twice a week basketball outings are a breeze.

Reflecting the fluidity of our rosters, in 2011 I joined Tom's team to compete in Houston. Playing in the super air-conditioned atmosphere of the Houston Astrodome to escape the sweltering Houston summer heat was memorable, but it was not the high point of the games for me. Rather, meeting a bunch of players, men and women between the ages of 75 and 86, left me with memories I will never forget.

Chapter Twenty-four

Notes from Houston: 2011 National Senior Games

The trip to Houston for the 2011 Senior Games started inauspiciously for me. I was dumped by American Airlines in Dallas with no ability to get to Houston that day—no flights and no available rental cars. I missed the 9 a.m. game entirely, and without my luggage, I had to settle for watching the 11 a.m. game against a tough opponent with a couple of guys in the 6'8" or 6'9" range. Our team did their best to cope, but it was a loss of about 12 points.

We lost our next game by 14 to another impressive squad from Missouri, but it was a moral victory since they ultimately won the championship. The Missouri team's star was John Brown, a 6'7" dynamo in the paint, around whom there was a lot of chatter on the sidelines and the snack tables. I heard that he'd scored over 30 points against Artis Gilmore. Intrigued by the sound bites (and his performance), I researched him and discovered he was an All-American at Missouri, seventh overall NBA pick in 1973 and NBA All-Rookie team in 1973-74. His seven year NBA career included stints with the Hawks, the Bulls and the Jazz, followed by ten years in Europe. Unlike most former NBA players, many of whom are hobbled by persistent injuries, he still had the "it." While the lines in his face revealed his 60 years, his body suggested someone in his thirties. I enjoyed sharing the court with him, but the real story of my odyssey to Houston had nothing to do with my own basketball play.

The Bulldogs and the Meteors

After our game against Missouri, our bench was taken over by the San Diego Meteors, four women in the 75 to 79 age bracket. Intrigued to know their backstory, I struck up a conversation with a couple of them. I discovered they hadn't played in college or high school—"no Title IX"—and had picked up the game later in life. Proudly, they pointed to one of their players—a tall redhead warming up on the court and told me she was a lawyer. I mentally filed that away as something to investigate later.

That morning the Meteors were playing the Bulldogs from Tennessee. I would have called them the Belles. These four women looked as if they had just stepped out of the beauty parlor. Many of the older women I saw at the tournament sported short 'practical' hairstyles, but each of the Bulldogs wore full make-up and elaborate silver hairdos. With their fashionable white uniforms, one might have thought they were headed to a garden party rather than to play basketball. How looks can be deceiving! They methodically destroyed the Meteors 36 to 18, a drubbing which was only slightly less impressive than their dismantling of the She Can Go from Illinois the previous day by a score of 42 to 11. This team of women in their late 70's scored 78 points in two games with 12 minute running time halves.

All aspects of their game hummed along like a Mercedes engine— offense, defense and rebounding. Most impressive was their leader, an extremely attractive player in her late 70's, who excelled at shooting and about everything else. Some of the shots she put in were truly amazing. I spoke to her after the game, and it was quite clear that as the defending champion her team was accustomed to winning. And win they did in Houston! In the entire tournament, the only remotely close score was a 7-0 forfeit for the championship game. Their opponent, the Oklahoma Golden Girls, presumably decided it was a futile effort to challenge the champions and headed home on an early flight.

The trip to Houston also had created a chance to dine that first evening with an old friend, fellow graduate student Gail Merel. Gail knew of my luggage woes and checked in with me the next day as I was watching the Meteors: "Clothes arrive?" I texted back "Am watching women 75-79." Her response: "I'm glad to know that when I'm 75-79 some man aged 64 may be watching me!!!!" In fact, I wasn't just watching, I was enthralled by these women, their skill and their mettle.

I was to have the privilege of watching more women's basketball in age brackets where we usually don't go hunting for spectator thrills. The Meteors' second game of the day was played mid-afternoon on the same floor as another game I was watching to scout an upcoming opponent. I periodically shifted my attention to the Meteors game and early in the second half I saw the lawyer who'd been pointed out to me earlier on the floor being attended to by a trainer. Several of the players from both teams formed a circle around her. She'd tripped over another player and landed face first on the floor—painful in any circumstance, particularly for someone over 75. The force of the impact was exacerbated by the fact that the floor lies over a concrete substructure. After a few minutes, she was helped off the court with a towel pressed on the large gash over her eye.

In the meantime, the Meteors were left with three players. Despite their reduced numbers, they did manage to win the game. As I left the gym late afternoon, I noticed the three of them warming up for their third game of the day—an incredible feat for of endurance for the septuagenarians (and they won that one too)! Two more games were scheduled for the Meteors the next day for a total of five in two days. In contrast, during those same two days, we youngsters in our early 60's played three games with six players. Fatigue finally overtook the iron women as they lost both games that day, managing to score a total of only 19 points, far below their average of more than 20 per game.

Joanne Garvey: Tax Lawyer with the San Diego Meteors

After watching my first Meteors game, I got my chance to chat with Joanne Garvey, the lawyer. She was by far the tallest member of the team, a big woman for that age group who walked with a slight limp. As we spoke, I recalled seeing her cross the lobby at my hotel and being struck by the sight of a woman in her 70's in her basketball uniform with a ball cradled firmly on her hip. To my surprise, I discovered that she was a fellow tax lawyer.

She also confessed she was a "ringer" from San Francisco playing on the San Diego team. Unlike many of the senior women who compete, Joanne was not a latecomer to the game. She began playing as a young girl on the playground, primarily with boys in her home town on the "other side of the Bay," Oakland. Playground basketball, she recalled, can develop some unique skills, such as how to get the ball to the hoop when there are tree branches in the way. Her early basketball was not limited to playing with boys. Several friends at her parochial school would play at a basket outside the school on Sunday mornings. With the hoop proximate to the church, it turned out that their play created an audible distraction from services so the pastor took action to terminate the Sunday morning basketball.

Her high school opportunities to play were limited since her years fell after the height of girls' basketball in the 1930's and before its later resurgence following enactment of Title IX. While there was no women's intercollegiate basketball at Berkeley, Garvey did play competitively. She was recruited to play on a travelling recreational team that competed in an informal women's league comprised of many of the area colleges, including Stanford, University of San Francisco and St. Mary's, and local military bases. At 5' 10 ½" she was a prized catch for a team. During her law school days at Berkeley's Boalt Law School, she continued playing in various leagues, but upon graduation she was away from the game for the next 35 years.

In 1994 she received a call from her younger sister who'd signed up Joanne to join a group of San Diego women forming a team to compete in senior competition. Joanne begged off the qualifying tournament, impressing upon her sister "I have a brief due." The team qualified without their center, and her sister called again advising her "to get into shape" since they were headed to the national tournament in San Antonio. Her senior basketball career had begun— one that lasted for 16 years as she travelled to every Nationals' venue until Houston. As she pointed out to me, the senior games circuit offered a sisterhood considerably more diverse than the legal fraternity she encountered daily` as a tax attorney.

When I returned home, I visited the website of her law firm, Sheppard Mullin, and discovered that she was excessively modest in the description of her legal career—she was a highly prominent attorney recognized as an authority on California state taxes and a trailblazer as a female attorney. Her career has been described as a series of "firsts." She was the first woman to be named a partner at a downtown San Francisco law firm and the first to hold various bar association executive positions; numerous publications are credited to her. In recognition of her prominence, she has been the recipient of many awards and honors, including one in her name. In 1994 the State Taxation Section, which she founded, established the Joanne M. Garvey Award for Lifetime Achievement. Subsequent awardees have included judges, law professors and distinguished practitioners in law firms. In 2003 she received the Margaret Brent Women Lawyers of Achievement Award by the American Bar Association, which honors outstanding women lawyers. Included among the group of prominent recipients is Hillary Rodham Clinton.

The American Lawyer Lifetime Achievement Award was presented to her in 2007 for her "tireless work in public service," particularly in improving access to legal services to all. The citation noted that she had headed the American Bar Committees devoted to legal aid. In her acceptance for this award, she self-deprecatingly commented that she had told "her friends that when you start getting awards like this, it means you're getting old." While there is some truth to that bit of wisdom, old people with undistinguished careers do not receive such awards. Besides, when she received the first of her awards in 1994, she was at most 60, and anyone of us who have passed that mark know that it is NOT old.

To the loss of all of us, that collision on the floor in Houston ended Joanne's competition at the Nationals. On September 11, 2014, she died at the age of 79 after a long bout with cancer. Along with the list of the achievements of this "women's mentor," the obituaries and tributes mentioned her "passion" for the game. As law professor Richard Pomp summarized it: "She was a class act—and a decent basketball player. She was nearly six feet—and had a better shot than me."

Oklahoma Sooner Gals

The Bulldogs and the Meteors had compelling stories, but truly the darlings of the tournament were the Sooner Gals of Oklahoma. I first came across them on Thursday morning for a 10 a.m. game when they played the Canyon Nets 80's from New Mexico. Decked out in their red, white and blue stars and stripes uniforms, the Sooners couldn't be missed. I knew it was a game in the women's 80+ division, and these three women did look old! In fact, they were 84, 85 and 86. That's right, there were only three of them: Jane, Juanita and Melba—no substitutes.

Why were they competing with only three players in a basketball tournament at their age? My friend Jim Viola couldn't resist asking. One responded rather sardonically: "Yes, we used to have six, but two died and one is now in the nursing home." Poignantly she had reminded us that at their age, it can be a remarkably short step from competing on the court to a trip to the graveyard or long term care. This uneasy relationship between mortality and basketball was emphasized by Melba, one of the three, in an interview she provided a month before to the *Tulsa World*. In explaining her devotion to playing, she expounded: "If you want to die really soon, just sit on the couch and watch TV…If you don't have a reason to get up in the morning and something important to do…then you are going to die."

I was particularly intrigued by Jane, the woman at the point; her white hair was piled on top of her head, she had a noticeable stoop at the shoulders, and she chewed gum while playing. At one point, Jane and one of the Canyons were fighting ferociously for control of the ball and nearly ended up in my lap in the first row. I commented on my voice memo—"This woman is really old and she is fighting for the ball as if she were twenty." At half-time the score was 10-0 with the Sooner Gals ahead. This was due primarily to the shooting skills of the 86-year-old Melba, who had scored 8 of the points, including one from 15 feet over the arms of the Canyon defenders. Although they did not score in the second half, their cushion was sufficient to prevail 10 to 6. The game was one of six played over four days. That included the unheard of two back-to-back, prompting one of them to comment in a later interview: "That makes it hard on a bunch of old gals."

Shortly after the game, the three of them began posing for photos. I decided to include myself, and one of them caught my eye as she pulled up her shorts to "show a little leg." I snapped the photo. It was obvious to all that they were the glamour team. The sidelines were filled with people documenting their feats, and a search on the web post-tournament produced numerous articles, photos and videos of the Gals in their red, white and blue. The photos included Jane with her hands folded in a saintly pose looking up to the heavens, Jane in a couple of instances fighting for the ball, Jane with her under the leg dribble and the three of them in a work-out with players from the Tulsa Shock of the Women's National Basketball League. My favorite was Jane standing with her battle-scarred arms on her hips and eyes scowling at the camera.

In another interview, Jane indicated that in addition to basketball, she intended to compete in a number of track and field events, including the discus, javelin, shot put, long jump, triple jump and hammer throw, most of which had earned her Senior Games medals previously. Whether because of her two broken ribs or conflicting schedules with the six basketball games, the results seem to indicate that she competed only in the hammer throw, for which she placed second with a throw of 11.07 meters or about 35 feet.

Jane recalled she didn't start playing basketball until she was 65 because when she was young "sports wasn't lady-like." Obviously, she was making up for all those lost opportunities of her youth to engage in un-ladylike behavior. The excitement engendered by their presence was heightened by an awareness that they'd decided this was to be their farewell performance. One of the Gals dryly commented she had decided it was time to take up golf!

While it was the last hurrah for the Sooner Gals, it was not Jane's last trip to the Senior Games. She returned in both 2013 and 2015 to compete in track and field, throwing the 8.82 pound hammer nearly 30 feet at age 88. She also managed to squeeze into her training schedule a trip to Washington D.C. in 2014 to receive a Congressional Medal for her contributions to the Civil Air Patrol during World War II.

Battle of the Octogenarians

And then there were the men. While there were several men in the 75-80 age group who were still "players," my attention was caught by the remarkable Bob Cisneros of the Ohio Greyhounds in the 80+ division. As I was walking along the sideline one afternoon, I spotted the handsome 5'9" guard warming up with his routine—draining three-pointers, shooting nearly flawlessly from the free throw line and driving to the basket with moves of a man 50 years younger. I inquired where he played college and he explained he was cut as the 11th man at one of the Ohio colleges. "I am certain that none of those 10 play nearly as well as you do now" I opined and could've added "probably none of them are still playing and some may be dead."

I had seen their opponents the Wisconsin 80's play the previous afternoon and had been impressed with Richard Lane, a smooth lanky forward type. During the first half, he had made a number of exquisite drives from the side into the paint, converting a few eye-popping baby hook shots. He had missed much of the action for the remainder of the game as he worked on stretching his back to loosen up a strain. Speaking with him briefly before facing the Greyhounds, I complimented him on his shots the previous day; "well, a couple made," was his dismissive and modest response. When I asked about the back, he responded: "I shouldn't be playing, but I'm planning to do it any way." Mind over matter at 80!

The first half was dominated by the eventual division champions Greyhounds, who were up 16 to 3 at the buzzer. Cisneros was the clear difference. At the break, I reported on my voice memo: "Cisneros made a few three-pointers, has been ferocious on defense and has been dribbling, shoveling and shooting."

Sitting in the stands I assumed the role of a play by play announcer for the second half, and what follows are excerpts from those 12 minutes of thrilling play:

Wisconsin passes it in, is stolen by Ohio, Cisneros dribbles, shoots and in.

Wisconsin gets the ball over to Lane, dribbles. Beautiful. He goes right by his guy for the lay-up.

Ball to Cisneros, beautiful pass to no. 9, back to Cisneros, fakes a pass, takes a couple of dribbles and let's go a running shot from inside the three point line; sinks it.

Cisneros to no. 12, back to him; takes the shot; missed that shot—first one I've seen him miss in a while.

Lane has it, passes it to no. 10, back to Lane; dribbles by everyone. Stop in action—I think he was fouled. Time-out!

Back over to Lane. Dribbles around and what an incredible shot! He went to his left and then banked it off the board.

Three-point-shot by Wisconsin is off; Lane grabs rebound and puts back up from about 4 feet. It is in.

Ohio has it; no. 12 to 11 and then Cisneros; great play: one, two, three and in.

Pass to Ohio no. 10; sinks it from 12 to 15 feet.

Over to Cisneros, then passes to no. 12 (Cisneros is an excellent passer); ball is knocked loose and Cisneros picks it up goes to his right. He's going to take it all the way in and is fouled. Makes the free throw. Misses the second; he doesn't miss many of these.

Tie up between Lane and Cisneros. Arrow points to Ohio.

Ohio misses; Lane has rebound and throws out to three-point line to clear; back to Lane, who come across the lane and does his hook shot. Falls short.

Back in play. Cisneros to 12, to 11 and then back to Cisneros. Shot from corner. Bingo—it is in.

Cisneros to 11; hands off to 12, back to Cisneros, then to 12 and 11, who passes to Cisneros—all by himself and of course two points.

Wisconsin shot missed—that's the end of the game: Greyhounds 29 to 13

As the play by play reveals, these octogenarians were engaged in a real game and were not merely old guys occupying space on the court. The play by play could have applied equally to the action of high school rivals, albeit at a reduced speed of play.

As with all the old folks I saw competing in Houston, they validated the claim this is a lifelong sport. On a personal level, they served as a source of inspiration to me. From time to time over the past several years, I've considered whether I should hang it up and retire from playing. After watching these guys (and gals), I'm convinced that sheer determination will get you pretty far and the chance to derive some pleasure from the playing competitively is enticement enough. I'm hoping to follow in their sneakers and to be at the Nationals when I'm eighty.

Chapter Twenty-five

To be Played, Not Remembered

I am painfully aware that my play today nowhere resembles what it was 30 years ago, or even 10 years ago, or for that matter two years ago. At times I need to strain my mind to recapture the feeling I had playing as a younger man. Nor can I expect improvement. It's only going to get worse.

I still go to the gym religiously and practice my shots with the same concentration and go through a series of drills to maintain flexibility and reflexes. From the neck up, I continue to focus on game strategies and attend to the smallest advantage the wisdom of playing experience can give me. But in testing my body in the heat of a game I know it's failing me incrementally. It's occasionally possible to fight the outgoing tide and see an opposite trend, that great day on the court—something to encourage me, but it never endures and its occurrence is becoming rarer..

Watching the Sooner Gals and feeling the excitement in the crowd as they played, it's hard not to be inspired. They've beaten the odds, and there is no reason the rest of us cannot follow, I reassure myself. Then I realize there's a reason that the number of teams competing in the 80+ divisions are a scant half dozen. The culprits of course are physical deterioration, injury, even death. No amount of inspiration will prevail against these to extend a basketball life. Those Sooner Gals are statistical marvels with luck and good genes on their side to add fuel to their determination.

Not that long ago, two of my dearest friends, who were work colleagues and fellow players, gave me a lesson in how to live with physical decline—when the body no longer obeys and you have to make peace with that fact. I met Jim Livesey, salesman extraordinaire and perennial optimist, when I first left law and entered the business world. He later joined my in a company I founded. Every day he walked in with a buoyant smile fresh from his early morning five-mile run. I noticed how our team counted on him to see the bright side of whatever we faced and he delivered that same energy to our basketball games where we were always led by his spirit, exemplified by that smile.

Beginning in 2003, Jim was afflicted with successive varieties of cancer, against which he fought valiantly for eight years, ultimately losing the battle at age 61. It was how he accommodated to the successive losses without giving up that taught me a powerful lesson—acceptance without capitulation, and never with bitterness.

A year and a half later, we lost the irrepressible Geoff MacDonald, my colleague and always the poster child for hearty determination and positivity and a believer in perfect physical conditioning. Geoff relished a physical challenge and sought them out, the bigger the better. He drew such obvious intense pleasure in exhorting the troops, leading the charge, and conquering the challenges, be they up a mountain, down a ski slope or on a basketball court. Beginning in 2010, Geoff began to show signs of a degenerative brain disease—initially evident in his speaking and then his physical movements and balance. There was no cure, and after a long and sustained period of deterioration, he died six months shy of his 65th birthday. Besides noting his business success, his unshakeable positive attitude and his love of life and people, his obituary commented that "in basketball games he was the player, coach, and referee—all in one!" That loss taught me that sharing in our common joy is paramount and that joy is a fleeting moment in time.

As Senior Games leader Ed Conway says when he kicks off a tournament, we should give thanks we still are able to play this game. And fortunate we are! As I've travelled around over the last few years for my "private reunions," I've discovered that most of those members of my former brotherhoods no longer are playing. While some simply decided to "hang up the sneakers," most I have spoken with sadly noted that they were forced to quit because of physical problems, a decision frequently dictated by a doctor. The high dropout rate is understandable. Basketball is a game that tests the physical limits of our constitution and asks much of the body. It can be exhausting running up and down the court, at times making me wonder if I can continue another thirty seconds. Gasping for air, continual movement with or without the ball, contending for rebounds, driving to the basket or contorting to block shots all constitute exceptional demands and are the royal road to injury.

When I stop and think about how few of us are still standing, I'm forced to not only ponder my luck but also savor the moment. For many years I was ferociously critical of my performance. Many post-game nights were spent methodically analyzing the details of the errors and bad plays of the evening rather than immediately falling asleep for a well-earned rest. "That was not a high percentage shot...my block-out against Joe was terrible on those two plays...poor positioning on that stupid foul...what was I doing getting involved in that argument," I would obsess as I lay in bed eyes wide open.

Today all that's changed. I've achieved my primary goal if I arrive home without a limp and can look forward to returning to the gym the following week. Rather than a topic to be subjected to critical analysis, each game has become a precious experience to be cherished. I'm well aware that at age 68 only a finite number of games remain for me. I'm thankful every time I walk through those doors to run up and down the court for an hour or so. And I pay attention to it, grateful for what I have rather than what I've lost.

Facing decline though, also leads to another perspective about whether to retire or not. If I continue to play, I'll witness the ongoing decline of my body and athletic skills. It's hard to risk memories of playing at or near my prime being dulled by all the growing difficulties. It's a dilemma that everyone faces. Some have opted to quit and retain those memories. If I'd walked away from the game after a favorable chapter such as the last game of the Upstarts, the departure from the New York Lawyers' League or the end of the second year of Over the Hill, I would've left with memories unencumbered with the not so memorable recent declines.

Yet, I would've been deprived of so much. I would have missed joining new brotherhoods and keeping my constant companion at my side as I confronted new chapters in life, and there would have been fewer private reunions the past five years with those who'd shared the past with me. I would've missed all those moments on the court during all these years playing the game I love. I would've given up part of my identity.

Once I leave that basketball on the court never to be picked up again, all that's left will be memories—they may be treasured, but nevertheless they will only be memories. As my inner voice reliably tells me when mired in an extended injury or coming home after a terrible day on the court, the game is to be played, not remembered.

ACKNOWLEDGEMENTS

Any project spanning five years can be successful only with the help of the proverbial village, and in my case it has been a very large one. I'm deeply indebted to the over 100 people with whom I've spoken in person or by phone to rehash memories of those games long past, and those authors who have inspired me with their works on basketball and their life, all of whom are cited in the **Notes.**

.A special thanks to each of my three sons, Brendan, Colin and Mike, who have fulfilled many roles in my basketball world: willing subjects of instruction in the game as young boys, fellow players, fans, and the original and patient audience for my stories.

My wife Susanne provided me with an invaluable sounding board that deepened my understanding and insight into what the game has meant to me. She collaborated with me through endless reviews and editing through her always critical and unsparing eye and played a major role in providing the structure and the tone of the book. Without her, this book would not have borne any resemblance to the finished product.

My gratitude to her extends far beyond the production of this book. For the entire 43 years she has known me, she has endured my fanaticism for the game, and she has lovingly tolerated all the time I have devoted to this, even when it added to her family responsibilities and duties (as it frequently did).

In addition, special thanks go out to those who reviewed portions of the manuscript and provided valuable comments: Jeff Wieand, Tom Powers, Erin Dowdall, Lorraine Loomis, Leo Berry, Marc Racicot, Lenny Kesten, Rick Killigrew, John Doerr, Carol Sutherland and Kate Blunt.

For my book cover, I am grateful for the efforts of Pat King and Joyce Alpert.

Finally, I want to thank the countless number who have shared with me the joys of the game of basketball all these years. They include all the members of my brotherhoods, but the three to whom I am most indebted for my basketball life did not spend that time on the playgrounds or in the gym with me—my parents, John Dowdall and Mary Tyvand, and my Grandmother Cecilia Kantack.

NOTES

For **chapter one**, I am indebted to Charlie Rose for our chats at the Boston Sports Club. His stories of Boston basketball in the 1960's gave me the original idea of this book. Also insights were gained from interviews with Bob Matosich, John Cheek and Bill Lowney. The Obama and basketball connection is chronicled in Alexander Wolff, *The Audacity of Hoop: Basketball and the Age of Obama* (Temple University: 2015). Inspiration was provided by the following basketball memoirs: Ira Berkow, *To the Hoop: The Seasons of a Basketball Life* (Basic Books: 1997); Bill Bradley, *Life on the Run* (Vintage Books: 1995); Pat Conroy, *My Losing Season* (Nan A. Talese-Doubleday: 2002); Phil Jackson and Hugh Delehanty, *Sacred Hoops: Spiritual Lessons of a Hardwood Warrior* (Hyperion: 1995). I also was influenced by Berkow in my choice of title. Berkow's is ironic in that he always pulled up for the jumper rather than go to the hoop while I probably passed up the jumper a few too many times.

My preparation for this book included reading a number of classic histories of the game. A particularly interesting one was Robert W. Peterson, *Cages to Jump Shots: Pro Basketball's Early Years* (Oxford: 1990). While purportedly the subject is the professional game, it captures well the grit and spirit of the game for the first forty years or so. Also influential were a couple of visits to the Basketball Hall of Fame, located in Springfield, Massachusetts.

For **chapters two and three**, a particular thanks to Evalyn Batten Johnson for providing a wonderful tour of Virginia City, introducing me to a number of former players under my father, authoring a terrific history of the town, *Virginia City* (Arcadia Publishing: 2011) and organizing the All School Reunion (August 29, 2013), for which she prepared the booklet *The Last Hurrah Memory Book*. Special thanks to my mother Mary Tyvand and her late husband Ben Tyvand for their perceptive insights on life in Virginia City and Dillon and high school basketball in the 1950's. Also thanks to former VC players, Norm Dixon, John Sprunger and Jerry Lightfoot and Carma Gilligan, wife of the late Dave. Invaluable information on Dillon came from interviews with George Scott, Max Hansen and Frank (Frog) Hull. Ron Losee's autobiography is *Doc* (Ballantine Books: 1994). The lyrics of the Beavers' fight song were supplied by Max Hansen and his daughter.

For **chapters four through eleven**, I express particular thanks to Tom White for generously sharing with me his compilation of the history of the Anaconda City Championship series and to Mike Vollmer for all the newspaper clippings for my junior year. I have benefitted from numerous interviews with friends and coaches from my Anaconda days. Of particular benefit were the four plus hours I spent with my former teammate and then rival John Cheek. His wife Debbie Cheek has been an enthusiastic supporter of the project and has provided me with contact information for her Copperhead classmates. Similarly, my classmate Leo Berry has been a valued supporter, making introductions and contacts and sending photos Also many thanks to Jeff Frank, Paul Greenough, Tom Greenough, Jim Gransbery, Jack Haffey, Ron Haffey, John Harold, Bill Hill, Archbishop Raymond Hunthausen, Joe Furshong, Bill Lowney, Jack Lowney, Bill Matosich, Bob Matosich, Tim McKeon, Pat McKittrick, Tim McKittrick, Jim Meredith, Bill Molendyke, Dave Neilson, Jack Oberweiser, Bill Shea, Bill Sullivan, Mike Vollmer and Tracy Walsh. I also received valuable insights from non-Anaconda opponents and observers: Frank (Frog) Hull, Chuck Johnson, Marc Racicot, Glen Smiley and Jim Smiley. Former head of the Anaconda Historical Museum Jerry Hansen provided me with a history of girls' basketball in Anaconda. The following books have provided significant background material: Keith L. Moran, *The Roll of Champions* (1969); Eleanor Olson, *Wayne Estes: A Hero's Legacy* (Publishers Press: 1991); Patrick F. Morris, *Anaconda Montana: Copper Smelting Boom Town on the Western Frontier* (Swann Publishing: 1997); Alice Finnegan, *Goosetown in Their Own Words* (Sweetgrass Books: 2012) (includes the Dowdall baby buggy story). I also have been provided much detail on games from back issues of the *Anaconda Standard, Anaconda Leader, Missoulian* and *Montana Standard*. As to various aspects of the history of the game referred to in these chapters, see John Christgau, *The Origins of the Jump Shot* (University of Nebraska Press: 1999); Linda Peavey and Ursula Smith, *Full Court Quest: The Girls from Fort Shaw Indian School Basketball Champions of the World* (U. of Oklahoma Press: 2008). As to the general history of women's basketball, see Pamela Grundy and Susan Shackelford, *Shattering the Glass* (The New Press: 2005). The *Sports Illustrated* article on Roger Rouse appeared November 13, 1967.

For **chapters twelve and thirteen**, I have received valuable assistance from the Notre Dame Archives, particularly with respect to back issues of *The Observer*. Special thanks to varsity veteran John Gallagher for his views from that perspective. Thanks to various players at the Rock who gave me their insights: Steve Effler, Jack Farrell, Mike Kelly, Tom McCloskey, Dick Reynolds, Dick Roddewig, Tom Rouse, Chris Stephan and Corky Sterling. Historical perspectives on Notre Dame basketball are found in Michael Coffey, *Echoes on the Hardwood* (Taylor Trade Publishing: 2004); Tim Neely, *Hooping it Up: The Complete History of Notre Dame Basketball* (Diamond Communications: 1985). The description of the Fieldhouse is in *Sports Illustrated*, January 16, 1961. The reflections on the hook shot are found in Tommy Heinsohn and Joe Fitzgerald, *Give 'em the Hook* (Prentice Hall Press: 1988). Regarding my activities in the arts, special thanks to Donald and Christine Costello for their perspectives and to

Kate Blunt, who provided me with some of my letters to her detailing my activities as an undergraduate at Notre Dame. Dick Roddewig also was helpful with his recollections of those years. Thanks also to John Corigliano for his thoughts on the premiere of his work.

For **chapters fourteen and fifteen**, thanks to John Garvey for his recollections. Also thanks to Jim Wilson for his many conversations on sports and Bill Kristol and Harvey Mansfield for their reflections on the Harvard Government Department and athletic games at that time. The *Sports Illustrated* article on the Harvard/ Yale academic game was in the December 9, 1974 issue. As to my law school years, special mention needs to be made for Tom Powers, to whom I have been inextricably linked to the game for 43 years, for providing me information and insights on these years. Former Miami mayor Xavier Suarez similarly provided valuable information and authored the *Harvard Law Record* article on Hemenway ball and playground ball, from which I have quoted. A particular thanks to the remaining members of the Upstarts for our conversations: Tom, Bob Dolian, Rick Drooyan and Scott Davis. Also thanks to Bart Campbell, John Gavin, Tim O'Brien and Sheldon Solow for reflecting on their Hemenway days. The *Harvard Law Record* and *The Harvard Crimson* were a valuable source for the history of the gym and our intramural league. The legal battles following Larry Inlow's death are chronicled principally in the *Indiana Business Journal*, the *IndyStar*. A detailed exposition and analysis of the extended litigation is found at http://www.shirleylaw.net/images/ArticlesOfInterestAttorneys/ArticleontheLegacyofLawrenceInlow5-13-15.pdf. And of course I want to express my indebtedness to the then Susanne Gossett, who forever changed my life when she entered it the same month as the Upstarts' first game.

For **chapters sixteen and seventeen**, special mention must go to Paul Mueller, whose efforts have been invaluable for chronicling those New York years. In addition to issues of THE BULL, he also prepared a detailed memorandum on our basketball program and included photos. Also thanks to my other former teammates for their recollections and our discussions of those happier times for Dewey Ballantine: Joe Angland, Ed Blythe, Richard Farren, Mike Kelly, Fran Morris and Joe Williams. George Pataki's perspectives on the firm and its basketball are found in *Pataki: An Autobiography* (Viking: 1998). The article on the New York Lawyers' League was in the *New York Times*, April 7, 1998. The incident of Stephenson/Food Bank incident was reported at www.thelegalintelligencer.com/id=1202425513701/Court-Tosses-Claim-by-Player-Punched-During-Lawyers-League-Game?slreturn=20160519173850 (*New York Law Journal* article). The story of the decline and bankruptcy of Dewey LaBoef was detailed in numerous news articles of *The New York Times* and the *Wall Street Journal*. The world of Wall Street firms in the 1970's is captured in Paul Hoffman, *Lions in the Street* (Saturday Review Press: 1973). For the Stafford Hilaire story, I relied upon articles from various Denver-based publications and legal decisions and other legal documents relating to his case. Of particular importance is the decision of *United States of America v. Carnagie and Hilaire*, 533 F.2d 1231 (10th Cir. 2008). The definition of conspiracy is found in *Black's Legal Dictionary*. Judge Learned Hand's comments on conspiracy are found in *Harrison v. United States*, 7 F.2d 259, 263 (2d Cir. 1925). For a perceptive study of the aggressiveness of prosecutors on a variety of fronts, including conspiracy, see Harvey Silverglate, *Three Felonies in a Day* (Encounter Books: 2011)

For **chapter eighteen**, I am indebted to Sheldon Fink of Sonnenschein for his extensive knowledge and wisdom about Chicago basketball. Also thanks to fellow Sonnenschein players Jim Lourgos, Rob Mark and Pat Moran for their time. Dick Roddewig and his fellow Ross Hardies teammates provided invaluable information about the powerhouses of the league. For the story of the Oak Ave pick-up, I am particularly indebted to John Herron with Dick Gleason, Sam Ramonosky and John Gavin adding colorful detail. The Erica Jong quote is found in Ira Berkow, *Court Vision: Unexpected Views on The Lure of Basketball* (U. of Nebraska Press 2004). The Berkow book incidentally is an interesting compendium of observations about basketball by noted artists, musicians, scientists, writers and other non-players from the perspective of their craft. The dynamics of jumping are chronicled well in Asher Price, *Year of the Dunk* (Crown Publishers: 2015). The Jeff Koons *Three Ball 50/50 Tank* is at the Museum of Modern Art.. His comments about inflatability are found at www.sothebys.com/en/auctions/ecatalogue/2014/contemporary-art-evening-sale-n09141/lot.62.html

For **chapter nineteen**, thanks to former Bingham players Dick Harter and Bob Miley, Dan Eastman and a favorite former client, Rich Balsbaugh. Also thanks to that unknown referee whose comment on managing partner inspired me ultimately to change careers. Thanks to Gabriel for introducing me to the international game, and of course another nod to Tom Powers.

For **chapters twenty through twenty-two**, there are so many to whom I'm grateful. Foremost is Larry Ingrassia, who shared so much of the experience with me that is outlined in these chapters. Also special mention goes to referee John 'Buck' Buckley, who shared with me so much about CYO basketball, the art of refereeing and life in general. John Bonsall provided much history of the CYO in Massachusetts, particularly the Framingham vicariate. I have benefitted immensely from the memories and insights of my fellow coaches and OTH-ers: Nick Bogard, Charlie Brown, Myles Brown, John Doerr, Terry Driscoll, Jim Ferry, Les Goldstein, Mike Holownia, Lenny Kesten, Rick Killigrew, Mike Montalbano, Mark Mullaney, Lonnie Powell, Chris Stevens, Leo Troy and Menno Verhave. Thanks also to Chris Stevens for the article published in the *Wellesley Townsmen*. Finally, a deep thanks to the hundreds of guys who joined me on the OTH courts during the last quarter century. My understanding of the OTH split has been aided by the perspectives of many of the participants. Thanks to Mark Mullaney for recounting his battle against cancer.

Notes

The George Dohrmann book cited at the end of chapter twenty is *Play Their Hearts Out* (Ballantine: 2012).

I've borrowed the term "geezer jocks" for the title of **chapter twenty three** from the name of a magazine that ran for a couple of years about a decade ago. Dedicated to the athletic exploits of senior athletes, the magazine's name was changed to *Master Athlete* in 2008 after some criticism of the former name's connotations. Shortly thereafter it went out of business.

For **chapters twenty three and twenty four,** thanks to fellow senior players Ed Conway, Irwin Grossman, Steve Leonard, Hank (Cowboy) Philbrick and Tom Winters for their thoughts. Carl Beal's unpublished essay on the history of senior basketball in Massachusetts has provided a thoughtful perspective on those seeking to make the game a lifelong sport. As to the "hot hand" controversy, see Thomas,Gilovich, Amos Tversky and Robert Vallone, "The Hot Hand in Basketball: On the Misperception of Random Sequences" in *Cognitive Psychology* 17, 295 (1985) for the original study positing the fallacy of the hot hand. Recent critiques of the Gilovich-Tversky-Vallone thesis include Andrew Bocskocsky, John Ezeowitz and Carolyn Stein, "The Hot Hand: A New Approach to an Old 'Fallacy,'" delivered at 8th Annual MIT Sloan Sports Analytics Conference (2014); Brett Green and Jeffrey Zwiebel, "The Hot Hand Fallacy: Cognitive Mistakes or Equilibrium Adjustments? Evidence from Baseball," Stanford Graduate School of Business (2013) Joshua Miller Adam Sanjurjo "A Cold Shower for the Hot Hand Fallacy," IGIER Working Paper No. 518. A special thanks to all the 2011 National Senior Games players I spoke with, particularly the late marvelous Joanne Garvey, Bob Cisneros, Richard Lane and members of the San Diego Meteors and the inimitable Oklahoma Sooner Gals, to whom I also am grateful for their consenting to pose for a photo. Articles on the Sooner Gals can be found at numerous internet news sites, including the *Tulsa News at 6*, the *Tulsa World* and the *Broken Arrow Ledger*. Some of the quotes from the Gals are found in these publications. The memorial for Garvey was reported at *State Tax Today*, September 15, 2014.

For **chapter twenty five**, I have been inspired by the lives of my former partners, Geoff MacDonald and Jim Livesey, and they are missed greatly.

INDEX

Index

Index

48038197R00197

Made in the USA
Middletown, DE
09 September 2017